REASONING PROCESSES IN HUMANS AND COMPUTERS

Theory and Research in Psychology and Artificial Intelligence

Morton Wagman

Westport, Connecticut
London

Library of Congress Cataloging-in-Publication Data

Wagman, Morton.
Reasoning processes in humans and computers : theory and research in psychology and
artificial intelligence / Morton Wagman.
p. cm.
Includes bibliographical references and indexes.
ISBN 0–275–97525–8 (alk. paper)
1. Reasoning (Psychology) 2. Reasoning (Psychology)—Data processing. 3. Artificial
intelligence. 4. Cognitive science. I. Title.
BF442.W34 2003
153.4'3—dc21   2002072848

British Library Cataloguing in Publication Data is available.

Library of Congress Catalog Card Number: 2002072848
ISBN: 0–275–97525–8

First published in 2003

Praeger Publishers, 88 Post Road West, Westport, CT 06881
An imprint of Greenwood Publishing Group, Inc.
www.praeger.com

Printed in the United States of America

The paper used in this book complies with the
Permanent Paper Standard issued by the National
Information Standards Organization (Z39.48–1984).

10 9 8 7 6 5 4 3 2 1

Contents

Tables and Figures

FIGURES

Table 4.1 (continued)

The second premise states the belief that things (the objects) are dissimilar in their vocal cords which the respondent may have been offered as an assertion about (hence the low certainty perhaps) or a statement. The final premise states the conclusion that makes us to be one of cords, which may then have been and instead being given. But it is a rule, for certainty of the conclusion, the assertion and nearer should have been fairly low claims certainty premise but for the final conclusion to be actual certainty.

Wallace posited an example to illustrate GPS-based such as transform. The first part states a belief that bananas grow because, among other things, the suitability (or of agriculture) product certain. Bananas are a fairly product that to represent the climate where they are grown as the vocal certainty value. The final premise asserts that the climate appropriate to a tropical bananas contains the places where they are grown fairly equally. The conclusion follows with moderate certainty that Honduras produces many tropical fruits, such as mangos and coconuts.

Preface

This book presents a critical analysis of current theory and research in the psychological and computational sciences directed toward an elucidation of reasoning processes and structures ranging from the domain of everyday plausible reasoning to the domain of scientific explanatory reasoning.

In the first chapter, theories and research in human reasoning and reasoning systems are examined. Experimental research in deductive and inductive reasoning, the nature of artificial intelligence reasoning systems, nonmonotonic and commonsense reasoning, and general types of reasoning in artificial intelligence are discussed in depth.

In the second chapter, a formal core theory of plausible reasoning processes is described, and relevant empirical human protocol evidence is presented. The formal core theory is discussed with respect to mental models, correctness of reasoning, statement transforms, derivation from mutual implications and dependencies, and transitivity inferences.

In the third chapter, theory and research concerned with the processes of human reasoning are examined. The use of abstract rules in reasoning is analyzed and compared with instance models in both symbolic and connectionist architectures.

The fourth chapter focuses on significant aspects of human reasoning. The probabilistic contrast model of causal reasoning is identified as a significant advance in the development of a mathematical conceptualization of human reasoning.

In the fifth chapter, experimental research in belief bias and logical reasoning is presented. The complex experimental effects of belief in the truth of the conclusion on the quality of the reasoning process in production and evaluation of paradigms are described. The chapter concludes with an information processing model of the resolution of logical inference and psychological belief.

In the sixth chapter, the course of inductive reasoning that led to the discovery of the cause of scurvy is described, and a computational simulation of the medical discovery is presented. The CHARADE system and the hypotheses about scurvy are discussed, including the rationale for the induction of scurvy cases and experimental tests that led to the confirmation of the cause of scurvy.

In the seventh chapter, Bayesian reasoning is examined. The conclusion, based on 25 years of research concerning judgment under uncertainty, that people do not possess a subjective calculus of probability and are therefore biased toward cognitive distortion can be overturned by replacing Bayesian probability with frequentistic probability. Frequentistic probability conforms to evolutionary and ecological processes which created a human brain that represents experiences in the world in frequentistic terms. In the second part of the chapter, theory and supporting experiments demonstrate the possibility that the human mind does possess Bayesian algorithms, but that their elicitation depends on presenting data in frequentistic rather than probabilistic formats. Frequentistic formats did result in Bayesian algorithmic reasoning and the overcoming of the cognitive bias toward base rate neglect.

In the eighth chapter, a theory of syllogistic reasoning that depends on the nature of representation of relations between classes of universal-particular statements and affirmative-negative forms is described in depth. Experimental protocols reveal that people use either spatial or verbal representations to solve syllogistic problems. The findings challenge the mental model theory of syllogistic reasoning that has wide currency.

In the ninth chapter, the robust theory of commonsense reasoning is described. In this theory, rule-based reasoning and similarity-based reasoning, usually viewed as separate and disparate, can be meaningfully integrated within a connectionist architecture that includes the CONSYDERR program that convincingly executes the robust theory of commonsense reasoning.

In the tenth chapter, temporal reasoning is examined. The concepts and methods of temporal abstraction and their embodiment in the RÉSUMÉ system, which achieves medical time management in patient care, are described.

In the eleventh chapter, similarity-based reasoning is considered. A critique of the similarity assumption in case-based reasoning is presented, including case-based reasoning (CBR) and the similarity assumption, approaches to the retrieval of adaptable cases, and the logic of adaptation-guided retrieval. The Déjà Vu system is discussed, including Déjà Vu and adaptation knowledge, adaptation capability knowledge in Déjà Vu, and adaptation-guided retrieval in Déjà Vu. Experiments with Déjà Vu and adaptation-guided retrieval are described, and implications for case-based reasoning and/or artificial intelligence are considered.

Appendix A presents an analysis of the n-factor problem.

Reasoning Processes in Humans and Computers: Theory and Research in Psychology and Artificial Intelligence is the most recent volume in a series of published and planned volumes whose consistent theme is that of developing an intellectual grounding for establishing the theoretical and research foundations and the psychological and philosophical implications of a general unified theory of human and artificial intelligence (Wagman, 1991a, 1991b, 1993, 1995, 1996, 1997a, 1997b, 1998a, 1998b, 1998c, 1999, 2000a, 2000b, 2002). Each of the volumes contributes important aspects of this enterprise, and each reflects new theory, research, and knowledge in both human and artificial intelligence across the domains of problem solving, reasoning, analogical thinking, learning, memory, linguistic processes, representation modes, creative processes, explanation theory, time cognition, consciousness and theory of mind, logic mechanisms, mathematical thought, theories of thinking, and scientific discovery.

All the volumes are mutually supportive, and all are directed to the same audience: scholars and professionals in psychology, artificial intelligence, and cognitive science. Graduate and advanced undergraduate students in these and related disciplines will also find the book useful.

ACKNOWLEDGMENTS

I wish to express my thanks to LaDonna Wilson for her assistance in preparing all aspects of the initial manuscript. I am grateful to Steve Wilson for his excellent work in assisting in the preparation of the tables and figures as well as in the production of the final complete manuscript. I am also grateful to Audrey Fisher, Bridget Young, Lori Seitz, and Kathleen Pritchett for their excellent typing of portions of the manuscript.

I am indebted to Sherman Stein, Jerome Rosovsky, and Michael Teitelman for their contributions to the solution of the n-factor problem (Appendix A). The proofs provided by Sherman Stein constitute original approaches that mutually reinforce the validity of the theorems. Jerome Rosovsky and Michael Titleman provided incisive and facilitating reviews and detected errors in earlier versions of the proof. Finally, Dean Hickerson contributed a general proof.

Table 2.1
Formal Representations of Derivations from Mutual Implication

Positive Derivation

Negative Derivation

Source: Collins, A. M., and Michalski, R. (1989). The logic of plausible reasoning: A core theory. *Cognitive Science 13*, p. 39. © Cognitive Science Society. Reprinted with permission.

of the place, and also that the average temperature is near 65 degrees at the equator and 0 degrees at the poles, then he might conclude that a place like Lumberton, which is about 40 degrees from the equator, has an average temperature of about 75 degrees. People have both more or less precise notions of how variables interact, and we have tried to preserve flexibility within our representation for handling these different degrees of precision. (Collins and Michalski, 1989, pp. 33–35)

1

Human Reasoning and Reasoning Systems

DEDUCTIVE REASONING

Logic and Psychology

Almost up to the close of the nineteenth century and until the work of Darwin (1872) and Spencer (1896), psychology was undifferentiated from philosophy. Rational man was held to think essentially in terms of the philosopher's logical calculus (Whitehead and Russell, 1910–1913). Man was perceived as obeying inevitably the laws of logical thought.

The work of Darwin, especially the *Descent of Man* (1871), placed psychology of thought in the general framework of evolution, survival, and environmental adaptation. In fact, in *Descent of Man* Darwin outlined a number of experimental designs intended to test the problem-solving or reasoning ability of animals. This opened a way to a long series of experiments in comparative psychology in which reasoning for a time came to be associated with the behavior of lower animals, including the rat (Heron and Hunter, 1922).

But human rationality was dethroned not only through Darwinian evolutionary perspectives but also through the work of Freud. In his "Doctrine of Psychosexual Evolutionism," Freud forever reduced everyday human behavior and mishaps to primitive and irrational motives and conflicts, a concept he elaborated in his *Psychopathology of Everyday Life* (Freud, 1966). Moreover, the Freudian view seemed to hold that the very rationality of man could sometimes be attributed to intellectual avoidances and defenses, sometimes with clear obsessional or compulsive symptoms (Fenichel, 1945). The early laboratory investigations of human reasoning ability and performance seemed to separate psychology as a science from its maternal source in philosophy and to extend the Freudian view of man's everyday psychopathology to the lofty realm of erroneous formal syllogistic reasoning.

Beginning sometime in the 1950s, experimental psychology of reasoning—under a general shift of psychological interest to cognition, prompted in the United States by the work of Bruner, Goodnow, and Austin (1956), in England by the work of Bartlett (1958), and beginning even earlier in Geneva, by the immense contributions of Piaget (1949) and his collaborators—dethroned Darwinism and Freudianism and relegated their legacies to secondary importance. The questions of the range and power of man's logical competencies and their underlying information processes were placed in a position of saliency without restoring the earlier philosophical description of human reasoning as *a priori* equivalent to the idealized forms described in various formal, logical systems.

During the last 100 years, philosophy and logic have not stood still. Logic as a major branch of philosophy has become a highly specialized science—held by some to be akin to mathematics and by others to be either the basis of mathematics or merely a set of transformations from which mathematical operations derived (Bourbaki, 1964; Church, 1956; Copi, 1967; Terrell, 1967). The difference between logic as a science and psychology as a science must be observed.

With regard to reasoning, psychology studies how people actually do reason, whereas logic is normative with respect to reasoning, providing a standard of valid reasoning. Valid reasoning and logic are contentless, very much like mathematical symbols in calculus and algebra are mathematically correct regardless of the reference of the symbols. This gives mathematics and logic both their power and their difficulty—power because of their range of application and difficulty because of their abstract character. Yet, logical operations—as part of the working tools of all scientists in their inferential behavior in drawing conclusions from their symbolized data—may also be an indispensable tool in studying people's everyday competence as they reason themselves into real or fantasized problem situations, grasp the implications of the reasoning problem more or less adequately, and reason themselves more or less clearly out of the perplexing quandary (Piattelli-Palmarini, 1994; Sutherland, 1992).

The Laws of Thought in Psychoanalysis and Philosophy

In psychology and philosophy, theories of the nature of human intellect have ranged between two extremes. In psychoanalytic psychology, they construe conscious reasoning as a functionary of unconscious defensive processes, as illogical, and as uninterested in reducing logical inconsistency and achieving logical validity. In philosophy, theories construe conscious reasoning as an autonomous process that seeks the establishment of truth in all conclusions. Whereas psychoanalysis (Freud, 1966) considered the laws of thought to be a disguise for

Table 1.1

Conclusion as a Function of Formal or Informal Reasoning Process and True or False Premises

Reasoning Process	True Premises	False Premises
Formal	Conclusion is necessarily valid, necessarily true, necessarily sound.	Conclusion is necessarily valid, necessarily false, necessarily unsound.
Informal	Conclusion is possibly valid, possibly true, possibly sound.	Conclusion is possibly valid, necessarily false, necessarily unsound.

Source: Wagman, M. (1991b). *Cognitive Science and Concepts of Mind: Toward a General Theory of Human and Artificial Intelligence*. New York: Praeger, p. 28. Reprinted by permission of Praeger Publishers, an imprint of Greenwood Publishing Group, Inc., Westport, CT.

the laws of unconscious irrationality, philosophy (Mill, 1874) considered the laws of thought to be coextensive with the laws of logic. Although John Stuart Mill admitted that human thought was sometimes illogical, he explained this as a mere slip in the logical machinery of the mind.

The Rules of Logical Inference and Their Violations

Contemporary philosophers of logic (Suppes, 1964) are not convinced of the inherent logical quality of thought, and they offer a set of concepts and criteria to evaluate the logical quality of any product of human intellect. Although there are many technical differences among the formal systems of logic (Church, 1956), they agree on the importance of the concepts of valid and fallacious (invalid) conclusions, sound and unsound conclusions, substantively true and false conclusions.

A sound conclusion results from effective, though not necessarily formal, reasoning with true premises. An unsound conclusion results either from ineffective reasoning or false premises, or both. A valid conclusion results from correct formal reasoning with either true premises or false premises. Table 1.1

summarizes the nature of the conclusion (necessary-possible, valid-invalid, true-false, sound-unsound) that results from the type of reasoning process (formal-informal) and the type of premises (true-false).

Logicians recognize that sound conclusions may follow from a reasoning process that differs from the rules of logical inference. Such a reasoning process is not logical in the sense that it does not follow the formal rules of inference. Logicians assert that their rules of formal logical inference guarantee valid conclusions, if they are followed, whereas informal or natural methods of reasoning do not inevitably result in valid conclusions (Macnamara, 1986).

Reasoning with Logical Implications

Rips and Marcus (1990) presented subjects with eight types of conditional reasoning problems. Each problem contained two premises and a conclusion. Subjects were asked to determine whether the conclusion was always true, sometimes true, or never true. Response percentages are given in Table 1.2. Correct answers to each type of problem are also given in the table.

Problem types 1 and 2 involve modus ponens, a valid form of logical implication; the perfect performance of subjects results from the perfect match of everyday reasoning with formal reasoning. Problem types 3 and 4 involve the denial of the antecedent, a fallacious form of logical implication; the imperfect performance of subjects results from imperfect knowledge of formal logic (Taplin, 1971).

Problems 5 and 6 involve the affirmation of the consequent, a fallacious form of logical implication; the less than perfect performance of subjects results from less than perfect knowledge of formal reasoning (Staudenmayer, 1975). Problems 7 and 8 involve modus tollens, a valid form of logical implication; the mediocre performance of subjects results from the counterintuitive form of the logical argument.

Reasoning with Modus Tollens

A significant category of logical negation is modus tollens, a method of establishing validity through the use of negation. Beginning with the work of Wason (1966), modus tollens has been intensively studied in the psychological laboratory (Bonatti, 1994; Cosmides, 1989; Dominowski, 1995; Evans, 1998; Evans, Barston, and Pollard, 1983; Green, 1997; Green and Larking, 1995; Green, Over, and Pine, 1997; Love and Kessler, 1995; Nickerson, 1996; Nisbett, 1993; Oaksford and Chater, 1994, 1996; Platt and Griggs, 1993; Rips, 1997; Roberts, 1993; Sloman, 1996; Sperber, Cara, and Girotto, 1995).

In deductive reasoning with conditional statements (if p, then q), there are two valid logical rules: (a) modus ponens (if p, then q, and p; therefore, q) and (b) modus tollens (if p, then q, and not q; therefore, not p). Research has indicated (Rips and Marcus, 1977) that modus ponens is directly understood by

Table 1.2
Percentage of Total Responses for Eight Types of Conditional Syllogisms

Syllogism	Always	Sometimes	Never
1. $P \supset Q$ P $\therefore Q$	100[a]	0	0
2. $\overline{P \supset Q}$ P $\therefore \sim Q$	0	0	100[a]
3. $\overline{P \supset Q}$ $\sim P$ $\therefore Q$	5	79[a]	16
4. $\overline{P \supset Q}$ $\sim P$ $\therefore \sim Q$	21	77[a]	2
5. $\overline{P \supset Q}$ Q $\therefore P$	23	77[a]	0
6. $\overline{P \supset Q}$ Q $\therefore \sim P$	4	82[a]	14
7. $\overline{P \supset Q}$ $\sim Q$ $\therefore P$	0	23	77[a]
8. $\overline{P \supset Q}$ $\sim Q$ $\therefore \sim P$	57[a]	39	4

[a]The correct response.

Source: Rips, L. J., and Marcus, S. L. Suppositions and the analysis of conditional sentences. In
J. R. Anderson, *Cognitive Psychology and Its Implications*, 3rd ed. New York: W. H. Freeman
and Co., p. 294.

most people but modus tollens is difficult. In modus ponens, deductions are
drawn from what is the case (*p*), but in modus tollens deductions are drawn
from what is not the case (not *q*). Reasoning with positive states of affairs is
familiar and makes the valid logical form of modus ponens seem natural, but
reasoning with negative states of affairs (what is not the case) is unusual and
makes the valid logical form of modus tollens seem strange.

From the perspective of formal logic, modus ponens and modus tollens are
equal in difficulty because they are formalisms in the same way that, in algebra,
positive values of *x* and negative values of *x* are equal in difficulty because they
are formalisms. With this explanatory introduction, we will describe Wason's
research (1966) with a conditional reasoning problem in which subjects fail to
use the valid logical form modus tollens.

Experimental Research with Modus Tollens Reasoning

The experimenter placed four cards in front of the subject. On the first card was the letter *e*, on the second card was the letter *k*, on the third card was the number 4, on the fourth card was the number 7. Subjects were informed that there was a number on one side of each card and a letter on the other side.

The subject's task was to evaluate the validity of the following rule: "If a card has a vowel on one side, then it has an even number on the other side." The subject's problem was to evaluate the validity of the rule by turning over only those cards that needed to be turned over.

The difficulty of the task is indicated by finding that 96 percent of the subjects made incorrect choices. Cards *e* and 4 were turned over by 46 percent of the subjects (turning over the 4 was incorrect because neither the presence of a consonant nor the presence of a vowel would have invalidated the rule). Card *e* was turned over by 33 percent of the subjects (partially correct but incomplete), and other incorrect selections were made by 17 percent of the subjects. Cards *e* and 7, the correct selections, were turned over by only 4 percent of the subjects. (The rule would have been invalidated by a vowel on the other side of the 7 or an odd number on the other side of the *e*.)

The logic of conditionals can be usefully applied to Wason's selection task. As indicated above, modus ponens and modus tollens are the two valid deductions that can be drawn from a conditional statement such as that given in the rule for Wason's selection task. The violation of either modus ponens or modus tollens would prove the rule false.

The symbolic form of the rule in the selection task is: if *p*, then *q*.

Applying modus ponens, we have: if *p* (vowel), then *q* (even number), and select *e* (vowel); then not *q* (odd number) on the other side of the card would violate modus ponens and thereby prove the rule false.

Applying modus tollens, we have: if not *q* (odd number), then not *p* (consonant), and select 7 (odd number); then *p* (vowel) on the other side of the card would violate modus tollens and thereby prove the rule false.

The power and difficulty of modus tollens as a reasoning tool is clearly demonstrated in Wason's card-selection experiment. In a review of this research, Wason and Johnson-Laird (1972) commented that many subjects showed an inability to comprehend modus tollens, even after lengthy explanation.

Many subjects developed an irreversibility in their cognitive approach to the experimental task. Initially, subjects select the *e* and the 4 because these cards match the rule (vowel and even number); and then they do not seem able to reverse their cognitive approach so as to consider the possibility of other card selections. In particular, these subjects could not project falsity and select the card with the 7 on it. Even after the correct selections were shown and explained to them, the subjects exhibited a type of protective evasiveness. Thus, although subjects might concur that an odd number on the other side of a vowel might invalidate the rule, they could not comprehend why a vowel on the other side of the 7 would also invalidate the rule.

Subsequent research (Griggs, 1983; Griggs and Ransdell, 1986) has generally confirmed Wason's findings, but some experimenters have designed experimental contexts that facilitate the apparent use of modus tollens. For example, the context might instruct subjects that they were to detect a violation of some type of government rule, thereby alerting them to the necessity of a contrafactual approach to the task.

For example, Johnson-Laird, Legrenzi, and Legrenzi (1972) showed subjects four envelopes. The first was flap side up and unsealed. The second was flap side up and sealed. The third was address side up with a 50-lire stamp. The fourth was address side up with a 40-lire stamp. Subjects were to imagine that they were clerks of the post office and that they were to detect whether there was a violation of the directive that sealed envelopes must have additional 10-lire postage. In particular, subjects were asked to verify the rule: "If a letter is sealed, then it has a 50-lire stamp on it." The subject's task was to determine which envelopes should be turned over.

Of the 24 subjects, 21 correctly turned over the sealed envelope and the 40-lire envelope. This finding contrasts with Wason's results; but as indicated earlier, the context of testing for a violation predisposes subjects to the use of modus tollens.

Conclusions and Implications

Generalizing from these and other experiments (Griggs and Cox, 1982; Hoch and Tschirgi, 1983; Rips, 1986), it appears that people do not command the extracontextual formal operation of modus tollens but seem to slide into the use of modus tollens when the context encourages a contrafactual cognitive approach (Markovits, 1988). Modus tollens is important in mathematics and science and in many forms of critical thought. Education in modus tollens and other aspects of formal logic (Wagman, 1978, 1984) is therefore useful.

EXPERIMENTAL MODIFICATION OF FALLACIOUS REASONING

A distinction can be drawn between the approach of psychology and the approach of logic in the study of reasoning. Psychology is concerned with describing how people reason, and perhaps why, but not with whether they reason correctly. Logic (Terrell, 1967) attempts to provide systematically the laws or principles that distinguish correct reasoning from incorrect. The science of psychology (Wason and Johnson-Laird, 1972) is concerned with how people reason and with establishing scientific laws descriptive or explanatory of that reasoning behavior.

Reasoning that violates a rule of logic is invalid or fallacious. A subclass of fallacious reasoning consists of informal fallacies in which the violations of the rule of logic result from certain linguistic or psychological factors that tend to deceive people into believing that they are reasoning accurately. The fallacies of amphiboly, composition, and division depend on linguistic ambiguities (Johnson-Laird, 1969). The fallacies of appeals to force, pity, or authority and similar emotional appeals depend on psychological rationalization (Feather, 1967). The abstract character of the terms involved in reasoning (Wilkins, 1929) may lead to invalid conclusions and encourage the fallacy of the illicit conversion (Simpson and Johnson, 1966).

For the most part, psychological research on fallacious reasoning has been concerned with group or individual differences in response to tests of logical reasoning (Morgan, 1956; Sharma, 1960; Stanovich, 1998) or with isolating the psychological process responsible (Chapman and Chapman, 1959; Janis and Frick, 1943; Polk and Newell, 1995; Sells, 1936). The present study is concerned with the possibility of modifying fallacious reasoning.

In an exploratory investigation, Wason (1964) found that the fallacious inferences involved in the affirmation of the consequent and denial of the antecedent could be inhibited by an experimental design that created a self-contradictory or *reductio ad absurdum* situation. Wason (1964) wondered whether this method had any generality or any superiority to a method resembling teaching-machine procedures. The present investigation (1) compared a didactic correction method with the self-contradiction method, (2) tested generality across content varying in personal-emotional or scientific-abstract significance, and (3) tested for transfer to an extraexperimental criterion.

Principles of logical inference in deductive reasoning (Terrell, 1967) stipulate that in a conditional statement having the form of if p, then q, that if p is true, then q is a correct inference; and if q is false, then p must be false. However, it is fallacious to conclude that if p is false, then q must be false, or if q is true, then p must be true. Both fallacies proceed from an inductive or probabilistic approach rather than from a deductive approach which requires that a drawn inference be certain (Thompson, 1995). Thus, whether inferences drawn from a conditional statement are valid or fallacious depends on whether the formal rules of deductive reasoning or the everyday rules of inductive reasoning are followed. In the present experiment, as in Wason's (1964) investigation, subjects were presented with specific information regarding the rule that holds without exception and permits the drawing of either valid or fallacious inferences. The fallacious inferences drawn by subjects can involve either the affirmation of the consequent or the denial of the antecedent.

Method

Subjects and Design

The subjects were 160 students who participated in the experiment as part of their introductory psychology course research requirements. They were randomly assigned to eight equal groups: for the antecedent condition, a self-contradiction, a didactic correction, and a control group; for the consequent condition, a self-contradiction, a didactic correction, and a control group; and two control groups for the test of logical inference, one for the antecedent form of the test and one for the consequent form.

The order of administration of experimental materials for subjects in the self-contradiction, didactic correction, and control groups of the antecedent (or consequent) condition was the antecedent (or consequent) form of the pretest of logical inference, the main experimental task, and the antecedent (or consequent) form of the posttest of logical inference.

Each subject was randomly assigned to one of the permutations of the order of the four types of material (Types A, B, C, and D). All procedures were individually administered and completed in a two-hour period.

Measures

Test of Logical Inference

To test for possible transfer effects of the methods of self-contradiction and didactic correction, a pre- and postlogical inference measure was administered. Printed in a booklet, the items of this test had a form that consisted of two premise statements, followed by a space in which the conclusion was to be written. Half the items had personal-emotional significance, and half were neutral-scientific in character. The personal-emotional items dealt with intelligence, grades, dating, physical attractiveness, and other personal, family, or vocational problems. The neutral-scientific items dealt with mechanics, economics, statistics, astronomy, meteorology, and anthropology.

Four forms of the test of logical inference were used: a pre- and postform for the antecedent task and a pre- and postform for the consequent task. Each form contained twenty items, two permitting valid and eighteen permitting fallacious inferences. For the antecedent task, the valid items were of the form: (1) if p, then q, (2) p, (3) therefore. . . . The fallacious items had the form: (1) if p, then q, (2) not p, (3) therefore. . . . For the consequent task, the valid items had the form: (1) if p, then q, (2) not q, (3) therefore. . . . The fallacious items had the form: (1) if p, then q, (2) q, (3) therefore. . . .

Control Group for the Logical Inference Test

The antecedent and consequent forms of the test of logical inference were administered to two control groups of subjects who, between pre- and postadministration of this test, took a test of common information. This test consisted of sixty-five items and covered everyday information in the fields of sports, art, music, science, literature, history, and current events. The intent was to control for experimental task time.

Procedure

The subjects were orally instructed as follows:

Your task is to try to find out the critical or missing grade point average (number of dates, age, q variable) in the rule. I will show you the IQs (ratings, distances, p variables) of a number of students (students, stars, xs), one at a time. After explaining the particulars of each, you will have to answer two questions about the critical grade point average (number of dates, ages, q variables) and then give your estimate of it. You will not be timed. Do you have any questions?

A subject who responded fallaciously on the first trial of a given type of material was queried until he or she gave a valid response. This procedure was not followed on successive trials. Subjects were permitted to keep the slips with the particulars of trial one, their answers to the two questions, and their estimates of the critical value missing in the rule so that they might have them for reference as they studied the particulars of trial two. After they completed their answers and estimates for trial two, the slips for trial one were collected, and subjects were permitted to keep the slips for trial two while they studied those of trial three, and so on for the remaining trials of a given type of material.

At each trial, the subject was required to answer two questions about the relationship between particulars of that trial. The estimate of the critical value missing in the rule was intended to motivate subjects and to furnish an index for the possibility that a subject might be drawing inferences in a haphazard or random fashion.

For the antecedent task, the following two questions were posed on each slip: "Could x be less than the critical grade point average (frequency of dating, age of star, q value) missing in the rule? Could x be more than the critical grade point average (frequency of dating, age of star, q value) missing in the rule?" Here, x represented the particular grade point average (frequency of dating, age of star, q value) on a given trial.

For the consequent task, the following two questions were asked: "Could x be more than the critical IQ (physical attractiveness rating, distance from the Earth, p value) missing in the rule? Could x be less than the critical IQ (physical attractiveness rating, distance from the Earth, p value) missing in the rule?"

For the even-numbered trials, the first of this pair of questions discriminated a valid inference and the second a fallacious inference. A *no* response to these questions indicated that a fallacious inference had been drawn, since it eliminated one of two possibilities. A *yes* response to these questions, which did not exclude either possibility, was therefore the correct answer when they permitted a fallacious inference to be drawn.

Antecedent Task

In the antecedent task, designed to encourage the fallacy of denial of the antecedent, subjects were given the following instructions verbally: "This is a reasoning task that requires a lot of concentration and careful thought. It begins like this: 'In a certain university, the following relationship between intellectual aptitude and grade point average held without exception.' " Subjects were shown a card on which was printed the following rule: "All students with an IQ of 130 or more earned a grade point average of at least _____." In a series of ten trials, subjects were shown the IQs and grade point averages of particular students from the university for which the rule held. Each trial consisted of a separate slip of paper that contained the following information: (1) the IQ and grade point average for a particular student; (2) two questions that asked subjects to determine whether a particular grade point average on the slip could be higher or lower than the grade point average missing in the rule; and (3) a statement that asked subjects to estimate the grade point average missing in the rule. On the first four trials, the grade point averages of students with IQs above 130 were higher than those of students with IQs below 130. It would be valid to infer that the grade point average missing in the rule could not be higher than that of any student whose IQ was more than 130, but fallacious to infer that it could not be less than that of any student having an IQ below 130.

Self-Contradiction

Beginning with the fifth trial and continuing through the tenth, the grade point averages of students were steadily dropped. This permitted a valid inference to be made on trials five, seven, and nine and permitted a fallacious inference to be made on trials six, eight, and ten. For example, on trial four, a student with an IQ of 128 had a grade point average of 3.7, but on trial five a student with an IQ of 135 had a grade point average of 3.5. Thus, the valid inference on trial five that the critical grade point average (the grade point missing in the rule) could not be more than 3.5 contradicted the fallacious inference on trial four that the critical grade point average must be more than 3.7. But on trial six a student with an IQ of 122 had a grade point average of 3.37. The fallacious inference on this trial that the critical grade point average could not be less than 3.37 was consistent with the valid inference on trial five that the critical grade point average could not be more than 3.5. Thus, the valid inferences on trials five, seven, and nine were consistent with the fallacious inferences on trials that succeeded them but inconsistent with fallacious inferences that preceded them.

Consequent Task

In the consequent task, subjects were presented with the following rule: "All students with an IQ of _____ or more earned a grade point average of at least

4.0." It would be valid to infer that all students with a grade point average of less than 4.0 must have an IQ less than that of the critical IQ. It would be fallacious to infer that all students with a grade point average of more than 4.0 must have an IQ higher than that of the critical IQ. On each of ten trials, subjects were presented with the IQ and grade point average of a specific student and required to answer two questions regarding the limits of the critical IQ, as well as to give their correct estimate of it. On trials one, two, three, and four, the IQs of students with grade point averages over 4.0 were all higher than those of students with grade point averages below 4.0. Thus, valid and fallacious inferences on these trials were consistent with each other. Trials one and three permitted valid inferences, and trials two and four, fallacious inferences.

Self-Contradiction

Beginning with trial five, however, the IQs on successive trials were steadily increased. Thus, on trial four, a student with a grade point average of 4.1 had an IQ of 132, but on trial five, a student with a grade point average of 3.9 had an IQ of 136. The valid inference on this trial, that the critical IQ could not be less than 136, contradicted the fallacious inference on trial four, that the critical IQ could not be more than 132. On trial six, however, a student with a grade point average of 3.7 had an IQ of 138. The fallacious inference on this trial that the critical IQ could not be more than 138 was consistent with the valid inference on trial five that the critical IQ could not be less than 136. Thus, valid inferences on trials five, seven, and nine were consistent with the fallacious inferences that followed them but inconsistent with fallacious inferences that preceded them.

Control Group

A control group of subjects was used in both the antecedent and consequent tasks. They differed from the experimental subjects in that the information presented on all ten trials permitted consistency between valid and fallacious inference.

Didactic Correction Method

The subjects in the didactic correction method received the same ten trials as subjects in the control groups. However, in addition, after their response to trial four, they were provided with an explanation of valid or fallacious conclusions for that trial. In the antecedent task, after subjects' responses to trials four, six, eight, and ten, a card was presented with the following information printed on it:

The rule does not say that a student with an IQ less than 130 must have a grade point average less than that of a student whose IQ is more than 130. The rule, in fact, says nothing about a student who has an IQ less than 130. For a student who does have an

IQ less than 130, his grade point average can be either higher or lower than the critical grade point average for the rule.

After trials five, seven, and nine, the following information was presented on a card: "Since the IQ on the slip of paper is above 130, the grade point average on the slip of paper must be above the grade point average for the rule."

In the consequent task, following trials four, six, eight, and ten, the following information was presented on a card: "The rule does not say that a student with a grade point average above 4.0 must have an IQ higher than that for the rule. For a student with a grade point average above 4.0, his IQ can be either higher or lower than the critical IQ for the rule."

Following trials five, seven, and nine, the following information was presented on a card: "Since the grade point average on the slip of paper is less than 4.0, the IQ on the slip of paper must be less than the IQ for the rule."

Material

Personal-Emotional Material (Types A and B)

The generality of the self-contradiction and didactic correction methods was tested across material varying in personal-emotional and scientific-abstract content. Type A material, which dealt with the relationship between IQ and grade point average, has been described. Type B was concerned with the relationship between ratings of physical attractiveness and frequency of dating. In a certain university, the following relationship between physical attractiveness and frequency of dating held without exception: "All men (women) with a physical attractiveness rating of 80% or higher went out on dates at least _____ times a month." For the consequent task, the following rule was used: "All men (women) with a physical attractiveness rating _____% or higher went out on dates at least 20 times a month."

Scientific-Abstract Material (Types C and D)

In a certain scientific study, the following relationship between a star's distance from the Earth and a star's age held without exception: "All stars which are 1,000 light-years or more from the Earth are at least _____ years old." In the consequent task, the rule was as follows: "All stars that are _____ light-years or more from the Earth are at least 3 billion years old."

Type D material involved symbolic and mathematical relationships: A certain group of mathematicians found that the following relationship between variables p and q held without exception: "All xs with a variable p equal to 150 or more had a q variable of at least _____." In the consequent task, the rule was as follows: "All xs with a variable p equal to _____ or more had a q variable of at least 5,000."

Table 1.3
Number of Subjects Initially Susceptible to Making Fallacious Inferences Who Resisted Making Subsequent Fallacious Inferences at Different Stages of the Task or Made the Maximum Number of Fallacious Inferences (i.e., Made No Corrections for Combined Types A, B, C, and D Materials)

Group	Antecedent Task		Consequent Task		Combined Antec. and Conseq. Tasks	
	Resist	No rev.	Resist	No rev.	Resist	No rev.
Self-Contradiction						
Number susceptible	42		52		94	
Sixth trial	7	6	2	0	9	6
Eighth trial	10	2	6	3	16	5
Tenth trial	8	0	4	0	12	0
No. making						
No Corrections	31		45		76	
Control						
Number susceptible	59		73		132	
Sixth trial	1	1	0	0	1	1
Eighth trial	1	0	1	0	2	0
Tenth trial	1	0	0	0	1	0
No. making						
No Corrections	58		72		130	
Didactic correction						
Number susceptible	16		32		48	
Sixth trial	6	5	22	19	28	24
Eighth trial	7	2	25	5	32	7
Tenth trial	8	0	27	1	35	1
No. making						
No Corrections	8		4		12	

Note: Resist refers to Ss who resisted on individual trials; No rev. refers to Ss who did not revert to fallacious reasoning.

Source: Wagman, M. (1984). *The Dilemma and the Computer: Theory, Research, and Applications to Counseling Psychology.* New York: Praeger, p. 110. Reprinted by permission of Praeger Publishers, an imprint of Greenwood Publishing Group, Inc., Westport, CT.

Results

Comparative Effectiveness of Didactic Correction and Self-Contradiction in Inhibiting Fallacious Inferences

The frequency distribution of "resist making fallacious inferences" (Table 1.3) was analyzed with the use of Whitfield's tau (Whitfield, 1947). The major findings were that the didactic correction method was significantly ($p < .001$) more effective than the self-contradiction method, which, in turn, was significantly ($p < .01$) more effective than the control group in inhibiting fallacious reasoning, whether the reasoning task involved scientific reasoning problems or personal reasoning problems.

Comparison of Treatment Groups on Pre-Posttest of Logical Inference

An ANCOVA (Analysis of Covariance) was performed on the eight treatment groups, with the post-score on the logical inference test as the dependent variate and the pre-score as the covariate. Adjusted mean scores (correct inferences) were as follows: didactic correction (antecedent fallacy) group equaled 15.23, didactic correction (consequent fallacy) group equaled 14.59, self-contradiction (antecedent fallacy) group equaled 7.14, self-contradiction (consequent fallacy) group equaled 6.91, pre-postcontrol (antecedent fallacy) group equaled 6.13, and pre-postcontrol (consequent fallacy) group equaled 5.71. The result of the AN-COVA was $F(7, 149) = 8.13$, $p < .01$. Tukey pairwise test comparisons indicated that the two didactic correction groups were significantly different ($p < .01$) from the other six groups. Subsequent separate analyses of scientific versus personal logical inference test items did not change the pattern of findings reported for the total test score.

Discussion

Discussion of Didactic Correction versus Self-Contradiction Method

The didactic correction method proved to be a very effective procedure for reducing fallacious reasoning. Its effectiveness was dependent on a cognitive information-feedback procedure. In a study concerned with the modification of fallacious reasoning with implication (if, then) logical problems, Leahey and Wagman (1974) also found a cognitive information-feedback procedure especially effective. In both the Leahey and Wagman study and the present investigation, it was demonstrated that effectiveness in modifying fallacious reasoning transferred to an external task. The self-contradiction method, though not as effective as the didactic correction method, did significantly reduce fallacious reasoning, as compared with control group performance. This method, however, was dependent on the self-recognition of inconsistency in response and the ability to avoid such self-contradiction in future reasoning responses. Such intellectual competence may well have been an excessive cognitive load for most research participants, and it certainly was more cognitively demanding than being repeatedly reminded by a printed card concerning what were valid and fallacious responses (didactic correction method).

Wason (1964), after demonstrating the effectiveness of the self-contradiction procedure, wondered whether the method would have generality and whether a method based on a teaching machine analogy might prove as effective. The present research demonstrated the generality of the self-contradiction method across reasoning problems with varying personal and scientific content. It also demonstrated the greater effectiveness of a method based on a teaching machine analogy, that is, the didactic correction method.

Wason's data for his combined antecedent and consequent conditions indicated that out of fourteen susceptible subjects in the self-contradiction group, five failed to make any corrections, whereas out of sixteen susceptible subjects in his control group, twelve failed to make any corrections. The respective percentages were 35.7 percent for the self-contradiction group and 75 percent for the control group. In the present research, for all types of material combined and for the antecedent and consequent conditions combined, 76 subjects out of 94 susceptible in the self-contradiction group; 12 out of 48 in the didactic correction group; and 130 out of 132 susceptible in the control group (98.5 percent) failed to make any corrections.

The subjects did not perform as well as Wason's in the self-contradiction and control condition. But subjects in the didactic correction condition performed substantially better than subjects in Wason's self-contradiction condition. The foregoing suggested that the task was especially difficult; 75 percent of Wason's control group and 98.5 percent of the present control group failed to make any corrections of fallacious reasoning.

Reverting to Fallacious Reasoning

Wason found that most of his subjects who, though initially susceptible to making fallacious inferences, successfully resisted making fallacious inferences on trial six or eight and tended to resist making fallacious inferences on the subsequent trials of this ten-trial experiment. In the present research, subjects responded to a total of 40 trials and, more particularly, to ten trials for each of the four types of material. It is of interest to learn whether subjects behaved like Wason's with respect to reverting or not reverting to fallacious reasoning. For this purpose, the data were tabulated (Table 1.3) with respect to the number of subjects who continued to resist fallacious reasoning after their initial correction of fallacious reasoning on a particular trial.

Wason's findings were confirmed for the self-contradiction group and the didactic correction group. Thus, for all four types of material combined and for antecedent and consequent conditions combined (Table 1.3), the appropriate frequencies for trials six, eight, and ten, respectively, were as follows: self-contradiction—6, 5, and 0; didactic correction—24, 7, and 1; control group—1, 0, and 0. It would thus be a moot point as to whether these data support Wason's claim of "insight" by his nonreverting self-contradiction group of subjects or whether they refute the claim and replace it by a "one-trial learning" explanation common to both self-contradiction and didactic correction procedures.

Test of Logical Inference

Although the discussion has thus far emphasized the clear superiority of the didactic correction method to the self-contradiction method in inhibiting fallacious inferences, it is of special interest to note what happened when the support given the didactic correction group by the presence of an explanatory correction card on each trial was removed during the administration of the test of logical inference. The didactic correction group maintained its superior effectiveness, as compared to the self-contradiction method, for both antecedent and consequent reasoning fallacies and for both personal and scientific reasoning content. This finding was unexpected. It had been thought that without the support of the cognitive feedback procedure, the didactic correction group would revert to fallacious reasoning and would thereby drop below the performance level of the self-contradiction group, whose insight into fallacious reasoning, developed by a *reductio ad absurdum* procedure, should be well-transferred to performance on the logical inference test.

Future Research

The present research has compared the relative effectiveness of the two methods for modifying fallacious reasoning. These methods were tested in a trial-by-trial experimental paradigm that required participants to retain information from previous trials. This memory load may have been especially disadvantageous to the self-contradiction method, as reported by several subjects in the postexperimental inquiry. Replacement of the trial-by-trial paradigm with an information array paradigm would eliminate the memory load and thus make possible a clearer competition between a method based on self-recognition and self-correction of inconsistency versus a method based on repetitive cognitive information feedback. It would also be valuable to extend the comparative effectiveness of the two methods to logical fallacies beyond those of denial of the antecedent and affirmation of the consequent.

Experimental Inquiry—Qualitative Aspects

The experimenter (E) administered a standard experimental inquiry to each subject (S) in an effort to learn more about the qualitative differences in approach to the tasks, in reasoning strategies, and in the effect of content on performance.

S-10: Didactic Correction Consequent Group

This S failed to follow the straightforward information given on the didactic correction cards and is a good example of rationalizing her inability to cope with the task demand by insisting that the didactic correction cards were incorrect.

E: Did the instructions given to you on the second task affect your performance on that task?

S-10: I wasn't sure if the [didactic correction] cards were right.

E: This is the correct reasoning for this task.

S-10: Are you trying to trick me or something? I think the cards are confusing. They make it [the task] more confusing rather than making it easier.

The E noted that this S was one of the skeptical ones; she was one of the few who failed to get the didactic correction right. She missed all the ones on that task because she did not understand the cards or she did not think they were right.

S-8: Didactic Correction Consequent Group

The E's notes for this S describe the increased task difficulty produced by the interacting effect of this type of material and the fact of its being administered initially.

E: Did the content have any effect on your answer to the two questions and to the estimates?

S-8: Somewhat. [The E noted that it was mainly Type C, his first type of material, that had a negative effect.] I didn't understand the stars very well.

In general, most people thought that the first type of material had a confusing effect and that the content had some effect on their answers. It was particularly hard to understand when *p*s and *q*s were administered first.

S-13: Didactic Correction Consequent Group

This S illustrates failure of transfer from the didactic correction procedure to the posttest of logical inference and an S for whom the concrete literal instructions on the didactic correction cards could not provide a general enough cognitive structure that would enable her to perceive the common logical inferential pattern involved in both the experimental task and the transfer task. The E noted that this S got the ABDC permutation, got all the pre- and posttest wrong, and "got it" on trial eight of Type A—which was the easiest. The S stated that the pretest had no effect on the posttest and no effect on the experimental task and that the experimental task had no effect on the posttest.

S-6: Self-Contradiction Antecedent Group

This was one of the few subjects who demonstrated excellent reasoning in the self-contradiction task and who gave a good explanation of her cognitive processes and of perceiving that, beginning with trial five, consequent values were steadily increased and that, for antecedent values below the critical value, the consequent value could be either more or less than the critical value missing from the rule. Apparently, then, self-contradiction served effectively to inhibit the drawing of fallacious inferences for all her subsequent experimental trials.

E: Did you have any difficulty in answering either or both of the questions ["Could it be more?" and "Could it be less?"] on the slip of paper on the experimental task?

S-6: I used the idea that there could be no exception. [This means that when she saw these contradictions, she considered those to be exceptions. A few other Ss also did this.] I think it was easier to answer the questions than it was to give the estimates. [The E noted that this was rather unusual—most people thought the reverse.] I think I estimated them pretty accurately and answered the questions well.

E: Was there anything strange about the numbers given on the ten-trial reasoning tasks?

S-6: Yes, on D [*p*s and *q*s, which was her third type of material] lower variables changed to higher variables. The *p*s and *q*s were the most difficult to reason about, but memory played a large part in the experimental task. I think I did better on the later ten-trial sequences—especially the last two.

E: Did the first ten trials have any effect on the next ten trials [the Wason task]?

S-6: It decided the way I graded the next ones. [So it did have some effect.]

E: What process of reasoning did you use?

S-6: The ones that were less than what was needed were yes-yes. [She "got it" on the eighth trial of the first type of B.]

S-16: Self-Contradiction Antecedent Group

In contrast to the previous S, this S, while he performs very well, is not able to give a very lucid account.

S-16: There was no effect of any of the tasks on the other.

E: Were you aware of any contradictions on the ten trials?

S-16: Yes, with the contradictions I worked down to a certain point on the estimates.

E: Did the contradictions have any effect on your answers to the two questions and on your estimate of the critical values?

S-16: Yes.

E: What do you think the task was getting at?

S-16: Logic—a reaction from a situation from something prior. [The S missed *some*. He was not very lucid about his speech, but he did quite well.]

S-3: Self-Contradiction Antecedent Group

An interesting and very frequent phenomenon was the tendency to average data of the ten trials and of sequential estimates, which interacted negatively with the effects of contradiction as illustrated in the following protocol.

E: Was there anything strange about the numbers given on the ten-trial reasoning task?

S-3: I couldn't pick out an average. [Several Ss wanted to average the numbers together in order to find out an estimate, but, of course, there was no average.] I thought there was a contradiction on the first ten, but not on the rest of the three types. [This was because he got it right after the first ten and did not see any contradictions.]

E: What did the contradictions mean to you?

S-3: I was looking for an average. After you [E] explained the first one of the Type C [his second type of material] to me, I got it. [The E queried Type C and explained the first one; E noted that evidently his explanation gave S a clue.]

S-18: Self-Contradiction Antecedent Group

This S, though she gave little in the way of explanation of her reasoning processes, performed perfectly on all trials for all four types of material. She also responded correctly to both the pre- and posttest of logical inference and was able to grasp the logical similarity of the three reasoning tasks. The E noted that this woman was not susceptible; she has had little math and no logic in her educational background. She got everything right on the Wason task.

S-18: I already knew how to do it [i.e., the instructions did not affect her performance].

E: Did the first task have any effect on the second task?

S-18: It used the same form—if-then.

E: Did content have any effect on your reasoning?

S-18: Some. The stars affected my reasoning a little bit because it was harder to think in light-years.

S-9: Self-Contradiction Antecedent Group

The protocol summary exemplifies a type of S best described as a "concrete responder." The E noted that this man got the permutation CADB (stars first). He "got it" on the fourth type of material, which was the dating, but S experienced some difficulty before he mastered it. The E queried C and D.

S-9: The first task made me more careful when I was reasoning on the second task. [The E noted that nothing else had any effect.] I didn't notice any contradictions on the experimental task. [The E explained to S what was contradictory.]

E: What effect, if any, did the contradictions have on your estimate of the critical values?

S-9: I couldn't figure some of it out, but figured it out on that last type. The dating was more understandable. The content had a large effect.

E: Did the content have any effect later on?

S-9: Definitely. The stars and the *p*s and *q*s confuse me.

S-23: Self-Contradiction Antecedent Group

The protocol for this S illustrates very well the effect of contradiction on fallacious reasoning. The E's notes also indicate that this S was well motivated and very much involved in the task, perhaps a requirement more than a desideratum for effectiveness on the contradiction procedure.

E: Did the contradictions on the experimental task affect your reasoning?

S-23: I noticed the contradictions on trial six or seven of Type D material [his first type].

E: What effect, if any, did the contradictions have on your answers to the two questions?

S-23: It reversed the yes-no in some cases and the yes-yes in others.

E: What effects did the contradictions have on your estimates—on your critical values?

S-23: It decreased them. [The E noted that this was the case.] After the first four trials, something seemed to click and I understood what was going on.

S-22: Self-Contradiction Antecedent Group

The inappropriate imposition of a mathematical structure on the particulars of each trial throws this S way off and blocks the working of contradiction. This S had the DCBA permutation—really the hardest in reverse order. The E included in his notes: "Well motivated—cynical—thought he knew everything about math." The S tried to convince the E that the entire experiment was set up wrong. The E had to argue at length with the S before he would even take the test.

The S got the Type D first, which played right into his hands because it was the math type. The trials were numbered X1, X2, X3, X4, . . . , X10, which is simply numbering the trials. It said for an X1 with a *p* variable equal to _____, it had a *q* variable equal to _____. The S was worried that X1 had to be less than X2.

E: Just forget the Xs and just start the trials.

S-22: You can't forget the Xs—they're an integral part of the whole thing. [The E noted that even though S did not think he did, this S got it all wrong.] The first test had a little bit of effect on the third test, but none of the other things had any effect.

E: Were you aware of any contradictions of the ten trials?

S-22: Not actually contradictory; the numbers were misarranged.

E: At what point did you notice that?

S-22: On the first series [Type D], it didn't bother me. Then I changed my answers.

E: What process of reasoning did you use to answer the two questions on the task?

S-22: Nothing would ever be less than a critical value—no relationship was ever established. [The E noted that the S was evidently looking for some mathematical relationship.]

S-11: Self-Contradiction Antecedent Group

The effect of self-contradiction in requiring the S to change her reasoning is indicated in the following protocol summary. The E's notes stated that S did "almost okay—got quite a few right on the Wason task." The E noted that S had a little logic and some math courses in high school.

E: What would you say was the effect of the first task on the second task?

S-11: It was just like syllogisms on both. It did have some effect [the first on the second task]. The other tasks did not have any effect on each other. I noticed the contradictions on the second task on the Type C material [which was the second type she got].

E: What did the contradiction mean to you?

S-11: It forced me to reason correctly [which was what we wanted her to say].

E: Did the content have any effect on your answers to the two questions and on your estimates?

S-11: Yes, the Type C material [stars] was the only one that had an effect. [The E did not have to query her at all. She got all of Type B right, which was the last type, and all of Type A right also, which was the second from the last. She got almost everything right except for the first type; that is, she did correct herself.]

S-1: Control Antecedent Group

This S was able to bypass the diverse content in the four types of material and to respond to their univocal structure. This S was "not susceptible to the Wason task; consequently, he got all the Wason task correct." The E noted that S knew a lot about logic, but he had had no course in it.

S-1: I don't think any of the tasks had any effect on any of the other tasks.

E: What did you think the task was getting at? [The E observed that S was able to explain this question relatively well.]

S-1: I think I made some mistakes on the second question [the second type of material. However, he did not.]

E: What was the effect of content on your answers to the two questions on the estimates?

S-1: Content had no effect. There was a pattern, and they were all logically the same—all the four types. [Evidently, he considered only the logical relationships.]

S-15: Control Antecedent Group

This protocol illustrates the case of a subject who reverts to fallacious reasoning and does so by reinterpreting relationships in the rule.

E: Did the first ten trials on the experimental task [Type B material] have any effect on the next ten, and those on the next ten, and so forth?

S-15: I didn't pay much attention on the second, third, and fourth types.

E: Why did you change from the yes-yes [the correct answer on the first type] to yes-no?

S-15: Because I reinterpreted the rule to mean no one with less than 80 percent rating could go out on more than the critical number of dates [i.e., she reverted to fallacious reasoning].

S-14: Control Antecedent Group

The S's protocol portrays the deleterious intrusion of personal feeling about the content of the task material into her reasoning processes. This S had the CBAD permutation.

E: What effect did the first task have on the third task?

S-14: I left more blanks on the first one. I was worried about personal feelings. It was hard to write down an answer if you don't agree with it, so I based most of my answers on common sense. [The E deduced that she had a more logical approach on the posttest since she did not leave as many blank, but her logic was wrong.]

E: What process of reasoning did you use to answer the two questions on the experimental task?

S-14: I really didn't see what you wanted. [Then, E explained and queried her on the Type B, which was her second type of material. She failed to understand the stars (her first type); she answered no-no to quite a few questions on it.] I inferred things [which refers to her personal feelings toward the dating type of material. She did not give any real explanation for the process of reasoning.] The content of the A [grade point average] and B [dating] types influenced my reasoning.

S-17: Control Antecedent Group

In contrast to the previous S, the protocol of this S indicated a detachment of content from logical operations and insight into the structure of valid and fallacious inferential behavior.

E: Did the second reasoning task have any effect on the last?

S-17: Yes, it confirmed my initial opinions. [Evidently, the "it" refers to the logic of the task.]

E: What would you say was the effect of the first task on the second task?

S-17: The first task gave me the impression that you shouldn't jump to conclusions. [The E noted that this seemed a good insight.] I didn't think that the first task had any effect on the last.

E: Did the first ten trials have any effect on the next ten?

S-17: Not as far as the questions; but with the estimates, yes, there was an effect. There definitely was a pattern involved. There never was a distinct lower value for q [on the Type D material]. Values can always be more than the critical number, but it could sometimes—in certain cases—be less. [The E observed that S was not susceptible. He knew what he was doing all through the experimental task.]

E: Did content enter into your reasoning?

S-17: No, not on a logical basis.

S-19: Control Antecedent Group

In contrast to both the previous Ss, this S declares that content is of no significance to her reasoning, she is highly confident that she was reasoning very well during the experiment, and, despite the fact that she had recently taken a university semester course in logic, she failed completely the logical requirements of the experimental task. The E had to query her on the first type of material, and she failed to get any of the answers right all through the experimental task, even though she did have a logic course.

S-19: I didn't think the questions on the slips of paper were very important. I thought the estimates were more so. I didn't have any difficulty reasoning about anything. The first ten trials made it easier for the next ten trials on the experimental task. [E noted that content had no effect on her reasoning. She seemed to be relatively confident about what she was doing, but she got them all wrong.]

S-21: Didactic Correction Antecedent Group

An example of cognitive rigidity is given in the following protocol summary of a subject who, rather than modifying her inferential behavior, chose to defend it by defying the explanations on the didactic correction cards. The E observed that this S got the experimental task completely wrong. Her background included some logic but only a small amount of math in high school.

E: Did you have any difficulty in answering either or both of the questions on the slips of paper on the experimental task?

S-21: Yes, I believed the instructions but defied the instructions. Still, I thought it would be less. I read the instructions thinking it could be either more or less, but I had it in my mind that the number could be less than the critical value or would have to be less than the critical value, and so I didn't change my reasoning. [The E indicated in his notes that she got everything wrong.] The ps and qs were the most difficult to reason about.

E: Did the didactic correction instructions affect your performance on the third task?

S-21: I disregarded them. They were presented too many times. [The E explained that they were presented after each trial, so she evidently tired of them.]

S-7: Didactic Correction Antecedent Group

The protocol notes for this S indicate an unusual grasp of the common logical structure of the three reasoning tasks and the associated disregard of content. This male S was run with the CDBA permutation. He had taken quite a bit of math in college, including differential equations; however, he had not studied logic. The E included in his notes that this man got it immediately on the experimental task. He seemed to really understand the pre- and posttests as well as the experimental task.

E: What effect did the experimental task have on the third task?

S-7: It was boring. There was no effect of the first on the second [the pre on the post] on the second time [the posttest]. I didn't read after p. I read only p, then q—not p. I only read as far as p, then looked at the second line to see if there was a not-p; and, if there was, I left it blank. [The E noted that S got those right.]

E: Did the instructions given on the experimental task [the didactic correction instructions] affect your performance on that task?

S-7: It was the same logic as the first test.

E: Did the content have any effect on your answers?

S-7: It was ridiculous! I was looking for a formula for the estimates throughout the four types of material. [Some of the people persisted, especially with the Type D, in looking for a formula all the way to the end. Later, on asking the E whether there was a mathematical relationship between the two, some Ss were rather surprised to find out there was not; but most of these were the ones who got it wrong. Most people who concentrated on the estimates seemed to get it wrong, but those who knew what they were doing did not spend much time on the estimates—they put down the same estimate almost throughout. The E queried this S on Type C (his first type of material). The E noted, however, that after S got the instructions, he got it immediately on the sixth trial.]

S-25: Didactic Correction Antecedent Group

A curious "reasoning by extremes" procedure is described in the following protocol summary of this S.

E: What process of reasoning did you use to answer the two questions on the experimental task?

S-25: I looked at the extremes. It couldn't be less, or more, or whatever. [The E observed that S fell into the pattern yes-no, no-yes, and reasoned it out in this manner, which was, of course, wrong.]

E: What did you think the task was getting at?

S-25: How well you can predict what one number will be, given others.

E: Did content have any effect on your reasoning?

S-25: Only on the grade point average (Type A). [The E noted that S got them all wrong on the last one.]

S-4: Control Consequent Group

The essential structuring given to the rule by the words "at least" is ignored by this S, and she fails on all trials.

E: What process of reasoning did you use?

S-4: I looked at the extreme values and eliminated them.

E: Did you notice any key words in the rules that were essential to the understanding of the problem?

S-4: No. [The E explained that the words noticed should be "at least" or "or more," and that most persons recognized at least one of the two possibilities. Content had no effect on the S's reasoning. The E recorded that this was a typical control S. Also, she did not get anything right on the experimental task.]

S-24: Self-Contradiction Consequent Group

This protocol illustrates a subject who, unlike many others, could both perceive inconsistency in the "strangeness" of the sequencing of information and respond to the inconsistency with a correct resolution.

E: Was there anything strange about the numbers that were given on the ten-trial sequences in the experimental task?

S-24: They set you up for a low number and then threw in a high number.

E: What process of reasoning did you use to answer the two questions on the task?

S-24: On the star material, if the particular number was above the limit, then I answered yes-yes. If the distance was less than 40 million light-years, then it was less than the represented amount.

S-29: Self-Contradiction Consequent Group

In contrast to the previous S, this S recognizes the inconsistency in the presented information but is unable to resolve it.

E: Was there anything strange about the numbers given on the ten-trial sequences on the experimental task?

S-29: There could be a high IQ with a low grade point average and a high rating with low dating. [The E noted that S evidently saw these numbers as something strange and contradictory.] I thought the *p*s and *q*s were the most difficult to reason about, because they were mathematical and because they were given first. I think I did best on the dating type.

E: Did the first ten trials have any effect on the next ten?

S-29: Yes, they were confusing.

E: Was there a pattern involved—generally? Was there a pattern in your yes-no responses, no-yes, or yes-yes, in your answers to the questions?

S-29: Not until the last ten (Type B material). [However, the E noted that she got the last type wrong anyway.]

E: Did you notice any keywords that were in the rules that were essential to the understanding of the problem?

S-29: Yes, "at least" or "or more."

E: Did you find what might be thought of as a solution or general statement you could make to summarize the main problems on the task? [The E asked either this question or "what was the process of reasoning you used."]

S-29: No. The A and B type of material was easier. [The E observed that she did not get anything right, had good motivation, good concentration, and was friendly.]

S-12: Self-Contradiction Consequent Group

The following protocol is of a subject who had two semesters of university calculus, perceived the common logical structure of the three experimental tasks, recognized the critical importance of "at least" or "more than," recognized the presence of changes in the consequent values, and yet failed completely to take account of the contradictions implied and consequently failed all trials. The E indicated in his notes that this S, who had no previous courses in logic, got the

ABCD permutation and gave no right answers on the experimental task. The E queried him on the first type of material (Type B).

E: Did the experimental task have any effect on the third task? Did the first task have any effect on the second task?

S-12: No, from the first to the third, there was a collective process. [The E noted that the S must have meant some sort of practice effect.] The third was easier. The first introduced you to the third.

E: To what degree were tasks one and two related?

S-12: To a high degree. Also, the experimental and the third to a high degree. One and three [the pre and post] were the same.

E: How important did you feel the two questions on each slip of paper were on the experimental task?

S-12: The importance was to see how my opinions could change. [The E noted that S was thinking in ratios, which was wrong. In fact, S even remarked that this was wrong on the first type of material, Type A.]

E: Did you have any difficulty in answering either or both the questions on the slips of paper?

S-12: No, not after Type A. [Nevertheless, S did get them all wrong.]

E: Was there anything strange about the numbers on the ten-trial sequences?

S-12: Some seemed completely extreme exceptions to the rule.

E: Were you aware of any contradictions to the ten trials? What was contradictory?

S-12: The extremes.

E: What effects, if any, did the contradictions have on your answers to the two questions?

S-12: None.

E: What effect, if any, did they have on your estimates?

S-12: None. I disregarded the extremes as exceptions.

E: What process of reasoning did you use in answering the two questions on the task?

S-12: I answered the questions from the estimates. I made the estimate first, then answered the question from that [which was a dangerous way to go about it].

E: Did there seem to be a pattern involved?

S-12: Yes, the last five got to be real high values.

E: How big a part would you say memory played in the experimental task?

S-12: Pretty big part—I had to remember the first. The dating was the most difficult to reason about. *P*s and *q*s were the easiest. All the materials were the same in logical sense.

E: Did the first ten trials have any effect on the next ten?

S-12: Yes, they familiarized me with the material.

E: What do you think the task was getting at?

S-12: How good a gin player you are. You can draw conclusions from certain facts.

E: Did you notice any key words in the rules that were essential to the understanding of the problem?

S-12: "At least" and "or more."

E: Did my correction of your answer in the first trial help you later in the task? [Earlier, S had asked E if this was an average, and E replied no.]

S-12: That helped.

E: Did the content have any effect on your reasoning?

S-12: On Type A it did—on Type D maybe. I started comparing my own grade point average with the ones in the tasks. [This S did not get any right.]

S-28: Self-Contradiction Consequent Group

The following protocol illustrates a subject for whom self-contradiction worked very effectively at an early point in the experimental trials and who, apparently, transferred this learning successfully to the posttest of logical inference. For this S, E's notes indicate that S corrected his reasoning on trial eight of his first type of material (Type C) and got [all] correct from there on; E did not query him at all. This S had two weeks of logic in high school and calculus and differential equations in college.

E: Did the experimental task have any effect on the third task?

S-28: I remembered the logic I had on the second task, and it helped me on the third. The first test had no effect on the experimental, and the first test had no effect on the third.

E: Was there anything strange about the numbers given on the ten-trial sequences?

S-28: Yes—high-low and 5. [The E noted that from trial four to trial five S noticed the contradiction of the high number with the low corresponding number.] It was the same on all trials—one that fit, one that didn't.

E: Were you aware of any contradictions, and what was contradictory?

S-28: On the first type there was a contradiction. [The E noted that evidently S did not notice any after that because he corrected his reasoning; that is, he noticed a contradiction of the first type and corrected his reasoning. From then on, there would not have been any contradictions.]

Summary

The relative power of two methods of changing fallacious reasoning was investigated in 160 male or female undergraduate university students. Subjects (Ss) were randomized among three experimental conditions: didactic correction method, self-contradiction method, and control. Resistance to committing the fallacies of affirmation of the consequent and denial of the antecedent was studied in an experimental reasoning task. The didactic correction method was significantly ($p < .001$) more effective than the self-contradiction method for both types of logical fallacies and for both scientific reasoning problems and personal reasoning problems. On a transfer task concerned with a reduction of errors in drawing logical inferences, the didactic correction method was significantly ($p < .01$) more effective than the self-contradiction method. It was concluded that the didactic correction method, based on repetitive cognitive information feedback procedures, was more effective in reducing fallacious reasoning than the self-contradiction method, based on self-recognition of inconsistency in inferential behavior. It was recommended that the comparative efficacy of the didactic correction and self-contradiction methods be studied in a fixed array rather than in a trial-by-trial paradigm in order to reduce memory load and that generality of method effectiveness be studied with type of logical fallacies beyond the affirmation of the consequent and the denial of the antecedent.

NATURAL REASONING AND HUMAN INTELLECT

The Concept of Natural Reasoning

The term *natural reasoning* has been used in several senses. In one sense, natural reasoning is contrasted with artificial reasoning, where artificial may refer either to contrived laboratory experiments in the psychology of human reasoning or to reasoning as it is performed by computers. In a second sense, natural reasoning is contrasted with technical reasoning, where technical may refer either to the tactics, strategies, and procedures of an art, craft, or profession or to the formal axioms and theorems of a system of logic or mathematics. In a third sense, natural reasoning is contrasted with academic reasoning, where natural reasoning refers to untutored, practical, everyday reasoning and academic reasoning refers to trained, abstract, and specialized reasoning. In a fourth sense, natural reasoning has been identified with animal reasoning, in contrast to human reasoning. In a fifth sense, natural reasoning has been identified with the Rousseauian doctrine (Cornford, 1945) of the wisdom of the preliterate, in contrast to the Platonic doctrine (Brumfitt and Hall, 1973) of the wisdom of the philosopher-king. These distinctive senses of natural reasoning should be kept in mind in the following discussion of natural reasoning and human intellect.

Elsewhere in this chapter, Thomas Hobbes is described as the proponent of the view that human reasoning is but computation. As this discussion makes clear, the Hobbesian doctrine may be in need of revision. *Artificial intelligence and not human reasoning is but computation.* Research appears to indicate that human reasoning is extramathematical, extralogical, and often biased by ineffective heuristics (Galotti, 1989).

Experimental Research in Natural Reasoning

Reasoning has been studied in the experimental psychology laboratory with both formal abstract problems and informal problems similar to experiences in everyday life (Rips, 1990). Formal or artificial problems that require application of rules of logical inference (see the earlier section on modus tollens and human intellect) are difficult because most people are not trained in symbolic logic. People respond to such problems with extralogical maneuvers, visualizing and recalling solutions to situations that resemble the problems (Evans, 1982; Johnson-Laird, 1983). How well do people perform with laboratory problems that resemble everyday situations? Such problems might concern estimating odds or making probability judgments, such as those involved in guessing some-one's occupation or in figuring the chances of becoming ill with a life-threatening disease. Another class of problems concerns practical matters such as subdividing a group of persons into a series of committees. Natural reasoning with such everyday problems often depends on rule-of-thumb cognitive opera-tions, termed *heuristics*, that enable an all-too-quick response to the requirements of the problems. Several examples of research with everyday natural reasoning problems are now discussed.

The Similarity Heuristic and Natural Reasoning

Kahneman and Tversky (1973) informed one group of subjects that a person had been picked at random from a group of people composed of 70 engineers and 30 lawyers. A second group of subjects was informed that a person had been picked at random from a group composed of 30 engineers and 70 lawyers. Subjects were required to estimate the probability that the person was an engi-neer. The mean estimate for the engineer-high group was .70, and the mean estimate for the engineer-low group was .30.

Next, the subjects were informed that another person was selected at random, and they were provided with the following summary description of the person.

Jack is a 45-year-old man. He is married and has four children. He is generally con-servative, careful, and ambitious. He shows no interest in political and social issues and spends most of his free time on his many hobbies, which include home carpentry, sailing, and mathematical puzzles. (Kahneman and Tversky, 1973)

Next, the subjects were required to provide probability estimates that the described person was an engineer. Subjects in the engineer-high group estimated that the chances were 90 out of 100 that Jack was an engineer, and subjects in the low group gave the same estimate.

The summary description of Jack was similar to the stereotype of an engineer and dissimilar to the stereotype of a lawyer. The similarity factor exercised an upward displacement on subjects' estimates. Subjects in the engineer-low group apparently permitted the similarity heuristic to block adequate consideration of the fact that the prior probability of Jack being an engineer was only .30.

Thus, natural reasoning resulted in a probability estimate of .90, although the base rate was only .30. In contrast to natural reasoning, formal reasoning—in

Table 1.4
The Derivation of Bayes's Theorem

The posterior probability of a hypothesis if given evidence E is

$$P(H \mid E) = \frac{P(H \cap E)}{P(E)} \tag{1}$$

where P(H ∩ E) is the probability of both H and E being true and P(E) is the probability of the evidence. We can express these as

$$P(H \cap E) = P(E \mid H)P(H) \tag{2}$$

and

$$P(E) = P(H \cap E) + P(\bar{H} \cap E) \tag{3}$$

where

$$P(\bar{H} \cap E) = P(E \mid \bar{H})P(\bar{H}) \tag{4}$$

In these equations, P($\bar{H}$ ∩ E) denotes the probability of both the hypothesis being false and the evidence still obtaining; P(E|H) is the conditional probability of the evidence if the hypothesis is true; P(E|$\bar{H}$) is the conditional probability of the evidence if the hypothesis is false; P(H) is the prior probability of the hypothesis; and P($\bar{H}$) = 1 - P(H). Substituting equations 2, 3, and 4 into equation 1, we get the form of Bayes's theorem that we have been using:

$$P(H|E) = \frac{P(E \mid H)P(H)}{P(E \mid H)P(H) + P(E \mid \bar{H})P(\bar{H})}$$

Source: Anderson, J. R. (1985). *Cognitive Psychology and Its Implications*, 2nd ed. New York: W. H. Freeman and Co., p. 300.

particular Bayes's mathematical probability theorem (see Table 1.4)—would require, based on the difference in prior probabilities for the two groups (.30 and .70), a distinctly smaller posterior probability for the engineer-low group than for the engineer-high group. Yet both groups gave a posterior probability of .90.

In a further phase of the research (Kahneman and Tversky, 1973), subjects were presented with a description of a person that contained no clues regarding possible professional identity.

Dick is a 30-year-old man. He is married with no children. A man of high ability and high motivation, he promises to be quite successful in his field. He is well liked by his colleagues. (Kahneman and Tversky, 1973)

Subjects in both the engineer-low group and the engineer-high group estimated that the posterior probability was .5 that Dick was an engineer. In this case, subjects apparently responded to the noninformative sketch by making the 50–50 estimate. Bayes's theorem (see Table 1.4) would provide that because no informative evidence was provided, the posterior probability is the same as the prior probability (.30 for the engineer-low group, .70 for the engineer-high group). Natural reasoning deviated from formal reasoning and produced the failure to consider prior probabilities.

In this research, natural reasoning was extramathematical, not in the sense of computationally deviating from Bayes's formula (see Table 1.4) but in a sense of conceptually deviating. That is, subjects should not be expected to compute mentally the posterior probability from the prior and conditional probabilities but should be expected to understand the interdependence of the concepts of prior probability, conditional probability, and posterior probability. Such understanding would advance reasoning an additional increment beyond the condition of Rousseauian natural reasoning (Nisbett et al., 1987).

The Availability Heuristic and Natural Reasoning

In natural reasoning, events that are easily remembered or easily computed are illusorily perceived as more common. For example, what comes readily to mind, for most persons, is judged as more common in occurrence, whereas what comes to mind with difficulty is judged as relatively rare. This illusory aspect of natural reasoning, termed the *availability heuristic*, has been widely investigated.

Kahneman and Tversky (1973) requested their subjects to judge the relative proportion of words in English that begin with the letter k or that have k as the third letter in a word. Subjects reported that k-beginning words came more readily to mind than did words with k as the third letter, and subjects judged the former to be more common than the latter.

The illusory judgment, the results of the availability heuristic, deviated sharply from the fact that k-beginning words are only one-third as common as words with k as the third letter. K-beginning words are more strongly associated in semantic memory, and more of them are recalled into mental content—from which the illusory conclusion is drawn of their higher prevalence in external reality. Analogously, words with k as the third letter are weakly associated in semantic memory, resulting in lower recall and in illusory judgment of lower representation in reality.

The memory aspect of the availability heuristic, in which events that are remembered more easily are judged to be more frequent in occurrence, was investigated by Slovic, Fischoff, and Lichtenstein (1976). Subjects were requested to judge the relative likelihood of occurrence of events: Death from accidents or death from strokes, from murder or from diabetes, from cancer or from heart disease. Subjects erroneously judged the first member of each pair to be more frequent. Dramatically and frequently reported in the communication media, cases of death from accident, homicide, or cancer are easily recalled from memory and illusorily judged more frequent than cases of death from stroke, diabetes, or heart disease.

Another example of the availability heuristic is that events that are easily computed are illusorily judged as more common. Kahneman and Tversky (1973) requested one group of subjects to estimate how many subcommittees of two persons each could be formed from a set of ten persons, and they asked a second group of subjects to estimate how many subcommittees of eight persons could be formed from a set of ten persons. The first group of subjects produced a median estimate of 70 subcommittees, and the second group of subjects produced a median estimate of 20 subcommittees. The correct answer to the two questions is identical: 45 subcommittees.

The reason for the identical answer derives from the symmetric conditions: Every eight-person subcommittee that is formed leaves a remainder of two persons who could form a different subcommittee, and every two-person subcommittee leaves a remainder of eight persons who could form a different committee.

Subjects in either group could have arrived at the correct answer of 45 subcommittees with a little knowledge of combinations and factorials: The number of combinations of k objects that can be formed from a set of n objects equals $n! / (k)! (n - k)!$. For the two-member subcommittee problem, $n = 10$, $k = 2$. For the eight-member subcommittee problem, $n = 10$, $k = 8$. Substituting these values reveals that the number of combinations (45) is identical for the two problems because the numerators (10!) are identical and the denominators (2!8!; 8!2!), except for the order of the factorials, are also identical.

The substantial deviations in the median estimates (70 two-member and 20 eight-member subcommittees) from the true value (45 subcommittees) suggest that most subjects possess neither verbal nor mathematical insight into the problems. The explanation offered by Kahneman and Tversky was that subjects were victims of their own availability heuristic that created illusory estimates. Subjects can easily form and retain different two-member subcommittees, and this facile productivity results in their overestimation of the number of possible subcommittees. On the other hand, subjects construct and retain different eight-member subcommittees with difficulty, and their low productivity rate leads them to an underestimation of the number of possible subcommittees.

REASONING AND A GENERAL THEORY OF INTELLIGENCE

The clear implication of the various research studies discussed is that natural reasoning is often biased by the uncritical use of the similarity and availability heuristics and that people do not understand or apply the relevant formal reasoning concepts (mathematical or logical) that could prevent illusory conclusions.

The power of formal reasoning has been challenged by some investigators who provide examples of how problems that might seem to require formal reasoning can be solved by other methods. These methods, in general, involve visualizing possible arrangements of elements in a problem or tying numerical concepts to specific physical objects and relationships.

In other instances, concrete mental models allow the performance of complex tasks that might be supposed to require abstract formal reasoning procedures. For example, Denny (1986) found that Ojibway and Inuit hunters successfully accomplish environmentally relevant quantitative reasoning even though their concepts of number and arithmetical operations are completely tied to the particular objects to which they are applied. Strikingly similar results were obtained in a very different setting by Scribner (1984) in a study of preloaders in an American dairy who accomplish the equivalent of mixed-base arithmetic by visualization of partial case lots without having to resort to counting. In both instances, the situational context, through the mediation of appropriate mental models, supports the accomplishment of tasks that would require much more sophisticated and difficult procedures to do out of context. (Oden, 1987, p. 218)

These examples deserve at least two comments. The first is that these may be examples not of reasoning but of extrareasoning imaginal and kinesthetic modes of problem approach and solution, analogous, to some extent, to the mental catalog of imaginal snapshots of typical chess positions and chess moves regularly used by expert and master chess players (de Groot, 1965, 1966). The second comment is that context-determined methods are task-limited (and, perhaps, in their reliance on habitual concrete imaginal mental models, cannot advance many increments beyond the Rousseauian doctrine of natural reasoning), whereas the essential power of formal reasoning (advanced logic and mathematics) is its generality of application, both to the given concrete examples and to far more complex and abstract problems (Eisenstadt and Simon, 1997; Rips, 1994).

A general theory of intelligence should embrace explanation ability or reasons for behavior, whether the behavior is that of human intellect or that of artificial intelligence (Wagman, 1997a). Explanations that consist of a sequence of steps or rules are common in the two realms of intelligence. However, the capacity to adjust explanation with respect to the intended audience may, at the present time, be restricted to the human realm. For example, expert systems, as a technological embodiment of artificial intelligence, are evaluated as deficient in this component of general intelligence:

> Explanation by human experts, in general, are tailored to their audiences. The details of reasoning as related to another expert in the same domain will be different from those related to a layman. This requires a kind of intelligent behavior not apparent in the explanation facilities of current expert systems. (Hayes-Roth, Waterman, and Lenat, 1983, p. 49)

From a historical perspective, it is interesting that three centuries before the era of expert systems, Decartes (1596–1650) had made a similar observation regarding the unadaptive and unintelligent speech of a mechanical automation: "It never happens that it [the automation] arranges its speech in various ways, in order to reply appropriately to everything that may be said in its presence, as even the lowest of man can do" (quoted in Wilson, 1969, p. 138).

It is of interest that the mathematical reasoning method used by Euclid and termed *reductio ad absurdum* was later used by Turing (1936) to establish that there can be no universal algorithm for proving the truth for all theorems in a broad class of mathematical problems. This algorithmic basis of artificial intelligence is thereby limited.

RATIONALITY AND PSYCHOLOGICAL RESEARCH

In previous sections, rationality has been examined in various contexts and with respect to tensions and antinomies between rationality both as formal deductive structure and as descriptive reality. In the present section, the tensions concerning the two versions of rationality are examined in the context of psychological research. In particular, the research of Kahneman and Tversky (Kahneman, Slovic, and Tversky, 1982; Kahneman and Tversky, 1982, 1984; Tversky and Kahneman, 1983) is discussed in a series of examples drawn from that research, with emphasis on the nature of the assumptions, interpretations, abstractions, criteria, and conclusions regarding human rationality.

Example One

Two groups of subjects were told either (Group A) that on the way to the theatre they lost tickets that cost $40 or (Group B) that on the way to the theatre they lost cash in the amount of $40. The groups were asked if they would buy new tickets. Group A less frequently responded that they would. Spending $80 in a theatre-going account was too extravagant. Group B subjects assigned their loss to a general cash account not tied specifically to theatre tickets.

The researchers asserted that Group A and Group B should not differ because the totality of expenditures ($80) would be identical. Clearly, this is an example of inappropriate mathematical abstraction that dissolved the differentiated cognitive structures (theater-going account, general cash account) of subjects (see

Table 1.5
Problematic Assumptions, Abstractions, and Conclusions in the Kahneman and Tversky Research on the Psychology of Rationality

I.   FOCUS OF STUDY
        The focus of study should be defining, describing, and measuring actual human reasoning with the psychological problem, rather than mathematical abstraction and idealization of the psychological problem.

II.   MATHEMATICAL ABSTRACTION

        The mathematical abstraction of the psychological problem requires drastic assumptions that essentially eliminate the psychological conditions of the human reasoner, which were supposed to be the object of the study.

III. SELECTION OF MATHEMATICAL STRUCTURES

        The particular mathematical formulae used by Kahneman and Tversky represent an arbitrary selection from a broad range of possible formulae. There are many versions of Bayes's theorem and Bayes's equations, and there are many versions of standard and nonstandard mathematical theorems of probability and probability equations (Mackie, 1973).

IV.   APPLICATION OF ACTUARIAL PREDICTION

        The theory of actuarial prediction is based on population samples with application to target sample, with probability statements having reference to the sample, with increasing error as size of sample diminishes, and with maximum error in application to the single case. Moreover, as the amount of definitive information regarding the single case increases, the value of and need for actuarial prediction diminishes rapidly.

V.   CRITERIA OF RATIONALITY AND ASSOCIATED CONCLUSIONS

        The criterion of adherence to abstract deductive structures is inappropriate and results in the unwarranted conclusion that human rationality is, in general, of low quality. The transformation of a complex psychological problem constituted of affective, conative, cognitive, situational, and cultural interacting components into a rationalized mathematical problem whose solution becomes the criterion for solution of the psychological problem and from which conclusions about human reasoning with psychological problems are drawn is, altogether, a highly dubious process.

Source: Wagman, M. (1991a). *Artificial Intelligence and Human Cognition: A Theoretical Inter-comparison of Two Realms of Intellect*. New York: Praeger, p. 34. Reprinted by permission of Praeger Publishers, an imprint of Greenwood Publishing Group, Inc., Westport, CT.

Section II of Table 1.5) and of an inappropriate imposition of a criterion of abstract rationality (see Section V of Table 1.5).

Example Two

Subjects were given a description of a 31-year-old woman, and then they were asked to assign probability estimates to statements about her. The description included the information that as a college student she majored in philosophy, became intensely interested in issues concerned with social equity, and actively participated in antinuclear and antidiscrimination demonstrations. Subjects were asked to rank a set of eight statements from the most probable to the least probable. Included in the set were items: (a) "she is a bank teller and active in the feminist movement," (b) "she is a bank teller," (c) "she is a psychiatric social worker."

The researchers found that 80 percent of the subjects ranked the first item as more probable than the second item, and they concluded that this was a violation of rationality because mathematical probability theory stipulates that given events X and Y, the probability of both X and Y is less than the probability of X alone or the probability of Y alone. According to the researcher, the subjects were biased or in error because they integrated the details of the woman's activist background with the detail of being a feminist. However, this integration of information is not in error, nor is it in violation of statistical probability, because the information is reasonably linked and not absolutely independent, as required in mathematical abstraction (see Section II of Table 1.5) and because increased knowledge of the single case renders abstract actuarial prediction less applicable (see Section IV of Table 1.5).

Example Three

Subjects were informed that in a court case a witness to a cab crash had identified the cab as green, that under the environmental conditions such witnesses can correctly distinguish green cabs from blue cabs 80 percent of the time, and that in a particular city the ratio of green cabs to blue cabs is 15 percent to 85 percent. The researchers then asked subjects to state the probability that the cab in the crash was actually a blue cab.

For the group of subjects, a median probability of .20 was found. The researchers claimed that the median probability estimate of .20 was incorrect because the subjects should have construed the problems as a mathematical abstraction and applied a statistical measure that takes account of base rates. In particular, the researchers contended that the subjects should have construed the problem in terms of Bayes's theorem (see Table 1.4), which does take into account base rates or a priori probabilities. In this case, the base rates of green cabs and blue cabs were quite different (15 percent green cabs, 85 percent blue cabs, information given to the subjects).

The researchers (Tversky and Kahneman, 1977) applied Bayes's theorem (see Table 1.4), assuming that the a priori probabilities were to be taken into account simply on the basis of the frequency of the blue and green cabs and regardless of whether blue and green cabs had any differential accident rates. Thus, the researchers computed the values for the terms in Bayes's equation (5) in Table 1.4 as follows:

$$P(H|E) = \frac{(.2)(.85)}{(.2)(.85) + (.8)(.15)} = \frac{.17}{.29} = .59$$

However, because no information was given regarding differential accident rates for blue and green cabs, their relative frequency can be disregarded, or, following LaPlace's rule, each a priori probability can be assigned a value of .5, in which case, $P(H) = P(H) = .5$. Therefore, the a priori probabilities are canceled out, yielding:

$$P(H|E) = \frac{(.2)(.5)}{(.2)(.5) + (.8)(.5)} = \frac{.2}{.2 + .8} = .2$$

We have presented the researchers' analysis and the subjects' analysis in terms of Bayes's theorem. Clearly, the researchers used Bayes's theorem (albeit incorrectly), but it is not at all clear that the subjects used Bayes's theorem, unless it so happened that they were simultaneously taking a course in statistics in which they had recently studied Bayes's equation. So it is most likely that the subjects (a) disregarded the disparity in number of blue and green cabs as having no bearing and (b) simply subtracted the correct identification value of .8 from 1.0 to yield the estimate of .2 that the cab was actually blue.

The experiment throws no light on what the subjects' actual cognitive processes were. It merely tells that they did not follow the experimenters' interpretation and application of Bayes's theorem (and that they probably did not use Bayes's theorem at all). But if we want to understand the nature of reasoning in everyday situations or in jurors evaluating witnesses' evidence in testimony in a court case, then the focus of research should not be on the question of whether subjects can or cannot apply a normative statistical measure but on what cognitive processes lead them to take account of, or not to take account of, base rates and how that information can be combined with the evaluation of the witnesses' testimony or evidence (see Section I of Table 1.5).

In reviewing their own extensive research involving "more than 3,000 subjects and dozens of problems," Tversky and Kahneman (1983, p. 309) reach a conclusion, in line with the present analysis (see Table 1.5), that mathematical abstraction, except for "the domain of random sampling" (p. 310) is not an appropriate standard or descriptor of everyday human rationality:

Judgements of probability vary in the degree to which they follow a decompositional or a holistic approach and in the degree to which the assessment and the aggregation of probabilities are analytic or intuitive. . . . At one extreme there are questions (e.g., What are the chances of beating a given hand in poker?) that can be answered by calculating the relative frequency of "favorable" outcomes. Such an analysis possesses all the features associated with an extensional approach: It is decompositional, frequentistic, and algorithmic. At the other extreme, there are questions (e.g., What is the probability that the witness is telling the truth?) that are normally evaluated in a holistic, singular, and intuitive manner. . . . Decompositions and calculation provide some protection against conjunction errors and other biases, *but the intuitive element cannot be entirely eliminated from probability judgements outside the domain of random sampling.* (Tversky and Kahneman, 1983, p. 310; italics added)

The tension between the normative and the descriptive accounts of rationality, introduced at the beginning of this section, and the inappropriateness of mathematical or logical modeling of everyday ordinary reasoning, discussed in the present section (and summarized in Table 1.5), are recognized reluctantly by Tversky and Kahneman (1983) in their admission of the problems entailed by a research model that studies deviations from normative mathematical and logical models of reasoning; problems that could be obviated by research that studies actual details of everyday reasoning with its myriad inconsistent but useful distinctions of judgments according to idiosyncratic contexts that cannot be modeled by formal mathematical abstractions (see Section I of Table 1.5):

Our studies of inductive reasoning have focused on systematic errors because they are diagnostic of the heuristics that generally govern judgement and inference. . . . The focus on bias and illusion is a research strategy that exploits human error, although it neither assumes nor entails that people are perceptually or cognitively inept. . . .

We have argued that intuitive judgements of all relevant marginal, conjunctive, and conditional probabilities are not likely to be coherent, that is, to satisfy the constraints of probability theory. . . .

The violations of the qualitative laws of geometry and probability in judgements of distance and likelihood have significant implications for the interpretation and use of these judgements. Incoherence sharply restricts the inferences that can be drawn from subjective estimates. . . . Furthermore, a system of judgements that does not obey the conjunction rule cannot be expected to obey more complicated principles that presuppose this rule, such as Bayesian updating, external calibration, and the maximization of expected utility. *The presence of bias and incoherence does not diminish the normative forces of these principles, but it reduces their usefulness as descriptions of behavior and hinders their prescriptive applications. Indeed, the elicitation of unbiased judgements and the reconciliation of incoherent assessments pose serious problems that presently have no satisfactory solution.* (Lindley, Tversky, and Brown, 1979; Shafer and Tversky, 1983; italics added)

The issue of coherence has loomed larger in the study of preference and belief than in the study of perception. . . . In the absence of an objective criterion of validity, the normative theory of judgement under uncertainty has treated the coherence of belief as the touchstone of human rationality. Coherence has also been assumed in many descriptive analyses of psychology, economics, and other social science. This assumption is attractive because the strong normative appeal of the laws of probability makes violations appear implausible. Our studies of the conjunction rule show that normatively inspired theories that assume coherence are descriptively inadequate, whereas psychological analyses that ignore the appeal of normative rules are, at best, incomplete. A comprehensive account of human judgement must reflect the tension between compelling logical rules and seductive nonextensional intuitions. (Tversky and Kahneman, 1983, pp. 313–314; italics added)

Conclusion

Formal constructs of rationality vary with respect to their existence as self-contained systems and with respect to impingement on and interaction with the empirical concerns of science and of ordinary, everyday reasoning. Systems of formal mathematics and formal logic may be essentially autonomous deductive structures with little or no interpretive applications. Systems of mathematics may have intimate and mutually dependent relationships with theoretical and applied science. Mathematical models may be viewed as conceptual tools directed toward the improvement of understanding in physics, economics, and psychology. As discussed above, mathematical modeling of psychological reasoning is especially difficult, and the balancing of formal criteria and heuristic criteria in judging the quality of human rationality constitutes, in itself, a significant and formidable problem in rational analysis (Anderson, 1993; Simon, 1982, 1991).

As self-involved reasoners investigating our own rationality, we may be forever limited by self-recursive cognition and the absence of a comparative standard. Comparison with the rationality of artificial intelligence may, to some extent and from certain perspectives, obviate the limitation (Wagman, 1999).

DEDUCTIVE REASONING AND ARTIFICIAL INTELLIGENCE

The Logical Foundation of Artificial Intelligence

The predicate calculus is the logical foundation of the rationality of artificial intelligence. The representation of knowledge in computers may take a variety of convenient forms, such as that of the semantic network; but these forms are theoretically reducible (Hayes, 1977) to the predicate calculus. The predicate calculus thus provides the general scope and power of the reasoning ability of artificial intelligence (McCarthy, 1988). However, the reasoning ability of artificial intelligence is restricted to formal rationality. The rationality of artificial intelligence, operating through the predicate calculus, is purely symbolic (Sterling and Shapiro, 1986).

Devoid of content and dependent only on formal logic structures and operations, artificial intelligence possesses an implacable and formidable rationality (Wagman, 1998a). Complex problems in an ever-expanding range of disciplines—including aspects of the humanities and (more centrally) the physical, biological, and social sciences—are construed in the indifferent language of the predicate calculus and reduced through a series of theorem-proving operations to a set of symbols consisting only of negative and affirmative disjuncts—completely empty of content but, through the general resolution method, yielding a solution to a problem. The significant question now arises: How shall we inter-compare the rationality of artificial intelligence and the rationality of human intellect?

Rationality in both artificial intelligence and human intellect has as its central theme the drawing of inferences, that is, coming to accept a fact based on another fact. Inferences that are logically correct are deductive inferences. The predicate calculus (originated by Frege, 1879) is a deductive system of logic that includes a technical language for the correct formulation of propositions (statements about facts) and a set of technical rules for correctly deducing new propositions or facts.

The Affinity of Logical Reasoning and Mathematics

This logical calculus reminds us of the affinity of mathematics (Michener, 1978) and logical reasoning. Leibniz, (along with Newton) the developer of the differential and integral calculus, envisioned the application of a philosophy of calculation (his "universal character") to reasoning about general fields of human knowledge.

In a similar vein, Hobbes (1588–1679) in his *Leviathan* (1651) pithily stated that "reasoning is but reckoning," where reckoning was for Hobbes a synonym for calculating. Hobbes's formulation is a classical statement of the modern rendition: Reasoning is but a computational transform.

Again, Boole (1815–1864) developed an algebra (based on the logical con-nectives and the binary number system) of thought (see Table 1.6). In the preface to his book (1854), Boole states: "The mathematics we have to construct are the mathematics of the human intellect."

Whereas Boole attempted to apply mathematics to reasoning, Euclid (fl. 300 B.C.) applied reasoning to mathematical theorem proving (Wos, 1983). In a way, we may cite Euclid's method of proof as a foreshadowing of the development of the general resolution theory of theorem proving in artificial intelligence (Robinson, 1965). Thus, Euclid's use of the logical deduction law *reductio ad absurdum* to prove that the square root of two is an irrational number is echoed in Robinson's use of *reductio ad absurdum* as the central logical mechanism by which the general resolution method in artificial intelligence accomplishes the goal of mathematical theorem proving and general problem solving (Genesereth, 1983).

The powerful mathematical reasoning method, *reductio ad absurdum*, used by many creative mathematicians (including Alan Turing) to establish the proof of a proposition or theorem, consists of a sequential logical procedure. The sequence begins with the assumption that the proposition or theorem is false, continues with mathematical deductions that follow from the initial assumption, and concludes with a demonstration that these deductions culminate in the con-tradiction of the initial assumption that the proposition or theorem was false.

Table 1.6
Boolean Algebra: Propositions as Equations

Proposition	Equation	Conditions of Final Interpretations
The class x	x	
The class not-x	1 − x	
All Xs are Ys All Ys are Xs	x = y	
All Xs are Ys	x(1 − y) = 0	
No Xs are Ys	xy = 0	
All Ys are Xs Some Xs are Ys	y = vx	vx = some Xs v(1 − x) = 0
No Ys are Xs Some not-Xs are Ys	y = v(1 − x)	v(1 − x) = some not Xs vx = 0
Some Xs are Ys	v = xy or vx = vy or vx(1 − y) = 0 v = x(1 − y)	v = some Xs or some Ys vx = some Xs, vy = some Ys v(1 − x) = 0, v(1 − y) = 0 v = some Xs or some not Ys
Some Xs are not Ys	or vx = v(1 − y) or vxy = 0	vx = some Xs, v(1 − y) = some not Ys v(1 − x) = 0, vy = 0

Source: Boole, G. (1854). *An Investigation of the Laws of Thought on Which Are Founded the Mathematical Theories of Logic and Probabilities.* New York: Macmillan, p. 62.

The General Resolution Method

Resolution is used to prove theorems (Chang and Lee, 1973) that are written in the predicate calculus. The predicate calculus, in turn, represents a state of affairs or problem state. Proving the theorem becomes equivalent to problem solving.

Contradiction or refutation is the goal in theorem proving by the general resolution method. Contradiction or refutation proves the falsity of the negation of a proposition and thus establishes its truth.

It has been pointed out that the establishment of contradiction is a major goal in both Euclid's proof and in general resolution. There are similarities and differences in Euclid's and resolution proof. In Euclid's proof, following the assumption of negation of the irrationality of the square root of two, a series of laws of elementary algebra are sequentially applied, terminating in the contradiction. The language is the language of algebra. In proof by resolution, a series of laws of logic is sequentially applied, terminating in the contradiction. The language is the language of the predicate calculus (Table 1.7).

The laws of commutation and association are common to both algebra and logic. In both, there are strategies for simplifying expressions. Algebraic terms that are identical except for a sign are dropped. Logical expressions in the form of conjunctions are reformulated as disjunctions. Disjunctions that are identical except for the sign are dropped.

One important difference between algebra and logic is that in the resolution method the negated proposition is included in the set of predicate calculus formulas (literals or clauses) and resolvants are then produced by application of logic rules (Table 1.8), whereas in Euclid's proof, the negation is not so included but is used to generate a contradictory finding through the laws of algebra.

The general strategy of resolution in a theorem-proving system involves a set of procedures that begins with the representation of a state of affairs in the language of the predicate calculus (see Table 1.7). The predicate calculus expressions are rewritten as groupings of logic symbols, termed *clauses*; the inference rules of resolution are then applied to the clauses (see Table 1.8).

These inference rules are directed toward a gradual simplification of the set of clauses (in large systems, thousands of clauses may be involved [Clocksin and Mellish, 1981]). Simplification involves the conversion, by means of rules of logic (see Table 1.8), of conjunctions into disjunctions and implications into disjunctions. Resolution is then applied to disjunctive clauses that are complementary in sign. These pairs of clauses are then resolved—eliminated from the set of clauses. The process continues with the elimination of further clauses until the nil (empty) clause is produced (no complementary disjunctions remain).

Table 1.7
The Predicate Calculus

The language of predicate calculus consists of these:

    A set of constant terms.

    A set of variables.

    A set of predicates, each taking a specified number of

        arguments.

    A set of functions, each taking a specified number of

        arguments.

    The connectives *if, and, or,* and *not*.

    The qualifiers *exists* and *for all*.

The terms of the language are these:

    constant terms.

    variables.

    functions applied to the correct number of terms.

The formulas of the language are these:

    A predicate applied to the correct number of terms.

    If p and q are formulas, then (if p q), (and p q)

        (or p q), and (not p).

    If x is a variable, and p is a formula, then *(exists (x) p)*,

        and *(for all (x) p)*.

Source: Charniak, E., and McDermott, D. (1985). *Introduction to Artificial Intelligence*. Reading, MA: Addison-Wesley, p. 19. Italics added.

Summary of the Resolution Method

The resolution method is designed to enable computer systems to solve problems by theorem proving. Then the logic of the theorem-proving problem and the resolution by refutation or contradiction can be briefly summarized.

From a set of propositions, prove some goal X. The first step is to negate the goal X. The second step is to add the negation of X to the set of propositions, thus forming an expanded set. The third step is to transform the expanded set of propositions into a set of clauses (groupings of predicate calculus expres-

Table 1.8
Clauses and Resolvents

	Parent Clauses	Resolvents	Comments
	P and $\sim P \vee Q$ (i.e., $P \Rightarrow Q$)	Q	Modus ponens
	$P \vee Q$ and $\sim P \vee Q$	Q	The clause $Q \vee Q$ "collapses" to Q. This resolvent is called a merge.
	$P \vee Q$ and $\sim P \vee \sim Q$	$Q \vee \sim Q$ and $P \vee \sim P$	Here, there are two possible resolvents; in this case, both are tautologies.
	$\sim P$ and P	Nil	The empty clause is a sign of a contradiction.
	$\sim P \vee Q$ (i.e., $P \Rightarrow Q$) and $\sim Q \vee R$ (i.e., $Q \Rightarrow R$)	$\sim P \vee R$ (i.e., $P \Rightarrow R$)	Chaining

Key: $\sim$ - negation, not
            $\vee$ - disjunction, or
            $\Rightarrow$ - implies

Source: Nilsson, N. (1980). *Principles of Artificial Intelligence*. Palo Alto, CA: Tioga, p. 45.

sions). The fourth step is to apply resolution to the set of clauses with the intended purpose of deriving a contradiction (the nil clause). From the contradiction, the final logical step is the negation of the negation of the goal X; that is, the proof of the theorem is established.

Resolution is the predominant method of inference in PROLOG (Amble, 1987). In relying on resolution instead of a variety of inference methods, PROLOG optimizes its efficiency and power in automatic theorem proving.

Forward and Backward Chaining

Linked inferences are referred to as a chain. A forward chain links interferences from a problem state to a solution state, from facts to a conclusion. A

Table 1.9
Some Characteristics of Forward and Backward Chaining

Forward Chaining	Backward Chaining
Planning, monitoring, control	Diagnosis
Present to future	Present to past
Antecedent to consequent	Consequent to antecedent
Data driven, bottom-up reasoning	Goal driven, top-down reasoning
Work forward to find what solutions follow from the facts	Work backward to find facts that support the hypothesis
Breadth-first search facilitated	Depth-first search facilitated
Antecedents determine search	Consequents determine search
Explanation not facilitated	Explanation facilitated

Source: Giarratiano, J., and Riley, G. (1989). *Expert Systems: Principles and Programming*. Boston: PWS-Kent Publishing Co., p. 161.

backward chain links inferences in a backward direction from hypotheses to the set of supporting facts, from the satisfaction of subgoals to the achievement of a goal. Table 1.9 systematically compares the distinguishing characteristics of forward chaining and backward chaining.

INDUCTIVE REASONING AND ARTIFICIAL INTELLIGENCE

The Nature of Nonmonotonic Reasoning

Nonmonotonic reasoning (Clark, 1978) is concerned with the relationship between given facts or premises and conclusions or drawn inferences. Monotonic reasoning results in necessary conclusions or inferences, whereas nonmonotonic reasoning results in plausible conclusions or inferences (Brewka, Dix, and Konolige, 1997). Classical formal systems of logic are monotonic. In monotonic logics, conclusions remain unchanged in the face of new data. In monotonic systems, rule-based inferences are not responsive to newly discovered exceptions to the rules.

In nonmonotonic systems of reasoning (Reiter, 1980), new data or new exceptions to the rules result in a changed or abandoned conclusion. The conclusion is said to have been "defeated." Conclusions capable of being defeated in the future are said to be "defeasible" (Pollock, 1987).

Default Reasoning

Default reasoning (Reiter, 1978) is a type of nonmonotonic reasoning. The logic of default reasoning is as follows: If there is no proof that X (object, person, situation, process, state, etc.) does not possess an attribute A, then it may be concluded that X does not possess attribute A. The conclusion of this pattern of logic is said to be "a default."

Less formally, unless demonstrated, known, or proven to be otherwise, the usual or default conclusion may be drawn. Defeasible reasoning is typical of everyday reasoning, including reasoning by experts in all fields. A computer expert program that models a human expert applies nonmonotonic reasoning to derive a plausible (a default) conclusion. A nonmonotonic expert reasoning program that diagnoses automobile engine trouble or human heart trouble or business investment trouble or psychological trouble may reach a satisfactory conclusion based on the assumption that there is no proof that nontypical conditions are present but may subsequently discover new data that require the rejection of the conclusion.

Theoretically, other things being equal, the likelihood of the occurrence of defeated conclusions increases as nonmonotonicity increases. Designers of expert systems may have to balance cost-benefit ratios in reducing the likelihood of defeated conclusions (McDermott and Doyle, 1980).

PROBABILISTIC REASONING AND ARTIFICIAL INTELLIGENCE

The Nature of Probabilistic Reasoning

In general, whereas knowledge in the physical sciences tends to be primarily deterministic, knowledge in the human sciences tends to be primarily probabilistic. Deterministic knowledge, in which facts are either true or false, is readily represented and processed in the language of the predicate calculus; but probabilistic knowledge, in which facts are uncertainly true or uncertainly false, requires special techniques.

Probabilistic reasoning is characteristic of cognition in situations of incomplete knowledge: scientific exploration, medical diagnosis, legal interpretation, and psychological counseling. Techniques of probabilistic reasoning in artificial intelligence range from direct application of mathematical probability equations (e.g., the use of Bayes's theorem in the PROSPECTOR system that locates mineral deposits [Duda, Gashnig, and Hart, 1980]) to heuristically guided knowledge rules (e.g., the production system MYCIN that diagnoses infections and recommends therapy [Shortliffe, 1976]).

Probabilistic Reasoning in a Counseling System

Let us consider the problem of the development of an artificial intelligence system for psychological counseling (Wagman, 1980, 1988). Like a human counselor, the artificial intelligence system would use evidence about the person and knowledge about the relevant environment of the person to formulate a set of problem diagnoses and solution recommendations. The counseling system would employ rule-based probabilistic reasoning.

Consider the problem of selecting a career goal for a university student. There is evidence of varying validity concerning not only the student's interests and abilities but also the characteristics of various university curricula. The lack of complete validity in the evidence indicates the need for probabilistic reasoning about possible career goals. The counseling system might employ rule-based probabilistic reasoning, as shown in Table 1.10.

The rule-based probabilistic reasoning system displayed in Table 1.10 indicates probabilities associated with curricula recommendations based on actuarial studies of relationships between predictor variables of ability and interest test scores and outcome variables of success in a variety of university curricula.

The predictor variables and the outcome variables do not reflect a deterministic domain of knowledge. However, within the psychological domain, beginning with the work of Meehl (1954), research has indicated that actuarial (statistical) prediction in which experience tables are followed is superior to clinical (individualized) prediction in which counselor judgments are followed. However, clinical prediction may be superior to actuarial prediction for situations in which student characteristics or environmental characteristics differ markedly from the characteristics of the actuarial population (nonmonotonicity).

The implication is that a counseling system like that sketched in Table 1.10 (only a suggestive trace is given) would be appropriate for most students but inappropriate for some students. The algorithmic intelligence of the counseling system constitutes both its strength as a general advisor (monotonicity) and its weakness as a special advisor (nonmonotonicity).

TYPES OF REASONING IN ARTIFICIAL INTELLIGENCE

Artificial intelligence research has developed multiple methods of inference. A summary of these reasoning methods follows:

Deduction: Logical reasoning in which conclusions must follow from their premises.

Induction: Inference from the specific case to the general.

Intuition: No proven theory. The answer just appears, possibly by unconsciously recognizing an underlying pattern. Expert systems do not implement this type of in-

Table 1.10
A Counseling System Using Rule-Based Probabilistic Reasoning

Rule 1: If there is evidence that the student has abilities a and b, then curriculum w probably ($p = .23$) should be selected.

Rule 2: If there is evidence that the student has interests c and d, then curriculum x probably ($p = .35$) should be selected.

Rule 3: If there is evidence that the student has abilities a and b, but lacks interests c and d, then curriculum y probably ($p = .49$) should be selected.

Rule 4: If there is evidence that the student has abilities a and b and has interests c and d, then curriculum z probably ($p = .75$) should be selected.

Rule 5: If the student is doing poorly in curriculum y and probably ($p = .81$) has abilities a and b and probably ($p = .78$) has interests c and d, then a transfer to curriculum z should probably ($p = .91$) be recommended.

Note: In Rule 1, evidence about interest is unavailable, and in Rule 2, evidence about ability is unavailable.

Source: Wagman, M. (1991b). *Cognitive Science and Concepts of Mind: Toward a General Theory of Human and Artificial Intelligence*. New York: Praeger, p. 51. Reprinted by permission of Praeger Publishers, an imprint of Greenwood Publishing Group, Inc., Westport, CT.

ference yet. ANS (Artificial Neural Systems) may hold promise for this type of inference since they can extrapolate from their training rather than just provide a conditioned response or interpolation. That is, a neural net will always give its best guess for a solution.

Heuristics: Rules of thumb based on experience.

Generate and test: Trial and error. Often used with planning for efficiency.

Abduction: Reasoning back from a true conclusion to the premises that may have caused the conclusion.

Default: In the absence of specific knowledge, assume general or common knowledge by default.

Autoepistemic: Self-knowledge.

Nonmonotonic: Previous knowledge may be incorrect when new evidence is obtained.

Analogy: Inferring a conclusion based on the similarities to another situation. (Giarratiano and Riley, 1989, p. 119)

COMMONSENSE REASONING AND ARTIFICIAL INTELLIGENCE

Human intelligence has adapted to the diverse, complex, rapidly changing demands of everyday life situations by means of a repertoire of commonsense reasoning strategies deployed both singly and in combination and taking account of nuances and contexts that require differential responses. Artificial intelligence research has developed types of reasoning that are eminently suited to rather clear-cut structured situations that can be described and represented with formal precision. Commonsense reasoning, however, constitutes a formidable challenge to artificial intelligence research:

While much of human reasoning corresponds to that of traditional logic, some important human commonsense reasoning is not monotonic. We reach conclusions from certain premises that we would not reach if certain other sentences were included in our premises. For example, learning that I own a car, you could conclude that it is appropriate on a certain occasion to ask me for a ride; but when you learn a further fact that the car is in the garage being fixed, you no longer draw that conclusion. . . .

As a more concrete example of nonmonotonic reasoning, consider the conditions under which a boat may be used to cross a river. Now consider things that might have no oars, no motor, or no sails, depending on what kind of a boat it is. It would be reasonably convenient to list some of these things in a set of axioms. However, besides these obstacles that we can expect to list in advance, human reasoning will admit still others should they arise, but it cannot be expected to think of them all in advance (e.g., a fence down the middle of the river). One can handle this difficulty by using circumscription to minimize the set of things that prevent the boat from crossing the river—that is, the set of obstacles to be overcome. If the reasoner knows of none in a particular case, he will conjecture that the boat can be used, but if he learns of one, he will get a different result when he minimizes.

This illustration shows that nonmonotonic reasoning is conjectural rather than rigorous. Indeed, it has been shown that certain mathematical logical systems cannot be rigorously extended, that they have a certain kind of completeness. (McCarthy, 1988, pp. 304–310)

2

Plausible Reasoning

THEORY OF PLAUSIBLE REASONING

In "The Logic of Plausible Reasoning," Collins and Michalski (1989) present an ambitious theory designed to formalize both the inferential patterns and the degree of certainty that characterize people's responses to everyday questions for which they do not possess immediate knowledge. The theory is complex and will be described in detail in this chapter. Following the descriptive account, a commentary on the theory will be presented.

General Characteristics

Collins and Michalski (1989) give the following account of the general characteristics of their theory of plausible reasoning:

The theory consists of three parts:

1. a formal representation of plausible inference patterns; such as deductions, inductions, and analogies, that are frequently employed in answering everyday questions;
2. a set of parameters, such as conditional likelihood, typicality, and similarity, that affect the certainty of people's answers to such questions; and
3. a system relating the different plausible inference patterns and the different certainty parameters.

This is one of the first attempts to construct a formal theory that addresses both the semantic and parametric aspects of the kind of everyday reasoning that pervades all of human discourse.

The goal of our research on plausible reasoning is to develop a formal system based on Michalski's (1980, 1983) variable-valued logic calculus that characterizes different patterns of plausible inference humans use in reasoning about the world (Collins, 1978a; Polya, 1968). Our work attempts to formalize the plausible inferences that frequently occur in people's responses to questions for which they do not have ready answers (Carbonell and Collins, 1973; Collins, 1978a, 1978b; Collins, Warnock, Aiello, and Miller, 1975). In this sense it is a major departure from formal logic and various nonclassical logics; for example, fuzzy logic (Zadeh, 1965), multiple-valued logic (Lukasiewicz, 1967), Dempster-Shafer logic (Shafer, 1976), intuitionist logic (Martin-Lof, 1982), variable-precision logic (Michalski and Winston, 1986), probabilistic logic (Nilsson, 1986), belief networks (Pearl, 1986), and default logic (Reiter, 1980; Yager, 1987). Being descriptive based, the theory includes a variety of inference patterns that do not occur in formal logic-based theories. The central goals of the theory are to discover recurring general patterns of human plausible inference and to determine parameters affecting the certainty of these inferences. Unlike other theories of plausible reasoning, the theory combines semantic aspects with parametric aspects captured by numeric or symbolic estimates of certainty. (Collins and Michalski, 1989, pp. 1–2)

Protocol Analysis

In developing a theory, Collins and Michalski (1989) recorded protocols of people's discourse as they asked and replied to questions. They then analyzed the protocols with respect to the presence of regularities in inferential plausible reasoning.

In order to analyze human plausible reasoning, Collins (1978b) collected a large number of people's answers to everyday questions, some from teaching dialogues and some from asking difficult questions to four subjects. These answers have the following characteristics:

1. There are usually several different inference patterns used to answer any question.

2. The same inference patterns recur in many different answers.

3. People weigh different evidence that bears on their conclusion.

4. People are more or less certain about their conclusion depending on the certainty of their information (either from some outside source or from memory), the certainty of the inference patterns and associated parameters used, and on whether different patterns lead to the same or opposite conclusions. (Collins and Michalski, 1989, p. 2)

Analysis of the First Protocol

Analysis of the first protocol reveals an inference pattern that in the taxonomy of Collins and Michalski (1989) is termed *derivation from a mutual implication.*

The first transcript comes from a teaching dialogue on South American geography (Carbonell and Collins, 1973) (T stands for teacher, and S stands for student):

T: There is some jungle in here (points to Venezuela) but this breaks into a savanna around the Orinoco (points to the Llanos in Venezuela and Colombia).

S: Oh right, is that where they grow the coffee up there?

T: I don't think that the savanna is used for growing coffee. The trouble is the savanna has a rainy season and you can't count on rain in general. But I don't know. This area around Sao Paulo (in Brazil) is the coffee region, and it is sort of getting into the savanna region there.

In the protocol the teacher went through the following reasoning. Initially, the teacher made a hedged "no" response to the question for two reasons. First, the teacher knew that coffee growing depends on a number of factors (e.g., rainfall, temperature, soil, and terrain), and that savannas do not have the correct value for growing coffee on at least one of those factors (i.e., reliable rainfall). In the theory this is an instance of the inference pattern called a *derivation from a mutual implication*, in particular the implication that coffee growing depends on reliable rainfall. Second, the teacher did not know that the Llanos was used for growing coffee, which the teacher implicitly took as evidence against its being a coffee region. The inference takes the form "I would know the Llanos produces coffee if it did, and I don't know it, so it probably does not." This is called a "lack-of-knowledge inference" (Collins et al., 1975; Gentner and Collins, 1981). This inference pattern is based on knowledge about one's own knowledge and hence is a meta-knowledge inference.

Then the teacher backed off the initial negative response, because positive evidence was found. In particular, the teacher thought the Brazilian savanna might overlap the coffee growing region in Brazil around Sao Paulo, and therefore might produce coffee. If the Brazilian savanna produces coffee, then by functional analogy (called a *similarity transform* in our theory) the Llanos might. Hence, the teacher ended up saying, "I don't know," even though the original conclusion was correct.

The teacher's answer exhibits a number of the important aspects of human plausible reasoning. In general, a number of inference patterns are used together to derive an answer. Some of these are inference chains where the premise of one inference draws on the conclusion of another inference. In other cases the inference patterns are triggered by independent sources of evidence. When there are different sources of evidence, the subject weighs them together to determine a conclusion and the strength of belief in it. ... It is also apparent in this protocol how different pieces of information are found over time. What appears to happen is that the subject launches a search for information starting with the words in the question (Collins and Loftus, 1975; Quillian, 1968). As pieces of information are found, they trigger particular inferences. Which inference pattern is applied is determined by the relation between the information found and the question asked. For the question about growing coffee in the Llanos, if the respondent knew that savannas are generally good for growing coffee, that would trigger a deductive inference. If the respondent knew of a similar savanna somewhere that produced coffee, that would trigger an analogical inference. In the protocol, the more accessible information about the unreliable rainfall in savannas was found before the less accessible information about the coffee growing region in Brazil and its relation to the Brazilian savanna. The search for information is such that the most accessible information is found first, as by a marker passing or spreading activation algorithm (Charniak, 1983; Quillian, 1968). (Collins and Michalski, 1989, pp. 3–4)

Analysis of the Second Protocol

Analysis of the second protocol discloses the presence of a *specialization transform* and of two *certainty parameters, frequency and typicality.*

The next protocol illustrates a plausible deduction (Q stands for questioner and R for respondent):

Q: Is Uruguay in the Andes Mountains?

R: I get mixed up on a lot of South American countries (pause). I'm not even sure. I forget where Uruguay is in South America. It's a good guess to say that it's in the Andes Mountains because a lot of countries are.

The respondent knew that the Andes are in most South American countries (seven out of nine of the Spanish-speaking countries). Since Uruguay is a fairly typical South American country, the respondent guesses that the Andes may be there, too. The respondent is wrong, but the conclusion was quite plausible. This kind of plausible deduction is called a *specialization transform* in the theory, based on the fact that Uruguay is a specialization of a South American country. This example illustrates two of the certainty parameters associated with it: *frequency* (respondent knows the Andes are in most countries), and *typicality* (Uruguay is a typical South American country). (Collins and Michalski, 1989, p. 4)

Analysis of the Third Protocol

Analysis of the third protocol discloses the important inference pattern termed *derivation from a mutual implication.*

The third protocol illustrates the other kinds of plausible deduction in the theory, called *derivation from a mutual implication* (in particular, rice growing implies warm weather, flat terrain, and fresh water):

Q: Do you think they might grow rice in Florida?

R: Yeah, I guess they could, if there were an adequate fresh water supply. Certainly a nice, big, warm, flat area.

The respondent knew that whether a place can grow rice depends on a number of factors, and also knew that Florida had the correct values on at least two of these factors (warm temperatures and flat terrain). The respondent therefore inferred that Florida could grow rice if it had the correct value on the other factor thought of (i.e., adequate fresh water). The respondent may or may not have been aware that rice growing also depends on fertile soil, but did not mention it here. Florida in fact does not produce rice in any substantial amount, probably because the soil is not adequate. This protocol shows how people make plausible inferences based on their approximate knowledge about what depends on what, and how the certainty of such inferences is a function of the degree of dependency between the variable in question (rice) and the known variables (i.e., terrain, climate, water). (Collins and Michalski, 1989, pp. 4–5)

Analysis of the Fourth Protocol

Analysis of the fourth protocol demonstrates the *similarity transform* and the *dissimilarity transform* in plausible reasoning.

The fourth protocol from a teaching dialogue illustrates two inferences in the core theory; a *similarity transform* and a *dissimilarity transform* (S stands for student, T for teacher):

S: Is the Chaco the cattle country? I know the cattle country is down there (referring to Argentina).

T: I think it's more sheep country. It's like western Texas, so in some sense I guess it's cattle country. The cattle were originally in the Pampas, but not so much anymore.

As in the first protocol, the respondent (teacher) is making a number of plausible inferences in answering this question, some of which lead to different conclusions. First, the teacher thinks that the Chaco is used for sheep raising, but there is some uncertainty about the information retrieved, which leads to a hedged response. This supports a *dissimilarity transform* and an implicit lack-of-knowledge inference (a meta-knowledge inference). The *dissimilarity transform* is based on the view that sheep country is distinct from cattle country, presumably in terms of its climate or vegetation, so that if the Chaco is sheep country it is not likely to be cattle country. The lack-of-knowledge inference takes the form: "I don't know that it's cattle country, and I would know if it were (e.g., I know about sheep), so it probably is not cattle country." But then the teacher noted a similarity between the Chaco and western Texas, presumably in terms of the functional determinants of cattle raising (e.g., climate, vegetation, terrain). Because western Texas is cattle country, this led the teacher to a very hedged affirmative response, based on a *similarity transform*. Finally the teacher alluded to the fact that the Pampas is the place in Argentina known for cattle, and the place the student was most likely thinking of. This argues against the Chaco having cattle based on another meta-knowledge inference, a "functional alternative inference" (Collins, 1978b; Pearl, 1987): "The Pampas is an Argentinian plain and the Pampas has cattle, so the fact that there are cattle in an Argentinian plain cannot be taken as evidence for cattle in the Chaco." In answering this question, then, two patterns of plausible inference led to a negative conclusion and one to a positive conclusion. (Collins and Michalski, 1989, p. 5)

Analysis of the Fifth Protocol

Analysis of the fifth protocol distinguishes the differential significance of distributed similarity and focused similarity. The *dissimilarity transform* and the *similarity transform* appear frequently in the analysis.

The fifth protocol again illustrates both a *similarity* and a *dissimilarity transform*, and more importantly, the distinction between inferences based on overall similarity and those based on similarity with respect to the functional determinants of the property question (Q stands for questioner, R for respondent):

Q: Can a goose quack?

R: No, a goose—well, it's like a duck, but it's not a duck. It can honk, but to say it can quack. No, I think its vocal cords are built differently. They have a beak and everything, but no, it can't quack.

The *similarity transform* shows up in the phrases, "It's like a duck" and "They have a beak and everything" as well as in the initial uncertainty about the negative conclusion. It takes the form, "A duck quacks and a goose is like a duck with respect to most features, so maybe a goose quacks." The certainty of the inference depends on the degree of similarity between ducks and geese.

But then two lines of negative inference led the respondent to a negative conclusion. First there is a lack-of-knowledge inference implicit in the statement "It can honk, but to say it can quack." The respondent knew about geese honking but not about their quacking. Therefore, the respondent would supposedly know about geese quacking, if in fact they did quack.

The second line of negative inference (apparently found after the respondent started answering) is the *dissimilarity transform* evident when it is stated, "I think its vocal cords are built differently." The *dissimilarity transform* takes on the form "Ducks quack, geese are dissimilar to ducks with respect to vocal cords, and vocal cords determine the sound an animal makes, so probably geese do not quack." This inference was enough to lead to a strong "no." Of course the respondent knew nothing about the vocal cords of ducks and geese, because they don't have any, and was probably thinking of the difference in the lengths of their necks. Our own hypothesis is that longer necks resonate at lower frequencies and hence honking can be thought of as deep quacking. (Collins and Michalski, 1989, p. 6)

Summary of Protocol Analyses

The general results of the protocol analyses are summarized in the following account:

These five examples illustrate a number of aspects of human plausible reasoning as it occurs in common discourse. They show how people bring different pieces of knowledge to bear on a question and how these pieces sometimes lead to the same conclusion and sometimes lead to different conclusions. Often knowledge is found after the respondent has started answering, so that the certainty of the answer seems to change in midstream. The examples also show how people's approximate functional knowledge of what depends on what often comes into play in different inferences such as deductions and analogies. Therefore these dependencies are a central part of the core theory we have developed. . . . We have collected many such protocols (Collins, 1978b) and these same patterns (as well as others) recur again and again in many different content domains and contexts. Any theory that is to account for such data will have to characterize these systematic patterns and the way that functional dependencies (e.g., coffee growing depends on reliable rainfall) interpenetrate these patterns of inference. (Collins and Michalski, 1989, pp. 6–7)

The Formal Character of the Core Theory

The core theory of plausible reasoning developed by Collins and Michalski (1989) is a general structure, domain-independent, and reflective of everyday psychological reasoning that departs from normative logic.

We should emphasize . . . that the scope of the theory is the kind of domain-independent, weak inferences (Newell, 1980) akin to the syllogistic forms of logic. The core theory attempts to specify the generalizations of syllogistic forms that reflect the way people actually reason, not how they should reason. This scope leaves out two kinds of plausible reasoning seen frequently in people's answers to questions: 1) domain-specific reasoning (e.g., "the language of Mexico is Mexican," which employs a special rule for forming language names); and 2) generalized weak methods that involve active search for information, such as means-ends analysis (Newell and Simon, 1972) and proof by cases (e.g., to estimate how many Catholics there are in the world, many people will consider different countries or continents and estimate how many in each). (Collins and Michalski, 1989, p. 7)

The Core Theory and Mental Models

Collins and Michalski (1989) believe that while reasoning often includes the manipulation of mental models or images, the essential nature of reasoning consists of the inferential patterns that control how mental models are manipulated. They explain their position in the following account:

Johnson-Laird (1980, 1983) has argued that the best account for human reasoning is not in terms of systematic rules or inference patterns, but rather in terms of the manipulation of mental models. While we agree that people manipulate mental models in their reasoning (Collins, 1985; Collins and Gentner, 1982, 1983, 1987; Stevens and Collins, 1980), their use of mental models is orthogonal to the systematic patterns described in this paper. In particular, the protocols we have collected often involve picturing different situations (e.g., a mental map of South America, images of savannas, or an advertisement showing Juan Valdez on his coffee plantation in Colombia). These images can be taken as evidence for the manipulation of mental models in Johnson-Laird's terms. But overlaying this manipulation of mental models are the systematic patterns in which they are deployed to support one's conclusions (cf. Rips, 1986). So while mental models may be part of the story of plausible reasoning, there is another critical part which the theory we propose addresses. (Collins and Michalski, 1989, p. 7)

The Core Theory and the Correctness of Reasoning

Collins and Michalski (1989) have developed a descriptive theory of reasoning and not a normative theory of correct reasoning in the context of decision making or the logical requirements for inferential validity (Wagman, 1978, 1993). They present their position in the following account:

The theory does not address the issue of whether people make systematic errors in their reasoning, as the psychological literature on decision making (Kahneman, Slovic, and Tversky, 1982) attempts to document. This issue does not arise in the theory because we are developing a formalism for representing the kinds of inferences people make and the parameters that affect their certainty, rather than a theory about how people make particular inferences. People may systematically ignore some kinds of information or undervalue particular certainty parameters—we have not attempted to determine whether they do or not. Instead we have tried to represent all the kinds of reasoning patterns and the kinds of certainty parameters that appear in the protocols we have analyzed (Collins, 1978a, 1978b). *In this regard it is worth pointing out that certain fallacies in logic, such as affirming the consequent (Haviland, 1974), become plausible inference patterns in the theory. . . . As will be seen, dependencies and implications are bidirectional in the theory and so derivations from them, such as affirming the consequent, are plausible but not certain inferences. The same point is made by Polya (1968).* (Collins and Michalski, 1989, pp. 7–8; italics added)

Statement Transforms

The formal representations of statement transforms together with examples are presented in Table 2.1. The transforms fall into four categories of relations: generalization (GEN), specialization (SPEC), similarity (SIM), and dissimilarity (DIS). The first two relations go up and down in a hierarchy, and the latter two connect any two comparable nodes in the hierarchy. Essential features of the statement transform examples are given in the following account:

We can illustrate GEN-based argument transforms with the inference that if chickens have gizzards, then birds in general may have gizzards. The first premise represents the belief that chickens have gizzards: presumably almost all chickens have gizzards, so the frequency (ϕ) and the certainty (γ) are high. Presumably, μ_a is also high because any internal organ tends to occur in many different animals. The second premise represents the belief that chickens are birds, and that they are typical with respect to their biological characteristics. As we pointed out earlier, the dominance (δ) of chickens among birds is low. The third premise states that the internal organs of a bird depend highly on the biological characteristics of the bird. The conclusion that birds in general have gizzards is fairly certain given the high values of the critical variables.

SPEC-based argument transforms are illustrated by an example from the beginning of the paper where the respondent inferred that the Andes might be in Uruguay. The respondent believed that the Andes are in most South American countries, so frequency (ϕ) was moderately high. With respect to the second premise, Uruguay is a typical South American country, which increases the likelihood that the Andes would be found there. But its low dominance (δ) in terms of the proportion of South America that Uruguay comprises makes the inference less likely. With respect to the third premise, the fact that Uruguay is typical of South American countries in general only weakly predicts that it will include the Andes Mountains. Altogether, the inference is fairly uncertain given the moderate frequency and the low dominance of Uruguay.

We can illustrate SIM-based argument transforms with the Chaco protocol from the beginning of the paper, where the respondent inferred that the Chaco might produce

Table 2.1
Formal Representations of Statement Transforms

---

(1)   GEN-based argument transforms

$d(a) = r: \gamma_1, \phi, \mu_a$
a' GEN a in CX (a', D(a')): τ, γ_2, δ
$D(a') < ----d(a'): \alpha, \gamma_3$

$d(a') = r: \gamma = f(\gamma_1, \phi, \mu_a, \tau, \gamma_2, \delta, \alpha, \gamma_3)$

Internal organ (chicken)={gizzard ...}: γ_1 = high, ϕ = high, μ_a = indeterminate
Bird GEN chicken in CX (bird, biological characteristics(bird)):
        τ = high, γ_2 = high, δ = low
Biological characteristics (bird) < ----- > Internal organ (bird):
        α = high, γ_2 = high

Internal organ (bird) = {gizzard ...}: γ = high

(2)   SPEC-based argument transforms

$d(a) = r: \gamma_1, \phi$
a' SPEC a in CX (a:D(a)): τ, γ_2, δ
$D(a) < ----- > d(a): \alpha, \gamma_3$

$d(a') = r: \gamma = f(\gamma_1, \phi, \tau, \gamma_2, \delta, \alpha, \gamma_3)$

Mountains (S.A. country)={Andes ...}: γ_1 = high, ϕ = high, μ_a = indeterminate
Uruguay SPEC S.A. country in CX (S.A. country; characteristics (S.A. country)):
        τ = high, γ_2 = high, δ = low
Characteristics (S.A. country) < ----- > Mountains (S.A. country):
        α = moderate, γ_3 = high

Mountains (Uruguay = {Andes ...}: γ = moderate

---

cattle given that west Texas did. In the first premise, the frequency (ϕ) with which different parts of west Texas have cattle is high, and the multiplicity (μ_a) of places with cattle is high, both of which make the inference more likely. The second premise asserts that the Chaco is at least moderately similar to west Texas in vegetation (or whatever variables the respondent had in mind). The third premise relates vegetation of a region to its livestock, which is a strong relation, given that cattle will usually be raised where the vegetation will support them. The fourth premise merely establishes the fact that west Texas and the Chaco are regions, in support of the second and third premises. The conclusion is only moderate in certainty, given our assumption of uncertainty about how similar the Chaco and west Texas are.

To illustrate DIS-based argument transforms, we chose the example from the protocol shown earlier as to whether a goose quacks. The first premise reflects the respondent's belief that ducks quack, which is very certain. Though almost all ducks quack (ϕ is high), very few other animals quack (μ_a is low), which makes the DIS inference more certain.

Table 2.1 (continued)

---

(3)   SIM-based argument transforms
$d(a) = r$: γ_1, ϕ, μ_a
a' SIM a in CX (A; D(A)): σ, γ_2
$D(A) < -----d(A)$: α, γ_3
a, a' SPEC A: γ_4, γ_5

$d(a') = r$: $\gamma = f(\gamma_1, \phi, \mu_a, \sigma, \gamma_2, \alpha, \gamma_3, \gamma_4, \gamma_5)$

Livestock (West Texas) = {cattle ...}: γ_1 = high, ϕ = high, μ_a = high
Chaco SIM West Texas in CX (region; vegetation(region)):
         ϕ = moderate, γ_2 = moderate
Vegetation (region) < -----> Livestock (region): α = high, γ_3 = high
West Texas, Chaco SPEC region: γ_4 = high, γ_5 = high

Livestock (Chaco) = {cattle ...}: γ = moderate

(4)   DIS-based argument transforms

$d(a) = r$: γ_1, ϕ, μ_a
a' DIS a in CX (A:D(A)): σ, γ_2,
$D(A) < -----> d(A)$: α, γ_2
a, a' SPEC A: γ_4, γ_5

$d(a') \neq r$: $\gamma = f(\gamma_1, \phi, \mu_a, \sigma, \gamma_2, \delta, \alpha, \gamma_3, \gamma_4, \gamma_5)$

Sound (duck) = quack: γ_1 = high, ϕ = high, μ_a = low
Goose DIS duck in CX (bird; vocal cords (bird)):
         σ = high, γ_2 = moderate
Vocal cords (bird) < -----> Sound (bird): α = high, γ_3 = low
Duck, goose SPEC bird: γ_4 = high, γ_5 = high

Sound (goose) $\neq$ quack: γ = low

The second premise states the belief that ducks and geese are dissimilar in their vocal cords which the respondent must have been at least a bit uncertain about (hence the low certainty assigned to the statement). The third premise relates the sound a bird makes to its vocal cords, which also must have been an uncertain belief given that it is not true. The certainty of the conclusion that geese do not quack should have been fairly low (though another inference led to the same conclusion in the actual protocol).

We have created an example to illustrate GEN-based referent transforms. The first premise asserts that Honduras produces bananas among other things (the multiplicity (μ_r) of agricultural products is high). Bananas are a fairly tropical fruit in terms of the climate where they are grown, as the second premise states. The third premise asserts that the climate appropriate for agricultural products constrains the places where they are grown fairly strongly. The conclusion follows with moderate certainty that Honduras produces many tropical fruits, such as mangos and coconuts.

Table 2.1 (continued)

---

(5) GEN-based referent transforms
$d(a) = \{r \ldots\}: \gamma_1, \phi, \mu_r$
r' GEN r in $CX(d; D(d)): \sigma, \gamma_2, \alpha$
$D(d) < -----A(d): \alpha, \gamma_3$
a SPEC $A: \gamma_4$

$d(a) = \{r' \ldots\}: \gamma = f(\gamma_1, \phi, \mu_r, \sigma, \gamma_2, \alpha, \gamma_3, \gamma_4)$

Agricultural product (Honduras) = {bananas ...}:
    γ_1 = unknown, ϕ = high, μ_r = high
Tropical fruits GEN bananas in CX (agricultural products,
    climate(agricultural products)): τ = high, γ_2 = high, δ = low
Climate (agricultural products) $< ----- >$ Place (agricultural products):
    α = high, γ_3 = high
Honduras SPEC place: γ_4 = high

Agricultural products (Honduras) = {tropical fruits ...}: γ = moderate

(6) SPEC-based referent transforms

$d(a) = \{r \ldots\}: \gamma_1, \phi,$
r' SPEC r in CX $(d:D(d)): \tau, \gamma_2, \delta$
$D(d) < ----- > A(d): \alpha, \gamma_3$
a SPEC $A: \gamma_4$

$d(a) = \{r' \ldots\}: \gamma = f(\gamma_1, \phi, \tau, \gamma_2, \delta, \alpha, \gamma_3, \gamma_4,)$

Minerals (South Africa) = {diamonds ...}: γ_1 = high, ϕ = high,
Industrial diamonds SPEC diamonds SPEC diamonds in CX (minerals;
    characteristics(minerals)): τ = high, γ_2 = high, δ = high
Characteristics (minerals) $< ---- >$ Place (minerals): α = moderate , γ_3 = high
South Africa SPEC place: γ_4 = high

Minerals (South Africa) = {industrial diamonds}: γ = high

We also created the example of SPEC-based referent transforms. The first premise states that South Africa produces diamonds. Industrial diamonds are a kind of low-quality diamond (used in drills) and they must be fairly dominant (δ) among diamonds given their low quality, though they are not particularly typical of what we think of as diamonds. Here is a case where high dominance compensates for low typicality. The third premise is somewhat irrelevant since the typicality is low. But the inference that South Africa produces industrial diamonds is quite certain given the high dominance of industrial diamonds among diamonds.

The example of SIM-based referent transforms is drawn from a protocol where the respondent, when asked whether wolves could bark, inferred they probably could (Collins, 1978b). One of his inferences derived from the fact that he knew wolves could

Table 2.1 (continued)

---

(7)   SIM-based referent transforms
       $d(a) = \{r \ldots\}$: γ_1, ϕ, μ_r
       r' SIM r in CX (d; D(d)): σ, γ_2
       $D(d) < \text{-----} A(d)$: α, γ_3
       a SPEC A: γ_4

       $d(a) = \{r \ldots\}$: $\gamma = f(\gamma_1, \phi, \mu_r, \sigma, \gamma_2, \alpha, \gamma_3, \gamma_4)$

       Sound (wolf) = {howl ...}: γ_1 = high, ϕ = high, μ_r = low
       Bark SIM howl in CX (sound; means of production(sound)):
            σ = high, γ_2 = high
       Means of production (sound) $< \text{-----} >$ animal (sound): α = high, γ_3 = high
       Wolf SPEC animal: γ_4 = high

       Sound (wolf) = {bark ...}: γ = moderate

(8)   DIS-based referent transforms

       $d(a) = \{r \ldots\}$: γ_1, ϕ, μ_r
       r' DIS r in CX (d:D(d)): σ, γ_2,
       $D(d) < \text{-----} > A(d)$: α, γ_3
       a SPEC A: γ_4

       $d(a) \neq \{r \ldots\}$: $\gamma = f(\gamma_1, \phi, \mu_r, \sigma, \gamma_2, \alpha, \gamma_3, \gamma_4)$

       Color (Princess phones) = {white, pink, yellow ...}:
            γ_1 = high, ϕ = high, μ_a = low
       Black DIS white & pink & yellow in CX (color; lightness(color)):
            σ = low, γ_2 = high
       Lightness (color) $< \text{-----} >$ phone type (color): α = low, γ_3 = high
       Princess phone SPEC phone: γ_4 = high

       Color (Princess phones) $\neq$ {black ...}: γ = moderate

---

Source: Collins, A. M., and Michalski, R. (1989). The logic of plausible reasoning: A core theory. *Cognitive Science, 13*, pp. 29–31. © Cognitive Science Society. Reprinted with permission.

howl, with both high frequency and certainty (but low multiplicity (μ_r) because most animals only make one or two sounds). He also thought that barking was similar to howling in terms of the way the sound is produced (a howl, as it were, is a sustained bark). Furthermore, the means of production of a sound constrains the type of animals that can make that sound, as the third premise states. It follows then with at least moderate certainty that a wolf can bark.

The example of DIS-based referent transforms is from a protocol where the respondent was asked if there are black princess telephones (Collins, 1978b). The respondent could remember seeing white, pink and yellow princess phones, as the first premise states. Here the frequency (ϕ) of these colors among those she had seen seemed quite high, which counts against the possibility of black princess phones. But the multiplicity of different colors among phones (μ_r) is moderate, which counts for the possibility of black princess phones. The second premise reflects that fact that black is quite dissimilar to those colors in terms of lightness. The third premise states that knowing the lightness only somewhat constrains the type of phone (α is low). The conclusion that princess phones are not black is uncertain given the low α in the third premise and the moderate μ_r in the first premise. (Collins and Michalski, 1989, pp. 28–33)

Derivation from Mutual Implications and Dependencies

Collins and Michalski (1989) present a systematic account of how statements can be plausibly derived from implications or dependencies.

[Table 2.2] illustrates the two types of *derivation from mutual implication* that occurred in the protocols shown in the beginning of the paper. The positive derivation illustrates how multiple conditions were ANDed together (i.e., a warm climate, heavy rainfall, and flat terrain) as predictors of rice growing. The belief that Florida has all three leads to a prediction that rice will be grown there. In the actual protocol the respondent was unsure about rainfall in Florida, and so concluded that rice would be grown if there were enough rain (i.e., Rainfall (Florida) = heavy <=> Product (Florida) = {rice . . . }).

The negative derivation illustrates the fact that if any of the variables on one side of a mutual implication that are ANDed together do not have the appropriate values, then you can conclude that the variable on the other side does not have the value assumed in the mutual implication. In the example, because the Llanos did not have reliable rainfall, the respondent concluded that the Llanos probably did not produce coffee. If variables are ORed together (e.g., either heavy rainfall or irrigation are needed for growing rice) a different pattern holds: Having one or the other predicts rice is grown and having neither predicts no rice is grown.

[Table 2.3] shows the equivalent representations for derivations from mutual dependencies. The inference patterns are different for positive and negative dependencies, so we have separated them in the table. It is possible to draw a negative conclusion from a mutual dependency simply by negating the second premise and the conclusion in either of the patterns shown.

The positive dependency represents the case where as one variable increases, the other variable also increases. In the formal analysis we have denoted the entire range of both variables by three values: high, medium, and low. When a positive dependency holds, if the value of the first variable is high, medium, or low, the value of the second variable will also be high, medium, or low, respectively. This is the weakest kind of derivation possible from a mutual dependency. In the example, if a person knows that the temperature of air predicts the water holding capacity of air, and he knows that temperature of the air outside is warm, then he can infer that the air outside could hold a lot of moisture. People make this kind of weak inference very frequently in reasoning about such variables (Collins and Gentner, 1987; Stevens and Collins, 1980).

The pattern for the negative dependency is reversed; if the value of one variable is high, the other is low, and vice versa. We have illustrated the derivation from mutual dependency in terms of a more precise dependency between two variables. If a person believes that the latitude of a place varies negatively (and linearly) with the temperature

Table 2.2
Formal Representations of Derivations from Mutual Implication

Positive Derivation

$d_1(a) = r_1 < == > d_2(a) = r_2, \alpha, \gamma_1$
$d_1(a') = r_1, \phi, \gamma_2$
$a' = $ SPEC a: γ_3

$d_2(a') = r_2: \gamma = f(\alpha, \gamma_1, \phi, \gamma_2, \gamma_3)$

Climate(place) = warm & Rainfall(place) = heavy & Terrain(place) = flat
    $< == >$ Product(place) = {rice ...}: α = high, γ_1 = certain
Climate(Florida) = warm: ϕ_1 = moderately high, γ_2 = certain
Rainfall(Florida) = heavy: ϕ_2 = moderate, γ_3 = uncertain
Terrain(Florida) = flat: ϕ_3 = high, γ_4 = certain
Florida SPEC place: γ_5 = certain

Product(Florida) = {rice ...}: γ = uncertain

Negative Derivation

$d_1(a) = r_1 < == > d_2(a) = r_2, \alpha, \gamma_1$
$d_1(a') \neq r_1, \phi, \gamma_2, \mu_r$
a' SPEC a: γ_3

$d_2(a') \neq r_2: \gamma = f(\alpha, \gamma_1, \phi, \gamma_2, \mu_r, \gamma_3)$

Rainfall(place) = reliable & climate(place) = subtropical $< == >$
    Product(place) = {coffee ...}: α = moderate, γ_1 = certain
Rainfall(Llanos) $\neq$ reliable: ϕ = high, γ_2 = fairly certain, μ_r = low
Llanos SPEC place: γ_3 = certain

Product(Llanos) $\neq$ {coffee ...}: γ = fairly certain

Source: Collins, A. M., and Michalski, R. (1989). The logic of plausible reasoning: A core theory. *Cognitive Science, 13*, p. 34. © Cognitive Science Society. Reprinted with permission.

of the place, and also that the average temperature is near 85 degrees at the equator and 0 degrees at the poles, then he might conclude that a place like Lima, Peru, which is about 10 degrees from the equator, has an average temperature of about 75 degrees. People have both more or less precise notions of how variables interact, and we have tried to preserve flexibility within our representation for handling these different degrees of precision. (Collins and Michalski, 1989, pp. 33–35)

Table 2.3
Formal Representations of Derivations from Mutual Dependencies

---

Derivation of Positive Dependency

$d_1(a) <-+-> d_2(a): \alpha, \gamma_1$
$d_1(a') = $ high, medium, low: ϕ, γ_2
a' = SPEC a: γ_3

$d_2(a') = $ high, medium, low: $\gamma = f(\alpha, \gamma_1, \phi, \gamma_2, \gamma_3)$

Temperature(air) $<-+->$ Water holding capacity(air): $\alpha = $ high, $\gamma_1 = $ certain
Temperature(air outside) = high: $\phi = $ high, $\gamma_2 = $ certain
Air outside SPEC air: $\gamma_3 = $ certain

Water holding capacity(air outside) = high: $\gamma = $ certain

Derivation from Negative Dependency

$d_1(a) <-\ -\ -> d_2(a): \alpha, \gamma_1$
$d_1(a') = $ high, medium, low: ϕ, γ_2
a' = SPEC a: γ_3

$d_2(a') = $ low, medium, high: $\gamma = f(\alpha, \gamma_1, \phi, \gamma_2, \gamma_3)$

Abs. Val. Latitude(place) $<-\ -> $ Aver. Temperature(place): linear;
    $0^\cdot, 85^\cdot, 90^\cdot, 0^\cdot; \alpha = $ moderate, $\gamma_1 = $ certain
Abs. Val. Latitude(Lima, Peru) = $10^\cdot$: $\phi = $ high, $\gamma_2 = $ fairly certain
(Lima, Peru) SPEC place: $\gamma_3 = $ certain

Aver. Temperature(Lima, Peru) = $75^\cdot$: $\gamma = $ moderately certain

---

Source: Collins, A. M., and Michalski, R. (1989). The logic of plausible reasoning: A core theory. *Cognitive Science, 13*, p. 35. © Cognitive Science Society. Reprinted with permission.

Transitivity Inferences

The logic of transitivity applied to a set of implications or dependencies results in the new inferences. Examples of this logic are given in the following account:

[Table 2.4] shows two forms of a *transitivity inference*, one based on mutual implication and the other based on mutual dependency. The example for mutual implication

Table 2.4
Formal Representations of Transitivity Inferences

On Mutual Implication

$d_1(a) = r_1 <==> d_2(a) = r_2: \alpha_1, \beta_1, \gamma_1$
$d_2(a) = r_2 <==> d_3(a) = r_3: \alpha_2, \beta_2, \gamma_2$

$d_1(a) = r_1 <==> d_3(a) = r_3: \alpha = f(\alpha_1, \alpha_2), \beta = f(\beta_1, \beta_3), \gamma = f(\gamma_1, \gamma_2)$

Aver. Temperature(place) = 85˚ $<==>$ Latitude(place) = equatorial:
    α_1 = high, β_1 = fairly high, γ_1 = certain
Latitude(place) = equatorial: $<==>$ Abs. Humidity(place) = high:
    α_2 = high, β_2 = moderate, γ_2 = certain

Aver. Temperature(place) = 85˚ $<==>$ Abs. Humidity(place) = high:
    α = high, β = low, γ = certain

On Mutual Dependency

$d_1(a) <--> d_2(a): \alpha_1, \beta_1, \gamma_1$
$d_2(a) <--> d_3(a): \alpha_2, \beta_2, \gamma_2$
$d_1(a) <--> d_3(a): \alpha = f(\alpha_1, \alpha_2), \beta = f(\beta_1, \beta_3), \gamma = f(\gamma_1, \gamma_2)$

Interest rates(country) $<----> $ Money supply growth(country):
    α_1 = high, β_1 = moderate, γ_1 = certain
Money supply growth(country) $<--+-->$ Inflation rate(country):
    α_2 = high, β_2 = high, γ_2 = certain
Interest rates(country) $<---->$ Inflation rate(country):
    α_3 = high, β_3 = low, γ_3 = certain

Source: Collins, A. M., and Michalski, R. (1989). The logic of plausible reasoning: A core theory. *Cognitive Science, 13*, p. 36. © Cognitive Science Society. Reprinted with permission.

states if a person believes an average temperature of 85° implies a place is equatorial, and that if a place is equatorial it will tend to have high humidity, then he can infer that if the average temperature of a place is 85° it will tend to have high humidity, and vice versa. . . . If one were to write the causal links for this example, it would probably go from equatorial latitude to high temperature to high humidity. But people do not systematically make a distinction between causal and diagnostic links, nor do they store things in such a systematic order. For example, they may not know that equatorial places, such as jungles, have high humidity and not link it explicitly to their high temperature. Thus, the inference in this example derives a more direct link (temperature $<=>$ humidity) from a less direct link (latitude $<=>$ humidity). It also should be noted that the diagnostic link in the first implication (temperature $=>$ latitude) may be more constraining than the causal link (latitude $=>$ temperature). That is, there are probably more equatorial places where the average temperature is not 85° (e.g., Ecuador) then places where the average temperature is 85° but are not equatorial.

The example for transitivity inference on mutual dependency illustrates how people reason about economics (Salter, 1983). Salter asked subjects questions, such as what is the effect of an increase in interest rates on the inflation rate of a country. People gave him chains of inferences like the one shown. If interest rates increase, then growth in the money supply will decrease, and that in turn will cause the inflation rate to decrease (the latter is a positive dependency). So an increase in interest rates will lead to a decrease in the inflation rate. This kind of reasoning is a major way that people construct new mutual implications and dependencies. (Collins and Michalski, 1989, pp. 35–37)

COMMENTARY

The core theory of human plausible reasoning developed by Collins and Michalski (1989) is an important contribution to scientific psychology for two reasons. The system has the merit of an inductive strategy in which the construction of logical forms is closely derived from and fitted to data. The system has the merit of a rational psychological synthesis of logical forms and certainty factors.

There are, however, two distinct limitations. The system is limited in that, while the theory purports to be applicable to "all of human discourse" (Collins and Michalski, 1989, p. 1), the data base for the theory consists of discussions of factual knowledge in geography, agriculture, and economics. Human discourse goes well beyond a rational, academic, and objective discussion of factual knowledge. The system is also limited in that the theory is tuned only to the surface appearance of the data. The theory naively assumes that surface appearance of discourse data can completely account for inferential patterns in plausible reasoning. Inferential patterns can be hidden in automatic cognition that largely supports conscious deliberative thought.

3

Abstract Rules and Reasoning

THE USE OF ABSTRACT RULES IN HUMAN REASONING

A central issue in comparing human and artificial reasoning concerns the employment of abstract rules of inference. Clearly, insofar as artificial intelligence employs the predicate calculus, its reasoning is abstract. It is also the case that logicians and mathematicians in their formal professional work use systems of deductive inference. But do they and people in general employ abstract rules in everyday reasoning and problem solving? Smith, Langston, and Nisbett (1992) addressed this important question:

A number of theoretical positions in psychology—including variants of case-based reasoning, instance-based analogy, and connectionist models—maintain that abstract rules are not involved in human reasoning, or at best play a minor role. Other views hold that the use of abstract rules is a core aspect of human reasoning. We propose eight criteria for determining whether or not people use abstract rules in reasoning, and examine evidence relevant to each criterion for several rule systems. We argue that there is substantial evidence that several different inferential rules, including modus ponens, contractual rules, causal rules, and the law of large numbers, are used in solving everyday problems. We discuss the implications for various theoretical positions and consider hybrid mechanisms that combine aspects of instance and rule models. (Smith, Langston, and Nisbett, 1992, p. 1)

Smith, Langston, and Nisbett (1992) state their general methodology in the following terms.

We propose eight criteria for deciding whether a given abstract rule is applied, where each criterion essentially embodies a phenomenon that is more readily explained by a rule-based approach than by an alternative model. We argue that use of these criteria indicates there is substantial evidence for people's use of several deductive and inductive inferential rules, all of which have in common that they are widely considered to be normatively required for correct reasoning. (Smith, Langston, and Nisbett, 1992, p. 2)

The First Criterion of Rule Use

The first criterion and its rationale are presented in the following account.

Criterion 1: Performance on Rule-Governed Items Is as Accurate with Unfamiliar as with Familiar Items

Rationale. The logic behind Criterion 1 stems from the idea that an abstract rule is applicable to a specific item because the item can be represented by some *special abstract structure* that also defines the rule (the special structure is the antecedent part of the rule). Because even novel items can possess this special structure, they can be assimilated to the rule (see Rips, 1990).

When a test item or problem is presented, it is coded in a form that is *sufficiently abstract* to lead to access of an abstract rule: Once accessed, if need be, the rule can be used for further abstract coding of the test item. The next stage is to instantiate, or bind, the variables in the rule with entities from the input. Finally, the rule is applied to yield the desired answer; that is, inspection of the instantiated representation reveals that the antecedent of the rule has been satisfied, thereby licensing the conclusion. There are therefore four stages: coding, access, instantiation (variable binding), and application.

We can illustrate the model with our "If gork then flum; gork?" example. When presented with this item, you might code it, in part, as an "If X, then Y" type item. This would suffice to access modus ponens. Next, you would instantiate p with "gork" and q with "flum." Then you would apply the rule and derive "flum" as an answer. Note that had you initially coded the item more superficially—say, as an "If-then claim"—this might still have sufficed to activate modus ponens, which could then have been used to elaborate the abstract coding. Though this is merely a sketch of a model, it is compatible with the general structure of rule-based models of deductive and inductive reasoning (e.g., Collins and Michalski, 1989; Rips, 1983).

With this sketch in hand we can be more explicit about how our criterion of equivalent accuracy for familiar and unfamiliar items fits with rule-following. If we assume that there is no effect of familiarity on the likelihood of coding an item sufficiently abstractly, then there will be no effect of familiarity on the likelihood of accessing an abstract rule. Similarly, if we assume there is no effect of familiarity on instantiating a rule or inspecting an instantiated representation, there will be no effect of familiarity on applying a rule. Both assumptions seem plausible, which makes the criterion plausible (i.e., familiar items should not lead to greater accuracy). Indeed, if anything, the more familiar an item is, the *less* likely it is to be coded abstractly. This is because familiarity often rests on frequency, and frequent presentations of an item might lead one to represent it in terms of its specific content.

For a criterion to be truly useful, of course, the phenomenon it describes must also be difficult to account for by a nonrule-based explanation. The major alternatives to rule models are instance models, and Criterion 1 is indeed hard to explain in terms of instances. To appreciate this point, consider a rough sketch of a prototypical instance model:

When a test item or problem is presented, it is first coded, and this representation serves to activate stored instances from memory. The basis for access is the similarity of the test item and stored instances. One or more of the stored instances then serve as an analog for the test item. More specifically, a mapping is made between certain aspects of the retrieved instance and known aspects of the test item; this mapping then licenses the transfer of other aspects of the retrieved instance to unknown aspects of the test item. There are, therefore, three major stages: coding, access, and mapping.

This sketch of a model captures the general structure of current analogy models (e.g., Gentner, 1983; Holyoak, 1984; Holyoak and Thagard, 1989). In applying the sketch to the phenomenon captured by Criterion 1, two critical questions arise. The first is whether the representation of an instance codes the special structure of the rule, or is instead restricted to more concrete information. To illustrate, suppose you have stored an instance of the statement, "If you drive a motorcycle in Michigan, then you must be over 17"; the question of interest amounts to whether your stored instance includes information equivalent to *If p implies q; p; therefore q.* If an instance representation does include such information, then it essentially includes the rule. This strikes us not only as implausible, but also as contrary to the intended meaning of "instance." In particular, one does not think of an instance as containing variables. In what follows, then, we will assume that instances do not encode the abstraction they instantiate, though often they may encode features that are correlated with the abstraction. Thus, instance models differ from rule models not just in whether the test item accesses an instance or rule, but also in how abstractly the test item is coded to begin with.

The second critical question for an instance model is how to compute the similarity between the test item and the stored instance. If the similarity is computed over all features, then the model cannot explain the phenomenon of equal accuracy for familiar and unfamiliar items, because there is no guarantee that the stored instances most similar to "gork implies flum" will be useful in dealing with the test item. Perhaps "glory and fame" will be retrieved, and this conjunction is of no use in dealing with the test item.

To salvage an instance model we must assume that the similarity between the test item and the stored instance is computed over very restricted features, namely, those correlated with the special structure of the rule. Consider again a stored instance of the regulation, "If you drive a motorcycle in Michigan, then you must be over 17." The representation of this instance may well contain features corresponding to the concepts *if* and *then*, where these features are correlated with modus ponens. If such features were given great weight in the similarity calculation, a useful analog might be retrieved. There are, however, three problems with the assumption of differential weighting. First, it is ad hoc. Second, it may be wrong, as a growing body of evidence indicates that the retrieval of analogs is influenced more by concrete features, like appearance and taxonomic category, than abstract ones (e.g., Gentner and Toupin, 1986; Holyoak and Koh, 1987; Ross, 1987). Third, for some rules there may be no obvious features correlated with the rule's special structure (a good example is the law of large numbers, as we will see later). In short, when it comes to explaining the phenomenon that accuracy is as high for novel rule-based items as for familiar ones, an instance model seems to be either wrong or ad hoc. As we will see, the same conclusion holds for many of the other phenomena we consider. (Smith, Langston, and Nisbett, 1992, pp. 8–10)

The Second Criterion of Rule Use

The second criterion and its rationale are presented in the following section.

Criterion 2: Performance with Rule-Governed Items Is as Accurate with Abstract as with Concrete Materials

Rationale. This criterion is similar to our first one. However, whereas Criterion 1 was concerned with unfamiliar or nonsensical items, Criterion 2 is concerned with abstract items that may in fact be very familiar. To appreciate Criterion 2, note that intuition suggests that the rule modus ponens can readily be applied to a totally abstract item, such as "If A then B; A; therefore, B." (This item is abstract in the sense of containing few features, and, possibly, in the sense of containing variables.) Good performance on this item fits with the sketch of the rule model we presented earlier, because there is no reason to expect that abstract items are less likely than concrete ones to access the modus ponens rule, and no reason to expect abstract items to fare less well than concrete ones in instantiating the rule or inspecting an instantiated representation. If anything, we might expect abstract items to be both more likely to access the rule and easier to instantiate, because abstract items are more similar to the rule than are concrete items. Note further that good performance on abstract items is quite difficult to explain in terms of an instance model, because the only thing that an abstract item and a retrieved instance can possibly have in common is the special structure of the rule. That is, the use of abstract items allows one to strip away all the content but the special structure, and consequently, performance must be based on the special structure alone (Rips, 1990). For these reasons, Criterion 2 is among the most diagnostic ones we will consider. (Smith, Langston, and Nisbett, 1992, pp. 14–15)

The Third Criterion of Rule Use

The third criterion and its rationale are given in the following account.

Criterion 3: Early in Acquisition, a Rule May Be Applied to an Exception (A Rule Is Overextended)

Rationale. In psycholinguistics, this criterion has figured prominently in studies of how children master the regular past-tense form of English verbs. The relevant rule is to add "ed" to the stem of verbs to form the past tense, such as "cook-cooked." A finding that has been taken as evidence for following this rule is the tendency of young children to overextend the rule to irregular forms, such as "go-goed," even though they had previously used the irregular form correctly (Ervin, 1964). The rule specifies a special structure—the stem of a verb—and the phenomenon arises because children apply the rule to items containing the special structure even though the items should have been marked as exceptions. In terms of our sketch of a rule model, early in acquisition, exceptional verbs are likely to be represented in a way that accesses the relevant rule, and once the rule is accessed it is instantiated and applied.

Perhaps for more than any other criterion, there has been a concerted effort to formulate nonrule-based accounts of overextension. Thus, Rumelhart and McCelland (1987) offered a connectionist account of the overextensions of classification rules (see, e.g., Medin and

Smith, 1981). In general, then, this criterion seems less diagnostic than the previous two we considered. We include it, though, because it may prove to be diagnostic in specific cases. Indeed, with regard to overextension of the past-tense rule, critiques of the Rumelhart and McCelland proposal by Pinker and Prince (1988) and Marcus et al. (1990) suggest that a rule-based theory still provides the fullest account of the data. The critics noted, for example, that children are no more likely to overgeneralize an irregular verb that is similar to many regular ones than to overgeneralize an irregular verb that is similar to few regular ones. Yet, in most connectionist models, as in instance models, generalization is based on similarity. The lack of similarity effects fits perfectly with a rule-based account, of course. Thus, in situations where the likelihood of overgeneralizing an exception does not depend on the similarity of the exception to the regular cases, the criterion is indeed diagnostic. (Smith, Langston, and Nisbett, 1992, pp. 16–17)

The Fourth Criterion of Rule Use

The fourth criterion and its rationale are presented in the following section.

Criterion 4: Performance on a Rule-Governed Problem Deteriorates as a Function of the Number of Rules That Are Required to Solve the Problem

Rationale. Criterion 4 essentially holds that rules provide the appropriate unit for measuring the complexity of a problem. We can illustrate the criterion by considering problems that vary in the number of times they require application of the rule modus ponens. Even after equating for reading time, deciding that Argument 2 is valid presumably would take longer and be more error prone than deciding that Argument 1 is valid, because Argument 2 requires one more application of modus ponens:

a. If it's raining, I'll take an umbrella
   It's raining
   _____

   I'll take an umbrella
b. If it's raining, I'll take an umbrella
   If I take an umbrella, I'll lose it
   It's raining
   _____

   I'll lose an umbrella

(Our example might suggest that the phenomenon is an artifact of the premises being more complex in Argument 2 than in Argument 1; however, using correlational techniques, Rips, 1983, found no evidence that premise complexity per se affects the accuracy of reasoning.)

The phenomenon of interest follows from our sketch of a rule model as long as one or more of the stages involved—coding, access, instantiation, and application—is executed less efficiently when it has to do $n + 1$ things than just n things. As many theorists have pointed out, this vulnerability to sheer number may disappear with extended practice. In Anderson's (1982) rule-based model of cognitive skills, for example, rules that are frequently applied in succession come to be "compiled" or chunked into a simple rule; in such a case, performance would be rule-based yet fail to meet Criterion 4. The diagnosticity of this criterion is further reduced by the fact that the basic phenomenon involved seems roughly compatible with an instance model: What needs to be assumed is that problems that supposedly require more rules are really just problems that generally have fewer or less accessible analogues in memory. Again, though, we include the criterion because it may prove very diagnostic in certain cases, for example in cases where there is a *linear* relation between the number of rules that a problem requires and the reaction time needed to solve the problem. Also, the criterion has a history of use in evaluating rule-based hypotheses. For example, in psycholinguistics, it figured centrally in testing the hypothesis that the complexity of a sentence was an increasing function of the number of transformational rules needed to derive the surface form of the sentence (Miller, 1962). (Smith, Langston, and Nisbett, 1992, pp. 18–19)

The Fifth Criterion of Rule Use

The fifth criterion and its rationale are given in the following account.

Criterion 5: Performance of a Rule-Based Item Is Facilitated When Preceded by Another Item Based on the Same Rule (Application of a Rule Primes Its Subsequent Use)

Rationale. The rationale for this criterion is that, once used, a mental structure remains active for a brief time period and during this period the structure is more accessible than usual. In terms of our rule model, the access stage has been facilitated. (Anderson, 1982, made a similar assumption relating recency of rule use to ease of subsequent access.) Our sketch of an instance model would be able to account for the phenomenon to the extent that successively presented rule-based items are also similar in content; but as we will see, the plausibility of this account depends on the specific findings involved. (Smith, Langston, and Nisbett, 1992, pp. 19–20)

The Sixth Criterion of Rule Use

The sixth criterion and its rationale are presented in the following section.

Criterion 6: A Verbal Protocol May Mention a Rule or Its Components

Rationale. The rationale for this criterion is based on the standard interpretation of protocol analysis. Presumably, the protocol is a direct reflection of what is active in the subject's short-term or working memory, when it may have been recently used. Or, to put it in terms of our sketch of a rule model, the products of the access, instantiation, or application stages may reside (perhaps only briefly) in working memory, which makes them accessible to report. There is no reason to expect an instance model to yield such reports. However, the protocol criterion is still of limited diagnosticity, given that there are cases of apparent rule following in which the rules cannot be reported (namely, in language), as well as cases of reported rules for tasks for which there is independent evidence that the rules were not followed (Nisbett and Wilson, 1977). (Smith, Langston, and Nisbett, 1992, pp. 20–21)

The Seventh Criterion of Rule Use

The seventh criterion and its rationale are given in the following account.

Criterion 7: Performance on a Specific Rule-Based Problem Is Improved by Training on an Abstract Version of the Rule

Rationale. The idea behind this criterion is that, because rule following is presumably what underlies performance on specific problems, practice on an abstract version of the rule (abstract in all senses we have considered) can improve performance on specific problems. In part, this should be true because training improves the rule—clarifies it, renders it more precise, and even changes its nature so as to make it more valid. From the perspective of our sketch of a rule model, practice on the rule in the abstract could also benefit performance by increasing the accessibility of the rule and perhaps also by facilitating the application of the rule. (To the extent that there were any examples in the training, there could be a facilitation of the instantiation stage as well.) From the perspective of an instance model, there is no obvious reason why such abstract training should have any effect on performance. Criterion 7 is therefore quite diagnostic. (Smith, Langston, and Nisbett, 1992, p. 22)

The Eighth Criterion of Rule Use

The eighth criterion and its rationale are given in the following account.

Criterion 8: Performance on Problems in a Particular Domain Is Improved as Much by Training on Problems Outside the Domain as on Problems Within It, as Long as the Problems Are Based on the Same Rule

Rationale. If a major product of training is an abstract rule that is as applicable to problems from one domain as to those from another, then subjects taught how to use the rule in a given context domain should readily transfer what they have learned to other domains. To put it in terms of our sketch of a rule model: The major products of training are increases in the accessibility of the rule and in the consequent ease with which the rule can be instantiated and applied, and all of these benefits should readily transfer to domains other than those of the training problems. The upshot is that domain-specificity effects of training might be relatively slight. To the extent such effects are slight, instance models are embarrassed because they naturally predict better performance for test problems that resemble training ones. Hence, Criterion 8 is very diagnostic of rule following. (Smith, Langston, and Nisbett, 1992, pp. 24–25)

Summary of Major Results

Smith, Langston, and Nisbett (1992) present the following summary for their major results.

Throughout most of this article we have been concerned with two interrelated matters: possible criteria for rule following and possible rules that are followed. Let us first summarize our progress regarding the possible criteria, then turn to what we have found out about rules.

Criteria. We have presented and defended a set of criteria for establishing whether or not a rule is used for solving a given problem. Satisfaction of the less diagnostic of these criteria—those concerned with overextension, number of rules, priming, and protocols—adds something to the case that a given rule is used for solving a given problem. Satisfaction of the more diagnostic criteria—those concerned with familiarity, abstractness, abstract training effects, and domain independence in training—adds even more to the case for rule following. And satisfaction of most or all of these criteria adds greatly to the case for rule following. These criteria can serve to put the debate between abstraction-based and instance-based reasoning into clearer perspective.

[Table 3.1] presents each of the eight criteria crossed with the five different rule systems we have examined in detail; broken lines indicate that the rule system failed the criterion of interest. [Table 3.1] makes it easy to see a pair of points concerning the criteria. One is that most of the criteria has been relatively haphazard, with many tests of a particular criterion for some rules and only one or two tests of a smattering of the other criteria. We suspect that the criteria used have been chosen relatively arbitrarily, and that investigators often have tested less powerful criteria than they might have, simply because they were not aware of the existence of the other, more powerful ones. Our overview of criteria and the rationales behind them should help to organize and direct research on the use of rules.

The other point about the criteria that is readily apparent from [Table 3.1] is that the criteria converge. That is, if a rule passes one criterion it generally passes any other criterion that has been applied. Conversely, if a rule fails one criterion it generally fails other criteria that have been applied. We have only one case of this convergence of failures—modus tollens—because our main concern has been with abstract rules that are likely to be in people's repertoires. If we turn our attention to unnatural rules, which are unlikely to be in people's repertoires, we should see other failures to satisfy the criteria. Consider, for example, work by Ross (1987), in which people are taught relatively unnatural rules from probability theory, such as the rule that specifies the expected number of trials to wait for a particular probabilistic event to occur (the "waiting-time" rule). Ross observed a strong violation of our domain-independence-of-training criterion; that is, performance on a test problem markedly depended on its similarity to a training problem. Recent results by Allen and Brooks (1991), who taught subjects artificial rules, make exactly the same point. These failures of unnatural rules to pass the criterion attest to the validity of the criteria.

Three qualifications of the criteria are also worth mentioning. First, for purposes of clarity we have stated some of our criteria in an absolute or all-or-none fashion, but probably it would be more useful to treat each criterion in a relative fashion. We can illustrate this point with Criterion 1, *performance on rule-governed items is as accurate with unfamiliar as familiar items.* Taking the criterion literally, there is evidence for rule-following only when there is absolutely *no* difference between unfamiliar and familiar items. But surely the phenomenon that underlies the criterion admits of degrees, perhaps because of moment-to-moment variations in whether an individual uses a rule. Given this, Criterion 1 is better stated as *the less the difference in performance between unfamiliar and familiar rule-governed items, the greater the use of rules.* Similar remarks apply to Criterion 2 (good performance on abstract items), Criterion 7 (abstract training effects), and Criterion 8 (domain independence of training). It is noteworthy that actual

Table 3.1
Criteria for Use of Abstract Rules for Reasoning and Evidence Base Relating to Them

Criteria	Modus Ponens	Modus Tollens	Rule Types Contractual (Permissions & Obligations)	Causal	Law of Large Numbers
1. Good performance on unfamiliar items	Byrne (1989)	/////////////// Cheng & Holyoak (1985) Numerous Others //// ///////////////	Cheng et al. (1986) Cheng & Holyoak (1985)	Morris et al. (1991)	Nisbett et al. (1983)
2. Good performance on abstract items	Evans (1977)	Wason (1966) ////// Numerous Others ////	Cheng & Holyoak (1985)		
3. Overextension early in training					Fong et al. (1986)
4. Number of rules and performance	Osherson (1975) Rips (1983) Braine et al. (1984)				
5. Priming effects			Langston et al. (1991)		
6. Protocols identify rules	Rips (1983)				Piaget & Inhelder (1951/1975) Jepson et al. (1983) Nisbett et al. (1983) Fong et al. (1986)
7. Abstract training effects	/////////////////////////////// /////////////////////////////// /////////////////////////////// ///////////////////////////////	Cheng et al. (1986)	Cheng et al. (1986)	Morris, Cheng, & Nisbett (1991)	Fong et al. (1986) Lehman & Nisbett (1990)
8. Domain independence of training					Lehman et al. (1988) Fong et al. (1986) Fong & Nisbett (1991)

Note: Broken lines indicate the rule system filled the criterion of interest.

Source: Smith, E. E., Langston, C., and Nisbett, R. E. (1992). The case for rules in reasoning. *Cognitive Science*, *16*, p. 28. © Cognitive Science Society. Reprinted with permission.

uses of these criteria tend to employ the relative interpretation (see, e.g., the Allen and Brooks, 1991, use of domain-independence-of-training effects).

A second qualification of the criteria stems from the fact that their diagnosticity has been measured in terms of how difficult they are to explain by models based on *stored* instances. But Johnson-Laird (1983) has championed a theoretical approach which holds that people reason by generating *novel* instances (in his terms, "reasoning by means of mental models"). To illustrate, suppose someone is told, "If gork, then flum." They would represent this conditional in terms of the following sort of mental model:

$$gork1 = flum1$$
$$gork2 = flum2$$
$$(flum3).$$

The equal sign indicates that the same instance is involved, and the parentheses indicate that the instance is optional. If now told there exists a gork, one can use this mental model to conclude there also exists a flum, and in this way implement modus ponens. What is important about this for our purposes is that a theory based on such novel instances seems more compatible with our criteria than theories based on stored instances. For example, there is no obvious reason why one cannot construct a mental model as readily for an unfamiliar item as for a familiar one, or as readily for an abstract item as a concrete one.

The final qualification is simply that the application of our criteria does not provide as definitive data on the rule-versus-instance issue as does a contrast of detailed models. Our criteria are needed mainly in situations where detailed reasoning models have not been developed: the usual case as far as we can tell. (An exception is Nosofsky, Clark, and Shin, 1989, who did contrast detailed rule and instance models, but who considered rules that are not abstract by our definitions.) Our criteria also provide useful constraints in developing detailed rule models; for example, any rule model that is concerned only with abstract rules ought to produce comparable performance for unfamiliar and familiar items, for abstract and concrete items, and so on.

Rules. [Table 3.1] also tells us about what rules are followed. We believe that the applications of the criteria to date serve to establish that people make use of a number of abstract rules in solving problems of a sort that occur frequently in everyday life. In particular, there is substantial evidence for at least three sorts of rule systems.

For modus ponens, there is evidence that people: (a) perform as well—that is, make inferences in accordance with the rule—on unfamiliar as on familiar material; (b) perform as well on abstract as on concrete material; (c) perform better if they must invoke the rule fewer rather than more times; and (d) sometimes provide protocols suggesting that they have used the rule. (On the other hand, there is some evidence that the rule cannot be trained by abstract techniques, but this evidence may merely indicate that the rule is already asymptotic.)

For contractual rules, namely permission and obligation rules, there is evidence that people: (a) perform as well on unfamiliar as on familiar material; (b) perform as well on abstract as on concrete material; (c) show priming effects of the rule, at least within a content domain; and (d) benefit from training in their ability to apply the rule to any material that can plausibly be interpreted in terms of it. There is also some evidence of a comparable kind for formally similar causal rules.

For the system of statistical rules under the rubric of the law of large numbers, it has been shown that people: (a) perform well with unfamiliar material; (b) overextend the rule early in training; (c) often mention the rule in relatively abstract form in justification of their answers for particular problems; (d) improve their ability to apply the rule across a wide number of domains by purely abstract training on the rule; and (e) improve their performance on problems outside the domain of training as much as on problems with it.

The demonstrations that people follow modus ponens and the law of large numbers are of particular interest in view of the fact that these two rules are normative and promote optimal inferential performance. Evidence for people following certain abstract inferential rules thus amounts to evidence for people manifesting aspects of rationality. Although there is less data about causal rules, what evidence there is suggests that people also follow these rules (see [Table 3.1]), which again are normative. And there is some recent evidence for the use of still another set of normative rules, those governing economic choices (Larrick et al., 1990; [1993]).

In contrast to the positive evidence summarized before, there are three lines of negative evidence on the question of whether people use modus tollens. It has been shown that people perform poorly: (a) with unfamiliar items; (b) with abstract items; and (c) even after formal training in the rule. We therefore believe that the consensus among students of the problem that most people do not use modus tollens is justified in terms of the criteria studied to date. This demonstration indicates that application of our criteria can cut both ways: Negative evidence relating to the criteria can cast substantial doubt on the use of a rule, just as positive evidence can buttress the case for its use.

Of course modus ponens, modus tollens, contractual rules, and the law of large numbers are just a handful of the many possible seemingly natural rules that people may follow in reasoning about everyday problems. There are, for example, numerous rules in propositional logic other than ponens and tollens that have been proposed as psychologically real (see, for instance, Braine et al., 1984). One such rule is *and-introduction*, which states *If p is the case and if q is the case then p and q is the case.* The obvious question is: How does and-introduction stack up against our eight criteria? The same question applies to other rules from propositional logic, and to rules that have figured in Piagetian-type research (including transitivity, commutativity, and associativity), as well as to rules that come from other bodies of work. The point is that all we have done in this article is sample a rule or two from a few major branches of reasoning—deduction, statistics, and causality—and there are other rules of interest in these and other branches of reasoning.

A final point to note about the evidence for rules is that the work to date shows not merely that people *can* follow rules when instructed to do so in artificial problem-solving situations, but that they *do* follow quite abstract inferential rules when solving ordinary, everyday problems. For example, in their studies of the law of large numbers, Fong et al. (1986) performed not merely laboratory experiments, but field studies in which subjects did not even know they were being tested. In one study, male subjects were called in the context of an alleged "survey of sports opinions." Subjects were enrolled in introductory statistics courses and were called either at the beginning of the course or at the end. After being asked a few questions about NBA salaries and NCAA rules, it was pointed out to them that although many batters often finish the first two weeks of the baseball season with averages of .450 or higher, no one has ever finished the season with such an average. They were asked why they thought this was the case. Most subjects responded with causal hypotheses such as, "the pitchers make the necessary adjustments."

Some, however, responded with statistical answers such as, "there are not many at-bats in two weeks, so unusually high (or low) averages would be more likely; over the long haul nobody is really that good." There were twice as many statistical answers from subjects tested at the end of the term as from subjects tested at the beginning.

Similarly, Larrick et al. (1990) found that subjects who were taught cost-benefit rules came to apply them in all sorts of life contexts, from consumer decisions about whether to finish a bad meal or a bad movie, to professional decisions about whether to pursue a line of work that was turning out to be disappointing, to hypothetical questions about institutional policy and international relations.

Thus, the work reviewed here establishes not merely that people can follow abstract rules self-consciously in appropriate educational, experimental, or professional settings, but that such rules play at least a limited role in ordinary inference. (Smith, Langston, and Nisbett, 1992, pp. 26–32)

Abstract Models and Instance Models

Smith, Langston, and Nisbett discuss the issue of abstract models and instance models in the following section.

Combining Rule and Instance Mechanisms

Our review indicates that pure instance models of reasoning and problem solving are not viable. There is too much evidence, stemming from the application of too many criteria, indicating that people use abstract rules in reasoning. On the other hand, there is also abundant evidence that reasoning and problem solving often proceed via the retrieval of instances (e.g., Allen and Brooks, 1991; Kaiser, Jonides, and Alexander, 1986; Medin and Ross, 1989; Ross, 1987). At a minimum, then, we need to posit two qualitatively different mechanisms of reasoning. Whereas some situations may involve only one of the mechanisms, others may involve both.

In addition to *pure-rule* and *pure-instance* mechanisms, hybrid mechanisms may be needed as well. In particular, hybrid mechanisms may be needed for the situations noted earlier in which people process instances deeply enough to encode some information about the relevant abstraction as well as about the concrete aspects of the instance. These are the situations that are the concern of most case-based reasoning models (e.g., Hammond et al., 1991; Kolodner, 1983; Schank, 1982). In such situations, people have essentially encoded both an instance and a rule, so a hybrid mechanism must specify how the two representational aspects are connected. We consider two possibilities.

One possibility is that a retrieved instance provides access to a rule. That is, when an item is presented, it first accesses similar instances from memory that the reasoner can use to access a rule. Then, the final stages of rule processing—instantiation and application—ensue, though the instance may serve as a guide for these two stages. We can illustrate this mechanism with the drinking version of the four-card problem. When presented the problem, presumably a subject uses this item to retrieve from memory an episode of a drinking event; this representation may contain the information that people below the drinking age are in violation of the law, and the concept of *violation* may be used to access the permission rule; from here on, processing would continue as specified in our sketch of a rule model except that the retrieved instance can be used to guide the instantiation and application stages. This hybrid process, which we will refer to as *instance-rule mechanism*, captures the intuition that we often understand an abstract rule in terms of a specific example.

The other possibility is that a rule provides access to a relevant instance (a *rule-instance* mechanism). That is, when an item is presented it is coded abstractly, and this abstraction accesses the appropriate rule (these are the first two stages of our sketch of a rule model). The rule then provides access to some typical examples, and these instances control further processing. Again, we can illustrate with the drinking version of the four-card problem. When presented the problem, a subject codes the item in terms of *permission*, and uses this code to access the permission rules. Associated with these rules are typical examples of *permission* situations, and one or more of these instances is used as an analog for the present problem (that is, it is used for the mapping stage.)

A few comments are in order about these mechanisms. Note that we are not proposing the two hybrid mechanisms as alternatives to the two pure mechanisms (rule and instance). Rather, we suspect that all four mechanisms can be used, albeit with different situations recruiting different mechanisms. (The experimental situations we reviewed in this article likely involved either the *pure-rule* or the *rule-instance* mechanism.) In situations where more than one mechanism is involved, presumably the processes operate simultaneously and independently of one another. Thus, the final answer may be determined by a kind of "horse race" between the operative mechanisms, with the mechanism that finishes first determining the final judgement.

Note further that our hybrid mechanisms allow for instance-type effects should they occur. Consider again Criterion 1, that novel rule-based items are treated as accurately as familiar ones. The available evidence is consistent with the criterion, but the criterion deals only with accuracy. Perhaps if one were to measure reaction times, familiar rule-based items might be processed faster than novel ones. Such a result could be handled easily by our *instance-rule* mechanism. Familiar items should be faster in accessing a relevant instance because familiar items are themselves likely to be instances. In addition, we have already seen an indication of instance effects even for accuracy. Such an effect appeared in connection with Criterion 5, that application of a rule primes its subsequent use. Recall that in the four-card problem, Langston et al. (1991) found evidence for priming of contractual rules only when the prime and target were similar in content. This pattern of results also fits nicely with the *instance-rule* mechanism. Only when the target and prime are similar in content does the target retrieve the prime instance, and only when the prime is retrieved does one gain access to the relevant rule. Thus, instance-type effects do not imply that rules were not involved.

Finally, another case of instance-type effects during rules use is provided by Ross (1987). Ross trained subjects on the waiting-time rule of probability theory and then had them solve new test problems with the rule present. Even though the rule was present, subjects appeared to rely on training problems when determining how to instantiate the rule. These results indicate that instances are used not just to access a rule but also to help instantiate it, as in the instance-rule mechanism. (These results, however, may depend in part on the fact that the rule involved was not a natural one.)

In short, the dichotomy between pure rules and pure instances is too simple. Hybrid mechanisms seem plausible, particularly in light of the role they play in current versions of case-based reasoning. (Smith, Langston, and Nisbett, 1992, pp. 32–34)

Types of Rule Following

Smith, Langston, and Nisbett (1992) discuss the issue of types of rule following in the following section.

Two Kinds of Rule Following

Until now we have acted as if explicit rule following is the only kind of rule following. But a critical observation suggests the need to consider a second kind. The observation (due to Douglas Medin, personal communication, April 1991) is that, when *linguistic* rules are stacked up against our eight criteria they seem to consistently fail three of them, namely verbal protocols, abstract training effects, and context independence in training. That is, people are notoriously unable to verbalize the linguistic rules they purportedly use, and they fail to benefit much from explicit (school) instructions on these rules. If linguistic rules meet only 5 of our criteria whereas reasoning rules (generally) meet all eight, perhaps the kind of rule following involved in language is different from that involved in reasoning.

Presumably there is a kind of rule following that is *implicit* rather than *explicit*; that is, the rule is never explicitly represented, which accounts for why it can neither be reported nor affected by explicit instruction. The rule might be implemented in the hardware, and is essentially a description of how some built-in processor works (see Pinker and Prince, 1988, Section 8.2). Implicit rules are close to what we earlier characterized as operating principles of a system, and rules like this may be part of our basic cognitive architecture. Such notions fit nicely with Pylyshyn's (1984) concept of *cognitive penetrability*. His basic idea is that anything that is part of the fixed cognitive architecture cannot be altered (penetrated) by goals, context, or instruction. If some linguistic rules are part of our basic architecture, they should not be affected by instruction, which means that our two instructional criteria should fail, as they in fact do. (The seeming imperviousness of modus ponens to instruction leaves open the possibility that this rule too may be represented implicitly.) (Smith, Langston, and Nisbett, 1992, p. 34)

Connectionist Models and Rule Use

Smith, Langston, and Nisbett (1992) analyze the meaning of their results with respect to the doctrine of connectionism in the following section.

Implications for Connectionist Models

Although we know of no limit, in principle, on the ability of connectionist models to code abstractions, the evidence we have presented for abstract rules does not fit well with the connectionist program.

For one thing, what seems to be the most straightforward account of much of the evidence involves concepts that are anathema to connectionism. The account we have in mind is that of explicit rule following: The rule and input are mentally represented explicitly, and application of the rule to the input involves an inspection of the input to determine whether the antecedent of the rule has been satisfied. Notions of *explicit data structures* and *inspection of explicit structures* simply lie outside the ontology of connectionism. Of course, connectionists may be able to develop alternative accounts of the data, but there is no reason to believe the resulting connectionist models will be as parsimonious as the sort of rule-based model we advocate. This is particularly the case given that the abstract rules that have to be modeled all involve variable bindings, which remains a difficult issue in connectionist work (for discussion, see Holyoak, 1991). In short, rule-based models provide a simple account of the data, and no comparable connectionist alternatives are thus far in sight.

In constructing alternative models of the evidence, connectionists face another difficulty. The evidence indicates that people can use two qualitatively different mechanisms in reasoning, which we have termed "rules" and "instances," whereas connectionist models can either blur the rule-instance distinction, in which case they are simply failing to capture a major generalization about human cognition, or they can somehow mark the distinction, in which case they may be merely implementing a rule-based model in a connectionist net. We say "merely" because it is not clear that such an implementation will yield any new important insights about reasoning.

The preceding points have been programmatic, but the remaining one is more substantive. According to rule models, the rationale for some rules hinges on a *constituency relation*—like that which holds between *If p then q* and *p*—but most current connectionist models lack true constituency relations. In discussing this issue, we need to keep separate *localist* connectionist models, in which a concept can be represented by a single node, and *distributed* models, in which a concept is represented by a set of nodes. We consider localist models first.

To understand the constituency issue, consider modus ponens. Given *If p then q* and *p*, the fact that the latter is a constituent of the former is part of why we can conclude *q*. To take an even simpler example, consider again and-introduction: *If p is the case and if q is the case then p and q is the case*. Here, it is clear that the basis of the rule is a constituency relation; the rule essentially states, *if each of its constituents is the case, then a conjunction is the case*. In contrast, localist connectionist models lack constituency relations, so such relations can never serve as the bases of rules.

The reason localist connectionist models lack constituency relations is that their nodes (their representations) lack any internal structure, including a part-whole structure. In a localist model for and-introduction, for example, there might be separate nodes for *p, q*, and *p and q*, which are connected in such a way that whenever the nodes for *p* and *q* are both activated, the node for *p and q* is activated. Importantly, the node for *p and q* has no internal structure, and in no sense contains the node for *p* or that for *q*. Hence, the relation between the *p* and *q* nodes on the one hand, and the *p and q* node on the other, is strictly causal (as opposed to constituency). That is, activation of *p* and *q* causes activation of *p and q* in exactly the same way that activation of a node for *fire* might cause activation of a node for *smoke*. Although we know of no data on whether constituency relations are perceived as the bases of some rules, our intuitions suggest they are, which favors the rule account. (For a fuller discussion of these issues, see Fodor and Pylyshyn, 1988.)

Distributed connectionist models seem better able to accommodate constituency relations because they at least have a part-whole structure. Thus, if *p and q* is represented by a set of nodes, then some part of that set can, in principle, represent *p* and another part *q*. However, current distributed connectionist models still have trouble capturing constituent structure, as Fodor and McLaughlin (1990) pointed out. The latter authors take up a proposal of Smolensky's (1988) in which a concept (rule) is represented in terms of a vector whose components represent the activity levels of the members of the relevant set of nodes. According to Smolensky, vector a is a constituent of vector b if there exists a third vector—call it x—such that $a + x = b$; a is a part of b because b is derivable from a ($+x$). But this proposal permits the possibility that b may be activated without a being activated. In the case of and-introductions, this means that p *and* q could be activated without p being activated. Such a thing should be impossible if p is a true constituent of p *and* q. Again, to the extent some rules are based on constituent structure, the rule account is favored over current connectionist rivals.

None of this is to suggest that connectionist models do not have an important role to play—they have been very successful in capturing aspects of perception, memory, and categorization, for example—but rather to suggest that some aspects of reasoning may be inherently rule-based, and hence, not naturally captured by connectionist models. Of course, a rule-based model, unlike a connectionist one, will not look like a biological model. Thus, to pursue rule-based models of reasoning is to give up the wish that all mental phenomena be expressive of biological phenomena rather than merely neural connections to abstract rules that seem metaphorically to sit astride the hustle and bustle of biological activity in the brain, altering and managing the results of such activity, and being modified by the mere words of outsiders and the ministrations of educators. We do not pretend to be able to make the leap from the known facts of the behavior of the nervous system to a plausible, emergent set of highly modifiable abstract rules. We claim merely that a correct theory of mind may have to do so. (Smith, Langston, and Nisbett, 1992, pp. 34–37)

COMMENTARY

A fourfold classification can be imposed on mechanisms in reasoning: pure rule-based, pure instance-based, hybrid rule-instance based, and hybrid instance-rule based. The class of rule-based mechanisms is mapped in the research of Smith, Langston, and Nisbett (1992). Their methodology with suitable adaptations should be applied to the other three classes, resulting in summary tables analogous to Table 3.1. The resulting set of summary tables would constitute a descriptive classification.

The next strategic research advance would move from a descriptive classification to a dynamic analysis focused on the simultaneity and interaction of the mechanisms that operate on extended reasoning and problem-solving tasks. This empirical analysis should be placed under the theoretical aegis of a hybrid symbolic-connectionist architecture.

4

Causal Reasoning

REASONING ABOUT CAUSES AND ENABLING CONDITIONS

Philosophical inquiry has for many centuries been directed toward the explication of the nature of causation. Contemporary psychological theory and research in human causal reasoning will be considered in this section. In particular, the important research of P. W. Cheng and L. R. Novick (1991) will be described, and then a general commentary will be presented.

Probabilistic Contrast Model

In an effort to distinguish causes from enabling conditions, Cheng and Novick (1991) developed and tested the probabilistic contrast model. Central to the model are the concepts of causes as the factors that covary with effects; enabling conditions as the factors that do not vary with effects; and a focal set of events that contain the positive factors, the enabling conditions, and the effects. A computational mechanism of causality is offered:

We propose that a single mechanism can account for the conception of causality . . . : the computation of covariation between potential causes and the effect in question over a *focal set*, a set of events implied by the context. Covariation is hypothesized to be computed over the focal set as specified by our *probabilistic contrast model* (Cheng and Novick, 1990a), which applies to discrete variables. Our model defines a *main-effect contrast* (specifying a cause involving a single factor) Δp_i, as follows:

$$\Delta p_i = p_i - p_{\bar{\imath}} \qquad\qquad\qquad\qquad\qquad\qquad\qquad (1)$$

where i is a factor that describes the target event, p_i is the proportion of cases for which the effect occurs when factor i is present, and $p_{\bar{\imath}}$ is the proportion of cases for which the effect occurs when factor i is absent. When Δp_i is greater than some (empirically determined) criterion, then there should be a causal attribution to factor i. In other words, a cause is a factor the presence of which (relative to its absence) noticeably increases the likelihood of the effect. Only factors that are psychologically prior to the event-to-be-explained are evaluated.

As a contrast cannot be computed for a factor that is constantly present in a focal set (owing to division by zero in the computation of the proportion of the effect in the absence of the factor), the causal status of such a factor cannot be determined by events in the focal set; instead, its status is determined by events in other focal sets. In our models, such a factor is: (a) an enabling condition if it does covary with the effect in another focal set (i.e., a set of events selected under another context), but (b) causally irrelevant if it does not covary with the effect in any other focal sets.

We also defined an *interaction contrast*, which specifies a cause involving a conjunction of factors (e.g., the simultaneous presence of positively charged clouds and negatively charged clouds as the cause of thunder). By analogy to statistical contrasts, a two-way interaction contrast involving potential causal factors i and i, Δp_{ij}, is defined as follows:

$$\Delta p_{ij} = (p_{ij} - p_{\bar{\imath}j}) - (p_{i\bar{\jmath}} - p_{\bar{\imath}\bar{\jmath}}) \qquad\qquad\qquad\qquad (2)$$

where p, as before, denotes the proportion of cases in which the effect occurs when a potential contributing factor is either present or absent, as denoted by its subscripts. To our knowledge, there has not been any explicit definition of conjunctive causes in terms of contrast in previous proposals on the distinction between causes and enabling conditions.

The definitions of contrasts in equations (1) and (2) apply to inhibitory factors (i.e., factors that decrease the likelihood of an effect) as well as facilitatory factors (i.e., factors that increase the likelihood of an effect). Positive contrasts specify facilitatory causes; negative contrasts specify inhibitory causes.

We assume that a factor that does not have a noticeable probabilistic contrast will be considered causally irrelevant, independent of the other constraints. That is, we assume that covariation is a necessary criterion. (Cheng and Novick, 1991, pp. 95–96)

The following extract illustrates the Cheng and Novick (1991) probabilistic contrast model as applied to distinguishing among causes, enabling conditions, and irrelevant causes in the case of a focal set of lightning and forest fire events:

Now, assume that lightning struck the forest at the place where the fire started immediately before it started. Applying our model to the focal set of events, we see that the proportion of cases for which fire occurs in the presence of lightning is greater than the proportion of cases for which fire occurs in the absence of lightning (i.e., lightning covaries with fire). Lightning is therefore a cause. In contrast, the corresponding difference in proportions cannot be computed for oxygen, because oxygen is present in every event in that set. Oxygen does covary with fire in other focal sets, however; it is therefore an enabling condition. Finally, the presence of stones in the forest, which does not covary with forest fire in any focal set, would be considered causally irrelevant. *Thus, covariation computed over a focal set of events can differentiate among causes, enabling conditions, and causally irrelevant factors for an abnormal event such as a forest fire.* (Cheng and Novick, 1991, p. 97; italics added)

In the following paragraphs, Cheng and Novick (1991) relate their probabilistic contrast model of causality to the logic of necessary and sufficient causes and argue for the predictive usefulness of this model:

Cheng and Novick (1990a, 1990b) drew a distinction between *data* on which the causal inference process operates and the *process* of inference computation itself. In the present context, one can entirely explain the paradoxical distinction between causes and enabling conditions by a shift in the set of data on which the distinction is based from the set of data on which the logical identity of causes and enabling conditions is based. *Although causes and enabling conditions hold the same relationship to the target effect in terms of necessity and sufficiency with respect to the universal set of events in one's knowledge base, they do not do so with respect to the focal set. The distinction between causes and enabling conditions therefore does not contradict the status of these factors in terms of necessity and sufficiency within the focal set.*

The computation of covariation over a focal set of events that are causally relevant to fires (for example), maximizes the predictive value of the causes so identified for the focal set. If a primary goal of causal explanation is prediction, then the computation of covariation over a focal set is clearly adaptive. Consider some candidate answers to the question on the cause of the forest fire mentioned above in the context of the goal of predicting the next forest fire. The answer "the presence of oxygen" (which would covary with fire if all events in one's knowledge base that are causally relevant to fires are considered) is clearly not predictive of when the next fire will occur in the forest, for the obvious reason that oxygen is always present for all events in the forest (the focal set with which the questioner is concerned). In contrast, the answers "the lightning" or "the unusual dryness of the weather", which are based on the computation over a pragmatically restricted subset of events, are much more predictive of the next fire in the forest. *The computation of covariation over a focal set therefore identifies causal factors that are more useful* among *those that are equally* true. (Cheng and Novick, 1991, pp. 97–98; italics added to selected sentences)

Focal Sets and the Computation of Covariation

The probabilistic contrast model provides for the influence of differing contexts on the differentiation of causes and enabling conditions by the computation of covariation of events in a particular focal set. [Figure 4.1] contains examples of the computational procedure:

The figure is assumed to represent the entire set of events that are relevant to a particular effect in a hypothetical person's knowledge base. In the figure, each letter (e.g.,

Figure 4.1
Computation of Covariation

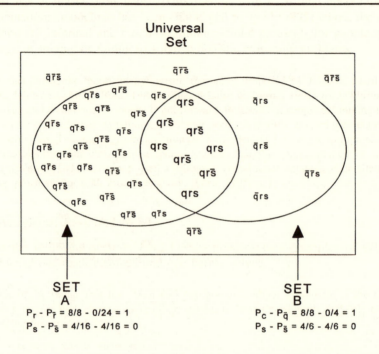

SET
A
$P_r - P_{\bar{r}} = 8/8 - 0/24 = 1$
$P_s - P_{\bar{s}} = 4/16 - 4/16 = 0$

SET
B
$P_c - P_{\bar{q}} = 8/8 - 0/4 = 1$
$P_s - P_{\bar{s}} = 4/6 - 4/6 = 0$

Note: This figure depicts computation of covariation within focal sets according to the probabilistic contrast model as an explanation of the distinction among causes, enabling conditions, and causally irrelevant factors. Each letter represents a factor. A bar above a letter denotes the absence of that factor. An event is represented by a sequence of letters denoting the conjunct of those factors in the event. The presence of the effect for an event is represented by placing the event in larger type. The absence of the effect for an event is represented by regular letters. Finally, loops enclosing the events denote focal sets.

Source: Cheng, P. W., and Novick, L. R. (1991). Causes versus enabling conditions. Reprinted from *Cognition*, *40*, p. 99, copyright 1991, with permission from Elsevier Science.

q) represents a *potential causal factor*. A bar above a letter (e.g., $\bar{q}$), denotes the *absence* of that factor. An *event* is represented by a sequence of letters (e.g., $\bar{q}rs$) denoting the conjunct of those factors in the event. The *presence of the effect* for an event is represented by placing the event in larger bold type. The *absence of the effect* for an event is represented by regular (small and non-bold) letters. Finally, loops enclosing events denote subsets of events selected under various contexts. That is, each enclosed subset represents a different focal set.

As can be seen in the figure, with respect to the universal set of events, factors q and r are individually necessary (i.e., $p_{\bar{q}} = p_{\bar{r}} = 0$) and jointly sufficient (i.e., $p_q < 1$, $p_r < 1$, but $p_{qr} = 1$) for the occurrence of the effect. Now consider subsets A and B. For each of these subsets, one factor covaries with the effect. For example, in set A, because p_r

= 1, and $p_{\bar{r}} = 0$, r should be perceived as a cause of the effect for that subset. (Factor r is sufficient and necessary for the effect within set A. For simplicity of exposition, only deterministic covariations are illustrated in the figure, but the model applies in the same manner to probabilistic covariations.) Factor q, however, remains constantly present in that focal set. A contrast for q therefore cannot be computed (within that set, q is insufficient for the effect and its necessity is undetermined). Factor q therefore should not be selected as a cause. But it is an enabling condition because it does covary with the effect in another focal set, set B. (It would have been causally irrelevant if it did not covary with the effect in any focal set.) Conversely, in set B, q covaries with the effect, as mentioned, whereas r remains constant. Only q, therefore, should be perceived as the cause of the effect for that subset. *Varying the relevant focal set thus alters which factor should be considered a cause and which an enabling condition.*

Notice that although s is sometimes present and sometimes absent in each subset, its presence or absence does not covary with the effect in either subset. Factor s is therefore causally irrelevant to the effect (at least for a person whose knowledge is represented in the figure). *Covariation over specified subsets therefore accounts for the distinctions among causes, enabling conditions, and causally irrelevant factors.* Recall that by comparison, the normality view requires a separate preliminary stage to discriminate conditions from causally irrelevant factors.

We have proposed that covariation computed over a focal set serves as the criterion for distinguishing among causes, enabling conditions, and causally irrelevant factors, regardless of the normality of the event to be explained. [Figure 4.1] illustrates this point. In set A, the presence of the effect is abnormal, whereas in set B it is normal. Contrasts regarding the presence of the effect for each set are illustrated in the figure. Contrasts can likewise be calculated regarding the absence of the effect, which of course have the *complementary* status with respect to normality in each set. (Cheng and Novick, 1991, pp. 98–100; italics added to selected sentences).

Experimental Tests of the Probabilistic Contrast Model

Overview

The distinction between causes and enabling conditions was tested in an experiment that compared the probabilistic contrast view with a normality view:

According to the normality view, causes are abnormal conditions within a given context, whereas enabling conditions are normal conditions within the context. In contrast, according to the probabilistic contrast model, causes are factors that covary with the effect within a relevant set of events (regardless of the normality of the factors); and enabling conditions are factors that remain constant within the focal set (hence their covariation with the effect cannot be computed for that set), but are known to covary with the effect in some other subset of events (i.e., are causally relevant). Normality per se, according to this view, should have no effect on the perception of causes versus enabling conditions. We report an experiment that tested these two views.

We tested our probabilistic contrast model by manipulating the focal set on which subjects were expected to compute their causal inferences. The focal sets were presented in the form of two scenarios, which differed in the factor that covaried with the effect and the factors that remained constant. In addition to manipulating the focal set, we manipulated normality, in both its statistical and idealistic senses. For each scenario, the covarying factor is prevalent (hence a default in one version but rare (hence not a default) in another). Furthermore, whereas one of the scenarios described a covarying factor that was desired (i.e., an ideal), the other scenario described a covarying factor that was not desired (i.e., a deviation from an ideal).

Both scenarios concerned plant growth. One was about the growth of a weed, dandelions, in a family yard (an undesired outcome) and the other was about the maturation of corn plants in corn fields (a desired outcome). In each scenario, one factor covaried with the effect. This factor differed across the scenarios (sunlight in the dandelion scenario vs. nutrients in the soil in the corn scenario). The remaining factors were held constant in each scenario: two of these factors were necessary for the effect according to subjects' prior knowledge (water in both scenarios in addition to one of the above two factors) and one of them was not (the presence of a house next to the plants). At the end of each scenario was a causal question about plant growth. Subjects were asked to indicate the causal status (cause, mere condition, causally irrelevant, and inhibitor) of each of the four factors.

Statistical normality was operationalized in the scenarios by specifying the positive value of the covarying factor as occurring in either most or few cases in the given context. For example, in the prevalent version of the ideal scenario, four out of five corn fields tended by a farmer had virgin soil (the positive value of the covarying factor) whereas the fifth had its soil depleted of nutrients by previous farming. To ensure that virgin soil was perceived as a default in the given context, the farmer was described in the scenario as a pioneer settling in a valley where few people had reached and farmed. In contrast, in the rare version of the scenario, many corn plants matured in only one of the five corn fields. This field had virgin soil whereas the other four fields had depleted soil. To ensure that virgin soil was not perceived as a default, the farm was described in the scenario as inherited through many generations of farmers in a poor country. Because our operational definition of statistical normality satisfies the more stringent interpretation of being a majority, it also satisfies the less stringent one of being a default (Kahneman and Miller, 1986).

Before subjects read the scenarios, they were given the brief explanation of the distinction between causes and mere conditions. . . . As mentioned earlier, because the example in the explanation fits the variants of the normality view as well as the probabilistic-contrast view, any results differentiating the two views must be due to subjects' intuitive understanding of the distinction.

To measure the perceived focal sets, subjects were asked to rate how accurately each of three expanded questions that specified different focal sets reflected their interpretation of the causal question in each scenario. To measure the perceived "default" values, subjects were asked to indicate the value of the covarying factor (e.g., rich soil vs. soil depleted of nutrients) that they expected in general in each scenario. (Cheng and Novick, 1991, pp. 109–110)

The following paragraphs provide an account of and the rationale for systematic experimental predictions:

The probabilistic-contrast view predicts that the two scenarios, which differ in the factor that yields a large probabilistic contrast (sunlight in the dandelion scenario vs.

nutrients in the corn scenario) and the factors that are constantly present in the scenario (all variables besides the one with the large contrast), will produce different causes and enabling conditions. Moreover, it predicts that the normality of the covarying factor in the focal set (whether it is prevalent or rare and whether it fits the ideal or deviates from it) will not influence judgments on the causal status of any factor. In particular, it predicts that a factor that covaries with the effect in the focal set, even a statistically or idealistically normal one, will be considered a cause and be distinguished from conditions that are constantly present in the focal set.

In contrast, the statistical normality view predicts that within each scenario (dandelion or corn), only in the rare (non-default) versions should the conditions be considered causes; in the prevalent (default) versions, they should be considered enabling conditions, despite large probabilistic contrasts for these factors within the focal set. The idealistic normality view, however, predicts that only conditions that deviate from an ideal (i.e., those in the dandelion scenario but not those in the corn scenario) should be considered causes. (Cheng and Novick, 1991, p. 110)

Method

Experimental subjects, procedure, materials, and design are presented in the following account:

Subjects and Procedure

The subjects were 78 UCLA students, who participated in partial fulfillment of requirements for their introductory psychology class. Each subject received a 6-page booklet as a distractor task in a memory experiment conducted on individual subjects. The subjects completed the task in 7–10 minutes.

Materials and Data

The first page of the booklet was the explanation of causes versus enabling conditions [distinction]. The last page of the booklet was the prior knowledge. The rest of the materials pertained to two brief scenarios, at the end of each of which was a question about an event in the scenario.

Subjects received the prevalent version of one scenario and the rare version of the other scenario, with the order of statistical normality and scenarios (i.e., idealistic normality) counterbalanced across subjects. Subjects were randomly assigned to one of the four combinations of the ordering of statistical normality and scenario by an experimenter who had no knowledge of the conditions. There were no order effects in the data; the order manipulations will therefore not be considered further.

Following is the prevalent version of the ideal scenario, in which amount of nutrients covaried with plant growth and the amounts of sunlight and water were constant within the focal set:

A young pioneer Greg built a cabin in a valley. He recently cleared an area next to his cabin, and planted corn in five fields. Although few other farmers had been in this valley, one of Greg's fields had had most of the nutrients in the soil depleted by several years of planting by a previous farmer. The other four fields were the ones that Greg had just cleared and had never been farmed before. At harvest time, Greg found that there were a lot of mature corn plants in the four new fields. But none of the corn plants in the old field matured. The plants in all five fields received the same amounts of water and sunlight since they were right next to each other. *What caused the corn plants to grow in the four recently cleared fields?*

The rare version of this scenario was identical to the above, with the exception that Greg, instead of being a pioneer settling in a valley with mostly virgin soil, "lives in a valley in the poor country, on a farm inherited through many generations in his family." Furthermore, the ratio of rich-to-depleted soil was reversed: four of Greg's fields had had most of the nutrients in the soil depleted by many years of planting by his predecessors, and the fifth was one that he had just cleared.

Following is the rare version of the non-ideal scenario, in which sunlight covaried with plant growth and the amounts of fertilizer and water were constant within the implied focal set:

A little boy Brad lives with his family in a wooded area. He noticed that there were dandelions covering the small open areas of his family's yard, but that there were no dandelions under the shade of the two large oak trees. He knows that sprinklers are distributed evenly over the yard. One day during a rainstorm he put jars out all over the yard and discovered that the amount of rain reaching the ground was roughly the same under the oak trees and in the open areas of the yard. He also found out that the soil was the same in all parts of the yard and that all parts of the yard had received the same amount of fertilizer. *What causes the dandelions to grow in the small open areas of the yard?*

The prevalent version of this scenario was identical to the above, with the exception that Brad, instead of living in a wooded area, lived in a barren area with few trees. In addition, the open areas of his yard were described as "large" and the oak trees were described as "small".

Questions and Predictions

Subjects were asked four questions about the scenarios they received. The first question asked subjects to indicate whether each of the four factors was a "cause (not a mere condition)", a "mere condition (not a cause)", or "irrelevant (neither a cause nor a mere condition)" for the growth of the respective plants (corn and dandelions). For the corn scenario, these factors were water, the farmer's house, sunlight, and nutrients in the soil. For the dandelion scenario, these factors were water, fertilizer, sunlight, and the boy's house. The probabilistic contrast model predicts that subjects will be more likely to pick a particular factor as a cause in the scenario in which it covaries with the effect in the implied focal set than in the scenario in which it remains constant. Neither statistical nor idealistic normality should affect subjects' responses. Necessary factors that remain constant should be mere conditions, and unnecessary factors should be causally irrelevant.

The second question asked whether each of four factors "inhibited" the growth of the respective plants in the given context. For the corn scenario, these factors were lack of water, the farmer's house, sunlight, and lack of nutrients in the soil. For the dandelion scenario, these factors were water, lack of fertilizer, lack of sunlight, and the boy's house. (Notice that two of the three necessary factors in each scenario were made negative by changing from the presence of the factor in the first question to the absence of the factor in the second question.) This question was included as a further test of the idealistic normality view. Asking about inhibition rather than facilitation reverses the desirability of the conditions. Whereas the presence of nutrients in the corn scenario (leading to the maturation of the plants) was desired, the absence of nutrients in one or more of the fields (leading to the failure of the plants to mature) was not. The idealistic normality view therefore predicts that whereas the desired presence of each necessary factor (e.g., nutrients in the corn scenario) would be an enabling condition, the undesired absence of the same factor in the identical scenario would be an inhibitory cause. Conversely, this view predicts that whereas the undesired presence of each necessary factor (e.g., sunlight in the dandelion scenario) would be a cause, the desired absence of the same factor in that scenario would not be an inhibitory cause. In contrast, the probabilistic-contrast view predicts that the factor that covaries with the effect in the focal set would be judged to be a cause, and the absence of that factor would be judged to be inhibitory, regardless of whether the presence or absence of that factor is desirable within the context.

The third question measured subjects' focal sets. It asked subjects to rate on a 7-point scale three expanded versions of the causal question in terms of how accurately each reflected their interpretation of the causal question (7 = very accurately, 1 = very inaccurately). Each expansion focused the causal question on a comparison along a different one of the three relevant dimensions mentioned in the scenario. For example, one of the expansions for the causal question in the sunlight scenario was: "What caused the dandelions to grow where there was ample fertilizer, compared to other places where there was not ample fertilizer (assuming that all places had roughly the same amounts of water and sunlight)?"

The fourth and final question asked subjects to indicate the value of the covarying factor that they expected in general in each scenario. In the corn scenario, the question was, "Do most places in the valley where Greg lived (including his fields) have rich soil or soil depleted of nutrients?" In the dandelion scenario, the question was, "Do most places in the area where Brad lives (including his yard) receive direct sunlight, or are most places in the shade?" This question was to ensure that our manipulation of prevalence was effective and that the prevalent covarying factors did fit the definition of normality in terms of being a default. (Cheng and Novick, 1991, pp. 111–113)

Results and Discussion

Table 4.1 presents the data bearing on the experimental predictions. Experimental findings are summarized and discussed in the following account:

We turn now to the critical question on causes versus mere conditions. The probabilistic contrast model predicts that subjects should be more likely to choose a particular factor as a cause in the scenario in which it covaried with the effect in the implied focal set than in the scenario in which it was constant, regardless of the prevalence of the desirability of the factor. The results were as predicted by this model [see Table 4.1]. Because the model specifies its predictions with respect to the focal set, our analyses below are restricted to subjects for whom our focal set manipulation was effective. An average of 90% of the subjects indicated nutrients to be a cause for the corn scenario, compared to only 7% who did so for the dandelion scenario, $X^2 (1, N = 69) = 43.8$, p $< .001$ for the prevalent version of each of the two scenarios, and $X^2 (1, N = 67) = 48.9$, p $< .001$ for the rare versions. Conversely, an average of 93% of the subjects indicated sunlight to be a cause for the dandelion scenario, compared to only 12% who did so for the corn scenario, $X^2 (1, N = 69) = 47.1$, p $< .001$ for the prevalent version of each of the two scenarios, and $X^2 (1, N = 67) = 42.0$, p $< .001$ for the rare versions. The third necessary factor, the presence of water, was constant in both scenarios. As

Table 4.1
Percentage of Subjects Indicating a Factor to Be a Cause or a Mere Condition in Experiment 2 for Prevalent and Rare Causes in an Ideal and a Nonideal Context

(a)   Context in which "nutrients" has a large contrast and other factors are constant (corn scenario–ideal).

Statistical Normality	N	Sunlight		Nutrients		Water		House	
		Cause	Mere Condition	Cause	Mere Condition	Cause	Mere Condition	Cause	Mere Condition
Prevalent	32	12	**88**	**91**	9	12	**88**	0	3
Rare	35	11	**77**	**89**	11	11	**77**	0	6

(b)   Context in which "sunlight" has a large contrast and other factors are constant (dandelion scenario--non-ideal).

Statistical Normality	N	Sunlight		Nutrients		Water		House	
		Cause	Mere Condition	Cause	Mere Condition	Cause	Mere Condition	Cause	Mere Condition
Prevalent	37	**95**	5	11	**81**	8	**84**	0	5
Rare	32	**91**	9	3	**84**	3	**88**	0	0

Note: Subjects whose ratings in the focal-set question reveal that they did not adopt the focal sets assumed by this analysis are excluded from this table. Numbers in **bold** type indicate the percentages of subjects who chose the responses predicted by the probabilistic contrast model.

Source: Cheng, P. W., and Novick, L. R. (1991). Causes versus enabling conditions. Reprinted from *Cognition, 40*, p. 110, copyright 1991, with permission from Elsevier Science.

predicted, it was indicated as a mere condition by most subjects (84%) in both scenarios. The fourth factor, the presence of the protagonist's house, was rarely indicated as a cause or a mere condition. They were indicated as irrelevant by most subjects in both the corn and the dandelion scenarios (96% and 97%, respectively).

As should be evident from a comparison of the results across the prevalent and rare versions of each scenario in [Table 4.1], the prevalence of a factor had no discernible effect on causal judgments for any of the four factors. The comparison was not statistically significant for any of the factors. Our results clearly show that subjects discriminated between prevalent factors that covary within the focal set (these were identified as causes) and prevalent conditions that were constant (these were identified as enabling conditions).

Recall that the idealistic normality view predicts that only conditions that deviate from the ideal should be selected as causes; that is, the presence of sunlight in the dandelion scenario should be the only cause, and the absence of nutrients in the corn scenario should be the only inhibitor. Contradicting these predictions but in support of the probabilistic contrast view, the positive values of both contextually covarying factors—the presence of nutrients in the corn scenario (a desired state) and the presence of sunlight in the dandelion scenario (an undesired state)—were judged to be causes (90% and 93%, respectively). Similarly, the negative values of both covarying factors—the absence of nutrients in the corn scenario (an undesired state) and the absence of sunlight in the dandelion scenario (a preferred state)—were judged to be inhibitors (94% and 96%, respectively). (Also as predicted by probabilistic contrasts, no other factor was considered an inhibitor in either scenario; less than 2% of the responses indicated other factors to be inhibitors.)

These results clearly show that factors that covaried with the effect in the set of events implied by the context, regardless of their prevalence or desirability, were perceived as causes (so identified by 92% of the subjects on average). In contrast, factors that remained constant in that focal set, but were nonetheless known to be necessary for the occurrence of the effect, were relegated to the status of mere conditions (so identified by 83% of the subjects on average). (Cheng and Novick, 1991, pp. 114–116; italics added)

Conclusion

The following presents the concluding analysis of the Cheng and Novick (1991) experimental research:

The results of our experiments support our probabilistic contrast model over a number of alternative explanations of the distinction between causes and enabling conditions. Let us briefly summarize the basis for this conclusion.

The normality, conversational, and probabilistic contrast views localize the explanation for the distinction between causes and enabling conditions at different stages. Both variants of the normality view explain the distinction at the inference stage. They hypothesize that people perceive a distinction between causes and enabling conditions despite their identity in terms of necessity and sufficiency because natural causal induction uses a rule that is not formulated in those terms. . . . Finally, the probabilistic contrast view traces the distinction to a stage before the process of inference begins. It explains the distinction by differences in the patterns of data that correspond to causes and enabling conditions for a focal set. Although causes and enabling conditions hold the same relationship with the target effect in terms of necessity and sufficiency with respect to the universal set of events in one's knowledge base, they do not do so with respect to the focal set. The probabilistic contrast view therefore resolves the puzzling deviation from characterization in terms of necessity and sufficiency by denying the existence of such a deviation.

Our results clearly support the probabilistic-contrast view. In [the experiment], we demonstrated the effect of patterns of data in the focal set on the distinction between the causes and enabling conditions. We manipulated the patterns of data in the focal set and confirmed the effectiveness of our manipulation by measuring subjects' identification of the contextually implied focal sets. Our results show that factors that covaried with the effect in the focal set were perceived as causes, and necessary factors that were kept constant in the focal set were perceived as enabling conditions.

Our results also provide evidence against the variants of the normality view. [The experiment] clearly shows that factors that covaried with the effect in the set of events implied by the context were perceived as causes, regardless of their prevalence or their status as a default or an ideal. By identifying the focal set, we have shown that the same inferential rules underlie the concept of causality in everyday life, where causes are typically statistically abnormal or deviate from an ideal, and in scientific situations, where causes are often statistically normal and do not deviate from an ideal. (Cheng and Novick, 1991, pp. 116–117)

COMMENTARY

Theories of causality have advanced from animistic superstition to rational analysis to mathematical functions. This development is most marked in the physical sciences, where the human concept of causation has been replaced by abstract mathematical symbols and equations. Philosophical accounts of causation—from Aristotle's typology of formal, final, material, and efficient causes to Mackie's theory of causal fields—are largely verbal constructions tied to everyday psychological experience. The mathematization of this common-sense psychology would mark an advancement in the development of a scientific psychology. The computational mechanisms that distinguish causes from enabling conditions are the most sophisticated components of Cheng and Novick's (1991) probabilistic-contrast model as it replaces verbal analysis with mathematical equations. The experimental research of Cheng and Novick (1991) supports their computational model, and replication and extension are warranted. However, in practical human affairs, as in legal reasoning, causation is psychologically mercurial and offers formidable challenges to its mathematization.

5

Logical Reasoning and Belief-Bias Effects

BELIEF-BIAS AND LOGICAL REASONING

Validity and Truth in Logic

It is important that research in the psychology of logical reasoning follows the principles of logic that govern the complex relationships between the validity-invalidity of arguments and the truth-falsity of premises and conclusions. Invalid argument patterns can consist of true premises and true conclusions, true premises and false conclusions, false premises and true conclusions, or false premises and false conclusions. Valid argument patterns can consist of true premises and true conclusions, false premises and true conclusions, or false premises and false conclusions. The pattern of valid arguments, true premises, and false conclusions is not extant in the principles of logic.

Experiment in Belief-Bias and Logical Reasoning

Overview

The research of H. Markovits and G. Nantel (1989) is summarized in the following account.

In this study, we examined whether adult subjects' beliefs regarding the empirical truth of a conclusion affected their production as well as their evaluation of a logical conclusion in a reasoning task. In addition, the relation between the ability to resolve an abstract reasoning problem correctly and the effect of belief-bias was examined. The subjects were given one of four paper-and-pencil reasoning tasks, two of them using an evaluation paradigm, and two of them using a production paradigm. Each paradigm comprised either neutral problems or belief problems. The neutral problems were constructed to be as similar as possible to the belief problems in order to control for extraneous factors. All four tasks also included an abstract reasoning problem. The results indicate a significant belief-bias effect for both the evaluation and the production tasks. Qualitative analysis indicated that the belief-bias effect was more pervasive in the production condition. In addition, the belief-bias effect was found to exist independently of the subjects' abstract reasoning ability. The results are discussed with reference to a two-stage model, in which belief is used to resolve uncertainties in inferentially produced conclusions. (Markovits and Nantel, 1989, p. 11)

Rationale

In a highly compact research format, Markovits and Nantel (1989) examined three significant aspects of the belief-bias effect in deductive reasoning. The rationale for the first aspect of their research is set forth in the following account.

One of the more interesting phenomena in the research on reasoning concerns *belief-bias* effect. Several researchers have claimed that subjects tend to evaluate the logical validity of deductive arguments on the basis of their personal beliefs regarding the empirical status of the conclusion. Specifically, subjects will tend to rate an argument as valid if they think that the conclusion is empirically true, and vice versa, irrespective of the textbook validity of the argument. The reality of the belief-bias effect has been questioned (Revlin and Leirer, 1978; Revlin, Leirer, Yopp, and Yopp, 1980), mainly on the grounds that some of the effects observed may be attributable to conversion effects due to subjects' idiosyncratic encoding of premises. However, Evans, Barston, and Pollard (1983) have demonstrated a strong belief-bias effect in experiments designed to control for both conversion and atmosphere effects.

The belief-bias effect has generally been found in paradigms for which subjects are presented with a specific conclusion (or a set of possible conclusions). It may be argued that, despite the most rigorous instructions, many subjects may be evaluating the empirical truth of the presented conclusion or conclusions and simply ignoring the premises, not because they cannot reason properly but because they do not properly understand the task (Henle, 1962). Such a possibility is certainly consistent with Evans et al.'s (1983) finding that subjects who accepted valid conclusions despite the influence of their beliefs referred more often to the premises than subjects who decided according to belief. One way of minimizing such a possibility and ensuring that subjects attend to the premises is to have subjects produce a conclusion. In other words, it may be argued that if the observed effects in evaluation tasks are due mainly to some process whereby subjects (mistakenly) examine only the conclusion of an argument, then forcing them to generate a conclusion from given premises should enable them to use their logical abilities more fully. Now, the effect of belief on the production of conclusions has been examined by Oakhill and Johnson-Laird (1985). They found that beliefs do tend to influence subjects' conclusion in a production task. However, they did not attempt to compare this effect with that found in an evaluation task. In addition, they compared subjects' performance with respect to believable as opposed to unbelievable conclusions, thus making the estimation of the magnitude of the effect somewhat difficult. *The main aim of the present study was therefore to replicate the effects of subjects' beliefs on the production of conclusions in a reasoning task, and to compare this effect with that found in a comparable evaluation task.* (Markovits and Nantel, 1989, p. 11; italics added)

The following rationale is provided for the second aspect of this research.

In the present study, we also attempted to address two further questions. First, studies in conditional reasoning have clearly shown that subjects' performance is often influenced by a variety of factors that are not directly related to the logic of the premises or the conclusion, and that it varies according to the specific logical form employed or the content of the premises. Conversion effects (Revlin et al., 1980), atmosphere bias (Woodworth and Sells, 1935), figural effects (Johnson-Laird and Steedman, 1978), and various forms of content effects (Guyote and Sternberg, 1981; O'Brien, Costa, and Overton, 1986) are all examples of such factors. Their existence makes comparisons among differing logical forms and contents somewhat hazardous. Note that Evans et al. (1983) explicitly controlled for conversion effects (as did Oakhill and Johnson-Laird, 1985), atmosphere bias, and the figural effect. While there is no evidence to suggest that their results might nonetheless have been affected by some such (as yet unknown) factor, we felt that it would be useful to replicate the basic belief-bias effect by using a method that attempted to control explicitly for both form and content effects as tightly as possible. The method chosen involved the construction of pairs of categorical syllogisms. Each syllogism involved an initial premise (major term) of the form "all A are B," which was identical for both. The second premise took one of the following forms: (1) "X is A," (2) "X is B," (3) "X is not A," and (4) "X is not B." In all cases, X was varied to produce two differing syllogisms: a neutral form that produced a conclusion for which the subject had no a priori beliefs with respect to the empirical truth; and a positive form that produced a conclusion for which the subject did have a clear belief regarding its empirical truth, and for which this belief contradicted the conclusion's logical status (i.e., if the subjects thought the conclusion was true, it was logically invalid, etc.). *By comparing the subjects' performance on the neutral and positive forms, it was felt that the belief-bias effect could be examined in a way that would eliminate any possible effects related to logical form and would minimize content variations.* (Markovits and Nantel, 1989, pp. 11–12; italics added)

The third aspect of the Markovits and Nantel (1989) research is summarized in the following terms.

The final question addressed by this study concerns the possible relation between logical competence and belief-bias. Evans et al. (1983) found evidence that subjects may oscillate between competing logical and nonlogical processes. This implies that subjects do attempt to consider the logical validity of an argument by examining the premises, when they are not led to employ other criteria such as their beliefs. Without entering into the problem associated with the nature of logical competence, it appears reasonable to suppose that if subjects have difficulty in reasoning correctly from premises that are relatively content-free or abstract, they might be more prone to use nonlogical indices when they are present. *Thus there should be a relation between the ability to reason correctly during a content-free task and the performance on a task for which a belief-bias effect may exist.* (Markovits and Nantel, 1989, p. 12; italics added)

Method

The experimental materials, subjects, and procedures are described in the following section.

Materials

Four paper-and-pencil questionnaires were constructed. The first page of each questionnaire, which was identical for each one, presented a series of four conditional reasoning problems with abstract content. At the top of the page was written:

Suppose it is true that:
    All the XAR's are YOF's
and answer the multiple choice questions.

After this came four multiple choice questions. The first one took the following format:

(A) If glock is an XAR, you can say
    (a) that it is certain that the glock is a YOF.
    (b) that it is certain that the glock is not a YOF.
    (c) that it is not certain whether the glock is a YOF or not.

The three other questions used the same format and presented the following statements: "(B) If a koy is a YOF, you can say"; "(C) If a glock is not a XAR, you can say"; "(D) If a koy is not a YOF, you can say." These four correspond to the logical forms *modus ponens, converse, inverse,* and *contrapositive.*

Note that in all cases, the abstract content questions preceded the syllogisms that were to examine the belief-bias effect. It has been shown that such a procedure encourages a *logical* reasoning mode in subjects that diminishes content effects (Hawkins et al., 1984; Markovits and Vashon, 1989). This procedure was thus designed to reduce any possible belief-bias effect and to facilitate the effect of subsequent instructions.

Two questionnaires used an evaluation paradigm. For these, the second page contained the following instructions (adapted from Evans et al., 1983):

You are going to receive a series of eight problems. You must decide whether the stated conclusion *follows logically* from the premises or not.

You must *suppose that the premises are all true* and limit yourself only to the information contained in these premises. This is very important.

At the top of the next page, the subjects received the following instructions (adapted from Evans et al., 1983):

For each problem, decide if the given conclusion *follows logically from the premises.* Circle YES if, and only if, you judge that the conclusion can be derived *unequivocally* from the given premises, otherwise circle NO.

For the *positive evaluation* questionnaire, subjects were then presented with the following eight syllogisms (four to a page):

(1)   Premise 1:   All things that are smoked are good for the health.

                Premise 2:   Cigarettes are smoked.

	Conclusion:	Cigarettes are good for the health.
(2)	Premise 1:	All unemployed people are poor.
	Premise 2:	Rockefeller is not unemployed.
	Conclusion:	Rockefeller is not poor.
(3)	Premise 1:	All flowers have petals.
	Premise 2:	Roses have petals.
	Conclusion:	Roses are flowers.
(4)	Premise 1:	All animals with four legs are dangerous.
	Premise 2:	Poodles are not dangerous.
	Conclusion:	Poodles do not have four legs.
(5)	Premise 1:	All mammals walk.
	Premise 2:	Whales are mammals.
	Conclusion:	Whales walk.
(6)	Premise 1:	All eastern countries are communist.
	Premise 2:	Canada is not an eastern country.
	Conclusion:	Canada is not communist.
(7)	Premise 1:	All animals love water.
	Premise 2:	Cats do not like water.
	Conclusion:	Cats are not animals.
(8)	Premise 1:	All things that have a motor need oil.
	Premise 2:	Automobiles need oil.
	Conclusion:	Automobiles have motors.

These syllogisms include two (1,5) of the form "all A are B, C are A, thus C are B," and two (4,7) of the form "all A are B, C are not B, thus C are not A." In each of them, the conclusions were rated as unbelievable by 37 independent subjects . . . and, in each case, the conclusion was logically valid. In addition, there are two syllogisms (3,8) of the form "all A are B, C are B, thus C are A," and two (2,6) of the form "all A are B, C are not A, thus C are not B." In each of these cases, the conclusions were rated as believable and were logically invalid. In the latter two cases, it should be noted that the forms are indeterminate—that is, there is no logically valid conclusion.

The second questionnaire that used the evaluation paradigm (*neutral evaluation*) was identical to the first, but with one major difference. In all cases, the minor premise of the eight syllogisms was altered in order to make the conclusion neutral with respect to belief. . . . The resulting conclusions were:

(1) Ramadions are good for the health.

(2) Hudon is not poor.

(3) Pennes are flowers.

(4) Argomelles do not have four legs.

(5) Lapitars walk.

(6) Sylvania is not communist.

(7) Selacians are not animals.

(8) Opprobines have motors.

In addition to the two questionnaires that used an evaluation paradigm, two more that used a production paradigm were constructed. The first page of these two questionnaires, as stated above, was identical to the one described previously: it contained a set of four conditional reasoning problems with abstract content. On the second page of both production questionnaires was written the following:

You are going to receive a series of eight problems. You must *produce* a conclusion which *follows logically* from the premises.

You must *suppose that the premises are all true* and limit yourself only to the information contained in these premises. This is very important.

At the top of the next page, the subjects received the following instructions:

For each problem, give the conclusion which *follows logically from the premises*. Formulate a conclusion only if you judge that it is possible to derive one *unequivocally* from the given premises. If you think that no conclusion can be logically and unequivocally derived from the premises, write NONE.

After this, one of the two series of eight syllogisms that were used in the evaluation questionnaires was presented (leading to two forms, *neutral production* and *positive production*), with the difference that no conclusion was presented. Space was provided for the subjects to write down a conclusion.

Procedure

The four forms of questionnaires were distributed at random among entire classes of university students. The subjects were informed that there was no time limit and that they could proceed until satisfied with their answers.

Subjects

A total of 186 French-speaking university students received one of four questionnaires. Of these, 44 received the positive production form; 48, the neutral production form; 43, the positive evaluation form; and 51, the neutral evaluation form.

Scoring

The subjects were scored on the abstract conditional reasoning problem and on the eight syllogisms with content. For those abstract problems, the subjects' responses were rated *conditional* (for those who responded correctly to all four forms), *intermediate* (correct response to modus ponens, incorrect response to one or more of the other three forms), or *biconditional* (responding to all four intermediate forms as if the relation were "if and only if"). In addition, two response patterns were taken to indicate difficulty in accepting the given premises (Markovits and Vashon, 1989). Thus those subjects who gave a response of uncertainty to modus ponens, or who responded by inverting the truth value of the minor premise in the conclusion (e.g., "If P then Q, Q is true, then P is false"), were rated as having given an *uncertain* response to the abstract conditionals. In the present context, the rationale for such a scoring schema derives from the following considerations: The logically correct response to the four conditional forms is the *conditional*. Previous studies have indicated that the probability that a subject will produce the logically correct response to subsequent problems varies with the response that the subject gives on an initial problem (Markovits, 1984; Markovits and Vashon, 1989), going from conditional, to intermediate, to biconditional, to uncertain. Thus, the scoring schema employed here explicitly uses the probability of producing the logically correct response to conditional syllogisms as an indication of reasoning ability.

Scoring on the positive evaluation syllogisms was as follows. The subjects were given one point for each time they decided that a believable response was valid or an unbelievable response was invalid. The scores thus ranged from 0 to 8. For the neutral evaluation syllogisms, the subjects were given a score of 1 for each time they gave a response equivalent to that which was scored on the positive form. Thus a subject who decided that "cigarettes are good for the health" was invalid on the positive form received 1 point while a subject who decided that "ramadions are good for the health" was invalid on the neutral form also received 1 point. The score on the neutral evaluation syllogisms thus indicates the number of times that the subjects chose the believable response for reasons related to either the logical form or the global content of the syllogisms used here, not to the believability of the conclusion.

Scoring on the positive production syllogisms was as follows—for the sake of brevity, in the following, the logical form will be referred to by the minor premise only (i.e., "A is B and C is A" will be designated by "C is A"): For the indeterminate forms ("C is B," "C is not A"), the subjects were given 1 point each time they produced a logically invalid but believable conclusion. For example, for the syllogism "all flowers have petals; roses have petals," the subjects who gave the conclusion "roses are flowers" would receive 1 point. For the other two forms ("C is A," "C is not B"), the subjects received 1 point each time they did not produce the logically valid but unbelievable conclusion. For example, for the syllogism "all things that are smoked are good for the health; cigarettes are smoked," the subjects received 1 point if they concluded that cigarettes are not good for the health, or if they did not give a firm conclusion (e.g., "cigarettes may or may not be good for the health"). For the neutral production syllogisms, the subjects were given 1 point each time they produced (or did not produce) responses equivalent to those for the positive syllogisms. These responses were identical to those in the positive form, with exception for the substituted term. For the two indeterminate syllogisms ("C is A," "C is not B"), subjects responding with, for example, "ramadions are not good for the health" or subjects not giving a firm conclusion received 1 point. Note that the scores on the production syllogisms are directly comparable to the scores on the evaluation forms, if one assumes that a subject who produces a given conclusion would evaluate that conclusion as valid would evaluate a different conclusion as invalid. For ease of reference, these scores will be referred to as *belief* scores. (Markovits and Nantel, 1989, pp. 12–14)

Results

The experimental findings are presented in the following account:

An analysis of variance using belief scores as the response variable, and type of syllogism (neutral or positive), form of presentation (evaluation or production), and performance on the abstract problems (conditional, intermediate, biconditional, or uncertain) as factors was performed. Following Conover (1980), this analysis was repeated after converting the scores on the syllogisms to rank orders. Since both analyses gave substantially the same results, only the first will be reported. This indicated significant main effects for type of syllogism . . . form of presentation . . . and performance on the abstract problem. . . . None of the interaction terms were significant. The first two main effects indicate that belief scores were higher for positive than for neutral forms, and higher for production than for evaluation. The third main effect is due to scores generally being lower for subjects giving conditional responses to the abstract problem . . . than for those giving intermediate responses . . . which were in turn lower than for subjects giving biconditional . . . or uncertain responses.

These results clearly support the general thesis of the existence of a belief-bias effect in reasoning. However, the idea that the production condition should generate a lower level of belief-bias is not supported. In accord with the results obtained by Marcus and Rips (1979), the production condition produced generally higher scores than the evaluation condition, although the effect of belief was present for both conditions. In this context, it is interesting to take a more qualitative look at the results. Four logical forms were examined with the eight syllogisms, two of each. . . . An initial question concerns the generality of the belief-bias effect across specific contents. The Mann-Whitney procedure was used to examine the effect of belief-bias for single items. This indicated that for the evaluation condition, a significant effect was found for two of the eight items. For the production condition, a significant effect was found for five of the eight items, and a sixth item was significant at the .06 level. The two items for which no significant difference was found for the production condition were those employing modus ponens (P is true), for which almost no belief-bias effect was obtained for either condition. Thus, overall the belief-bias effect is generalized across the various contents employed here.

[For] the evaluation condition, the major effect of belief-bias is concentrated on the two indeterminate forms ("C is not A," "C is B"). Mann-Whitney procedures indicate that for each of these, the scores are significantly higher for the positive than for the neutral forms. . . . This is consistent with previous results (Evans et al., 1983; Oakhill and Johnson-Laird, 1985). Note that while many subjects had difficulty reasoning with the "C is not B" form . . . the effect to belief was quite small. . . . In the production condition, the effect of belief is also significant for the indeterminate forms, "C is not A" . . . and "C is B." . . . In this case, however, there is a marginally significant difference for the "C is not B" form.

In addition to verifying the existence of belief-bias effects, the method employed here permits some evaluation of the extent to which belief-bias exerts an influence on reasoning independently from any other variable. . . . [The] subjects examined here produced an overall error rate of close to 30% in reasoning with syllogisms for which possible conclusions were neither believable nor unbelievable (neutral forms), in both the evaluation and production conditions. A direct comparison of overall error rates indicated that the presence of belief-bias produced an increase of 30% in the error rate in the evaluation condition, and a corresponding increase of 63% in the production condition. This suggests that while the presence of belief-bias does significantly influence adult reasoning, it is clearly the case the belief-bias alone cannot account for the majority of the errors that subjects make on items for which belief-bias may be present. These overall results must be qualified as a function of the specific logical form examined. If one considers the two indeterminate forms for which the effect of belief-bias was significant for both the evaluation condition and the production conditions, the relative increases in the error rate due to belief-bias were 49% and 80%, respectively.

In addition, these results, coupled with previous data concerning the differences for individual items, suggest that belief-bias appears to be more pervasive in the production task than in the evaluation task. In the latter case, the effects of belief are more limited, both in overall scope and in the number of specific items significantly affected.

Now, in the evaluation condition, the judgement that a conclusion is invalid could imply that the subject feels that there is no valid conclusion, or that the subject feels that a conclusion other than the one presented is valid. In the production condition, subjects must produce a specific conclusion, and this condition thus permits a more specific coding of the results than does the evaluation condition. . . . [For] the two determinate forms ("C is A," "C is not B"), the effect of belief results in a higher proportion of no specific conclusion, not in any tendency to produce the overtly believable response. This is consistent with results obtained by Oakhill and Johnson-Laird (1985). For example, for the syllogism, "all eastern countries are communist; Canada is not an eastern country," subjects tend to give no firm conclusion other than to produce the believable conclusion that "Canada is not communist." . . . [There] appears to be at least a rough relation between problem difficulty as measured by the proportion of logically correct responses on the neutral form and the effect of belief. The "C is A" form has the highest proportion of logically correct responses and the "C is B" has the lowest such proportion. These forms show, respectively, the least and greatest effect of belief.

Finally, the relation between the belief-bias effect and reasoning ability merits a more detailed examination. . . . [Belief] scores for positive content increase as reasoning performance on the abstract task decreases. However, part of this increase is attributable to the fact that less able subjects tend more often to fall into reasoning errors when belief does not play a part. Although the difference between belief scores for neutral and those for positive content does increase somewhat with decreasing performance on the abstract problem, this effect is not significant. (Markovits and Nantel, 1989, pp. 14–15)

COMMENTARY

The scientific work of Markovits and Nantel (1989) is an impressive demonstration of the technical specification of the interactive effects of belief-bias and logical reasoning. The effects of beliefs were demonstrated in both the production and evaluation of logical conclusions. The belief-bias effect was pervasive in the various experimental conditions. It must not be supposed that the experimental findings possess mere academic significance. A dramatic example of the vast significant effect of premise beliefs on logical conclusions can be found in Abraham Lincoln's debate with Judge Stephen Douglas concerning the Dred Scott decision that required the return of escaped slaves to their owners:

[W]hat follows is a short and even syllogistic argument from it [i.e., from the Dred Scott decision]. I think it follows, and submit it to the consideration of men capable of arguing, whether as I state it in syllogistic form the argument has any fault in it:

Nothing in the Constitution or laws of any State can destroy a right distinctly and expressly affirmed in the Constitution of the United States. The right of property in a slave is distinctly and expressly affirmed in the Constitution of the United States. Therefore, nothing in the Constitution or laws of any State can destroy the right of property in a slave.

I believe that no fault can be pointed out in that argument; assuming the truth of the premises, the conclusion, so far as I have the capacity at all to understand it, follows inevitably. There is fault in it as I think, but the fault is not in the reasoning; but the falsehood in fact is a fault of the premises. I believe that the right of property in a slave *is not* distinctly and expressly affirmed in the Constitution, and Judge Douglas thinks it *is*. I believe the Supreme Court and the advocates of that decision [the Dred Scott decision] may search in vain for the place in the Constitution where the right of property in a slave is distinctly and expressly affirmed. I say, therefore, that I think one of the premises is not true in fact.

6

Inductive Reasoning

Inductive reasoning has been regularly used in the establishment of simple numerical laws in physics, chemistry, and astronomy by artificial intelligence discovery systems. Symbolic induction in the discoveries did not extend to the search for *explanations* of the quantitative laws they established. An important new application of symbolic induction is the exploration of causal hypotheses as in the inductive experiments of Corruble and Ganascia (1997) on the causes of scurvy. Their research will be described in this section, and, then, a brief commentary will be presented.

SYMBOLIC INDUCTION AND DISCOVERY OF THE CAUSES OF SCURVY

Concise History of Scurvy

Corruble and Ganascia (1997) survey the history of scurvy in the following account:

Scurvy has been the cause of over a million of [*sic*] deaths aboard commercial and navy ships, and also on land, though to a lesser extent (Barker, 1992; Roddis, 1951). The disease took on an increased importance in the 15th century, with the development of long circumnavigations (Carpenter, 1986), and also in the 17th and 18th century, with the development of long missions in European navies, which involved numerous seamen. It is striking to note that scurvy is said to have caused more deaths in the French navy than combat with other European navies.

Consequently, research on the causes of scurvy attracted the brightest minds of the time. Among them, James Lind is famous for his remarkable *Treatise of the Scurvy* (Lind, 1753). From the 17th to the 20th century (when the actual cause of the disease, i.e., the lack of vitamin C, was discovered), dozens of theories were put forward on the origins of the disease. Many of these were totally disconnected from the real cause such as those referring to the psychological effect of being at sea, far away from home. Other theories were quite close to finding the real cause, especially the one that became widely accepted, which said that scurvy was the result of the conjunction of the humidity in the air and of the lack of fresh fruits and vegetables in the diet.

The lack of fresh fruits and vegetables was eventually accepted as the only cause of scurvy in the early 20th century. A first explanation for this late discovery is the lack of a concept necessary for a global understanding of the disease. The concept of vitamin, i.e., the idea that a small quantity of a chemical has a great influence on the functioning of the human body, is a key to the comprehension of the mechanism leading to scurvy. However, knowing that seamen were acquainted with the importance of fresh fruits and vegetables as early as the 15th century, it is surprising that a practical cure was not widely accepted earlier. To put it into more formal terms, though the lack of an *explanatory adequate theory* of scurvy is easily understandable due to the necessity of the concept of vitamin, the reason for the absence of a *descriptively adequate theory* (i.e., a theory establishing only the conditions of the development of the disease) is unclear.

This last question provided a good motivation to try modern inductive techniques on observational data available in the 19th century, before the actual discovery was made. This attempt is described in the following section. (Corruble and Ganascia, 1997, pp. 208–209)

Rationale for the Induction of Scurvy Cases

Corruble and Ganascia (1997) outline their rationale for inductive experimentation as follows:

A first experiment makes the assumption of pure inductivism: only the descriptions of cases are given to the inductive system. The rules induced are then analyzed according to a number of steps. The next sections detail the process of data collection, and the algorithm used. A third section focuses on the method used for the analysis of results proposed by the algorithm. (Corruble and Ganascia, 1997, p. 209)

Procedure for the Collection of Data

Corruble and Ganascia (1997) discuss data collection, training examples, and related issues in their inductive simulation of the etiology of scurvy in the following account:

In order to give our work a real simulation value, it has been necessary to use as training examples case descriptions that were as close as possible to the descriptions that were made before the discovery of the causes of scurvy. Therefore, the examples used all come from the 1880 *Dictionnaire Encyclopédique des Sciences Médicales* (Mahé, 1880), which provides relatively detailed descriptions of 25 cases of scurvy. During the

Figure 6.1
List of Attributes with Their Characteristics

Attribute	Type	Domain
year	integer	N*
location	string	NA
temperature	ordered set	severe-cold < cold < average < hot < very-hot
humidity	ordered set	low < high < very-high
food-quantity	ordered set	starvation < severe-restrictions < restrictions < OK
food-variety	ordered set	low < average < high
hygiene	ordered set	very-bad < bad < average < good < very-good
type-of-location	unordered set	land, sea
fresh_fruits/vegetables	Boolean	yes, no
disease-severity	integer	(0, 1, 2, ..., 5)

Source: Corruble, V., and Ganascia, J. G. (1997). Induction and the discovery of the causes of scurvy: A computational reconstruction. Reprinted from *Artificial Intelligence, 91*, p. 210, copyright 1997, with permission from Elsevier Science.

necessary translation of these natural language descriptions into the description language of the inductive system, one main objective was to remain as close as possible to the original, without modifying the description by using our own knowledge of the disease.

Ten features which constitute the description language given to the inductive system were found in most historical cases. They are summarized in [Figure 6.1]. Besides the date and location of the case, they include the temperature, the humidity in the air, the hygiene level, the quantity of food, its variety, the use or absence of fresh fruits and vegetables, the type of location (at sea or on land), and, lastly, the severity of the disease. Each of these attributes is defined by a type (ordered or unordered set, integer, etc.) and domain, thus enabling the induction process to take full advantage of the structure of the data. It is important to notice that the choice of features used for our representation is done based on syntactical analysis of the historical text. If a feature is present in the historical descriptions of more than a very few cases, then it is included in the description language of all the cases. Also, the induction system used does not require a value for every attribute and each case, so that missing values did not have to be filled arbitrarily with estimates.

Note that no attribute in the description language refers to the time spent at sea. The main reason for this is that the original descriptions found in the literature did not usually contain this information, or when they did, it was in a very qualitative way, difficult to reuse. These descriptions, however, often mention that the disease severity has developed over time, in which case the value chosen for the disease severity attribute is the one observed at the end (the beginning being seen as a transition phase). In some other cases, the disease can develop in a first phase, and then decrease or even disappear in the second phase. Since the second phase usually corresponds to new environmental conditions (new values for the other attributes), the phenomenon has been represented by creating two training cases: one corresponding to the first phase, and one for the second

Figure 6.2
An Example of Saturation on One Training Case

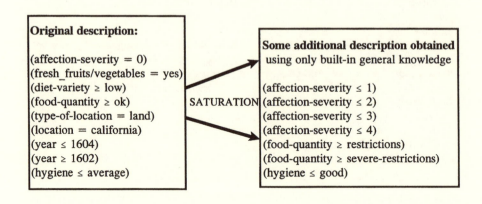

Source: Corruble, V., and Ganascia, J. G. (1997). Induction and the discovery of the causes of scurvy: A computational reconstruction. Reprinted from *Artificial Intelligence, 91*, p. 211, copyright 1997, with permission from Elsevier Science.

phase. These cases of remission are particularly useful in providing "negative" examples of the disease to the system, necessary for any supervised learning ([Figure 6.2] contains such a negative example). Also, by providing two training cases which are relatively similar except for a few attributes, each case of remission greatly helps the inductive process.

Examples of training cases will be given in the following sections but it is necessary first to provide some details on the inductive system used. (Corruble and Ganascia, 1997, pp. 209–210)

THE CHARADE SYSTEM AND HYPOTHESES ABOUT SCURVY

The CHARADE Induction System

Corruble and Ganascia (1997) describe CHARADE, a symbolic induction system, used as a mechanism of experimentation in the historical reconstruction of reasoning about the causes of scurvy.

CHARADE (Ganascia, 1987, 1991) is a symbolic inductive system which extracts logical rules expressing empirical regularities between attributes in a set of examples. More precisely, CHARADE can be classified as a k-DNF learner, which means that it generates sets of formulae of the type $d1$ & $d2$ & ... & $dn \rightarrow c$. These rules correspond to regularities observed on a set of training examples. CHARADE is able to generate all non-redundant regularities, but it can also be restricted to generate rules verifying some particular properties corresponding to what is called a *learning bias* in the area of machine learning (see for instance, [Ganascia, 1991; Russel and Grosof, 1990; Utgoff, 1986]). The aim of this paper is not to explain the theory of CHARADE; those interested are referred to the previous papers to obtain more details. However, some interesting features of CHARADE are highlighted in this section.

One of the main advantages of CHARADE is that most of its learning bias is explicit. CHARADE takes as input a description language which defines all attributes, their type (unordered set, ordered set, etc.), and their domain. Another point is the set of training examples. Also, a feature of particular interest here is the possibility of formalizing some domain knowledge using axioms. This knowledge (entered as production rules), as well as some built-in general knowledge about the types of attributes, is taken into account during the first phase, named saturation. This phase is used to enrich the description of each training case, as illustrated in [Figure 6.2] using example #6 from the database.

The inductive process takes advantage of the lattice structure of the search space to produce all logical IF-THEN rules consistent with the training examples that can be expressed with some conjunctions of elements of the descriptions. Some algebraic properties of this lattice are taken into account to cut out of the search some of the large parts of this lattice (an exponential search space), which are known not to contain any new rules. The algorithm finds the rules that do not have any exceptions: a rule does not need to cover all the examples to be produced, but if at least one of the examples contradicts the candidate rule, the rule will not be produced. Even if a training case has been successfully classified as a rule, the system will continue searching for other rules for this example, hence providing alternative rules for each case. This last feature of CHARADE is useful to our study here, which is based on the empirical comparison of competing induced theories.

The last type of bias which can optionally be defined by the user is the desired structure of the output rules. It is possible to restrict the search to all the rules that conclude on one group of attributes. For instance, in the case of scurvy, the rules which are searched for are the ones that conclude on the severity of the disease, because this is what we want to predict or explain. (Corruble and Ganascia, 1997, pp. 210–212)

Analysis of CHARADE's Output

Corruble and Ganascia (1997) describe their operations on the rules produced by the CHARADE system in the following section.

What the inductive algorithm outputs is a rule base. These rules do not have a specific ordering or structure; they are proposed in the order in which they were found. This section presents the three steps of analysis performed manually in our experiments.

• *Regrouping of rules.* The rule set obtained is partitioned in a number of subsets. Two rules are put in the same subset, if (1) their premises use the same factor for prediction, and (2) they are consistent (they should not contradict each other). Note that a rule using two different attributes in its condition could potentially be assigned to two subsets according to this procedure. Then, it is possible either to assign the rule to both subsets (in which case this step does not lead to a partition), or to assign the rule only once to a new subset of rules combining these two factors. This situation did not occur in our experiments on scurvy.

Figure 6.3
**Rules Proposed by CHARADE Regrouped According to the Factor They Put
Forward**

Set I: Rules 3, 4, 8 use in their premises the variety of the diet.
R3:   IF diet-variety ≥ high   THEN disease-severity ≤ 0   [5]
R4:   IF diet-variety ≤ average   THEN disease-severity ≥ 3   [4]
R8:   IF diet-variety ≥ average   THEN disease-severity ≤ 2   [11]

Set II: Rules 7, 10 use in their premises the presence (or absence)
                of fresh fruits and vegetables in the diet.
R7:   IF fresh_fruits/vegetables = no   THEN disease-severity ≥ 2   [5]
R10:   IF fresh_fruits/vegetables = yes   THEN disease-severity ≤ 2   [13]

Set III: Rule 2 uses in its premises the quantity of food available.
R2:   IF food-quantity ≥ ok   THEN disease-severity ≤ 0   [4]

Set IV: Rules 5, 6, 9, 12 use in their premises the level of hygiene.
R5:   IF hygiene ≤ bad   THEN disease-severity ≥ 3   [3]
R6:   IF hygiene ≤ average   THEN disease-severity ≥ 2   [4]
R9:   IF hygiene ≥ average   THEN disease-severity ≤ 2   [7]
R12:   IF hygiene ≥ good   THEN disease-severity ≤ 1   [6]

Set V: Rules 1, 11 use in their premises the temperature.
R1:   IF location = land, temperature ≥ hot   THEN disease-severity ≤ 0   [4]
R11:   IF temperature ≤ severe-cold   THEN disease-severity ≥ 1   [5]

Note: Note the number between brackets at the right of each rule stating how many examples it
    covers (i.e., the number of examples that match the premises of the rule). *Disease severity* is
    a ranking from 0 (no disease at all) to 5 (most severe).

Source: Corruble, V., and Ganascia, J. G. (1997). Induction and the discovery of the causes of
    scurvy: A computational reconstruction. Reprinted from *Artificial Intelligence, 91*, p. 213, copy-
    right 1997, with permission from Elsevier Science.

Each subset of rules obtained this way can then be considered a proto-theory because of its
coherence (in the factor put forward, and in the predictions of the rules). An application of this
step is found in [Figure 6.3].

• *Evaluation of explanatory power*. The evaluation here is not done according to the formal method
advocated by statistics or most machine learning work (prediction on new data). We are here
more interested in an informal, exploratory prior-assessment as done in medical research to decide
which hypothesis to pursue (the concepts of prior-assessment and pursuit are well explained in
[Schaffner, 1993]). Therefore, we use the number of individual cases explained by each *subset* of
rules as a criterion. This is indirectly related to the concept of *consilience* (Thagard, 1988) and
verisimilitude (Popper, 1959) except (this is a significant difference) that these refer to *classes* of
facts explained rather than *individual* cases. On the practical side, it is important to see that the
cover of a subset is not obtained by adding the covers of each individual rule of the subset (this

would count more than once cases covered by more than one rule). Instead, the cover is the cardinal of the union of the sets of examples covered by each rule in the subset.

• *Correspondence with history.* The last step is to look at the correspondence with history. Does each proto-theory correspond to a theory proposed in history? Reciprocally, does each theory proposed in history find a corresponding theory in our reconstruction? This notion of correspondence, essential to the enterprise of rational reconstruction, is peripheral to our first experiment, and becomes central in the second one. Here correspondence does not aim at a full isomorphism between history and our simulation. Our reconstruction, in our first and also in our second experiment, does not take into account *all* the facts, knowledge and beliefs about scurvy available to physicians in the 18th and 19th century. Our reconstructions are therefore a simplification from a psychological standpoint. Yet they are powerful means for evaluating hypotheses about the nature of the discovery process, both prescriptively (e.g., how inductive could this discovery have been?) and descriptively (e.g., why was this wrong theory defended for so long?). (Corruble and Ganascia, 1997, pp. 212–213)

EXPERIMENTS IN INDUCTIVE DISCOVERY

Results of the First Experiment

Corruble and Ganascia (1997) present the method and results of their first experiment in the following account.

Our first experiment was done without giving any domain knowledge to the system. This "pure" induction produced 12 logical rules which are provided in [Figure 6.3] with some analysis. These 12 rules were then manually regrouped according to the factor they put forward to predict disease severity. Each group constructed this way can be interpreted as a proto-theory on the cause of the disease.

The first point of interest is the parallel between the rules produced by CHARADE and the competing explanations proposed for the disease until the end of the 19th century and provided in Mahé (1880). Every group of rules produced by the system corresponds to an explanation from the medical literature. In [Figures 6.4.–6.7], the corresponding explanation from history is given just above each group of rules.

The second striking observation is obtained by looking at the number of examples covered by each subset of rules. The three main factors causing scurvy are, according to CHARADE, the presence of fresh fruits and vegetables in the diet, the variety of the diet (closely linked to the previous factor), and the hygiene level. A bar graph plotting the number of examples covered by each proto-theory is given in [Figure 6.8]. The lack of fresh fruits and vegetables covers $13 + 5 = 18$ examples, i.e., more than two-thirds of the total. So, THE factor set forth by CHARADE (according to this criterion) is the real cause of scurvy. It is important to remember that these results have been obtained without any domain knowledge. Nevertheless, in this case, one can say that CHARADE obtains better results than the scientists of the past centuries, in the sense that it puts forward the real cause of scurvy while physicians were misled until the end of the last century toward other theories.

Furthermore, it is useful to realize the existence of a bias in the previous prior-assessment of the various hypotheses. Since the data used for the experiment are real data, the descriptions are not all standardized. Hence, some cases are not described with the same level of detail; some attribute values are missing. A direct consequence is that an hypothesis putting forward a factor cannot explain a case for which this factor is not

Figure 6.4
Excerpts from the 1880 *Medical Encyclopedia* Followed by the Corresponding
Rules Proposed by CHARADE for Food Variety

DIET (*food variety*):
It was J. F. Bachstrom (1734) who first expressed the opinion that "Abstinence of vegetables is the only, the true, the first cause of scurvy" (Mahé, 1880)

Set I: Rules 3, 4, 8 use in their premises the variety of the diet.
R3:   IF diet-variety ≥ high   THEN disease-severity ≤ 0   [5]
R4:   IF diet-variety ≤ average   THEN disease-severity ≥ 3   [4]
R8:   IF diet-variety ≥ average   THEN disease-severity ≤ 2   [11]

Set II: Rules 7, 10 use in their premises the presence (or absence)
                of fresh fruits and vegetables in the diet.
R7:   IF fresh_fruits/vegetables = no   THEN disease-severity ≥ 2   [5]
R10:   IF fresh_fruits/vegetables = yes THEN disease-severity ≤ 2   [13]

Source: Corruble, V., and Ganascia, J. G. (1997). Induction and the discovery of the causes of scurvy: A computational reconstruction. Reprinted from *Artificial Intelligence, 91*, p. 214, copyright 1997, with permission from Elsevier Science.

Figure 6.5
Excerpts from the 1880 *Medical Encyclopedia* Followed by the Corresponding
Rules Proposed by CHARADE for Food Quantity

DIET (*food quantity*):
We are lead to conclude that a decrease in quantity of food, or to speak clearly, starvation, can occasionally serve the cause of scurvy, but it cannot produce it by itself (Mahé, 1880)

Set IV: Rule 2 uses in its premises the quantity of food available.

R2:   IF food-quantity ≥ ok   THEN disease-severity ≤ 0   [4]

Source: Corruble, V., and Ganascia, J. G. (1997). Induction and the discovery of the causes of scurvy: A computational reconstruction. Reprinted from *Artificial Intelligence, 91*, p. 214, copyright 1997, with permission from Elsevier Science.

known. This evaluation procedure is therefore biased in favor of well-informed attributes. An alternative prior-assessment mechanism which does not have this bias is proposed next; it is based on the cover as the previous one, but is defined as a percentage: the ratio of the former cover over the *potential* cover (i.e., the number of examples for which the factor is known). The results of this relative prior-assessment are given in [Figure 6.9]. It

Figure 6.6
Excerpts from the 1880 *Medical Encyclopedia* Followed by the Corresponding Rules Proposed by CHARADE for Hygiene

---

HYGIENE:
If Cook's crews were entirely spared from scurvy, in a relatively large extent considering the times, it is thought that these great results were precisely the happy consequence of the care given to the cleanliness and drying of the ships. (Mahé, 1880)

Set II:	Rules 5, 6, 9, 12 use in their premises the level of hygiene.		
R5:	IF hygiene ≤ bad	THEN disease-severity ≥ 3	[3]
R6:	IF hygiene ≤ average	THEN disease-severity ≥ 2	[4]
R9:	IF hygiene ≥ average	THEN disease-severity ≤ 2	[7]
R12:	IF hygiene ≥ good	THEN disease-severity ≤ 1	[6]

Source: Corruble, V., and Ganascia, J. G. (1997). Induction and the discovery of the causes of scurvy: A computational reconstruction. Reprinted from *Artificial Intelligence, 91*, p. 215, copyright 1997, with permission from Elsevier Science.

Figure 6.7
Excerpts from the 1880 *Medical Encyclopedia* Followed by the Corresponding Rules Proposed by CHARADE for Climate

---

CLIMATE:
Spring and winter are obviously the seasons of predominance for scurvy. (Mahé, 1880)

Set III:	Rules 1, 11 use in their premises the temperature.		
R1:	IF location = land, temperature ≥ hot	THEN disease-severity ≤ 0	[4]
R11:	IF temperature ≤ severe-cold	THEN disease-severity ≥ 1	[5]

Source: Corruble, V., and Ganascia, J. G. (1997). Induction and the discovery of the causes of scurvy: A computational reconstruction. Reprinted from *Artificial Intelligence, 91*, p. 215, copyright 1997, with permission from Elsevier Science.

can be seen that the hypotheses putting forward the role of the diet (either its variety, or more specifically the lack of fresh fruits and vegetables) stand out even more; 100% of the cases *potentially explainable with these factors* are covered by these two hypotheses.

Though all the rules proposed by CHARADE correspond to some explanations of the scurvy found in the medical literature, there are some explanations from the literature which are not produced by CHARADE. Among these, the most important one is undoubtedly the explanation referring to the humidity of the air as the main predisposing cause of scurvy. This theory was for a long time the most widely accepted, and was defended by people such as Lind. It is also the theory which is favored by the authors of the medical encyclopedia from which the examples are extracted. Therefore, it is surprising, considering the overall similarity, that it does not appear, at least marginally,

Figure 6.8
Absolute Cover of Causal Hypotheses

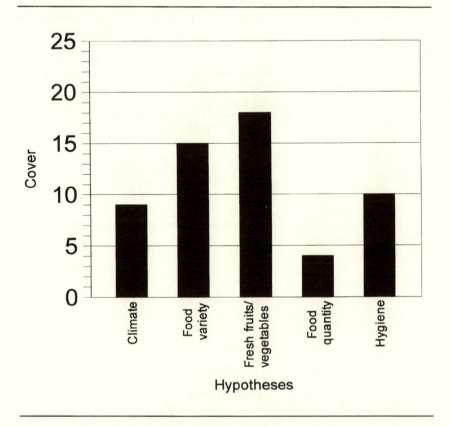

Source: Corruble, V., and Ganascia, J. G. (1997). Induction and the discovery of the causes of scurvy: A computational reconstruction. Reprinted from *Artificial Intelligence, 91*, p. 215, copyright 1997, with permission from Elsevier Science.

in the rules produced by CHARADE. The next section attempts to provide a computational explanation for this phenomenon through a simulation. (Corruble and Ganascia, 1997, pp. 213–217)

Testing the Blocked Perspiration Hypothesis

Corruble and Ganascia (1997) describe their symbolic reconstruction and testing of a false historical theory, namely, the blocked perspiration theory of scurvy, in the following section.

> The influence of a cold and humid atmosphere has been said to be the key factor for the apparition of scurvy. "Air humidity is the main predisposing cause of this disease," according to Lind (Mahé, 1880).

Figure 6.9
Relative Cover of Causal Hypotheses

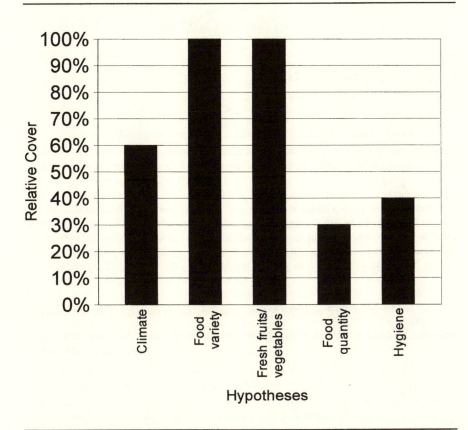

Source: Corruble, V., and Ganascia, J. G. (1997). Induction and the discovery of the causes of scurvy: A computational reconstruction. Reprinted from *Artificial Intelligence, 91*, p. 216, copyright 1997, with permission from Elsevier Science.

CHARADE does not conclude that the humidity of the air has any impact on the presence or absence of the disease, even though this was the most widely accepted theory in the 18th and 19th century. A possible explanation could be that, to reach this conclusion, the scientists had an inductive bias: maybe they had some *a priori* knowledge on the issue which biased their judgement on the origin of the disease.

A good way to test this hypothesis would be to have the inductive system reproduce the "wrong" induction of the scientists by formalizing the implicit knowledge that they used while working on the subject. This task is greatly assisted by the work of historians of medicine who have tried to reconstitute the conceptual and reasoning framework of physicians like Lind. In Carpenter (1986) for instance, it appears that the system of *blocked perspiration* was very widely accepted by the medical community at Lind's times (see [Figure 6.10]). In this system, the body is made mainly of solid tissues and fluids.

Figure 6.10
The Blocked Perspiration Theory Described in Carpenter (1986)

< < Lind's theory was based on the concept that a cold, wet climate (and also an unhappy psychological state and inactivity) could result in either a constriction or clogging of the pores in the skin and a consequent reduction in <u>insensible perspiration</u>. The idea that the skin was a major route of excretion of <u>undesirable "vapors and humors"</u> from the body dates back to Galen's time, but was very much developed by Sanctorius in the early 1600s. The idea that obstruction, caused by cold and damp, could result in a variety of putrid diseases became increasingly popular in the mid-eighteenth century and was put forward as the cause of fevers and cholera in military units. Another Edinburgh physician wrote in 1759: "There is no discovery next to that of circulation of blood, that has so much affected our reasoning in Medicine as that of insensible perspiration. The origin of most diseases and the operation of most medicines are accounted for it."

To return to Lind, he began his argument by pointing out that with the uninterrupted circulation of the body's fluids, the friction and mutual interaction with the solid tissues resulted in sweet and healthful components being "abraded and degenerated" into "various degrees of acrimony and corruption." Just as food had to be ingested to replace these components, so had the end products to be excreted. This seems a reasonable statement for someone to make in a period dominated by the success of physical (i.e., mechanical) theories in explaining different natural phenomena. He went on to say that minerals and acid salts we mostly excreted in the urine, but that a greater part of the total excretion was through the skin. He was impressed (we would say overly impressed) by the quantitative experiments that were supposed to have proved this beyond doubt. They involved a subject weighing his food and drink and also his excreta over a period, and also himself at the beginning and end. If the intake weighed more than the urine and feces, together with any gain in body weight, it was said that the excess was lost by perspiration. If the subject had not visibly sweated, this loss was entirely "invisible perspiration." It was possibly the quantitative aspect that particularly appealed to Lind, but of course, there was no measure of the carbon dioxide gas and water vapor lost in the air from the lungs. [...] > >

Source: Corruble, V., and Ganascia, J. G. (1997). Induction and the discovery of the causes of scurvy: A computational reconstruction. Reprinted from *Artificial Intelligence, 91*, p. 218, copyright 1997, with permission from Elsevier Science.

The fluids naturally tend to become corrupted. An important function of all the excretions, and especially of perspiration, is to evacuate these corrupted fluids from the body to keep only healthy fluids inside. If the perspiration is blocked, the corrupted fluids act as a poison and produce diseases. One can fight against the poisonous effect of the corrupted fluids by eating fruits whose acidity acts as a "detergent." This being accepted as a reasoning framework, the explanation of the role of humidity becomes clearer: humidity tends to block the pores of the skin; therefore, it prevents good perspiration and is the main cause of scurvy.

    The major steps of the reasoning framework in which the blocked perspiration theory could be articulated have been formalized into a set of axioms presented in [Figure 6.11].

Figure 6.11
Axiom Set Describing the "Blocked Perspiration" Theory

IF	(humidity = high)	THEN (perspiration ≥ hard)
IF	(hygiene ≥ good) (humidity = high)	THEN (perspiration ≤ hard)
IF	(humidity ≥ very-high)	THEN (perspiration ≥ blocked)
IF	(perspiration ≤ hard)	THEN (fluids ≤ healthy)
IF	(fresh_fruits/vegetables = yes)	THEN (fluids ≤ healthy)
IF	(fresh_fruits/vegetables = yes) (perspiration ≥ blocked)	THEN (fluids ≥ corrupted)
IF	(hygiene ≤ average) (location = sea)	THEN (humidity ≥ very-high)
IF	(hygiene ≥ good)	THEN (humidity ≤ high)

Source: Corruble, V., and Ganascia, J. G. (1997). Induction and the discovery of the causes of scurvy: A computational reconstruction. Reprinted from *Artificial Intelligence, 91*, p. 218, copyright 1997, with permission from Elsevier Science.

As seen in the figure, two new concepts (the perspiration quality, and the fluids quality) had to be added in the description language. Indeed, these two concepts, presented in [Figure 6.12] are not obtained through direct observations. The axioms state how the two theoretical concepts are logically linked to the observable features according to the theory.

Also, we want to point out that these axioms do not constitute a global theory of scurvy, since they do not express how the disease severity is logically linked to the observable features by a series of deductions. They introduce only the abstract concepts proposed by the blocked perspiration theory. The role of fresh fruits and vegetables appears in the conditions of the two rules, because, as noted above, the blocked perspiration theory considered that the acidity from the fruits could have a cleaning effect on corrupted fluids. Also the last two axioms are related to the blocked perspiration theory and express some 19th century common-sense knowledge left implicit in the literature. They concern the link between humidity and the level of hygiene in a ship; one of the main hygiene measures taken aboard ships consisted, especially since Cook, in keeping them dry.

We repeated the previous experiment giving this set of axioms to CHARADE. The aim was to observe the behavior of the system within the conceptual framework of the blocked perspiration theory given as domain knowledge to the system. To illustrate how CHARADE practically uses the domain knowledge, [Figure 6.13] shows how the saturation is done in this experiment on example #6. It can be compared to [Figure 6.2] when only general built-in knowledge on the types of attributes was used.

The results confirm our hypothesis about the importance of implicit knowledge. The rules produced (cf. [Figure 6.14]) correspond very well to the explanations given by 18th and 19th century physicians: the humidity appears (in conjunction with other factors) as an important predictor. Moreover, considering the number of examples covered, the rules using the *fluids quality* in their premise override the simpler (and true) rule found in the previous experiment condemning the lack of fresh fruits and vegetables. They indeed cover $14 + 9 = 23$ examples out of 25 instead of $13 + 5 = 18$ for the rules putting

Figure 6.12
Definitions of the Two New Concepts

Attribute	Type	Domain
perspiration	Ordered set	normal < hard < blocked
fluids	Ordered set	healthy < corrupted

Source: Corruble, V., and Ganascia, J. G. (1997). Induction and the discovery of the causes of
    scurvy: A computational reconstruction. Reprinted from *Artificial Intelligence, 91*, p. 218, copy-
    right 1997, with permission from Elsevier Science.

Figure 6.13
Saturation on One Example with Some Domain Knowledge

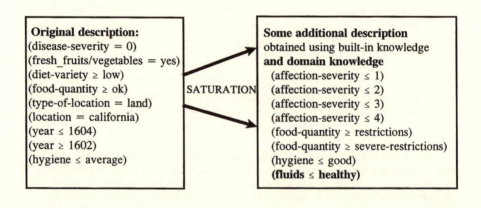

Source: Corruble, V., and Ganascia, J. G. (1997). Induction and the discovery of the causes of
    scurvy: A computational reconstruction. Reprinted from *Artificial Intelligence, 91*, p. 219, copy-
    right 1997, with permission from Elsevier Science.

forward fresh fruits and vegetables. This is illustrated by the new plot comparing the
cover of the competing hypotheses in [Figure 6.15]. In this experiment, since the new
factor (the quality of fluids) has a potential cover of 23, the *relative* cover of the new
hypothesis is 100%, which places it at the same level as the one based on diet variety
on the relative scale.

Figure 6.14
New Rules Produced When the Domain Knowledge Is Given to the System

---

IF humidity ≥ high,		
fresh_fruits/vegetables = unknown	THEN disease-severity ≥ 2.	[4]
IF humidity ≤ high, hygiene ≥ average	THEN disease-severity ≤ 1.	[6]
IF perspiration ≤ hard	THEN disease-severity ≤ 1.	[6]
IF fluids ≥ corrupted	THEN disease-severity ≥ 2.	[9]
IF fluids ≤ healthy	THEN disease-severity ≤ 2.	[14]

Source: Corruble, V., and Ganascia, J. G. (1997). Induction and the discovery of the causes of scurvy: A computational reconstruction. Reprinted from *Artificial Intelligence, 91*, p. 219, copyright 1997, with permission from Elsevier Science.

This phenomenon has been analyzed within a machine learning framework. It can also be explained in epistemological terms. In other words, the induction bias constituted by the domain knowledge can be seen as a hypothesis (implicit 19th century writings) about the effect of the environment on some internal functions of the human body. The induction itself is then an attempt to generate some rules from examples using this hypothesis. Therefore, the rules produced and the evaluation can be seen as a test of the explanatory or descriptive power of the hypothesis. In our case, the fact that the rules which use the abstract concepts cover a larger number of examples than the ones that we found in our first experiment is a sign of their greater explanatory power. We think that this might provide a good explanation for the importance given to humidity over the lack of fresh fruits and vegetables until the end of the nineteenth century. This analysis meets the point of view expressed in Thagard and Nowak (1990) about the role of explanatory power of a theory to explain its acceptance by the scientific community at a given time, given a particular conceptual framework. (Corruble and Ganascia, 1997, pp. 217–220)

Discussion of the Inductive Experiment

In the following section, Corruble and Ganascia (1997) interpret the results of their specific symbolic induction experiment and suggest use of computational modeling to overcome inductive bias in contemporary medical research.

There are two axes to the work just presented. The first one is the use of symbolic induction for discovery. In the case study that we have treated here, pure induction on 25 scurvy cases gave surprisingly good results in bringing forward the real cause of scurvy. However, this pure induction did not produce the theory that was the most widely accepted in the 18th and 19th century. The idea of reproducing these explanations expresses what we pursue in a second, descriptive axis of research: the reconstruction of reasoning as it took place in history. A second experiment in which some domain knowledge was given to the system eventually produced the missing explanation. This shows the importance of taking into account the conceptual framework of the scientists—even

Figure 6.15
Absolute Cover of Causal Hypotheses, with A Priori Knowledge

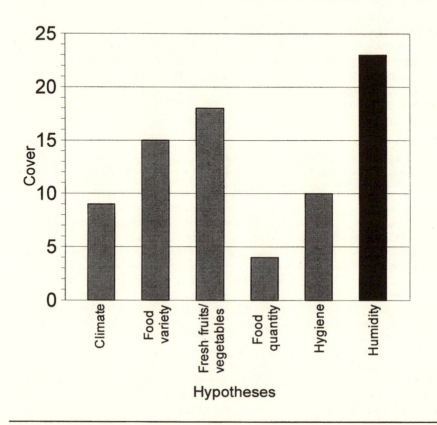

Source: Corruble, V., and Ganascia, J. G. (1997). Induction and the discovery of the causes of scurvy: A computational reconstruction. Reprinted from *Artificial Intelligence, 91*, p. 220, copyright 1997, with permission from Elsevier Science.

in a science which has reputedly relied only on observation since the beginning of the 19th century—to understand their reasoning.

The analysis of experimental results has used two explanatory criteria for the prior-assessment of causal hypotheses. The first one is a straight-forward count of examples covered by consistent subsets of rules. It was useful in bringing forward the real cause of scurvy, and then the cause put forward historically given appropriate *a priori* knowledge. This criterion, however, showed a bias in favor of well-described attributes. A second relative criterion, less biased by the quality of the data, uses a ratio of the previous criterion over the potential cover of the factor. It is even more efficient in bringing forward the real cause of scurvy, but does not put forward the cause favored in history as effectively, even with the appropriate background knowledge. Therefore, even though this second relative criterion seems more appropriate from a normative standpoint, it appears less useful from a descriptive standpoint; in our experiment, it is the absolute criterion, which does not take into account the quality of the data, that leads to the selection of the same hypothesis as the one selected by physicians in the 18th and 19th century.

In these experiments, the inductive bias seems to have a harmful effect, since it hides the real cause of scurvy. However, it is obviously not our goal to convince the reader that the inductive bias is harmful by nature. We know (especially from machine learning research [Mitchell, 1982]) that in most cases of induction, even more importantly in cases of human induction, a bias is necessary to constrain the search space. However, a lesson from our research is that it is critical to take into account one's induction bias to understand one's reasoning. In order to do so, it seems necessary to render this bias explicit since it is often the result of implicit knowledge, especially in medicine. It is our belief that computer simulation can be very helpful in this task.

From our experiments on scurvy, it seems that, in one case of a major medical discovery, artificial induction can be useful to reproduce or assist the reasoning of a physician, both normatively and descriptively. Even though many discoveries in medicine are not the result of such an inductive process (e.g., the ones resulting from a unique observation with a microscope), more experimentation has been carried out on other historical medical discoveries in etiology. We obtained similar results in the simulation of the discovery of the causes of leprosy as an inductive process, though this required using a new inductive algorithm (PASTEUR) designed to model exceptions explicitly (Corruble and Ganascia, 1996).

Similar ideas are currently being applied to joint projects with physicians to aid contemporary medical research. The first project involves a collaboration with hematologists working on leukemia research. From patient data collected in a number of US hospitals, we use the same type of computational induction presented here to come up with new hypotheses on the reasons why only some of the patients affected with myelodysplasia (often named pre-leukemia) develop acute leukemia. In this project, we hope that, as for the discovery of the causes of scurvy and the discovery of the causes of leprosy, the limitations in our understanding of the disease are more the results of erroneous reasoning than of a lack of necessary data. If this hypothesis proves true, then computational modeling and simulation of experts' inductive reasoning on leukemia should prove useful to elucidate the dogmas which limit our ability to reason on this particular problem (Corruble and Ganascia, 1994). A look at the recent history of leukemia research (Bernard, 1994), or at other areas of cancer research (Hellman, 1993) suggests that these dogmas are still numerous. Another project applies this approach to psychiatric research on human depression.

The main issue in moving from historical reconstruction to contemporary research is, apart from the scaling up in the complexity of the problems tackled, the absence of an important resource available in historical work; the analyses performed over time in the field of history of medicine. An exciting research direction is therefore to use the type of modeling and simulation presented in this article as a tool to aid this elucidation process. (Corruble and Ganascia, 1997, pp. 220–222)

COMMENTARY

In the philosophy of science, induction is viewed as the fallible process of the accumulation of evidence. Induction thus is opposed to deductive reasoning which, given the truth of premises, can guarantee valid conclusions. Deductive reasoning is valid if it is logically impossible for the conclusions to be false if the premises are true. However, there is something about the logic of deductive reasoning that makes it, in a sense, unnatural and artificial. As Bertrand Russell has said: Logic would be true even if there were no human beings. Inductive reasoning is the product of human evolution, a survival mechanism that has built into it the idea that the past is a good predictor of the future.

To bridge the gap between the fallibility of inductive reasoning and the certainty of deductive reasoning, algorithmic induction can be introduced. This, in effect, is what Corruble and Ganascia (1997) have done with their application of the algorithmic intelligence of CHARADE to the problem of the causes of scurvy. The computational logic of CHARADE is a deductive logic applied to an inductive task.

This bridging effectiveness of algorithmic induction is an appropriate antidote to the position against inductionism taken by Karl Popper (1959) in *The Logic of Scientific Discovery*, for it preserves the value of natural induction while permitting application of Popper's formal logic as conjectures and refutations that rely on the logical argument of *reductio ad absurdum* to establish logical contradiction and thereby the reputation of any particular scientific conjecture. The bridging power of algorithmic induction is demonstrated by the application of CHARADE to the reconstruction of the inductively false hypothesis that scurvy was due to the problem of humidity and blocked perspiration as discussed earlier in this chapter. Moreover, the method of algorithmic induction can be applied to test many of the steps and pathways that must be traversed in the quest for scientific discoveries.

7

Bayesian Reasoning

THE MATHEMATICAL LAW OF NATURAL SELECTION
AND BAYESIAN FREQUENCIES

In 1763, Thomas Bayes presented a number of equations for computing various types of probability. From the standpoint of evolutionary theory, the most important of these equations states that the probability of a single event can be computed by dividing the frequency of favorable results by the sum of frequency of favorable results plus frequency of unfavorable results. *This equation can be considered the mathematical law of natural selection.* Thus, the mathematical law of natural selection is a law of probability which states that as the ratio of frequency of favorable results to the sum of frequency of favorable results plus frequency of unfavorable results increases to a value greater than zero, specific biological mechanisms, structures, and behavior contributing to favorable adaptive results are selected.

The mathematical law of natural selection does not specify how the organisms from simple bacteria to complex cells to multicellular organisms "compute" the mathematical ratio. Perhaps it is not a matter of computation but of registering favorable and unfavorable results in cellular physiology and ensuing biochemical events that occur on their own physical terms guided and conforming, in all cases, by Maxwell's electromagnetic theory, that do the work. Thus, ethologists and evolutionary psychologists who describe animals in natural foraging as computing frequencies and Bayesian algorithms are only using a mathematical metaphor.

The use of this mathematical metaphor is central in the theory advanced in the research of Gigerenzer and Hoffrage (1995) and Cosmides and Tooby (1996), as described in this chapter.

BAYESIAN INFERENCE AND FREQUENCY REPRESENTATION

Psychological research indicates that people have difficulty in Bayesian reasoning using standard probability formats. In an effort to understand this difficulty and to provide a means of improving Bayesian reasoning, Gigerenzer and Hoffrage (1995) constructed a theoretical analysis of the relationship between the type of information format (standard or frequentistic) and the cognitive algorithms involved in Bayesian reasoning. Their theory and its application directed toward improving performance in Bayesian reasoning tasks will be presented in the following section, and, then, a brief commentary will be offered.

The Improvement of Bayesian Reasoning: Overview

Gigerenzer and Hoffrage (1995) present the following succinct account of their research.

Is the mind, by design, predisposed against performing Bayesian inference? Previous research on base rate neglect suggests that the mind lacks the appropriate cognitive algorithms. However, any claim against the existence of an algorithm, Bayesian or otherwise, is impossible to evaluate unless one specifies the information format in which it is designed to operate. The authors show that Bayesian algorithms are computationally simpler in frequency formats than in the probability formats used in previous research. Frequency formats correspond to the sequential way information is acquired in natural sampling, from animal foraging to neural networks. By analyzing several thousand solutions to Bayesian problems, the authors found that when information was presented in frequency formats, statistically naive participants derived up to 50% of all inferences by Bayesian algorithms. Non-Bayesian algorithms included simple versions of Fisherian and Neyman-Pearsonian inference. (Gigerenzer and Hoffrage, 1995, p. 684)

The Laws of Probability and the Laws of the Mind: Historical Background

Gigerenzer and Hoffrage (1995) present a brief intellectual history of the relationship between the laws of human thought and the laws of mathematical probability.

Is the mind, by design, predisposed against performing Bayesian inference? The classical probabilists of the Enlightenment, including Condorcet, Poisson, and Laplace, equated probability theory with the common sense of educated people, who were known then as "hommes éclairés." Laplace (1814/1951) declared that "the theory of probability is at bottom nothing more than good sense reduced to a calculus which evaluates that which good minds know by a sort of instinct, without being able to explain how with precision" (p. 196). The available mathematical tools, in particular the theorems of Bayes and Bernoulli, were seen as descriptions of actual human judgement (Daston, 1981, 1988). However, the years of political upheaval during the French Revolution prompted Laplace, unlike earlier writers such as Condorcet, to issue repeated disclaimers that probability theory, because of the interference of passion and desire, could not account for all relevant factors in human judgement. The Enlightenment view—that the laws of probability are the laws of the mind—moderated as it was through the French Revolution, had a profound influence on 19th and 20th-century science. This view became the starting point for seminal contributions to mathematics, as when George Boole (1854/1958) derived the laws of algebra, logic, and probability from what he believed to be the laws of thought. It also became the basis of vital contributions to psychology, as when Piaget and Inhelder (1951/1975) added an ontogenetic dimension to their Enlightenment view of probabilistic reasoning. And it became the foundation of contemporary notions of rationality in philosophy and economics (e.g., Allais, 1953; L. J. Cohen, 1986).

Ward Edwards and his colleagues (Edwards, 1968; Phillips & Edwards, 1966; and earlier, Rouanet, 1961) were the first to test experimentally whether human inference follows Bayes' theorem. Edwards concluded that inferences, although "conservative," were usually proportional to those calculated from Bayes' theorem. Kahneman and Tversky (1972, p. 450), however, arrived at the opposite conclusion: "In his evaluation of evidence, man is apparently not a conservative Bayesian: he is not Bayesian at all." In the 1970s and 1980s, proponents of their "heuristics-and-biases" program concluded that people systematically neglect base rates in Bayesian inference problems. "The genuineness, the robustness, and the generality of the base-rate fallacy are matters of established fact" (Bar-Hillel, 1980, p. 215). Bayes' theorem, like Bernoulli's theorem, was no longer thought to describe the workings of the mind. But passion and desire were no longer blamed as the causes of the disturbances. The new claim was stronger. The discrepancies were taken as tentative evidence that "people do not appear to follow the calculus of chance or the statistical theory of prediction" (Kahneman & Tversky, 1973, p. 237). It was proposed that as a result of "limited information-processing abilities" (Lichtenstein, Fischhoff, & Phillips, 1982, p. 333), people are doomed to compute the probability of an event by crude, nonstatistical rules such as the "representation heuristic." Blunter still, the paleontologist Stephen J. Gould summarized what has become the common wisdom in and beyond psychology: "Tversky and Kahneman argue, correctly I think, that our minds are not built (for whatever reason) to work by the rules of probability" (Gould, 1992, p. 469).

Here is the problem. There are contradictory claims as to whether people naturally reason according to Bayesian inference. The two extremes are represented by the Enlightenment probabilists and by proponents of the heuristics-and-biases program. Their conflict cannot be resolved by finding further examples of good or bad reasoning; text problems generating one or the other can always be designed. Our particular difficulty is that after more than two decades of research, we still know little about the cognitive processes underlying human inference, Bayesian or otherwise. This is not to say that there have been no attempts to specify these processes. For instance, it is understandable that when the "representativeness heuristic" was first proposed in the early 1970s to explain base rate neglect, it was only loosely defined. Yet at present, representativeness remains a vague and ill-defined notion (Gigerenzer & Murray, 1987; Shanteau, 1989; Wallsten, 1983). For some time it was hoped that factors such as "concreteness," "vividness," "causality," "salience," "specificity," "extremeness," and "relevance" of base rate information would be adequate to explain why base rate neglect seemed to come and go (e.g., Ajzen, 1977; Bar-Hillel, 1980; Borgida & Brekke, 1981). However, these factors have led neither to an integrative theory nor even to specific models of underlying processes (Hammond, 1990; Koehler, [1996]; Lopes, 1991; Scholz, 1987).

Some have suggested that there is perhaps something to be said for both sides, that the truth lies somewhere in the middle: Maybe the mind does a little of both Bayesian computation and quick-and-dirty inference. This compromise avoids the polarization of views but makes no progress on the theoretical front.

In this article, we argue that both views are based on an incomplete analysis: They focus on cognitive processes, Bayesian or otherwise, without making the connection between what we will call a *cognitive algorithm* and an *information format*. We (a) provide a theoretical framework that specifies why frequency formats should improve Bayesian reasoning and (b) present two studies that test whether they do. Our goal is to lead research on Bayesian inference out of the present conceptual cul-de-sac and to shift the focus from human errors to human engineering (see Edwards and von Winterfeldt, 1986): how to help people reason the Bayesian way without even teaching them. (Gigerenzer and Hoffrage, 1995, pp. 684–685)

Information Representation and Cognitive Algorithms

Algorithms and representations are intimately connected. Different mathematical or logical algorithms may be equivalent in the sense that they lead to equivalent solutions to problems, but their execution depends on the nature of the information representation on which the algorithm acts and the type of information representation that can influence information processing efficiency. In the following section, Gigerenzer and Hoffrage (1995) elaborate their position on cognitive algorithms and information representations.

Our argument centers on the intimate relationship between a cognitive algorithm and an information format. This point was made in a more general form by the physicist Richard Feynman. In his classic *The Character of Physical Law*, Feynman (1967) placed a great emphasis on the importance of deriving different formulations for the same physical law, even if they are mathematically equivalent (e.g., Newton's law, the local field method, and the minimum principle). Different representations of a physical law, Feynman reminded us, can evoke varied mental pictures and thus assist in making new discoveries: "Psychologically they are different because they are completely unequivalent when you are trying to guess new laws" (p. 53). We agree with Feynman. The assertion that mathematically equivalent representations can make a difference to human understanding is the key to our analysis of intuitive Bayesian inference.

We use the general term *information representation* and the specific terms *information format* and *information menu* to refer to *external* representations, recorded on paper or on some other physical medium. Examples are the various formulations of physical laws included in Feynman's book and the Feynman diagrams. External representations need to be distinguished from the *internal* representations stored in human minds, whether the latter are propositional (e.g., Pylyshyn, 1973) or pictorial (e.g., Kosslyn & Pomerantz,

1977). In this article, we do not make specific claims about the internal representations, although our results may be of relevance to this issue.

Consider numerical information as one example of external representations. Numbers can be represented in Roman, Arabic, and binary systems, among others. These representations can be mapped one to one onto each other and are in this sense mathematically equivalent. But the form of representation can make a difference for an algorithm that does, say, multiplication. The algorithms of our pocket calculators are tuned to Arabic numbers as input data and would fail badly if one entered binary numbers. Similarly, the arithmetic algorithms acquired by humans are designed for particular representations (Stigler, 1984). Contemplate for a moment long division in Roman numerals.

Our general argument is that mathematically equivalent representations of information entail algorithms that are not necessarily computationally equivalent (although these algorithms are mathematically equivalent in the sense that they produce the same outcomes; see Larkin & Simon, 1987; Marr, 1982). This point has an important corollary for research on inductive reasoning. Suppose we are interested in figuring out what algorithm a system uses. We will not detect the algorithm if the representation of information we provide the system does not match the representation with which the algorithm works. For instance, assume that in an effort to find out whether a system has an algorithm for multiplication, we feed that system Roman numerals. The observation that the system produces mostly garbage does not entail the conclusion that it lacks an algorithm for multiplication. We now apply this argument to Bayesian inference. (Gigerenzer and Hoffrage, 1995, p. 685)

Standard Probability Formats

The standard probability format has been regularly used in cognitive psychology research concerned with judgment under uncertainty. The judgment required is a single-point estimate or a single-event probability and the equation is one of many that have been developed since the original exposition by Thomas Bayes (1763). The results of the psychological research have been discouraging, and many cognitive psychologists have concluded that the human mind does not or cannot contain Bayesian algorithms. Gigerenzer and Hoffrage (1995) discuss the standard probability format, in detail, in the following section.

In this article, we focus on an elementary form of Bayesian inference. The task is to infer a single-point estimate—a probability ("posterior probability") or a frequency—for one of two mutually exclusive and exhaustive hypotheses, based on one observation (rather than two or more). This elementary task has been the subject of almost all experimental studies on Bayesian inference in the last 25 years. The following "mammography problem" (adapted from Eddy, 1982) is one example:

Mammography problem (standard probability format)

The probability of breast cancer is 1% for a woman at age forty who participates in routine screening. If a woman has breast cancer, the probability is 80% that she will get a positive mammography. If a woman does not have breast cancer, the probability is 9.6% that she will also get a positive mammography. A woman in this age group had a positive mammography in a routine screening. What is the probability that she actually has breast cancer? ____%

There are two mutually exclusive and exhaustive hypotheses (breast cancer and no breast cancer), there is one observation (the positive test), and the task is to arrive at a single-point probability estimate.

The information is represented here in terms of *single-event probabilities*: All information (base rate, hit rate, and false alarm rate) is in the form of probabilities attached to a single person, and the task is to estimate a single-event probability. The probabilities are expressed as percentages; alternatively, they can be presented as numbers between zero and one. We refer to this representation (base rate, hit rate, and false alarm rate expressed as single-event probabilities) as the *standard probability format*.

What is the algorithm needed to calculate the Bayesian posterior probability p(cancer|positive) from the standard probability format? Here and in what follows, we use the symbols H and $-$H for the two hypotheses or possible outcomes (breast cancer or no breast cancer) and D for the data obtained (positive mammography). A Bayesian algorithm for computing the posterior probability p(H|D) with the values given in the standard probability format amounts to solving the following equation:

$$p(H|D) = \frac{p(H)p(D|H)}{p(H)p(D|H) + p(-H)p(D|-H)}$$

$$= \frac{(.01)(.80)}{(.01)(.80) + (.99)(.096)} \tag{1}$$

The result is .078. We know from several studies that physicians, college students (Eddy, 1982), and staff at Harvard Medical School (Casscells, Schoenberger, & Grayboys, 1978) all have equally great difficulties with this and similar medical disease problems. For instance, Eddy (1982) reported that 95 out of 100 physicians estimated the posterior probability p(cancer|positive) to be between 70% and 80%, rather than 7.8%.

The experimenters who have amassed the apparently damning body of evidence that humans fail to meet the norms of Bayesian inference have usually given their research participants information in the standard probability format (or its variant, in which one or more of the three percentages are relative frequencies; see below). Studies on the cab problem (Bar-Hillel, 1980; Tversky & Kahneman, 1982), the light-bulb problem (Lyon & Slovic, 1976) and various disease problems (Casscells et al., 1978; Eddy, 1982; Hammerton, 1973) are examples. Results from these and other studies have generally been taken as evidence that the human mind does not reason with Bayesian algorithms. Yet this conclusion is not warranted, as explained before. One would be unable to detect a Bayesian algorithm within a system by feeding it information in a representation that does not match the representation with which the algorithm works.

In the last few decades, the standard probability format has become a common way to communicate information ranging from medical and statistical textbooks to psychological experiments. But we should keep in mind that is only one of many mathematically equivalent ways of representing information; it is, moreover, a recently invented notation. Neither the standard probability format nor Equation 1 was used in Bayes' (1763) original essay. Indeed, the notion of "probability" did not gain prominence in probability theory until one century after the mathematical theory of probability was invented (Gigerenzer, Swijtink, Porter, Daston, Beatty, & Krüger, 1989). Percentages became common notations only during the 19th century (mainly for interest and taxes), after the metric system was introduced during the French Revolution. Thus, probabilities and percentages took millennia of literacy and numeracy to evolve; organisms did not acquire information in terms of probabilities and percentages until very recently. How did organisms acquire information before that time? We now investigate the links between information representation and information acquisition. (Gigerenzer and Hoffrage, 1995, pp. 685–686)

Natural Sampling of Frequency

The evolution of cognitive mechanisms can be considered as part and parcel of the evolutionary development of physiological mechanisms in general. These cognitive mechanisms are essential to adaptive problem solving in changing environments and are dependent on the simplest and most general type of calculation, that is, the physiological registration of the frequency of event sequences. The standard probability format would be complex. Indeed, it can be demonstrated that probabilities expressed as percentages can be expressed as frequencies and that a priori probabilities can be ignored, all of which simplifies computation and clarifies understanding. In particular, the standard probability format can be replaced by the following: frequency of unfavorable results/frequency of unfavorable results plus frequency of favorable results or the complement: frequency of favorable results/frequency of favorable results plus frequency of unfavorable results.

Evolutionary theory asserts that the design of the mind and its environment evolve in tandem. Assume . . . that humans have evolved cognitive algorithms that can perform statistical inferences. These algorithms, however, would not be tuned to probabilities or percentages as input format, as explained before. For what information format were these algorithms designed? We assume that as humans evolved, the "natural" format was *frequencies* as actually experienced in a series of events, rather than probabilities or percentages (Cosmides & Tooby, 1996; Gigerenzer, 1991, 1993). From animals to neural networks, systems seem to learn about contingencies through sequential encoding and updating of event frequencies (Brunswik, 1939; Gallistel, 1990; Hume, 1739/1951; Shanks, 1991). For instance, research on foraging behavior indicates that bumblebees, ducks, rats, and ants behave as if they were good intuitive statisticians, highly sensitive to changes in frequency distributions in their environments (Gallistel, 1990; Real, 1991; Real & Caraco, 1986). Similarly, research on frequency processing in humans indicates that humans, too, are sensitive to frequencies of various kinds, including frequencies of words, single letters, and letter pairs (e.g., Barsalou & Ross, 1986; Hasher & Zacks, 1979; Hintzman, 1976; Sedlmeier, Hertwig, and Gigerenzer, 1995).

The sequential acquisition of information by updating event frequencies *without* artificially fixing the marginal frequencies (e.g., of disease and no-disease cases) is what we refer to as *natural sampling* (Kleiter, 1994). Brunswik's (1955) "representative sampling" is a special case of natural sampling. In contrast, in experimental research the marginal frequencies are typically fixed a priori. For instance, an experimenter may want to investigate 100 people with disease and a control group of 100 people without disease. This kind of sampling with fixed marginal frequencies is not what we refer to as natural sampling.

The evolutionary argument that cognitive algorithms were designed for frequency information, acquired through natural sampling, has implications for the computations an organism needs to perform when making Bayesian inferences. Here is the question to be answered: Assume an organism acquires information about the structure of its environment by the natural sampling of frequencies. What computations would the organism need to perform to draw inferences the Bayesian way?

Imagine an old, experienced physician in an illiterate society. She has no books or statistical surveys and therefore must rely solely on her experience. Her people have been afflicted by a previously unknown and severe disease. Fortunately, the physician has discovered a symptom that signals the disease, although not with certainty. In her lifetime, she has seen 1,000 people, 10 of whom had the disease. Of those 10, 8 showed the symptom; of the 990 not afflicted, 95 did. Now a new patient appears. He has the symptom. What is the probability that he actually has the disease?

The physician in the illiterate society does not need a pocket calculator to estimate the Bayesian posterior. All she needs is the number of cases that had both the symptom and the disease (here, 8 and the number of symptom cases (here, 8 + 95). A Bayesian algorithm for computing posterior probability p(H|D) from the frequency format (see [Figure 7.1], left side) requires solving the following equation:

$$p(H|D) = \frac{d\&h}{d\&h + d\& - h} = \frac{8}{8 + 95} \qquad (2)$$

where *d&h* (data and hypothesis) is the number of cases with symptom and disease, and *d& −h* is the number of cases having the symptom but lacking the disease. The physician does not need to keep track of the base rate of the disease. Her modern counterpart, the medical student who struggles with single-event probabilities presented in medical textbooks, may on the other hand have to rely on a calculator and end up with little understanding of the result (see [Figure 7.1], right side). Henceforth, when we use the term *frequency format*, we always refer to frequencies as defined by the natural sampling tree in [Figure 7.1].

Comparison of Equations 1 and 2 leads to our first theoretical result:

Result 1: Computational demands. Bayesian algorithms are computationally simpler when information is encoded in a frequency format rather than a standard probability format. By "computationally simpler" we mean that (a) fewer operations (multiplication, addition, or division) need to be performed in Equation 2 than in Equation 1, and (b) the operation can be performed on natural numbers (absolute frequencies) rather than fractions (such as percentages).

Equations 1 and 2 are mathematically equivalent formulations of Bayes' theorem. Both produce the same result, p(H|D) = 0.078. Equation 1 is a standard version of Bayes' theorem in today's textbooks in the social sciences, whereas Equation 2 corresponds to Thomas Bayes' (1763) original "Proposition 5" (see Earman, 1992).

Equation 2 implies three further (not independent) theoretical results concerning the estimation of a Bayesian posterior probability p(H|D) in frequency formats (Kleiter, 1994).

Result 2: Attentional demands. Only two kinds of information need to be attended to in natural sampling: the absolute frequencies d&h and d& −h (or, alternatively, d&h and d, where d is the sum of the two frequencies). An organism does not need to keep track of the whole tree in [Figure 7.1], but only of the two pieces of information contained

Figure 7.1
Bayesian Inference and Information Representation (Natural Sampling of Frequencies and Standard Probability Format)

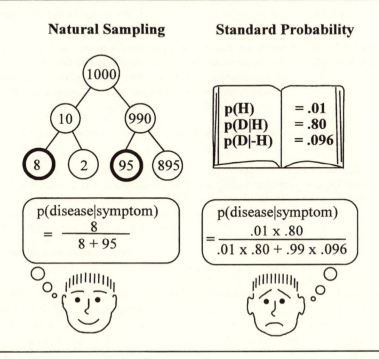

Source: Gigerenzer, G., and Hoffrage, U. (1995). How to improve Bayesian reasoning without instruction: Frequency formats. *Psychological Review, 102 (4)*, p. 687. Copyright © 1995 by the American Psychological Association. Adapted with permission.

in the bold circles. These are the hit and false alarm *frequencies* (not to be confused with hit and false alarm *rates*).

Result 3: Base rates need not be attended to. Neglect of base rates is perfectly rational in natural sampling. For instance, our physician does not need to pay attention to the base rate of the disease (10 out of 1,000; see [Figure 7.1]).

Result 4: Posterior distributions can be computed. Absolute frequencies can carry more information than probabilities. Information about the sample size allows inference beyond single-point estimates, such as the computation of posterior distributions, confidence intervals for posterior probabilities, and second-order probabilities (Kleiter, 1994; Sahlin, 1993). In this article, however, we focus only on single point estimation.

For the design of the experiments reported below, it is important to note that the Bayesian algorithms (Equations 1 and 2) work on the final tally of frequencies (see [Figure 7.1]), not on the sequential record of updated frequencies. Thus, the same four results still hold even if nothing but the final tally is presented to the participants in an experiment. (Gigerenzer and Hoffrage, 1995, pp. 686–687)

Information Format and Menu

In the following section, Gigerenzer and Hoffrage (1995) discuss the theoretical results that follow from delineating the intersection of two information formats and two information menus.

We propose to distinguish two aspects of information representation, *information format* and *information menu*. The standard probability format has a *probability format*, whereas a *frequency format* is obtained by natural sampling. However, as the second result (attentional demands) shows, there is another difference. The standard probability format displays three pieces of information, whereas two are sufficient in natural sampling. We use the term *information menu* to refer to the manner in which information is segmented into pieces within any format. The standard probability displays the three pieces p(H), p(D|H), and p(D| − H) (often called base rate, hit rate, and false alarm rate, respectively). We refer to this as the *standard menu*. Natural sampling yields a more parsimonious menu with only two pieces of information, d&h and (d&−h) (or alternatively, d&h and d). We call this the *short menu*.

So far we have introduced the probability format with a standard menu and the frequency format with a short menu. However, information formats and menus can be completely crossed. For instance, if we replace the probabilities in the standard probability format with frequencies, we get a standard menu with a frequency format, or the *standard frequency format*. [Table 7.1] uses the mammography problem to illustrate the four versions that result from crossing the two menus with the two formats. All four displays are mathematically equivalent in the sense that they lead to the same Bayesian posterior probability. In general, within the same format information can be divided into various menus; within the same menu, it can be represented in a range of formats.

To transform the standard probability format into the standard frequency format, we simply replaced 1% with "10 out of 1,000," "80%" with "8 out of 10," and so on (following the tree in [Figure 7.1]) and phrased the task in terms of a frequency estimate. All else went unchanged. Note that whether the frequency format actually carries information about the sample size (e.g., that there were exactly 1,000 women) or not (as in [Table 7.1], where it is said "in every 1,000 women") makes no difference for Results 1 to 3 because these relate to single-point estimates only (unlike Result 4).

What are the Bayesian algorithms needed to draw inferences from the two new format-menu combinations? The complete crossing of formats and menus leads to two important results. A Bayesian algorithm for the *short probability format*, that is, the probability format with a short menu (as in [Table 7.1]), amounts to solving the following equation:

$$p(H|D) = \frac{p(D\&H)}{p(D)}$$

(3)

This version of Bayes' theorem is equivalent to Equation 1. The algorithm for computing p(H|D) from Equation 3, however, is computationally simpler than the algorithm for computing p(H|D) from Equation 1.

What Bayesian computations are needed for the standard frequency format? Equation 2 specifies the computations for both the standard and short menus in frequency formats. The same algorithm is sufficient for both menus. In the standard frequency format of the

Table 7.1
Information Formats and Menus for the Mammography Problem

Format and menu	Description of problem
Standard probability format	The probability of breast cancer is 1% for women at age forty who participate in routine screening. If a woman has breast cancer, the probability is 80% that she will get a positive mammography. If a woman does not have breast cancer, the probability is 9.6% that she will also get a positive mammography. A woman in this age group had a positive mammography in a routine screening. What is the probability that she actually has breast cancer? _____ %
Standard frequency format	10 out of every 1,000 women at age forty who participate in routine screening have breast cancer. 8 of every 10 women with breast cancer will get a positive mammography. 95 out of every 990 women without breast cancer will also get a positive mammography. Here is a new representative sample of women at age forty who got a positive mammography in routine screening. How many of these women do you expect to actually have breast cancer? _____ out of _____
Short probability format	The probability that a woman at age forty will get a positive mammography in routine screening is 10.3%. The probability of breast cancer _and_ a positive mammography is 0.8% for a woman at age forty who participates in routine screening. A woman in this age group had a positive mammography in a routine screening. What is the probability that she actually has breast cancer? _____ %
Short frequency format	103 out of 1,000 women at age forty get a positive mammography in routine screening. 8 out of every 1,000 women at age forty who participate in routine screening have breast cancer _and_ a positive mammography. Here is a new representative sample of women at age forty who got a positive mammography in routine screening. How many of these women do you expect to actually have breast cancer? _____ out of _____

Source: Gigerenzer, G., and Hoffrage, U. (1995). How to improve Bayesian reasoning without instruction: Frequency formats. *Psychological Review, 102 (4),* p. 688. Copyright © 1995 by the American Psychological Association. Adapted with permission.

mammography problem, for instance, the expected number of actual breast cancer cases among positive tests is computed as 8/(8 + 95). Thus, we have the following two important theoretical results concerning formats (probability vs. frequency) and menus (standard vs. short):

Result 5: With a probability format, the Bayesian computations are simpler in the short menu than in the standard menu.

Result 6: With a frequency format, the Bayesian computations are the same for the two menus.

If the two pieces of information in the short menu are d&h and d, as in [Table 7.1], rather than d&h and d&−h, then the Bayesian computations are even simpler because the sum in the denominator is already computed. (Gigerenzer and Hoffrage, 1995, pp. 687–688)

Relative Frequency Format

In the following section, Gigerenzer and Hoffrage (1995) discuss the computational characteristics of the relative frequency format.

Several studies of Bayesian inference have used standard probability formats in which one, two, or all three pieces of information were presented as relative frequencies rather than as single-event probabilities—although the task still was to estimate a single-event probability (e.g., Tversky & Kahneman's, 1982, cab problem). For instance, in the following version of the mammography problem, all information is represented in relative frequencies (in %).

Relative frequency version (standard menu)

1% of women at age forty who participate in routine screening have breast cancer. 80% of women with breast cancer will get positive mammographies. 9.6 % of women without breast cancer will also get positive mammographies. A woman in this age group had a positive mammography in a routine screening. What is the probability that she actually has breast cancer? _____%

Is the algorithm needed for relative frequencies computationally equivalent to the algorithm for frequencies, or to that for probabilities? The relative frequency format does not display the absolute frequencies needed for Equation 2. Rather, the numbers are the same as in the probability format, making the Bayesian computation the same as in Equation 1. This yields the following result:

Result 7: Algorithms for relative frequency versions are computationally equivalent to those for the standard probability format.

We tested several implications of Results 1 through 7 (except Result 4) in the studies reported below. (Gigerenzer and Hoffrage, 1995, pp. 688–689)

The Single-Point Estimate Format

Gigerenzer and Hoffrage (1995) discuss probabilistic and frequentistic approaches to single-point estimates in the following section.

Whether estimates relate to single events or frequencies has been a central issue within probability theory and statistics since the decline of the classical interpretation of probability in the 1830s and 1840s. The question has polarized subjectivists and frequentists, additionally subdividing frequentists into moderate frequentists, such as R. A. Fisher (1955), and strong frequentists, such as J. Neyman (Gigerenzer et al., 1989). A single-point estimate can be interpreted as a probability or a frequency. For instance, clinical inference can be about the probability that a particular person has cancer or about the frequency of cancer in a new sample of people. Foraging (Simon, 1956; Stephens & Krebs, 1986) provides an excellent example of a single-point estimate reasonably being interpreted as a frequency. The foraging organism is interested in making inferences that lead to satisfying results in the long run. Will it more often find food if it follows Cue X or Cue Y? Here the single-point estimate can be interpreted as an expected frequency for a new sample. In the experimental research of the past two decades, participants were almost always required to estimate a single-event probability. But this need not be. In the experiments reported below, we asked people both for single-event probability and frequency estimates.

To summarize, mathematically equivalent information need not be computationally and psychologically equivalent. We have shown that Bayesian algorithms can depend on information format and menu, and we derived several specific results for when algorithms are computationally equivalent and when they are not. (Gigerenzer and Hoffrage, 1995, p. 689; italics added)

The Algorithms of Bayesian Inference

At least three types of possible algorithms are available for solving Bayesian inference problems: equations, graphical (pictorial) representations, and shortcut procedures that approximate the precision of equations.

How might the mind draw inferences that follow Bayes' theorem? Surprisingly, this question seems rarely to have been posed. Psychological explanations typically were directed at "irrational" deviations between human inference and the laws of probability; the "rational" seems not to have demanded an explanation in terms of cognitive processes. The cognitive account of probabilistic reasoning by Piaget and Inhelder (1951/ 1975), as one example, stops at the precise moment the adolescent turns "rational," that is, reaches the level of formal operations.

We propose three classes of cognitive algorithm for Bayesian inference: first, the algorithms corresponding to Equations 1 through 3; second, pictorial or graphical analogs of Bayes' theorem, as anticipated by Bayes' (1763) billiard table; and third, shortcuts that simplify the Bayesian computations in Equations 1 through 3. (Gigerenzer and Hoffrage, 1995, p. 689)

Predictions for Two Studies

Derived from their theoretical results, Gigerenzer and Hoffrage (1995) assert a set of experimental predictions.

We now derive several predictions from the theoretical results obtained. The predictions specify conditions that do and do not make people reason the Bayesian way. The predictions should hold independently of whether the cognitive algorithms follow Equations 1 through 3, whether they are pictorial analogs of Bayes' theorem, or whether they include shortcuts.

Prediction 1: Frequency formats elicit a substantially higher proportion of Bayesian algorithms than probability formats. This prediction is derived from Result 1, which states that the Bayesian algorithm is computationally simpler in frequency formats.

Prediction 2: Probability formats elicit a larger proportion of Bayesian algorithms for the short menu than for the standard menu. This prediction is deduced from Result 5, which states that with a probability format, the Bayesian computations are simpler in the short menu than in the standard menu.

Prediction 3: Frequency formats elicit the same proportion of Bayesian algorithms for the two menus. This prediction is derived from Result 6, which states that with a frequency format, the Bayesian computations are the same for the two menus.

Prediction 4: Relative frequency formats elicit the same (small) proportion of Bayesian algorithms as probability formats. This prediction is derived from Result 7, which states that the Bayesian algorithms are computationally equivalent in both formats. (Gigerenzer and Hoffrage, 1995, pp. 691–692)

Operational Criteria for Studies 1 and 2

To determine whether subjects in two studies were engaged in Bayesian inference, two interlocking criteria were used: outcome and process.

The data we obtained for each of several thousand problem solutions were composed of a participant's (a) probability or frequency estimate and (b) on-line protocol ("write aloud" protocol) of his or her reasoning. Data type (a) allowed for an outcome analysis, as used exclusively in most earlier studies on Bayesian inference, whereas data type (b) allowed additionally for a process analysis. . . .

We classified an inferential process as a Bayesian algorithm only if (a) the estimated probability or frequency was exactly the same as the value calculated from applying Bayes' theorem to the information given (outcome criterion), and (b) the on-line protocol specified that one of the Bayesian computations defined by Equations 1 through 3 or one (or several) of the Bayesian shortcut algorithms was used, either by means of calculation or pictorial representation (process criterion). We applied the same strict criteria to identify non-Bayesian cognitive algorithms. . . .

Statistical reasoning often involves pictorial representations as well as computations. Neither are easily expressed verbally, as in "think aloud" methods. Pictorial representations and computations consequently are usually expressed by drawing and writing down equations and calculations. We designed a "write aloud" technique for tracking the reasoning process without asking the participant to talk aloud either during or after the task.

The "write aloud" method consisted of the following steps. First, participants were instructed to record their reasoning unless merely guessing the answer. We explained that a protocol may contain a variety of elements, such as diagrams, pictures, calculations, or whatever other tools one may use to find a solution. Each problem was on a separate page, which thus allowed ample space for notes, drawings, and calculations. Second, after a participant had completed a problem, he or she was asked to indicate whether the answer was based on a calculation or on a guess. Third, when a "write aloud" protocol was unreadable or the process that generated the probability estimate was unclear, and the participant had indicated that the given result was a calculation, then he or she was interviewed about the particular problem after completing all tasks. This happened only a few times. If a participant could not immediately identify what his or her notes meant, we did not inquire further.

The "write aloud" method avoids two problems associated with retrospective verbal reports: that memory of the cognitive algorithms used may have faded by the time of a retrospective report (Ericsson & Simon, 1984) and the participants may have reported how they believe they ought to have thought rather than how they actually thought (Nisbett & Wilson, 1977).

We used the twin criteria of outcome and process to cross-check outcome by process and vice versa. The outcome criterion prevents a shortcut algorithm from being classified as a Bayesian algorithm when the precondition for the shortcut is not optimally satisfied. The process criterion protects against the opposite error, that of inferring from a probability judgement that a person actually used a Bayesian algorithm when he or she did not.

We designed two studies to identify the cognitive algorithms and test the predictions. Study 1 was designed to test Predictions 1, 2, and 3. (Gigerenzer and Hoffrage, 1995, p. 692; italics added)

Study 1: Information Format

Gigerenzer and Hoffrage (1995) present their intensive research on the relationship between information representation (formats and menus) and Bayesian reasoning in the following section.

We used two formats, probability and frequency, and two menus, standard and short. The two formats were crossed with the two menus, so four versions were constructed for each problem. There were 15 problems, including the mammography problem (Eddy, 1982; see [Table 7.1]), the cab problem (Tversky & Kahneman, 1982), and a short version of Ajzen's (1977) economics problem. The four versions of each problem were constructed in the same way as explained before with the mammography problem (see [Table 7.1]). In the frequency format, participants were always asked to estimate the frequency of "h out of d"; in the probability format, they were always asked to estimate the probability p(H|D). [Table 7.2] shows for each of the 15 problems the information given in the standard frequency format; the information specified in the other three versions can be derived from that. . . .

Prediction 1: Frequency formats elicit a substantially higher proportion of Bayesian algorithms than probability formats. Do frequency formats foster Bayesian reasoning? Yes. Frequency formats elicited a substantially higher proportion of Bayesian algorithms than probability formats: 46% in the standard menu and 50% in the short menu. Probability formats, in contrast, elicited 16% and 28%, for the standard menu and short menu, respectively. These proportions of Bayesian algorithms were obtained by the strict joint criteria of process and problems. Note that 50% Bayesian algorithms means 50% of all answers, and not just of those answers where a cognitive algorithm could be identified.

Table 7.2
Information Given and Bayesian Solutions of the 15 Problems in Study 1

Task: Estimate p(H|D)		Information (standard frequency format)[a]						Bayes[b]
H	D	H		D|H		D|H̄		p(H|D)
Breast cancer	Mammography positive	10	1,000	8	10	95	990	7.77
Prenatal damage in child	German measles in mother	21	10,000	10	21	50	10,000	16.70
Blue cab	Eyewitness says blue	15	100	12	15	17	85	41.38
AIDS	HIV test positive	100	1,000,000	100	100	1,000	1,000,000	9.09
Heroin addict	Fresh needle prick	10	100,000	10	10	190	100,000	5.00
Pregnant	Pregnancy test positive	20	1,000	19	20	5	980	79.17
Car accident	Driver drunk	100	10,000	55	100	500	9,900	9.91
Bad posture in child	Heavy books carried daily	50	1,000	20	50	190	950	9.52
Accident on the way to school	Child lives in an urban area	30	1,000	27	30	388	970	6.51
Committing suicide	Professor	240	1,000,000	36	240	120,000	1,000,000	0.03
Red ball	Marked with star	400	500	300	400	25	100	92.31
Choosing course in economics	Career oriented	300	1,000	210	300	350	700	37.50
Active feminist	Bank teller	5,000	100,000	20	5,000	2,000	95,000	0.99
Pimp	Wearing a Rolex	50	1,000,000	40	50	500	1,000,000	7.41
Admission to school	Particular placement test result	360	1,000	270	360	128	640	67.84

Notes: [a]The representation of the information is shown only for the standard frequency format (frequency format and standard menu). The other representations (see Table 7.1) can be derived from this. The two numbers for each piece of information are connected by an "out of" relation; for example, the information concerning H in the first problem should read as "10 out of 1,000." [b]Probabilities are expressed as percentages.

Source: Gigerenzer, G., and Hoffrage, U. (1995). How to improve Bayesian reasoning without instruction: Frequency formats. *Psychological Review, 102 (4),* p. 693. Copyright © 1995 by the American Psychological Association. Adapted with permission.

The percentage of identifiable cognitive algorithms across all formats and menus was 84%. . . .

The individual problems mirror the general result. For each problem, the standard probability format elicited the smallest proportion of Bayesian algorithms. Across formats and menus, in every problem, Bayesian algorithms were the most frequent. . . .

Prediction 2: Probability formats elicit a larger proportion of Bayesian algorithms for the short menu than for the standard menu. The percentages of Bayesian algorithms in probability formats were 16% and 28% for the standard menu and the short menu, respectively. Prediction 2 holds for each of the 15 problems. . . .

Prediction 3: The proportion of Bayesian algorithms elicited by the frequency format is independent of the menu. The effect of the menu largely, but not completely, disappeared in the frequency format. The short menu elicited 3.7 percentage points more Bayesian algorithms than the standard menu. The residual superiority of the short menu could have the following cause: Result 2 (attentional demands) states that in natural sampling it is sufficient for an organism to monitor either the frequencies d&h and d or d&h and d&-h. We have chosen the former pair for the short menus in our studies and thus reduced the Bayesian computation by one step, that of adding up d&h and d&-h to d, which was part of the Bayesian computation in the standard but not the short menu. This additional computational step is consistent with the small difference in the proportions of Bayesian algorithms found between the two menus in frequency formats.

How does the impact of format on Bayesian reasoning compare with that of menu? The effect of the format was about three times larger than that of the menu (29.9 and 21.6 percentage points difference compared with 12.1 and 3.7). Equally striking, the largest percentage of Bayesian algorithms in the two probability menus (28%) was considerably smaller than the smallest in the two frequency menus (46%). . . .

Summary of Study 1

The standard probability format—the information representation used in most earlier studies—elicited 16% Bayesian algorithms. When information was presented in a frequency format, this proportion jumped to 46% in the standard menu and 50% in the short menu. The results of study 1 are consistent with Predictions 1, 2, and 3. Frequency formats, in contrast to probability formats, "invite" Bayesian algorithms, a result that is consistent with the computational simplicity of Bayesian algorithms entailed by frequency. (Gigerenzer and Hoffrage, 1995, p. 695; italics added)

Cognitive Algorithms for Probability Formats

In the following study, Gigerenzer and Hoffrage (1995) focus on the relationship between formats and probabilistic reasoning in an effort to clarify the findings of previous research concerning base rate neglect.

In this study we concentrated on probability and relative frequency rather than on frequency formats. Thus, in this study, we explored cognitive algorithms in the two formats used by almost all previous studies on base rate neglect. Our goal was to test Prediction 4 and to provide another test of Prediction 2.

We used two formats, probability and relative frequency, and three menus: standard, short, and hybrid. The hybrid menu displayed p(H), p(D|H), and p(D), or the respective relative frequencies. The first two pieces come from the standard menu, the third from the short menu. With the probability format and the hybrid menu, a Bayesian algorithm amounts to solving the following equation:

$$p(H|D) = \frac{p(H)p(D|H)}{p(D)} \tag{4}$$

The two formats and the three menus were mathematically interchangeable and always entailed the same posterior probability. However, the Bayesian algorithm for the short menu is computationally simpler than that for the standard menu, and the hybrid menu is in between; therefore the proportion of Bayesian algorithms should increase from the standard to the hybrid to the short menu (extended Prediction 2). In contrast, the Bayesian algorithms for the probability and relative frequency formats are computationally equivalent; therefore there should be no differences between these two formats (Prediction 4). . . .

We used 24 problems, half from Study 1 and the other half new. For each of the 24 problems, the information was presented in three menus, which resulted in a total of 72 tasks. Each participant performed all 72 tasks. We randomly assigned half of the problems to the probability format and half to the relative frequency format; each participant thus answered half the problems in each format. All probabilities and relative frequencies were stated in percentages. The questions were always posed in terms of single-event probabilities. . . .

The procedure was the same in Study 1, except that we had participants do an even larger number of inference problems and that we did not use the "write aloud" instruction. However, participants could (and did) spontaneously "write aloud." After a student had completed all 72 tasks, he or she received a new booklet. This contained copies of a sample of 6 tasks the student had worked on, showing the student's probability estimates, notes, drawings, calculations, and so forth. Attached to each task was a questionnaire in which the student was asked, "Which information did you use for your estimates?" and "How did you derive your estimate from the information? Please describe this process as precisely as you can." Thus, in Study 2, we only had limited "write aloud" protocols and after-the-fact interviews available. . . .

We could identify cognitive algorithms in 67% of the 1,080 probability judgements. . . .

Prediction 4: Relative frequency formats elicit the same (small) proportion of Bayesian algorithms as probability formats. [Results] show that the number of Bayesian algorithms is not larger for the relative frequency format (60) than for the probability format (66). Consistent with Prediction 4, the numbers are about the same. More generally, Bayesian and non-Bayesian algorithms were spread about equally between the two formats. Therefore, we do not distinguish probability and relative frequency formats in our further analysis.

Prediction 2 (extended to three menus): The proportion of Bayesian algorithms elicited by the probability format is lowest for the standard menu, followed in ascending order by the hybrid and short menus. Study 2 allows for a second test of Prediction 2, now with three menus. Bayesian algorithms almost doubled from the standard to the hybrid menu and almost tripled in the short menu. . . .

Summary of Study 2

Our theoretical results were that the computational complexity of Bayesian algorithms varied between the three probability menus, but not between the probability and relative frequency formats. Empirical tests showed that the actual proportion of Bayesian algorithms followed this pattern; the proportion strongly increased across menus but did not differ between the probability and the relative frequency formats, which is consistent with Predictions 2 and 4. (Gigerenzer and Hoffrage, 1995, pp. 695–697)

General Discussion

In the following paragraph, Gigerenzer and Hoffrage (1995) conclude that the human mind is tuned not to sophisticated Bayesian inference but to specific algorithms tuned to specific frequency formats. Previous research had neglected the distinction and had, inappropriately, relied on the mathematical equivalence of the two formats, overlooking the need for a concrete match between algorithm and format. Finally, a frequency format fits practical evolutionary adaptation, and sophisticated Bayesian inference does not.

We return to our initial question: Is the mind, by design, predisposed against performing Bayesian inference? The conclusion of 25 years of heuristics-and-biases research would suggest as much. This previous research, however, has consistently neglected Feynman's (1967) insight that mathematically equivalent information formats need not be psychologically equivalent. An evolutionary point of view suggests that the mind is tuned to frequency formats, which is the information format humans encountered long before the advent of probability theory. We have combined Feynman's insight with the evolutionary argument and explored the computational implications: "Which computations are required for Bayesian inference by a given information format and menu?" Mathematically equivalent representations of information can entail computationally different Bayesian algorithms. We have argued that information representation affects cognitive algorithms in the same way. We deduced four novel predictions concerning when information formats and menus make a difference and when they do not. Data from more than 2,800 individual problem solutions are consistent with the predictions. Frequency formats made many participants' inferences strictly conform (in terms of outcome and process) to Bayes' theorem without any teaching or instruction. These results were found for a number of inferential problems, including classic demonstrations of non-Bayesian inference such as the cab problem (Bar-Hillel, 1980; Tversky & Kahneman, 1982) and the mammography problem (Eddy, 1982).

The results of the 15 problems in Study 1 constitute most of the data available today about Bayesian inference with frequency information. We know of only a few studies that have looked at Bayesian inference through frequency formats. Christensen-Szalanski and Beach (1982) sequentially presented symptom and disease information for 100 patients and asked participants to estimate p (disease/positive). Thus, their format was mixed: natural sampling of frequencies with a single-event probability judgment (see also Gavanski & Hui, 1992). The means from the natural sampling condition conformed better to Bayes' theorem than those from the standard probability version; however, only means—and not individual judgments or processes—were analyzed. Cosmides and

Tooby (1996) constructed a dozen or so versions of the medical problem presented by Casscells et al. (1978). They converted, piece by piece, probability information into frequencies and showed how this increases, in the same pace, the proportion of Bayesian answers. They reported that when the frequency was mixed—that is, when the information was represented in frequencies, but the single-point estimate was a single-event probability, or vice versa—the effect of the frequency format was reduced by roughly half. Their results are consistent with our theoretical framework.

At the beginning of this article, we contrasted the belief of the Enlightenment probabilists that the laws of probability theory were the laws of the mind (at least for *hommes éclairés*) with the belief of the proponents of the heuristics-and-biases program that the laws of probability are not the laws of the mind. We side with neither view, nor with those who have settled somewhere in between the two extremes. Both views are based on an incomplete analysis: They focus on cognitive algorithms, good or bad, without making the connection between an algorithm and the information format it has been designed for. (Gigerenzer and Hoffrage, 1995, pp. 697–698)

ECOLOGICAL AND EVOLUTIONARY APPROACHES TO BAYESIAN REASONING

Baconian Probability: Weight of Evidence

Whereas 25 years of cognitive psychology research concerned with people's deviation from a Bayesian calculus of probability has led to a conclusion of mental limitation in Bayesian reasoning—that subjects do not conform to subjective probability of the Bayesian calculus—it may be that subjects unschooled in matters of statistical inference may be using ecologically valid, evolutionarily determined, cognitive mechanisms that register frequency of favorable and unfavorable results in a series of experiences and that this automatic unconscious cognitive mechanism gives rise to a subjective estimate of confidence that is a weighted consequence of judgment concerning what has happened or may have occurred as in the establishment of probable cause or expected likely future outcome.

Baconian probability depends on a frequentistic concept of probability, the processing of frequency information by evolved cognitive mechanisms, and the report in working memory of a weighted-evidence confidence judgment. The formulation that has just been presented has been investigated in a series of experiments by Cosmides and Tooby (1996). Their theory, research, and implications will be presented and, then, a brief commentary will be offered.

Ecological Probability and Its Frequentistic Foundation: Overview

Cosmides and Tooby (1996) present the following cogent précis of their research.

Professional probabilists have long argued over what probability means, with, for example, Bayesians arguing that probabilities refer to subjective degrees of confidence and frequentists arguing that probabilities refer to the frequencies of events in the world. Recently, Gigerenzer and his colleagues have argued that these same distinctions are made by untutored subjects, and that, for many domains, the human mind represents probabilistic information as frequencies. We analyze several reasons why, from an ecological and evolutionary perspective, certain classes of problem-solving mechanisms in the human mind should be expected to represent probabilistic information as frequencies. Then, using a problem famous in the "heuristics and biases" literature for eliciting base rate neglect, we show that correct Bayesian reasoning can be elicited in 76% of subjects—indeed, 92% in the most ecologically valid condition—simply by expressing the problem in frequentist terms. This result adds to the growing body of literature showing that frequentist representations cause various cognitive biases to disappear, including overconfidence, the conjunction fallacy, and base-rate neglect. Taken together, these new findings indicate that the conclusion most common in the literature on judgement under uncertainty—that our inductive reasoning mechanisms do not embody a calculus of probability—will have to be reexamined. From an ecological and evolutionary perspective, humans may turn out to be good intuitive statisticians after all. (Cosmides and Tooby, 1996, p. 1)

Ecological Probability and Its Frequentistic Foundation: Basic Concepts

In the following section, Cosmides and Tooby (1996) argue that since there is evidence for statistical inference in the adaptive behavior of lower organisms, it is plausible to hypothesize that evolutionarily determined mechanisms achieving Bayesian reasoning exist in people as well.

Behavioral ecologists who study foraging have found evidence of very sophisticated statistical reasoning in organisms with nervous systems that are considerably simpler than our own, such as certain birds and insects (e.g., Real, 1991; Real & Caraco, 1986). Moreover, John Staddon (1988) has argued that in animals from sea snails to humans, the learning mechanisms responsible for habituation, sensitization, classical conditioning and operant conditioning can be formally described as Bayesian inference machines.

This evidence suggests that bird brains and insect minds are capable of performing statistical calculations that some psychologists have assumed human brains are "too limited" to perform. But if a bird brain can embody a calculus of probability, why couldn't a human brain embody one as well? We are not arguing here that humans *must* have well-designed mechanisms for statistical inference—we are merely arguing that the prevailing arguments for why we should *not* have such mechanisms are not substantial. As long as chance has been loose in the world, animals have had to make judgements under uncertainty. If an adaptive problem has endured for a long enough period, and is important enough, then mechanisms of considerable complexity can evolve to solve it. When seen in this light, the hypothesis that humans have inductive reasoning mechanisms that embody a calculus of probability, just like other organisms do, doesn't seem so intrinsically improbable. . . . In short, in contrast to the standard view that the human cognitive architecture does not embody either a calculus of probability or effective statistical completeness, we suggest that the human mind may contain a series of well-engineered competencies capable of being activated under the right conditions, and that a frequentist competence is prominent among these. . . .

Suppose people do have reliably developing mechanisms that allow them to apply a calculus of probability, but that these mechanisms are "frequentist": they are designed to accept probabilistic information when it is in the form of a frequency, and to produce a frequency as their output. Let us then suppose that experimental psychologists present subjects with problems that ask for the "probability" of a single event, rather than a frequency, as output, and that present the information necessary to solve the problem in a format that is not obviously a frequency. Subjects' answers to such problems would not appear to have been generated by a calculus of probability, even though they have mechanisms designed to do just that.

One way to see if this is the case is to compare performance on tests that ask for the probability of a single event to similar tasks that ask for the answer as a frequency. "Errors" that are reliably elicited by the single-event task should disappear on the frequency task.

That seems to be just what happens (for review, see Gigerenzer, 1991). For example, Klaus Fiedler (1988) showed that the "conjunction fallacy" virtually disappears when subjects are asked for frequencies rather than single-event probabilities (see [Table 7.3]). Whereas 70–80% of subjects commit the conjunction fallacy when asked for the probability of single events, 70–80% of the subjects *do not* commit the conjunction fallacy when asked for relative frequencies (a finding for which there is also evidence in Tversky & Kahneman's [1983] original study).

The same manipulation can also cause the "overconfidence bias" to disappear. "Overconfidence" is usually defined as a discrepancy between one's degree of belief (confidence) in a single event and the relative frequency with which events of that class occur. But such a discrepancy is not a violation of frequentist theories of probability. When one compares subjects' judged frequencies with actual frequencies, as Gigerenzer, Hoffrage, and Kleinbölting (1991) did, "overconfidence" disappears; subjects' judgements turn out to be quite accurate. According to their *probabilistic mental model* theory, one's confidence in a single answer is an estimate of the ecological validity of the cues used in providing that answer, not an estimate of the long-run relative frequency of correct answers. Indeed, by assuming that people accurately encode and store frequency information from the environment, Gigerenzer et al.'s theory allowed them to predictably elicit well-calibrated performance, overestimation, or underestimation, depending on whether the questions asked were a random sample from the subjects' reference class, selected to be difficult, or selected to be easy.

This result fits well with the literature on automatic frequency encoding. One would expect an organism that relies on frequency information in making judgements under uncertainty to be constantly picking up such information from the environment in a way that does not interfere with the organism's ongoing activities. Hasher, Zacks, and colleagues have found evidence for just such a mechanism. People encode frequency information very accurately, and they appear to do so automatically. Their performance on frequency discrimination tasks is unaffected by the kinds of factors that affect more "effortful" processes, such as free recall. For example, frequency performance is not hindered by competing task demands, it is not affected by the amount or appropriateness of practice, and it is not affected by the accuracy of the subject's test expectations. Moreover, there are no stable individual differences in performance, and second-graders

Table 7.3
Single-Event and Frequency Versions of Fiedler's (1988) Conjunction Problems

Single-Event Version	Frequency Version
Linda is 31 years old, single, outspoken and very bright. She majored in philosophy. As a student, she was deeply concerned with issues of discrimination and social justice, and also participated in anti-nuclear demonstrations.	Linda is 31 years old, single, outspoken and very bright. She majored in philosophy. As a student, she was deeply concerned with issues of discrimination and social justice, and also participated in anti-nuclear demonstrations. To how many out of 100 people who are like Linda do the following statements apply?
Please rank order the following statements with respect to their probability:	
	Linda is a bank teller
Linda is a bank teller	Linda is a bank teller and active in the feminist movement
Linda is a bank teller and active in the feminist movement	

Note: For both versions, several other statements had to be judged as well (e.g., "Linda is a psychiatric social worker"), but the crucial comparison is between the two statements listed above. For any two categories, A and B, instances of A should be judged more frequent than instances of A & B. In the above case, there are more bank tellers than there are bank tellers who are feminists because the category "bank tellers" includes both feminists and nonfeminists.

Source: Cosmides, L., and Tooby, J. (1996). Are humans good intuitive statisticians after all? Rethinking some conclusions from the literature on judgement under uncertainty. Reprinted from *Cognition, 58*, p. 19, copyright 1996, with permission from Elsevier Science.

do just as well as adults: just what one would expect of a reliably developing, automatic mechanism (see Alba, Chromiak, Hasher, & Attig, 1980; Attig & Hasher, 1980; Hasher & Chromiak, 1977; Hasher & Zacks, 1979; Hintzman & Stern, 1978; Zacks, Hasher, & Sanft, 1982). (Cosmides and Tooby, 1996, pp. 18–20)

The Medical Diagnosis Problem: Experimental Rationale and Results

Cosmides and Tooby (1996) conducted several experiments using the classical medical diagnosis problem in order to test their general hypothesis that frequentist versions of the problem can dramatically improve subjects' reasoning performance. The general background, rationale, and results of these experiments are summarized in the following section.

The mounting evidence that people are good "intuitive statisticians" when they are given frequencies as input and asked for frequencies as output, suggests that the issue of whether our inductive reasoning mechanisms embody a calculus of probability should be reopened. To this end, we conducted a particularly strong test of Gigerenzer's hypothesis that our inductive reasoning mechanisms were designed to operate on and to output frequency representations (henceforth called the "frequentist hypothesis"). We conducted a series of experiments to see whether casting a single-event probability problem in frequentist terms would elicit [B]ayesian reasoning. If it does, then the conclusion that our inductive reasoning mechanisms do not embody a calculus of probability—that they consist of nothing more than a few quick-and-dirty rules-of-thumb—will have to be re-examined.

The Medical Diagnosis Problem

If a test to detect a disease whose prevalence is 1/1000 had a false positive rate of 5%, what is the chance that a person found to have a positive result actually has the disease, assuming that you know nothing about the person's symptoms or signs? ____%

The above reasoning problem is called the medical diagnosis problem, and it was designed to assess whether people engage in [B]ayesian reasoning. It is famous in the literature on judgment under uncertainty for eliciting base rate neglect even from technically educated subjects. Casscells et al. (1978) asked a group of faculty, staff and fourth-year students at Harvard Medical School to solve this problem. Only 18% of them answered "2%," which is the correct [B]ayesian number under most interpretations of the problem. Forty-five percent of them answered "95%." Because "95%" is inconsistent with a population base rate for the disease of 1 in 1000, Casscells et al. concluded that their subjects were violating Bayes' theorem by ignoring the base rate. The usual explanation for base rate neglect is the operation of a representativeness heuristic, but this cannot account for base rate neglect in the medical diagnosis problem (Tversky & Kahneman, 1982, p. 154). Accordingly, Tversky & Kahneman use the results of Casscells et al.'s study to make the point that judgmental biases are widespread and difficult to eradicate:

Evidently, even highly educated respondents often fail to appreciate the significance of outcome base rate in relatively simple formal problems. . . . The strictures of Meehl and Rosen (1955) regarding the failure to appreciate base rates are not limited to clinical psychologists; they apply to physicians and other people as well. (Tversky & Kahneman, 1982, p. 154)

Physicians are taught statistics so that they will know how to evaluate diagnostic test results of the kind presented in the medical diagnosis problem. If even they fail to use a calculus of probability, then it seems compelling to argue that the human mind does not embody one.

We wanted to stand this experimental logic on its head. We chose the medical diagnosis problem for our experiments precisely because it had elicited such low levels of correct [B]ayesian reasoning *even* from statistically educated subjects. We wanted to see what would happen if the same problem were posed in frequentist terms—that is, if the problem information was presented as frequencies and the answer was asked for as a frequency. Could a frequentist version of the medical diagnosis problem elicit correct [B]ayesian reasoning "even" from undergraduates, most of whom have had little or no training in statistics? That would be strong evidence for the hypothesis that we do have mechanisms that embody some aspects of a calculus of probability, but that frequency representations are their natural format.

The remainder of this article is divided into three parts. In Part I we show that very high levels of [B]ayesian reasoning are elicited by frequentist versions of the medical diagnosis problem. In Part II, we show that simply clarifying non-frequentist versions of the problem does *not* produce these high levels of [B]ayesian reasoning. In Part III, we successively eliminate various elements of the frequentist problem to determine which are critical for producing high levels of [B]ayesian reasoning, and show that the crucial elements are (1) asking for the answer as a frequency rather than as a single-event probability, and (2) presenting the problem information as frequencies. . . .

In short, all the predictions of the frequentist hypothesis were confirmed: (1) inductive reasoning performance differed depending on whether subjects were asked to judge a frequency or the probability of a single event; (2) performance on frequentist versions of problems was superior to non-frequentist versions; (3) the more subjects could be mobilized to form a frequentist representation, the better their performance was; and (4) performance on frequentist problems satisfied those constraints of a calculus of probability that we tested for (i.e., Bayes' rule). Taken together, the results of Parts I–III support the hypothesis that frequentist representations activate mechanisms that produce [B]ayesian reasoning, and that this is what accounts for the very high levels of [B]ayesian performance elicited by the pure frequentist problems that we tested. (Cosmides and Tooby, 1996, pp. 21–22, 59)

Evolutionary Theory and Cognitive Mechanisms

Cosmides and Tooby (1996) conclude their research on the general hypothesis that the mind does possess a frequentist mechanism that provides a substrate to evolutionary adaptive decision making in the following account.

If the body of results indicating well-calibrated statistical performance continues to grow, then a new analytic framework may be required to organize and explain the literature on judgment under uncertainty (see, for example, Gigerenzer, 1991; Gigerenzer & Murray, 1987; Tooby & Cosmides, 1992). Highly organized, well-calibrated performance cannot occur in the absence of well-designed cognitive mechanisms, so any new analytic framework must admit and explain the existence of such mechanisms. The evolutionary-functional framework proposed by Marr is particularly promising: one looks for a mesh between the nature of the adaptive problem to be solved and the design of the algorithms and representations that evolved to solve it. Mathematics and evolutionary biology provide a broad assortment of alternative normative theories of statistical inference, appropriate to different kinds of adaptive problems. These can help one discover what cognitive processes govern inductive reasoning in various domains, and why they have the functional design they do. By locating functionality in its evolutionary and ecological context, performance that had previously looked erratic and erroneous may begin to look orderly and sophisticated.

It may be time to return to a more Laplacian view, and grant human intuition a little more respect than it has recently been receiving. The evolved mechanisms that undergird our intuitions have been subjected to millions of years of field testing against a very rich and complexly structured environment. With only a few hundred years of normative theorizing under our belts, there may still be aspects of real-world statistical problems that have escaped us. Of course, no system will be completely error-free, even under natural conditions. But when intuition and probability theory appear to clash, it would

Table 7.4
Cognitive Mechanisms and Adaptive Problems

Cognitive Function	Reference
Language acquisition	Pinker & Bloom (1990)
Representation and perception of the motion of objects	Shepard (1984); Freyd (1987)
Reasoning differentially about people's mental states versus physical objects	Atran (1990); Baron-Cohen (1994); Leslie (1987); Carey & Gelman (1991)
Cordical representation of speech	Mazoyer, Tzourio, Frak, Syrota, Murayama, Levrier, Salamon, Dehaene, Cohen, & Mehler (1993)
Memory processing	Petrides, Alivisatos, Evans, and Meyer (1993)
Acquisition and retrieval of verbal episodic memory	Shallice, Fletcher, Frith, Grasby, Fracowiak, and Dolan (1994)
Brain basis of theory of mind	Baron-Cohen, Ring, Moriarty, Schmitz, Costa, and Ell (1994)
Figurative aspects of language	Bottini, Corcoran, Sterzi, Paulesu, Schenone, Scarpa, Frackowiak, and Frith (1994)

seem both logical and prudent to at least consider the possibility that there may be a sophisticated logic to the intuition. We may discover that humans are good intuitive statisticians after all. (Cosmides and Tooby, 1996, pp. 68–69)

COMMENTARY

In recent decades, cognitive neural science has identified many brain structures that provide specific adaptive mechanisms for an impressively wide array of adaptive behaviors. So it may be that the cognitive mechanism for a frequentistic competence hypothesized by Cosmides and Tooby (1996) will also be mapped.

Table 7.4 illustrates the domain-specific cognitive mechanisms that have been identified in the literature.

8

Syllogistic Reasoning

SYLLOGISTIC REASONING AND MODES OF REPRESENTATION

The Affinity of Syllogistic Reasoning Problems to Mathematical Problems

Syllogistic reasoning problems can be viewed as a subset of mathematical problems with respect to mode of representation, method of solution, and logical validity criteria. The syllogistic problem is a subset because unlike the great variety of mathematical problems, syllogisms are restricted to a pair of verbally stated premises containing terms with two value quantifiers (universal-particular) and two value signs (negative-affirmative). As in the case of mathematical problems, syllogistic problems can depend for their solution on graphical or linguistic (including symbolic) representation and on the application of specific operations that meet the constraints of valid deduction. In mathematics, the specific operation of substitution of terms is a familiar and powerful problem-solving mechanism. In syllogistic problems, the substitution operation is equally powerful.

Two Theories of Syllogistic Reasoning: Overview

Aristotle included in his *De Anima* a tract on the dicology of syllogistic reasoning, including its theory and practice in political and legal argumentation. It was not, however, until the emergence of experimental psychology that scientific studies of syllogistic reasoning could be undertaken. The voluminous literature developed during the twentieth century made use of a broad variety of theories and methods. In recent decades, the mental model theory of Johnson-Laird has achieved prominence. This theory, with its formal annotations and computational modeling, has been challenged by Ford (1995) whose theory and method are informal and based on thinking-aloud protocols for people as they engage in solving or failing to solve syllogistic reasoning problems.

In this paper, the theory of syllogistic reasoning proposed by Johnson-Laird (1983, 1986; Johnson-Laird & Bara, 1984; Johnson-Laird & Byrne, 1991) is shown to be inadequate and an alternative theory is put forward. Protocols of people attempting to solve syllogistic problems and explaining to another person how they reached their conclusions were obtained. Two main groups of subjects were identified. One group represented the relationship between classes in a spatial manner that was supplemented by a verbal representation. The other group used a primarily verbal representation. A detailed theory of the processes for both groups is given. (Ford, 1995, p. 1)

Syllogisms: Easy and Hard

In the following section, Ford (1995) presents two examples of syllogism problems: one readily solved and one barely solved.

One of the things that has fascinated psychologists about syllogisms is the fact that while some are very easy to solve others appear to be extraordinarily difficult. Consider the syllogism given in (1).

(1)   None of the atheists are bankers
       All of the bankers are chessplayers

Hardly anyone solves this particular type of syllogism. Most people, according to Johnson-Laird (1986; Johnson-Laird & Bara, 1984; Johnson-Laird & Byrne, 1991), conclude that "None of the atheists are chessplayers" or, conversely, "None of the chessplayers are atheists". The correct conclusion is "Some of the chessplayers are not atheists". In contrast, virtually everyone solves the type of syllogism given in (2).

(2)   Some of the atheists are bankers
       All of the bankers are chessplayers

The correct conclusion for (2) is "Some of the atheists are chessplayers" or its converse "Some of the chessplayers are atheists." (Ford, 1995, pp. 1–2)

Syllogisms: Moods and Figures

In the following section, Ford (1995) presents the set of syllogism moods and figures.

On the face of it, the difference in difficulty between syllogisms seems quite remarkable because all 64 forms of possible syllogisms contain two of the only four different types of premises. These four types of premises (or moods) are given in (3).

(3) All of the Xs are Ys
    Some of the Xs are Ys
    None of the Xs are Ys
    Some of the Xs are not Ys

For any syllogism, the two premises contain a term in common and another term that is distinct for the two premises. Accordingly, there are only four "figures" in which a syllogism can occur. These are given in (4), where B represents the common term and A and C represent the distinct terms.

(4)	Figure 1	Figure 2	Figure 3	Figure 4
	A – B	B – A	A – B	B – A
	B – C	C – B	C – B	B – C

(Ford, 1995, p. 2)

Syllogisms: Some Theories of the Reasoning Process

Theories of the reasoning process in syllogistic problems are summarized in the following section.

Presumably, the differences in difficulty between syllogisms are due to our reasoning processes. Several theories of reasoning processes have thus been put forward to account for the data. Johnson-Laird and Bara (1984) criticized existing hypotheses, such as the atmosphere hypothesis (e.g., Begg & Denny, 1969; Woodworth & Sells, 1935; Woodworth & Schlosberg, 1954), the conversion hypothesis (e.g., Chapman & Chapman, 1959; Revlis, 1975), the transitive-chain theory (Guyote & Sternberg, 1981), and theories based on Euler circles (Erickson, 1974, 1978). Johnson-Laird and Bara put forward their own theory which grew out of work carried out over a number of years by Johnson-Laird and his colleagues (Johnson-Laird, 1975, 1980, 1982, 1983; Johnson-Laird & Steedman, 1978; Wason & Johnson-Laird, 1972). Johnson-Laird and Byrne (1991) updated their theory slightly, giving a different annotation for representing premises. While Johnson-Laird and his colleagues claim that their theory accounts for performance in making syllogistic inferences, and while it seems to have somewhat wide acceptance (e.g., Burton & Radford, 1991; Darley, Glucksberg, & Kinchla, 1988; Lee & Oakhill, 1978) there are a number of problems with the work. The present paper gives a critique of the work and reports on a study which suggests a quite different view of reasoning processes. For a review of Johnson-Laird's (1983) work on mental models see Ford (1985). (Ford, 1995, pp. 2–3)

Ford's Critique of the Johnson-Laird Theory of Syllogistic Reasoning

In the following section, Ford (1995) presents a description and critique of the Johnson-Laird view of the nature of syllogistic reasoning.

At the heart of Johnson-Laird's work (Johnson-Laird & Bara, 1984; Johnson-Laird & Byrne, 1991) is the belief that what underlies rational thought is not formal rules of logic but the ability to construct, manipulate, and evaluate mental models. It will be shown that the mental representations assumed in the theory are inadequate to account for reasoning performance and that reasoning processes are quite different from those proposed. Moreover, it will be shown that it is wrong to group all people together as though they basically reason in the same fashion.

When Johnson-Laird and his colleagues talk of mental models, they have a particular kind of representation in mind. Mental models, in their sense, are mental representations that are computable, finite, and contain sets of elements that are related in some way to some other sets of elements. They are "structural analogues of the world" (Johnson-Laird, 1983, p. 165), having "a structure that corresponds directly to the structure of the state of affairs that the discourse describes" (Johnson-Laird, 1983, p. 125). A mental model is "an internal tableau containing elements that stand for the members of sets" (Johnson-Laird, 1983, p. 97). A mental model contains "one finite set of individual tokens mapped into another" (Johnson-Laird, 1983, p. 125). The representations that Johnson-Laird & Bara and Johnson-Laird & Byrne give for the four types of premises used in syllogisms are given in the left and right hand columns of (5)–(8), respectively.

(5)   All of the Xs are Ys   X = Y   [X] Y
                                     X = Y   [X] Y
                                       0Y   . . .
(6)   Some of the Xs are Ys   X = Y   X Y
                                     X = Y   X Y
                                     0X 0Y   . . .
(7)   None of the Xs are Ys   X   [X]
                                     X   [X]
                                     ‾
                                     Y   [Y]
                                     Y   [Y]
                                                  . . .
(8)   Some of the Xs are not Ys X   X
                                     X   X
                                     ‾‾‾
                                     0X   Y   X   [Y]
                                          Y   [Y]
                                                  . . .

The zero sign in the left hand representations indicates an uncertainty as to whether or not the relevant individual exists. Thus, for example, in (5), the 0Y indicates that it is uncertain whether a Y that is not an X exists. In the right hand representations, the square brackets indicate that a set has been exhaustively represented. Thus, for example, in (5), X can only occur in the presence of Y. The three dots allow for other sorts of individuals not yet made explicit. For both representations, the exact number of Xs and Ys is irrelevant.

Let's consider the theory in detail by considering syllogism (1), and using the current notation of the theory. The premises of (1) and the mental model of both are given in (9), with the dots omitted for convenience.

(9)   None of the atheists are bankers
              [atheist]
              [atheist]

                          [banker]
                          [banker]

All of the bankers are chessplayers
        [banker]   chessplayer
        [banker]   chessplayer

Step 1. A crucial assumption of the theory is that for any syllogism that does not have a figure A − B, B − C, the reasoner first performs certain operations to make sure that the second term of the model for the first premise considered is B and that the first term of the model for the other premise is also B. This, it is claimed, makes the integration of the information in the two premises easier. Since the syllogism represented in (9) is in the figure A − B, B − C, there is no need for the reasoner to perform any operations to allow for the easy integration of the two premises. A single model of the information in the premises can be constructed immediately. One possible model is that given in (10).

(10) MODEL 1   [atheist]
                  [atheist]
                          [[banker]   chessplayer]
                          [[banker]   chessplayer]

Step 2. The model is scanned to determine the relation between the distinct terms, A and C. Given the model in (10), the reasoner could conclude "None of the atheists are chessplayers" or, conversely, "None of the chessplayers are atheists". The theory assumes that the first information put into working memory tends to be the first taken out and that the natural way to order the terms in a conclusion is the order in which they entered working memory. The former conclusion, "None of the atheists are chessplayers", would be preferred due to this, "first in, first out" principle.

Step 3. The reasoner determines whether a change can be made to the model which would refute the conclusion while not violating the two initial premises. Such a model is given in (11).

(11) MODEL 2   [atheist]
                  [atheist]   chessplayer
                          [[banker]   chessplayer]
                          [[banker]   chessplayer]

Step 4. Again, the reasoner would attempt to draw an informative conclusion relating the distinct terms. The model in (11) falsifies the conclusion drawn from (10). From (11), the reasoner could conclude that "Some of the atheists are not chessplayers" or, conversely, "Some of the chessplayers are not atheists".

Step 5. Again the reasoner would attempt to construct a model that refuted the conclusion reached in the previous step, while keeping the meaning of the initial premises intact. The model in (12) refutes the conclusion "Some of the atheists are not chessplayers".

(12) MODEL 3   [atheist]   chessplayer
                  [atheist]   chessplayer
                          [[banker]   chessplayer]
                          [[banker]   chessplayer]

Step 6. While the model in (12) rules out the conclusion "Some of the atheists are not chessplayers", it supports the conclusion "Some of the chessplayers are not atheists".

Step 7. The reasoner would attempt to develop another model of the combined premises which refuted the conclusion just reached. However, no model can be constructed which refutes the conclusion reached in step 6, and so this conclusion is accepted.

For the difficult syllogism, then, it is necessary to construct three models. It turns out that for the easy syllogism (2) only one model needs to be constructed. According to Johnson-Laird (Johnson-Laird & Bara, 1984; Johnson-Laird & Byrne, 1991), the theory correctly predicts that two main factors should affect performance on syllogistic reasoning—first, the number of models that must be constructed to represent the information in the two premises and, second, the figure of the syllogism. The greater the number of models needed to solve a syllogism, the greater the likelihood that one of the crucial models will not be considered and that an invalid conclusion will be reached. The figure of a syllogism has two effects—one concerning the preferred order of terms in a conclusion and one concerning level of difficulty.

Let's consider the figural effect, illustrated in [Figure 8.1], and described in detail by Johnson-Laird and Bara (1984, pp. 32–34). [Figure 8.1] shows what operations are required, according to Johnson-Laird and Bara, to get the terms of the models in the assumed preferred order. It is claimed that the operations become progressively more difficult moving from the figure on the left to the figure on the right. Given the "first in, first out" principle assumed in the theory, it is predicted that for the A − B, B − C figure the preferred order of terms in the conclusion should be A − C. For syllogisms with the B − A, C − B figure, the C term will be put into memory first because the model of the second premise would be considered first, thus leading to a preference for a conclusion with the terms in a C − A order. For both the A − B, C − B and the B − A, B − C figures, there are two ways to construct a mental model of the information in the two premises, with the two methods each yielding a different preferred order of terms in the conclusion and thus leading to no general preferred order for these two figures.

Although it might seem from analyses presented by Johnson-Laird and Bara (1984) and Johnson-Laird and Byrne (1991) that the major factors affecting performance on syllogisms are the figure and the number of models to be constructed, there are a number of problems which call the theory into question.

In the data Johnson-Laird and Bara (1984) present, there is one 1-model syllogism in the B − A, B − C figure where performance is exceptionally low, with no one giving the correct conclusion. Johnson-Laird and Bara attribute the poor performance to the figure of the syllogism. However, this seems unlikely as the zero score is vastly different from the two other one-model cases of the same figure, with the percentage of correct responses on these being over 50%. In fact, the zero score is more in line with the results for three-model cases. In Johnson-Laird and Byrne (1991), the syllogism is classified, without comment, as now being a three-model case. But why would a change in annotation lead to a change in the number of models required for one syllogism? In fact, there is no justification for the syllogism being classified as a three-model case. Consider (13) which presents the models of the premises for the syllogism, using the 1984 and 1991 annotations on the left and right, respectively.

(13)   All of the Bs are As   B = A   [B] A
                                  B = A   [B] A
                                   0A   . . .

Figure 8.1
The Figural Effect

Figure of Syllogism

	A – B B – C	B – A C – B	A – B C – B	B – A B – C
Operations to yield B as term 2 of the first premise considered and term 1 of the second premise considered	nothing required	build the model of premise 2 first	switch the order of the terms in the model of premise 2 OR build the model of premise 2 first, then switch the order of the terms in the model of the other premise	switch the order of the terms in the model of premise 1 OR build the model of premise 2 first, then switch the order of the terms in that model
Preferred order of terms in the conclusion	A – C	C – A	no preference	no preference
Level of difficulty	easy ──────────────────────────────────────→ difficult			

Source: Ford, M. (1995). Two modes of mental representation and problem solution in syllogistic reasoning. Reprinted from *Cognition, 54,* p. 6, copyright 1995, with permission from Elsevier Science.

    All of the Bs are Cs   B = C   [B] C
                                B = C   [B] C
                                 0C   . . .

When the terms in the model of the first premise are switched and integrated with the model of the first premise, the models in (14) are obtained.

(14)   A = B = C   A [B] C
        A = B = C   A [B] C
        0A   0C   . . .

Leaving out the irrelevant B term, the models in (15) are obtained.

(15)   A = C   A C
        A = C   A C
        0A   0C   . . .

Given the models in (5)–(8), it is quite clear that for both the 1984 and 1991 representations the correct conclusion "Some of the As are Cs" would be drawn from the one straightforwardly obtained model. For some reason, though, Johnson-Laird and Byrne present the three models illustrated in (16).

(16)   A C   A C   A C
       A C   A C   A C
                 A   C

Johnson-Laird and Byrne are apparently "fleshing out" the model obtained in (15). However, if one were to flesh out the model in (15) correctly, then four models would be obtained, the fourth being that in (17).

(17)   A
       A C
       A C
       C

In fact, though, there is no need to flesh out the one model of (15). The correct conclusion is clear from the model in (15) and there is no model that can be built which refutes the conclusion. The syllogism in question is the only one where Johnson-Laird and Byrne needlessly flesh out a model to obtain more models. Thus, for example, for a syllogism where the model obtained is [[*athlete*] *baker*] *canoeist*, they say,

It follows that one way of fleshing out the model explicitly is consistent with the set of athletes being properly included in the set of canoeists, and another way of fleshing out the model explicitly is consistent with the two sets being co-extensive. It is not necessary, however, to flesh out the model in order to draw the parsimonious conclusion:

        All of the athletes are canoeists

and there is no way of fleshing out the model to refute this conclusion: it is valid and depends on the construction of just one model. (Johnson-Laird and Byrne, 1991, p. 121)

The same can be said of the syllogism (13) and its model in (14) and (15). It should thus remain classed as a 1-model case just like the one Johnson-Laird and Byrne discuss in the given quotation.

    The second problem concerns the mental model given for one of the four forms of a premise. The premise in question is that given in (8). Both the 1984 and 1991 models of the premise are inappropriate because they imply, invalidly, that "Some of the Ys are not Xs", whereas in fact *all* of the Ys could be Xs even if some Xs are not Ys. Johnson-Laird and Byrne (1991, p. 120) note that their model "supports the converse assertion—a common fallacy—but it is falsified by constructing the alternative model [given in 18]."

(18)   X
       X
       X [Y]
       X [Y]

Similarly, you could give the model in (19) for the 1984 representation.

(19)   X
       X
       ——————
       0X Y
       0X Y

It turns out that if the representations in (8) are used, then the syllogisms with these premises are two-model cases. If the representations in (18) or (19) are used then the syllogisms are one-model cases.

A third problem concerns the "figural effect". Johnson-Laird and Bara (1984) noticed an unexplained effect for what they called the "symmetrical figures" A − B, C − B and B − A, B − C. They found that when the conclusion was in the same form as one of the premises, there was a tendency for the A or C term in the conclusion to be given in the same position as it had been in the premise of the same form. Johnson-Laird and Bara were not perturbed by the effect. But the problem raised by the effect is far greater than they assume. The problem is that *whatever is causing the effect in the symmetrical figures would also lead to a preference for A − C conclusions for syllogisms with the A − B, B − C figure and for C − A conclusions for syllogisms with the B − A, C − B figure*. That is, if the conclusion for an A − B, B − C syllogism is in the same form as one of its premises and there is a tendency to put the A or C term in the same position as it was in the premise, then an A − C conclusion will result. In the same way, there will be a preference for C − A conclusions for the B − A, C − B syllogisms. That is, the unexplained effect applies to the results for *all* of the figures not just the symmetrical figures and, moreover, it leads to the "figural effect". Johnson-Laird and Bara's account of preferred responses, which does not account for the symmetric figures anyway, is thus superfluous.

Let's consider how strong the tendency is to put an A or C term in the same position as it was in the premise that has the same form as the conclusion. It should first be pointed out that for premises that have the form "Some of the Xs are not Ys" a number of subjects seem to take this to mean "Some of the Xs are Ys." Johnson-Laird and Bara (1984) specifically classify 127 responses as dependent on this Gricean implicature, with the subjects giving inappropriate responses of the form "Some of the Xs are Ys." (Also see Grice, 1975.) It turns out that in *every* instance where responses were dependent on Gricean implicature, the A or C term in the conclusion was in the same position as it was in the premise of the form "Some of the Xs are not Ys". This was true for all four figures, leading to A − C conclusions for syllogisms with the A − B, B − C figure, C − A conclusions for syllogisms with the B − A, C − B figure, and for A − C or C − A conclusions for the symmetrical figures depending on the position of the A or

Table 8.1
Percentage of Conclusions for Each Figure with Respect to the Form of the Conclusion and the Position of the A and C Terms

Form of the conclusion and position of the A and C terms with respect to the premises	Figure of syllogism			
	A – B B – C	B – A C – B	A – B C – B	B – A B – C
	Percentage of responses in each category together with the percentage of correct responses (in parentheses)			
	n = 378	n = 326	n = 219	n = 192
Same form, same position	92.3 (27.8)	75.1 (27.8)	83.1 (32.4)	70.8 (37.5)
Same form, different position	6.1 (17.4)	22.1 (15.3)	14.6 (53.1)	26.0 (24.0)
Different form, same position	1.3 (100.0)	2.5 (100.0)	n.a.	n.a.
Different form, different position	0.3 (100.0)	0.3 (100.0)	n.a.	n.a.
Different form, position irrelevant	n.a.	n.a.	2.3 (80.0)	3.1 (83.3)

Note: The data were tabulated from examining responses to all 64 syllogisms given in the appendix of raw data by Johnson-Laird and Bara (1984).

Source: Ford, M. (1995). Two modes of mental representation and problem solution in syllogistic reasoning. Reprinted from *Cognition, 54*, p. 10, copyright 1995, with permission from Elsevier Science.

C term in the premise of the form "Some of the Xs are not Ys". Now let's consider Johnson-Laird and Bara's data for syllogisms where the Gricean implicature was irrelevant or was apparently not made.

Responses where subjects referred to A and C terms in their conclusion and where the Gricean implicature was irrelevant or not made were classified according to five categories. (1) *Same form, same position*. For these responses, the conclusion given has the same form as one of the premises, and the A or C term of the conclusion is the same position as it was in the premise. (2) *Same form, different position*. The conclusion given has the same form as one of the premises, but the A or C term is in a different position from what it was in the premis. (3) *Different form, same position*. The conclusion given has a different form from either of the premises, but the A and C terms keep their same relative positions. This category is relevant only to the non-symmetrical figures—because it is only in these cases that the A and C terms have different positions in the premises. (4) *Different form, different position*. The conclusion has a different form from either of the premises, and the A and C terms do not keep their same relative positions. Again, this is relevant only to the non-symmetrical figures. (5) *Different form, position irrelevant*. This conclusion has a different form from either of the premises. The position of the A and C terms in the conclusion is irrelevant because they both occupied the same position in both premises. This category, of course, is relevant only to the symmetrical figures. [Table 8.1] gives the percentage of responses for each figure that falls into the different categories and also gives the percentage of each of the conclusions in the different categories which were in fact correct.

Clearly, there is an overwhelming tendency to put the A or C term of the conclusion in the same position as it was in the premise of the same form. It is also clear that there is an overwhelming tendency to give a conclusion that has the same form as one of the premises. For all figures the vast majority of conclusions are in the category *same form, same position*. It is also clear that reasoners are giving such responses despite the fact that they are inappropriate most of the time. For all figures, the responses in the category *same form, same position* are correct only approximately one-third of the time.

A particularly striking feature of the data is that responses where the conclusion is in a *different* form from either of the premises are extremely rare, but when subjects do give such a response it is usually correct. Now, it turns out that *all* the three-model cases require a conclusion that is in a different form from either of the premises. None of the two-model cases do. Of the 1-model cases, there is one syllogism that does require a conclusion in a different form from either of the premises. That syllogism is the one that was classified as a one-model case in 1984 and then reclassified, seemingly unjustly, as a three-model case in 1991. The performance for this syllogism is closest to three-model cases—and what this syllogism has in common with the three-model cases is that the form required in the conclusion is different from the form of either of the premises.

Another point must be raised here, which Johnson-Laird and his colleagues do not note. There is something which the two- and three-model cases have in common which the one-model cases do not. All two- and three-model cases require a conclusion of the form "Some of the Xs are not Ys". Unlike the three-model cases, though, the two-model cases have a premise in that form. (Ford, 1995, pp. 3–11)

Ford's Research in Syllogistic Reasoning: Rationale

Given the critique of the Johnson-Laird theory of syllogistic reasoning presented in the previous section, Ford (1995) outlined the rationale for a novel approach to the study of syllogistic reasoning in the following account.

It seems that the theory proposed by Johnson-Laird and his colleagues may not be capturing the processes involved in syllogistic reasoning. Thus, questions remain: How do people represent and solve syllogistic problems? Is there any evidence that when solving syllogisms people do use mental models that are structural analogues of the state of affairs they represent, with finite elements standing for members of sets? Johnson-Laird and his colleagues dismiss other types of representation such as any that would be isomorphic to Euler circles whereby a representation of a class, not the finite members of the class, are given (e.g., Erickson, 1974, 1978). Do people use representations that emphasize the class itself and not the finite members of the class? Are the representations people use more verbal than Johnson-Laird and his colleagues would have?

The aim of the present paper was to determine how people represent and solve syllogistic problems. A study was carried out where subjects were given all 27 syllogisms that have a valid conclusion and were asked, first, to solve each syllogism saying aloud what they were thinking and then, second, to solve each syllogism again, but this time using a pencil and paper to explain to an interviewer how they were reaching their conclusion. To date, no study has been carried out which carefully analyzes protocols of people solving syllogisms. In fact, such protocols are not usually obtained. Subjects are usually asked simply to give a conclusion or to say which among a number of possible alternatives is the correct conclusion. (Ford, 1995, pp. 11–12; italics added)

Ford's Research in Syllogistic Reasoning: Method

The subjects, materials, and procedures of Ford's experiment are presented in the following section.

The subjects were 20 paid volunteers from the Stanford University community. There were 10 males and 10 females. None had ever taken a logic class . . .

The subjects met individually with a research assistant and were given the following instructions:

This is an experiment on how people combine information in order to draw conclusions from it. You will be given a series of pairs of statements about different groups of people. You are to read the statements and figure out what, if anything, follows necessarily from these premises about the people. Your conclusion should be based solely on the information in the premises, and not on plausible suppositions or general knowledge. Because we are trying to find out how people solve these problems, it is VITAL that you "think aloud" while working out your answer, so there should not be any silent periods on the tapes. Also, if you would like to use a pen and paper to help you come to your answer, please do so. When you have reached your conclusion, simply state your conclusion.

There are 27 pages in the booklet you will be given. Each page has a pair of statements about different groups of people on it. You are to read the statement aloud and then proceed to work out what conclusion, if any, follows from the premises. Remember, it is important to "think aloud": don't sit there being silent. Feel free to use a pen and paper. You can use the space below the statements. Once you have finished with the first pair of statements go on to the next page and the next problem. Take as much time as you need to figure out the problems.

The subjects were given two practice items. Each test booklet contained all 27 syllogisms that have a valid conclusion, with the syllogisms in a random order in each booklet. The distinct terms of the syllogisms were the names given to people having certain hobbies or persuasions, for example *gymnasts* or *vegetarians*, while the common terms were the names given to people having certain occupations, for example *lawyers*.

When the subjects finished the booklet they were asked to go through it again, but this time to explain to the interviewer, using pencil and paper, how they were reaching their conclusion. The interviews were tape recorded. (Ford, 1995, pp. 12–13)

The Verbal Reasoners: Syllogisms Are Like Algebraic Equations

From the protocols produced by subjects as they try to solve syllogistic problems, Ford identified two separate groups: verbal reasoners and spatial reasoners. The verbal reasoners appear to approach the syllogisms as though they were equations that could be treated with the operations of algebra:

Let's first consider the group who manipulated the verbal form of the syllogisms as though doing algebraic problems (Ss 12–19). Some of the subjects themselves recognized that what they were doing could be likened to algebra. They seem correct in their intuition. Consider the simple algebraic problem given in (26).

(26) $x = 5$
       $y = 20/x$
       Conclusion: $y = 20/5$ therefore $y = 4$

One line asserts a value for the common term ($x = 5$). To come to a conclusion about the unknown, y, the asserted value is substituted in the other line, yielding the conclusion ($y = 20/5$, therefore $y = 4$). Now consider the syllogism in (27).

(27)   Some of the blood donors are pilots
       All of the pilots are movie buffs

Using the algebraic analogy, one could say that the second premise allows one to give the value of "movie buffs" to "pilots". The value "movie buffs" can then be substituted for "pilots" in the first premise, giving the correct conclusion "Some of the blood donors are movie buffs". This characterization of solving syllogisms in the algebraic manner certainly does capture an important essence of the subjects' reasoning. However, the reasoning process is somewhat more complicated. A statement such as "All of the pilots are movie buffs" does not mean *pilots = movie buffs* in the sense of all pilots being movie buffs and all movie buffs being pilots. The subjects all recognize that to a varying degree.

Let's consider the syllogism in (28), which unlike (27) is a very difficult syllogism.

(28)   All of the historians are weavers
       None of the historians are tennis club members.

Reasoning in the same manner shown for (27), one might think you could say the first premise allows one to give the value of "weavers" to "historians" and that the value "weavers" could then be substituted for "historians" in the second premise, yielding the conclusion "None of the weavers are tennis club members". In fact, this conclusion is popular, as Johnson-Laird and his colleagues have noted, though it is incorrect because there may be weavers who are not historians and who therefore may be tennis club members. The subjects in the present study often showed a recognition of the fact that simple substitution was not always valid. Of the 8 "verbal" subjects being considered here, 7 showed such recognition through either giving the correct answer for one or more syllogisms similar to (28) or by indicating for such syllogisms that when the premise says "All the Xs are Ys" there could be Ys who are not Xs. The excerpt in (29) is typical.

(29)   HILARY (8A)

       All of the historians are weavers
       None of the historians are tennis club members

       PROTOCOL:

       "Since it's all for none then you know that none of the weavers are tennis club members
       wait all of the historians are weavers none of the historians well you actually can't conclude
       that because you might have another some one else like a philosopher who could be a weaver
       who might be a tennis club member so you really can't conclude that that ah all the weavers
       are not tennis club members ah oh well actually yeah like if you look at it simply then you

could say that none of the weavers are tennis club members but you might have somebody else who is also anoth' another person in a profession who's also a weaver who could be a tennis club member so you really can't conclude that"

CORRECT CONCLUSION:

"Some of the weavers are not tennis club members"

Since the subjects were for the most part aware that the syllogisms involved more than the simple substitution needed to solve the algebraic problem in (26), what principle was guiding their substitution? It is proposed that the subjects manipulating the verbal form of the syllogisms do, as in the algebraic problem in (26), take one premise as having a term that needs to be substituted with another term and the other premise as providing a value for that substitution. The premise that provides the value for substitution acts as a rule relating membership of class C to a property P, while the premise containing the term that needs to be substituted acts as a case of specific objects, O, whose status with regard to either C or P is known. It is proposed that the subjects are struggling for the principle given in (30) to guide their substitution.

(30)   A. If a rule exists affirming of every member of the class C the property P then

      (i) whenever a specific object, O, that is a member of C is encountered it can be inferred that O has the property P.

      (ii) whenever a specific object, O, that lacks property P is encountered it can be inferred that O is not a member of C.

   B. If a rule exists denying of every member of the class C the property P, then

      (i) whenever a specific object, O, that is a member of C is encountered it can be inferred that O does not have the property P and

      (ii) whenever a specific object, O, that possesses the property P is encountered it can be inferred that O is not a member of C.

The application of an affirming or denying rule to a particular instance using (i) is equivalent to modus ponens, while using (ii) it is equivalent to modus tollens. Modus ponens and modus tollens are inference rules that have been well known in logic for over 2000 years. It is claimed that the verbal subjects are struggling to use these principles to guide their substitution in trying to solve the syllogisms. The principle in (30) leads to simple substitution where simple substitution is valid, but is subtle enough to allow more sophisticated substitution where necessary. (Ford, 1995, pp. 19–21; italics added)

The Verbal Reasoners: Simple Substitution

In the following section, the use of the simple substitution process in a solution of syllogism problems is described in detail.

Consider (27) again, repeated here for convenience.

(27)   Some of the blood donors are pilots
     All of the pilots are movie buffs

The second premise of (27) affirms of every member of the class of pilots C that they have the property of being movie buffs P. It is thus the premise that provides the value for substitution (movie buffs). The first premise readily identifies "some of the blood donors" as specific objects O whose status with regard to C, pilots, is known. It therefore contains the term that needs to be substituted (pilots). Thus, (27) can be thought of in the manner illustrated in (27a).

(27a)   Some of the blood donors (O) are pilots (C)
        All of the pilots (C) are movie buffs (P)

Given (30Ai) we can infer that O (some of the blood donors) have the property P (the property of being movie buffs) and we can conclude that "some of the blood donors are movie buffs".

Leaving aside, for the moment, syllogisms that have a premise of the form "Some of the Xs are not Ys", there are 11 valid syllogisms where (30) can be applied directly, leading to simple substitution. However, these 11 syllogisms vary in a number of ways. Of the 11, there are 10 that can be solved by applying (30) to the first or the only universal premise and there is one where (30) must be applied to the second universal premise. Consider one where (30) must be applied to the second universal premise. Consider the syllogism in (31).

(31)   All of the vegetarians are lawyers
       All of the lawyers are stamp collectors

In attempting to apply (30) to the first universal premise, one would say that the first premise affirms of every member of the class of vegetarians C that they have the property of being lawyers P. This would lead one to think of (31) in the manner illustrated in (31a).

(31a)   All of the vegetarians (C) are lawyers (P)
        All of the lawyers (P) are stamp collectors

But notice that the second premise does not directly identify objects that are either members of C, vegetarians, or lack the property P, of being lawyers. To solve (31) by a direct use of (30), it is necessary to apply (30) to the second premise of (31). The second premise of (31) affirms of every member of the class of lawyers C that they have the property of being stamp collectors P. Now the first premise can be used to identify objects O, "All of the vegetarians," that are members of C, lawyers. This manner of thinking about syllogism (31) is shown in (31b).

(31b)   All of the vegetarians (O) are lawyers (C)
        All of the lawyers (C) are stamp collectors (P)

Given (30Ai), we can conclude that those objects O identified as being members of C must have the property P, of being stamp collectors, leading to the conclusion "All of the vegetarians are stamp collectors", with *stamp collectors* being substituted for *lawyers* in the first premise.

Now, of the 11 syllogisms being considered to which (30) can be applied directly, there are 7, such as (27) and (31), where the conclusion can be given in the same form as one of the premises, with the common term of the syllogism for that premise simply being replaced by the distinct term of the other premise—thus, for (27), "Some of the blood donors are pilots" becomes "Some of the blood donors are movie buffs" and, for (31), "All of the vegetarians are lawyers" becomes "All of the vegetarians are stamp collectors". However, for the other 4 syllogisms the conclusion must be given in a different form from either premise, with the second, and common, term in the Some premise being replaced by a negation of the distinct term from the other premise. Consider the syllogism in (32).

(32)   None of the butchers are winedrinkers
       Some of the foreigners are butchers

The first premise denies of every member of the class C, butchers, the property P of being a winedrinker. The second premise identifies objects O, "some of the foreigners", who are members of the class C of butchers. Thus, syllogism (32) can be thought of in the manner illustrated in (32a).

(32a)   None of the butchers (C) are winedrinkers (P)
        Some of the foreigners (O) are butchers (C)

Using (30Bi), it can be inferred that the objects O, "some of the foreigners", do not have the property P of being winedrinkers, thus leading to the conclusion "Some of the foreigners are not winedrinkers", where "not winedrinkers" has been substituted for "butchers". (Ford, 1995, pp. 22–23)

The Verbal Reasoners: Sophisticated Substitution

Conditions under which sophisticated substitution rather than simple substitution appear to be appropriate are described in the following section.

For 9 syllogisms, (30) cannot be applied so directly. Consider the difficult syllogism (28) again.

(28)   All of the historians are weavers
       None of the historians are tennis club members

The first premise of (28) affirms of every member of the class of historians C that they have the property of belonging to the class of weavers P. The second premise can then be considered in light of (30A). The second premise of (28) does not directly refer to objects that lack the property of being weavers. Nor does the premise refer to specific objects who are members of the class historians in the way that the first premise of (27) referred to objects who are members of the class "pilots"—"some of the blood donors are pilots". The premise does, however, refer to the class of historians itself. Thinking of the premise in this way is illustrated in (28a).

(28a)   All of the historians (C) are weavers (P)
        None of the historians (C) (O) are tennis club members

Now (30Ai) states that "whenever a specific object O, that is a member of C is encountered it can be inferred that O has the property P". If great care is not taken, one could be tempted to say that the O (historians) must have the property P (that of being weavers) so just replace "historians" with "weavers" in the second premise. Let's call this naive substitution. The protocol in (33) demonstrates naive substitution nicely, as does the protocol from Hilary already given in (29).

(33)   CATHERINE (26B)
       All of the historians are weavers

None of the historians are tennis club members

PROTOCOL:

H = W

H = TC

W = TC could have a weaver that is not a historian and is a TC member

"So we should be able to go that uh ok wait um I was gonna say that some of the tennis club members are not weavers ok ok ok you can replace h with w so you should be able to put weavers are not tennis club members (phone rings) I'll just go on with this weavers are not tennis club members you all of the historians are weavers none of the historians are tennis club members so I'm saying the weavers are not tennis club members but there could be weavers that are not historians and and therefore could be tennis club members so I don't think you can really conclude with this one 'cause you could have a weaver ok I'll just write this down you could have a weaver who's not a historian and is a tennis club member so you know (inaudible):

CORRECT CONCLUSION:

"Some of the weavers are not tennis club members"

Catherine is tempted to substitute "weavers" for "historians" in the second premise but realizes this would not be valid. What (30Ai) allows one to say, given (28a), is that "None of the historians are tennis club members and these historians are weavers". That is, (30Ai) and (28a) together let us infer that the historians in the second premise are weavers but that knowledge by itself really says nothing about the relationship between weavers as a whole and tennis club members—as both Catherine and Hilary fully recognize. The mistake they make is to take this recognition as grounds for saying you cannot draw a conclusion. [In] a sense Catherine and Hilary give up too early. To come closer to a solution one must pursue the relationship between the weavers of the second premise, that is, the historians, and the weavers as a whole and relate it to tennis club members. Having recognized that the historians of the second premise are weavers and that these possibly account for only some of all the weavers one could characterize the historians of the second premise as historian weavers and say "None of the historian weavers are tennis club members". This is one way of phrasing the correct conclusion, given usually as "Some of the weavers are not tennis club members". That is, it is picking out a subset of weavers and saying they are not tennis club members. Geoff nearly reaches the correct conclusion by the use of modification but he accidentally modifies the wrong term. He says "there are no historian tennis club members who are weavers". His conclusion makes no sense as there is no such thing as a historian tennis club member, given the second premise. He should have said that there are no historian weavers who are tennis club members. For syllogisms like (28), some subjects did manage to relate two terms by using modification. Thus Amy, for example, says for (28) "so that means that the weavers which are historians are not tennis club members".

Instead of attempting to use modification in reaching a solution, an alternative is reformulation of a premise. Thus, if one realizes that "All of the historians are weavers" implies that "Some of the weavers are historians", syllogism (28) can be reformulated as in (28b).

(28b)   Some of the weavers are historians
        None of the historians are tennis club members

Using (30b) we can say that the second premise of (28b) is one that denies of every member of the class of historians C the property of being tennis club members P. Now we need to consider the first premise to determine whether reference is made to any objects O who are either members of the class historians C or who possess the property of being tennis club members P. The first premise readily identifies "some of the weavers" as members of the class of historians. Thus, (28b) can be thought of in the manner illustrated in (28c).

(28c)   Some of the weavers (O) are historians (C)
        None of the historians (C) are tennis club members (P)

Now we can apply (30Bi), which states that "whenever a specific object, O, that is a member of C is encountered it can be inferred that O does not have the property P". We know that some of the weavers are objects O who are historians C, so we can infer that some of the weavers are not tennis club members. The protocol in (34) is an example where the realization that "All of the historians are weavers" implies that "Some of the weavers are historians" is used in reaching a conclusion.

(34)   ERIC (5B)

       All of the historians are weavers
       None of the historians are tennis club members
       PROTOCOL:

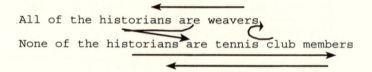

"all of the historians are weavers but we have this none thing here it's it's hard to say because you can't it's hard to make connections between the weavers and the tennis club members because if we have all the historians are weavers you know it doesn't it goes this way but it doesn't go this way I mean I don't know what the what the what the logic of the term for that is but (inaudible) you can have weavers and then you know weavers come from all walks of life some of them are are probably um I don't know linguists and um those linguists you know it doesn't say anything about linguists in here so those linguists may very well tennis club members so we can't going this way we can't say anything about weavers you know weavers you can't say much we can't say anything positive about it let's think about this um all the historians are weavers we don't know if there's any historians ok but if there are any historians like suppose there's two historians right that means there are two weavers who are also historians so we can say some of the weavers are historians um but this thing here if we want to get something out of this we can say none of the historians are tennis club members we can turn this around we can say this is going this way but we can go this way we can say we can say all the tennis club members are not historians ok so we have all of the tennis club members are not historians all the historians are weavers going backwards like this we could say that all the tennis club let's see about this go backwards here all the tennis club members are not historians all the historians are weavers um I sort of lost my thread of my argument there I can't (inaudible) all the historians are weavers none of the historians are tennis club members there may be some weavers (inaudible) we can maybe get like (inaudible) saying that all these um (inaudible) there are weavers there are historians so we can say that some of the weavers are not yeah we can go this way ok like that you can say some of the weavers are not tennis club members ok and and I don't know whether we can say that or not I mean I'm not sure how i' i' if you say all the historians like does that mean well yeah if you say all the historians that means you know there are some historians or maybe you just mean all of these hypothetical historians maybe there aren't any at all you know but assuming we've got historians then it seems to me we can pretty well say some of the weavers are not tennis club members"

CORRECT CONCLUSION:

"Some of the weavers are not tennis club members"

Eric was the only verbal reasoner who drew a conclusion in the form "Some of the Xs are not Ys" for the *All/None* syllogisms where such a conclusion was appropriate. Other verbal subjects who drew valid conclusions modified one of the terms. Eric was also the only subject who explicitly reformulated the premise "All of the Xs are Ys" as "Some of the Ys are Xs".

We see, then, that syllogisms such as (28) require sophisticated substitution in that one of the premises needs to be reformulated in order to apply (30) or modification must be used. The syllogism in (35) is another that can be solved by sophisticated substitution.

(35)   All of the engineers are sculptors
       All of the engineers are alcoholics

The first premise of (35) affirms of every member of the class of engineers C that they have the property of being sculptors P. The second premise must then be examined to see whether specific objects are mentioned who are either members of the class of engineers or who are not sculptors. Individuals who are not sculptors are not mentioned. The class of engineers itself is mentioned, so (35) could be thought of in the manner illustrated in (35a).

(35a)   All of the engineers (C) are sculptors (P)
        All of the engineers (C) (O) are alcoholics

It could also be thought of in the way shown in (35b), if (30) is applied to the second premise.

(35b)   All of the engineers (C) (O) are sculptors
        All of the engineers (C) are alcoholics (P)

Just as for (28), there is a temptation to do naive substitution—to say, taking (35a) for example, that the O (engineers) must have the property P (of being sculptors) so just replace "engineers" with "sculptors" in the second premise. So, for example, Hilary says "since everyone who is an engineer is a sculptor and everyone who is an engineer is an alcoholic you know that all the sculptors are alcoholics". What (30Ai) really allows one to say is that "All of the engineers are sculptors and they are also alcoholics". Some of the 8 subjects being considered got as far as this in their reasoning. So, for example, Shawna says "that means that all the engineers are sculptors and all the engineers are alcoholics that just means that all the engineers are sculptors and alcoholics 'cause you're not saying that all the sculptors are engineers just that all the engineers are sculptors ok".

Just as Catherine and Hilary gave up too early for (28), Shawna and the others who drew the same conclusion as her gave up too early for (35). To come closer to a solution, again taking (35a) as the example, one must pursue the relationship between the sculptors of the second premise, that is, the engineers, and the sculptors as a whole and relate it to alcoholics. Having recognized that the engineers of the second premise are sculptors and that these possibly account for only some of all the sculptors one could characterize the engineers of the second premise as engineering sculptors and say "All of the engineering sculptors are alcoholics", thus picking out a subset of sculptors and saying that they are alcoholics. Alternatively, taking (35b), one could say "All of the engineering alcoholics are sculptors". Once again Geoff nearly reaches the correct conclusion by using modification—he says "all of the alcoholic engineers are also sculptors" whereas he should have said "all of the engineering alcoholics are also sculptors".

Again, once it is recognized that a statement such as "All of the engineers are sculptors" does not mean that all of the sculptors are necessarily engineers one could reformulate the premise as "Some of the sculptors are engineers". Thus, the syllogism could be reformulated as (35c).

(35c)   Some of the sculptors are engineers
        All of the engineers are alcoholics

Given (30Ai), the syllogism could be thought of in the manner illustrated in (35d).

(35d)   Some of the sculptors (O) are engineers (C)
        All of the engineers (C) are alcoholics (P)

Eric, who was the only subject who explicitly reformulated the *All* premise to a *Some* premise for syllogisms like (28), was the only one amongst the 8 verbal reasoners who had any success with syllogism (35). His first attempt is given in (36).

(36)   ERIC (12A)
        All of the engineers are sculptors
        All of the engineers are alcoholics
        PROTOCOL:
        "you can have um other people who are alcoholics and you can have other people who are sculptors it doesn't say that all alcoholics are painters so you can't necessarily say that all sculptors are alcoholics but one thing you can say about this is that if there are any engineers at all then you have sculptors who are alcoholics and you have alcoholics who are sculptors but doesn't say there are any engineers at all maybe there's no engineers and if there's no engineers then there's not necessarily any sculptors who are alcoholics but if there are some engineers then you can say some sculptors who are alcoholics but it doesn't say there are any engineers at all maybe there's no engineers and if there are no engineers then there's not necessarily any sculptors who are alcoholics but if there are some engineers then you can say some sculptors are alcoholics and alcoholics are sculptors"
        CORRECT CONCLUSION:
        "Some of the sculptors are alcoholics" or, alternatively, "Some of the alcoholics are sculptors"

In (36), Eric concludes correctly that "some sculptors are alcoholics" though he made the mistake of then saying "alcoholics are sculptors". On his second attempt, he does not make this mistake, but says "some sculptors are alcoholics some alcoholics are sculptors". Although he does not say explicitly that he used reformulation for syllogism (35), he may very well have done so.

It is not only the "All" type of premise which sometimes needs to be reformulated or for which a subset must be chosen by modification. Consider the syllogism in (37).

(37)   None of the bankers are tennis club members
        Some of the bankers are gymnasts

The first premise of (37) denies of every member of the class of bankers, C, the property of being a tennis club member, P. The second premise can then be considered in light of (30B) and examined to see whether specific objects are mentioned who are either members of the class of bankers or who have the property of being tennis club members. The only way the second premise refers directly to bankers is by referring to "some of the bankers". Thus, (37) can be thought of in the way shown in (37a).

(37a)   None of the bankers (C) are tennis club members (P)
          Some of the bankers (C) (O) are gymnasts

Thinking of the syllogism this way and attempting to apply (30Bi) is not helpful. Instead, one must pursue the task of finding, in the second premise, specific objects who have the property of being bankers, other than "some of the bankers" themselves. When one realizes that "Some of the bankers are gymnasts" implies that "Some of the gymnasts are bankers", then progress can be made—the gymnasts who are bankers, or in other words, some of the gymnasts, are the objects O that were being sought and, using (30Bi), it can be inferred that "Some of the gymnasts are not tennis club members". Thus, for example, Amy says simply on her first attempt "then the banking gymnasts aren't tennis club members" and on her second attempt "some bankers are gymnasts then the gymnasts that are bankers are not tennis club members". So, too, Lisa L says "there are no tennis club members in those that are bankers and some of the bankers are gymnasts so if they're both the gymnasts that are bankers are not tennis club members". By reformulating the "Some" premise of (37), so that the syllogism is thought of as (37b), a solution can be achieved without the use of modification.

(37b)   None of the bankers (C) are tennis club members (P)
          Some of the gymnasts (O) are bankers (C)

Using (30Bi), it can be inferred that "Some of the gymnasts are not tennis club members".

As shown in (38), Eric specifically reformulates the *Some* premise in a syllogism with similar properties to (37) and reaches the correct conclusion.

(38)   ERIC (24A)

          None of the sculptors are columnists
          Some of the columnists are movie buffs

          PROTOCOL:

          "Um so we can say that none no we can't say that either these none and somes are pretty (inaudible) hard to get much out of some of the sculptors are movie buffs no sorry some of the columnists are movie buffs wait a minute that means that we have some movie buffs who are columnists is that right some of the columnists are movie buffs we have movie buffs who are columnists and those columnists are surely not sculptors so I think we can say here that some of the movie buffs are not sculptors some of the columnists are movie buffs (inaudible) we have columnists we have movie buffs we have movie buffs who are columnists so some of the sc' movie buffs are columnists and none of the sculptors are columnists means the same as it seems to me that all the columnists are not sculptors ok that's right so we have some movie buffs who are not sculptors"

          CORRECT CONCLUSION:

          "Some of the movie buffs are not sculptors"

It would be expected that the 9 syllogisms requiring more effort in identifying O when applying (30) would be more difficult for the verbal reasoners than the syllogisms where

identifying O is straightforward and where simple substitution can therefore take place. This is certainly borne out by the data.
(Ford, 1995, pp. 25–33)

The Spatial Reasoners and Euler Circles

A traditional aid in the solution of syllogistic problems was developed by the great mathematician Euler. The premises and conclusions of syllogisms can be represented by different types of Euler circles that do or do not intersect and do or do not contain one or more smaller circles within a large circle.

The spatial reasoners used shapes in different spatial relationships to represent different classes and their relationships. The representations were similar to the traditional Euler circle representations of syllogistic premises given in [Figure 8.2]. Thus, the spatial subjects used a type of representation specifically dismissed by Johnson-Laird and his colleagues, where the class itself and not the finite members of the class is represented. Johnson-Laird and Bara state:

Mental models represent finite sets by finite sets of mental tokens, and they can accordingly be mapped one-to-one onto the states of affairs that they represent. However, Euler circles . . . have no such direct mapping onto the state of affairs that they represent. In particular, Euler circles . . . represent finite sets in terms of non-denumerable infinites of points in the Euclidean plane. (Johnson-Laird & Bara, 1984, p. 28)

They go on to say:

A mental model of assertion:

> All of the accountants are pianists

contains a set of tokens that corresponds to the set of accountants, a set of tokens that corresponds to the set of pianists, and a set of identity relations between the tokens that corresponds to identifies between the entities:

accountant = pianist
accountant = pianist
                0pianist

Beyond this isomorphism, we make no strong assumptions about the way in which the information is specifically represented. . . . As the example illustrates, it is parsimonious to represent the fact that there may be certain individuals—pianists who are not account-ants—by introducing special tokens to stand for them, since in this way *one* model captures the content of the assertion in contrast to the need for two separate Euler dia-grams, one representing set

A included in set B and the other representing the two sets as co-extensive. The mental model does not lead to a combinatorial explosion, because anything that is predicated of pianists will apply to pianists in the uncertain category, too, and will not increase the number of possibilities. Mental models can therefore directly represent these referential indeterminacies in a way that is computa-tionally tractable, i.e., there is not exponential growth in complexity. (Johnson-Laird & Bara, 1984, pp. 28–29)

Figure 8.2
The Traditional Representation of Syllogistic Premises with Euler Circles

All of the Xs are Ys

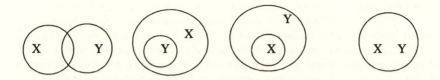

Some of the Xs are Ys

None of the Xs are Ys

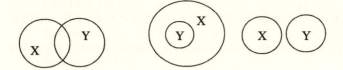

Some of the Xs are not Ys

Source: Ford, M. (1995). Two modes of mental representation and problem solution in syllogistic reasoning. Reprinted from *Cognition, 54*, p. 41, copyright 1995, with permission from Elsevier Science.

Now, the Euler circles in [Figure 8.2] represent all the possibilities that could logically exist if the premises were true and it is correct that if one attempted to solve syllogisms using these Euler circles a problem of combinatorial explosion would result. However, when subjects drew shapes to represent premises they did *not* give all possibilities. The subjects, when representing a premise, usually drew the relationship given in the first column of [Figure 8.2] for each of the premises. This does not mean that the subjects did not recognize the possibilities depicted in the traditional Euler circles. What seems to be the case is that the spatial subjects are giving representations that have a somewhat different interpretation from traditional Euler circles. In traditional Euler circles, each distinct representation of a relation is made on the assumption that the parts enclosed by the circles are not empty. Thus, for "All of the Xs are Ys," for example, the two relations depicted are quite distinct because the relation in the first column depicts the situation where there are Ys that are not Xs and the relation in the second column depicts the situation where there are no Ys that are not Xs. If one assumes that parts enclosed by the circles *can* be empty then it turns out that the representations in column 1 of [Figure 8.2] are the most general representations of the premises. This is illustrated in [Figure 8.3].

Notice that the spatial representations given by subjects in the present study are not sufficient alone to be unambiguous. For example, the preferred spatial representations the subjects gave for "Some of the Xs are Ys" and "Some of the Xs are not Ys" are the same. Similarly, the preferred representation of "All of the Xs are Ys" could also represent a special case of "Some of the Xs are Ys" and "Some of the Ys are Xs". When referring to the pictures, though, the subjects did have the verbal tags provided by the premises to keep the nature of the relationship in mind. Essentially, these tags serve as a reminder of which parts enclosed by circles cannot be empty, if Xs exist. Thus, for example, for "Some of the Xs are Ys", area 2 cannot be empty, while for "Some of the Xs are not Ys" it is area 1 that cannot be empty.

Of past theories, the Euler circle theory of Erickson (1974, 1978) comes close to supplying a representation like that of the spatial reasoners. However, it must be emphasized that the present account contends that the spatial reasoners do not interpret Euler circles in Erickson's manner, but instead prefer to give a representation that is the most general, where parts enclosed within the circles can be empty—a feature equivalent to the 0Y and 0X of Johnson-Laird and Bara's (1984) mental models. It is also contended that the spatial reasoners maintain a verbal tag for representations of the premises. Like the theory of Johnson-Laird and Bara, the present theory thus avoids the problem of combinatorial explosion, with one model representing one premise. (Ford, 1995, pp. 41–44)

The Spatial Reasoners: Totally Restrained Representations

Spatial representations for the premises of certain syllogisms are bound by the relationships between classes contained in the premises.

When attempting to solve a syllogism, the spatial reasoners appear to consider the relationship between the two classes mentioned in one premise and then to add the third class from the other premise, making sure it has the correct relationship to the class which is in common with the other premise. There are 6 syllogisms, all one-model cases in the Johnson-Laird system, where the resulting representation is such that the bound-

Figure 8.3
The Relationship Between Spatial Representation of Syllogistic Premises and Traditional Euler Circles

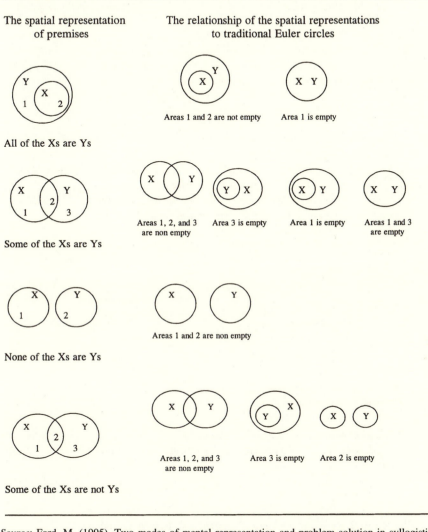

The spatial representation of premises

The relationship of the spatial representations to traditional Euler circles

Areas 1 and 2 are not empty   Area 1 is empty

All of the Xs are Ys

Areas 1, 2, and 3   Area 3 is empty   Area 1 is empty   Areas 1 and 3
are non empty   are empty

Some of the Xs are Ys

Areas 1 and 2 are non empty

None of the Xs are Ys

Areas 1, 2, and 3   Area 3 is empty   Area 2 is empty
are non empty

Some of the Xs are not Ys

aries of the classes are constrained to be one way and no other. Consider (44), repeated here for convenience.

(44) All of the bookworms are doctors
      None of the doctors are beekeepers

Given the preferred representation of "All of the Xs are Ys", the relationship between *bookworms* and *doctors*, for example, would be expressed as in (47).

(47)

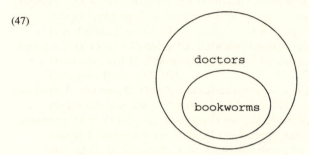

Verbal tag: All of the bookworms are doctors

The other premise would then be considered and the new class mentioned, *beekeepers*, would be placed in spatial relationship to the already considered classes. Since the premise says "None of the doctors are beekeepers", there is no choice but to place *beekeepers* in relation to *doctors* and *bookworms* in the manner shown in (48).

(48)

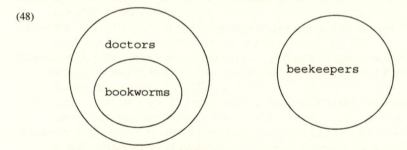

Verbal tag: All of the bookworms are doctors,
None of the doctors are beekeepers

The relationship between the two distinct terms, *bookworms* and *beekeepers*, is obvious and the conclusion "None of the bookworms are beekeepers" can be drawn. (Ford, 1995, pp. 44–45)

The Spatial Reasoners: Less Constrained Representations

In the following section, Ford (1995) analyzes the *All/Some* syllogisms with respect to problems of representation.

Now let's consider syllogism (21), repeated here for convenience.

(21)   Some of the playwrights are stamp collectors
       All of the playwrights are bookworms

The relationship between *playwrights* and *stamp collectors* could be considered and expressed as in (49), given the preferred spatial representation of "Some of the Xs are Ys".

(49)

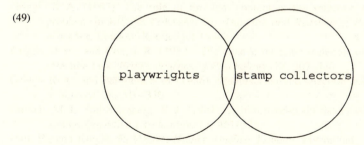

Verbal tag: Some of the playwrights are stamp collectors

The other premise would then be considered and *bookworms* must be placed in the correct relationship, given the expressed relationship between *playwrights* and *bookworms*. Given the preferred representation of "All of the Xs are Ys" there are 2 possible ways of relating *bookworms* to *playwrights* and *stamp collectors*. These are given in (50a) and (50b).

(50)

a.

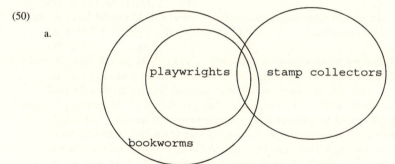

Verbal tag: Some of the playwrights are stamp collectors, All of the playwrights are bookworms

b.

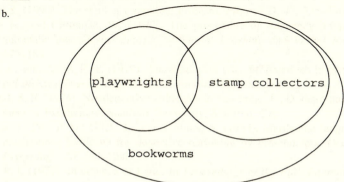

Verbal tag: Some of the playwrights are stamp collectors, All of the playwrights are bookworms

Under the interpretation of spatial representations where parts enclosed by circles can be empty, (50a) is the more general representation of syllogism (21), since the area of *stamp collectors* outside *bookworms* can be considered empty making it equivalent to (50b). In all, there are 4 syllogisms which present the same two types of choices as (21). All of these are one-model cases in Johnson-Laird's system. It is interesting to consider what spatial subjects draw. Of the 29 diagrams drawn by the subjects for the 4 syllogisms, only 2 were simply of the non-general representation given in (50b). These were given by two subjects, Steve and Tom, and in neither case did they reach the correct conclusion. There were 5 diagrams, given by 2 subjects, Tom and Carolyn, where both possible representations were presented and in all 5 instances the correct conclusion was given. The remaining 22 drawings, given by 6 of the 8 spatial subjects, gave a general spatial representation of the syllogisms. Sometimes these were identical to (50a). However, sometimes there were markings to show that the exact boundary of a line was uncertain, as in (51).

(51)   PETER (25B)

Some of the playwrights are stamp collectors
All of the playwrights are bookworms

PROTOCOL:

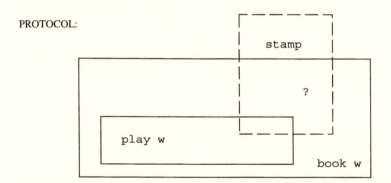

"and some of them are stamp collectors I don't know if there is any common ground between stamp collectors and bookworms or not because they could be right here and not anything or this could be right on the edge"

CORRECT CONCLUSION:

"Some of the stamp collectors are bookworms" or, alternatively, "Some of the bookworms are stamp collectors"

Sometimes a boundary that was uncertain was completely omitted, as in (52).

(52)   MIKE (22A)

All of the politicians are potters
Some of the politicians are chessplayers

PROTOCOL:

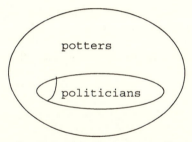

"ok so we have a large class of potters and you know that um all politicians are inside this class so put politicians here so if all the politicians are potters some of the politicians are also chessplayers so that means that um some of the chessplayers are potters and in particular we know for sure that um politicians that play chess (inaudible)"

CORRECT CONCLUSION:

"Some of the chessplayers are potters" or, alternatively, "Some of the potters are chessplayers" (Ford, 1995, pp. 46–48)

The Spatial Reasoners: All of the Xs Are Ys, All of the Xs Are Zs

In the following section, Ford (1995) presents an interesting comparison of spatial reasoners' performance with Johnson-Laird's model of the same difficult syllogism.

Next consider syllogism (35), which is the syllogism classified by Johnson-Laird and Bara (1984) as a one-model case and then reclassified by Johnson-Laird and Byrne (1991) as a three-model case.

(35)   All of the engineers are sculptors
       All of the engineers are alcoholics

The relationship between *engineers* and *sculptors*, for example, could be expressed as in (53).

(53)

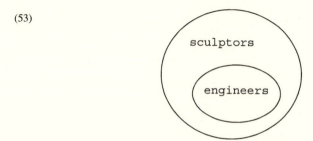

Verbal tag: All of the engineers are sculptors

The relationship of the class of *alcoholics* to the other two classes would then be expressed given the relationship holding between *engineers* and *alcoholics*. Considering the preferred representation of premises of the form "All of the Xs are Ys", there are four possible ways of relating *alcoholics* to *engineers* and *sculptors*. These are represented in (54a)–(54d).

(54)

a.

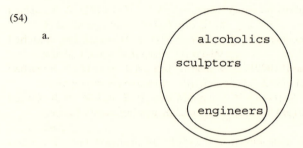

Verbal tag: All of the engineers are sculptors, All of the engineers are alcoholics

b.

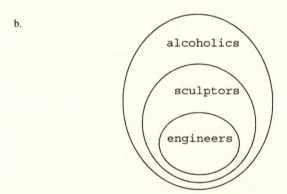

Verbal tag: All of the engineers are sculptors, All of the engineers are alcoholics

c.

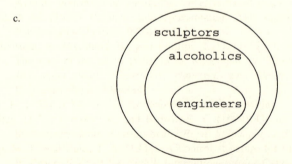

Verbal tag: All of the engineers are sculptors, All of the engineers are alcoholics

d.

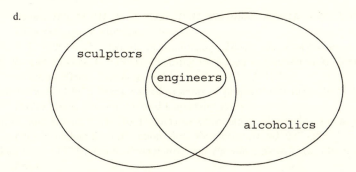

Verbal tag: All of the engineers are sculptors, All of the engineers are alcoholics

Given the interpretation of spatial representations where parts enclosed by circles can be empty, the representation in (54d) is the most general representation of syllogism (35). This is illustrated in [Figure 8.4].

Let's consider the representations drawn by the 8 spatial reasoners for syllogism (35). Not one subject drew the representation in (54a). One subject, Lisa M, drew only the representation in (54b) and gave the incorrect conclusion "All of the sculptors are alcoholics". One subject, Carolyn, drew a representation depicting (54b), (54c), and (54d) and gave the correct conclusion. Four of the other 6 spatial reasoners, Peter, Richard, Fran, and Mike, on at least one of their attempts at solving the syllogism, drew only the representation in (54d). (Ford, 1995, pp. 49–52)

The Spatial Reasoners: None/Some and All/None Syllogisms

Multiple ways of representing the terms of syllogistic premises are analyzed in the following section.

There are two groups of syllogisms where there are three ways of representing the relationship between the three terms of the syllogism, given the preferred representations of the premises. There are 8 *None/Some* syllogisms and 4 *All/None* syllogisms. Consider the syllogisms in (55)–(56), together with their representations.

Figure 8.4
The Most General Spatial Representation of "All of the Xs Are Ys, All of the Xs Are Zs" and Its Relationship to Other Representations

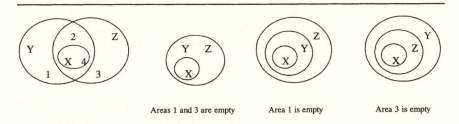

Source: Ford, M. (1995). Two modes of mental representation and problem solution in syllogistic reasoning. Reprinted from *Cognition, 54*, p. 51, copyright 1995, with permission from Elsevier Science.

(55)   Some of the poets are prizewinners, None of the poets are hikers

a.

Verbal tag: Some of the poets are prizewinners, None of the poets are hikers

b.

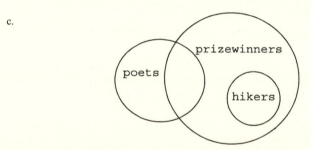

Verbal tag: Some of the poets are prizewinners, None of the poets are hikers

c.

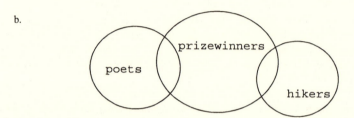

Verbal tag: Some of the poets are prizewinners, None of the poets are hikers

(56)   None of the clerks are weavers, All of the clerks are skaters

a.

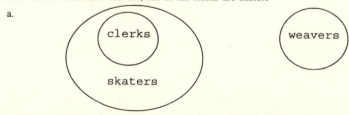

Verbal tag: None of the clerks are weavers, All of the clerks are skaters

b.

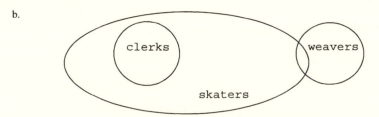

Verbal tag: None of the clerks are weavers, All of the clerks are skaters

c.

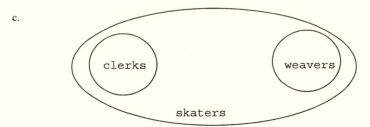

Verbal tag: None of the clerks are weavers, All of the clerks are skaters

The *b* versions of (55) and (56) are the most general representations of the syllogisms, as illustrated in [Figure 8.5].

It is important to note that the *b* versions are the most general representations *if* the intersecting Y and Z circles are taken as a representation of "Some of the Ys are not Zs". If the intersecting Y and Z circles are taken as a representation of "Some of the Ys are Zs" then the *b* versions are *not* the most general representation. For intersecting circles representing "Some of the Ys are Zs" the intersection cannot be considered empty. Thus the *a* versions of the representations could not be captured by the *b* versions. The protocols show that the subjects tend to treat the intersecting circles as representing "Some of the Ys are Zs". Consider first the responses of Mike, and Carolyn given in (57) and (58), respectively.

(57) MIKE (1b)

None of the bankers are tennis club members
Some of the bankers are gymnasts

PROTOCOL:

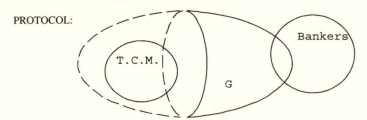

"None of the bankers are tennis club members ok so that tells me that there's a class of tennis club members ok then it says none of the bankers are tennis club members that's like saying none of the bankers belong to this class of tennis club members ok so now we draw

Figure 8.5
**The Most General Spatial Representation of the *Some/None* and *All/None*
Syllogisms Having Three Representations**

The most general spatial representations   The relationship of the most general spatial

representation to the other representations

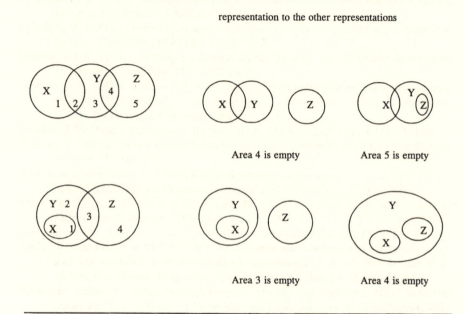

Area 4 is empty   Area 5 is empty

Area 3 is empty   Area 4 is empty

Source: Ford, M. (1995). Two modes of mental representation and problem solution in syllogistic
reasoning. Reprinted from *Cognition, 54*, p. 54, copyright 1995, with permission from Elsevier
Science.

this circle out here of bankers which doesn't intersect the tennis club members because you
can think of people being inside of here and people inside of here and people can be both
tennis club members and bankers ok alright so then we know that some of the bankers are
gymnasts so that tells us that there's another we can draw another circle round here that has
to intersect the circle of bankers ok this is the circle of gymnasts ok now other than that we
don't have any information about what th' what the class of what the relationship of the class
of gymnasts is to tennis club members because this can either go across like this in which
case none of the gymnasts are tennis club members or it could go like this in which case
some of them would be or of course you know it could go all the way out here and all the
tennis club members could be could be gymnasts and so the what conclusion then did I draw
none of the bankers are tennis club members ok some of the bankers are gymnasts and so
you can just really you can't really draw a conclusion"

CORRECT CONCLUSION:

"Some of the gymnasts are not tennis club members"

(58)   CAROLYN (16A)

All of the historians are weavers

None of the historians are tennis club members

PROTOCOL:

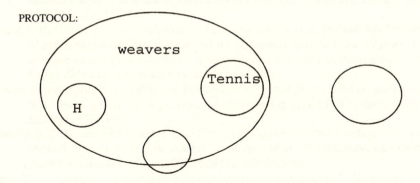

"good ok so tennis club members can't intersect but the way it is is that it could be the tennis the historians wait none of the historians are tennis club members ok so tennis club members could be inside of weavers it could be that all tennis club members are weavers it could be that some tennis club members are weavers or it could be that no tennis club members are weavers we really don't know all we know is that none of the historians are tennis club members"

CORRECT CONCLUSION:

"Some of the weavers are not tennis club members"

Mike and Carolyn give the *a*, *b*, and *c* versions of the representations, but because they see the intersecting Y and Z circles as representing "Some of the Ys are Zs" they cannot draw a conclusion that encompasses all three representations—the representations are just seen as conflicting. Next consider the responses of Richard and Peter, given in (59) and (60), respectively.

(59) RICHARD (14B)

Some of the poets are prizewinners
None of the poets are hikers

PROTOCOL:

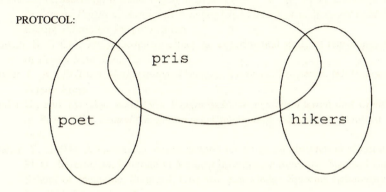

"some of the poets are prizewinners here's a poet here's a prizewinner but none of the poets are hikers but some of the prizewinners can possibly be hikers those that aren't poets therefore I cannot reach any conclusion here"

CORRECT CONCLUSION:

"Some of the prizewinners are not hikers"

(60)   PETER (14B)

>   None of the clerks are weavers
>   All of the clerks are skaters

PROTOCOL:

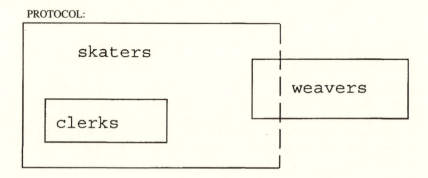

"so (inaudible) weavers so I guess we say that some of the weavers could be skaters but we're not for sure"

CORRECT CONCLUSION:

"Some of the skaters are not weavers"

Both Richard and Peter gave the *b* versions of the representations, with intersecting Y and Z circles. But, just like Mike and Carolyn, they see a conflict. They take the possible intersection of the Y and Z circles as meaning "Some of the Ys are Zs", while at the same time recognizing that, given the premises, they need not intersect. Since it cannot be true both that "Some of the Ys are Zs" and that "None of the the Ys are Zs", all they are left with is the inconclusive "Some of the Ys could be Zs".

Not surprisingly, then, for all the *None/Some* syllogisms and all of the *All/None* syllogisms which have three representations, the spatial reasoners performed poorly. . . . It seemed from the protocols that success was achieved only when subjects changed their focus away from the fact that a circle could be totally outside, totally within, or partially intersecting another circle. In order to solve the syllogisms the subjects had to see what the three potential representations would have in common. The protocols in (61)–(64) show examples of spatial subjects recognizing what commonality would exist for the different representations and thereby reaching the correct conclusion.

(61)   CAROLYN (3B)

>   None of the bankers are tennis club members
>   Some of the bankers are gymnasts

PROTOCOL:

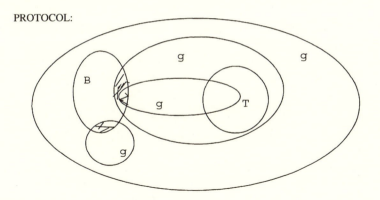

"you have a none you know that the two circles will not intersect so you have you'd label them and then what you do know is that some of the bankers are gymnasts so the alternatives would be you have an intersecting circle then you could look at it and say well how many different ways could I draw a circle which does intersect with bankers and you could say well it would be possible for me to draw one that intersects with both circles it would be possible for me to draw one which completely encloses that circle ah in fact it would be im' possible possible to draw a huge one and therefore then you can start by saying ok so what can you say about gymnasts and whenever you have this many alternatives you say ok prac' practically nothing and then you just go and list them you say ok obviously both could all be gymnasts ah some could be gymnasts some of both could be gymnasts it could also be true that none of the tennis club members were gymnasts what you do know for sure is that you're given that at least some of the bankers are gymnasts and therefore you know that at least some so what you can say about this little intersection here that you know about might be a good way to do it because if you shade in you know what has to be and you can say well that at least some of the gymnasts are not tennis club members and that's how you'd come to the conclusion"

CORRECT CONCLUSION:

"Some of the gymnasts are not tennis club members"

Carolyn not only recognizes the three possibilities that exist if the preferred representations of the premises are given, but also incorporates a diagram that reflects a specific case of "Some of the bankers are gymnasts"—where all bankers are gymnasts. At first she believes that you can only make a list of possibilities because *gymnasts* can either totally encompass, partially intersect, or be totally outside of *tennis club members*. Then, on considering the fact that for each of the three representations the *gymnast* circle intersects the *bankers* circle she realizes that there is a commonality, that there is a critical area that cannot be empty, and she goes on to give the correct conclusion—"Some of the gymnasts are not tennis club members".

(62) FRANCESCA (16B)

     None of the sculptors are columnists
     Some of the columnists are movie buffs

PROTOCOL:

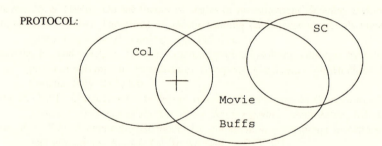

(Author's note: the circles and labels were drawn on the first (unsuccessful) attempt at solving the syllogism and the cross was added on the second (successful) attempt).

"so we have to do separate circles for columnists and sculptors and some of the columnists are movie buffs some of the columnists are movie buffs I know there's that there are people in that intersection columnists and movie buffs that means that there definitely some of the columnists are not sculptors wait none of the none of the yeah some of the columnists sculptors "s" "c" confused me ok all not only are all of the columnists not sculptors but some of the movie buffs are not sculptors that's the conclusion that some of the movie buffs are not sculptors"

CORRECT CONCLUSION:

"Some of the movie buffs are not sculptors"

Francesca draws the most general representation of the syllogism. Her protocol shows that it is the recognition of the significance of the intersection of *columnists* and *movie buffs* that is important—any *movie buffs* within *columnists* cannot be *sculptors*. This would be true for all three of the specific representations.

(63) MIKE (21)

Some of the poets are prizewinners
None of the poets are hikers

PROTOCOL:

"ok so class of hikers none of the poets are hikers um ok so the class of poets then doesn't intercept the class of hikers and some of the poets are prizewinners ok so at least some of the prizewinners are not hikers at least some and the smallest class would be the class that that intersects prizewinners with poets"

CORRECT CONCLUSION:

"Some of the prizewinners are not hikers"

Mike also does not draw the three possibilities. Rather, he draws a diagram which represents the section that all three possibilities would have in common and quite easily gives the correct conclusion.

(64)   RICHARD (2B)

   None of the clerks are weavers
   All of the clerks are skaters

PROTOCOL:

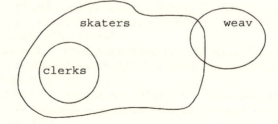

"so if this is weavers and these are clerks there's um non are both but all the clerks are skaters ok if so if skaters may be larger and it may also encompass weavers um that's not defined but you know then that um there are some skaters who are not weavers because um the skaters who are clerks are not weavers".

CORRECT CONCLUSION:

"Some of the skaters are not weavers"

Richard draws the most general representation of the syllogism. His comments and the wiggly lines of the *skaters* circle show, though, that he recognizes at least one of the other specific possibilities. He also recognizes that it does not really matter where you draw the line because the *skaters* who are *clerks* cannot be *weavers*. (Ford, 1995, pp. 52–62)

The Spatial Reasoners: Some of the Xs Are Not Ys

The interesting interpretations that spatial reasoners may give to the premise "Some of the Xs are not Ys" are presented in the following section.

As we have already seen, there is a tendency for people to take "Some of the Xs are not Ys" to mean "Some of the Xs are Ys". Effectively, when spatial reasoners do this they are either altering the verbal tag of the premise or adding a second verbal tag, leading to 2 conclusions. Thus, for example, Steve says "All of the psychologists are gymnasts . . . some of the psychologists are not skaters so some of the psychologists are skaters". He then goes on to draw two conclusions—one the correct conclusion, "Some of the gymnasts are not skaters", and one appropriate for the transformed syllogism, that is, "Some of the gymnasts are skaters". Performance is no doubt influenced by the confusion. Let's consider what else could influence performance for the spatial reasoners.

The 4 syllogisms with a premise of the form "Some of the Xs are not Ys" fall into 2 basic types. There are 2 with one premise of the form "Some of the Xs are not Ys" and another premise of the form "All of the Xs are Zs". Given the preferred representations of the 2 premises, there are 2 representations for these syllogisms. These are given in (65a) and (65b), with *a* being the more general representation since the area of Y outside of Z can be considered empty.

(65)

a.

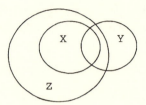

Verbal tag: Some of the Xs are not Ys, All of the Xs are Zs

b.

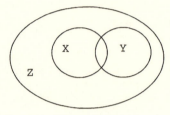

Verbal tag: Some of the Xs are not Ys, All of the Xs are Zs

The 2 other syllogisms have one premise of the form "Some of the Ys are not Xs" and another premise of the form "All of the Zs are Xs". Given the preferred representation of the 2 premises, there are 3 representations for these syllogisms. These are given in (66a)–(66c), with *b* being the most general representation because either the area Z intersecting Y or the area of Z outside of Y can be considered empty, yielding the *a* and *c* versions respectively.

(66)

a.

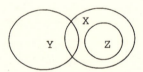

Verbal tag: Some of the Ys are not Xs, All of the Zs are Xs

b.

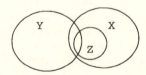

Verbal tag: Some of the Ys are not Xs, All of the Zs are Xs

c.

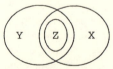

Verbal tag: Some of the Ys are not Xs, All of the Zs are Xs

. . . The results show that the spatial subjects find the *Some-Not* syllogisms quite difficult. One factor may be the confusion about the premise "Some of the Xs are not Ys". However, from examining the protocols it seemed there was another factor at play. Consider the syllogisms in (67) and (68).

(67)   All of the teetotalers (Z) are reporters (X)
       Some of the artists (Y) are not reporters (X)

(68)   Some of the soccer players (Y) are not professors (X)
       All of the blood donors (Z) are professors (X)

Both of these syllogisms would have representations given in (66), given the preferred representations of the premises. However, when attempting to solve the syllogisms with a spatial representation the experience is different depending on which premise is represented first. Let's say one attempts to solve syllogism (68) and represents the first premise first. One would begin with the representation in (69).

(69)

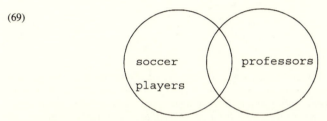

Verbal tag: Some of the soccer players are not professors

When the second premise "All of the blood donors are professors" is considered, it is a matter of deciding where, exactly, to place *blood donors*—it could be within *professors* but not intersecting *soccer players*, within *professors* but intersecting *soccer players*, or within *professors* and also totally within *soccer players*. Notice that the focus here is where to put *blood donors* in relation to *soccer players* and, as anything is possible, it seems confusing.

Now, let's consider syllogism (68) again, but taking the second premise first, which would make it equivalent to syllogism (67). In this case, one would begin with the representation in (70).

(70)

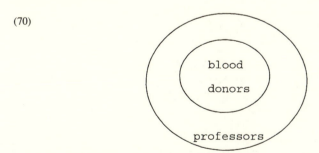

Verbal tag: All of the blood donors are professors

Now, when the premise "Some of the soccer players are not professors" is considered one would start to draw a circle which represents *soccer players* and is partially outside *professors*. Notice that now the focus is on *soccer players* and, moreover, that the relationship of *soccer players* to *blood donors* that is required in the correct conclusion— "Some of the soccer players are not blood donors". This sometimes seems to be immediately obvious to subjects. Thus, for example, consider the protocol of Mike in (71), solving syllogism (68), where he says he will consider the second premise first.

(71)   MIKE (11B)

      Some of the soccer players are not professors
      All of the blood donors are professors

      PROTOCOL:

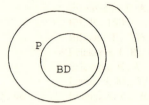

"ok some of the soccer players are not professors here's an example where that one's hard to deal with so go to the second one to start with where you're told that all of the blood donors are professors so then I draw my class of professors and I put the blood donors inside them and then you're told that some of the soccer players are not professors so you you know the class of soccer players has at least some of its members outside the class of professors and so that means at least some of the soccer players are not blood donors"

CORRECT CONCLUSION:

"Some of the soccer players are not blood donors"

    Now compare this with Francesca's protocol, in (72), where she considers the first premise first.

(72)   FRANCESCA (9B)

      Some of the soccer players are not professors
      All of the blood donors are professors

      PROTOCOL:

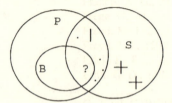

"so there's a professor's circle and there's some soccer players that are there are definitely some soccer players outside all of the blood donors are professors so that means that is all of the blood donors are professors then blood donors and may or may not be some of the same people (inaudible) because if if some of the soccer players are not are not professors and you knew that um you're still n' you're still n' then that means that I mean (inaudible) assuming then some of them are professors but well not even necessarily that but cer' if if some of them aren't professors they still wouldn't have to be the professors that are blood donors (inaudible) that's all for the conclusion"

CORRECT CONCLUSION:

"Some of the soccer players are not blood donors"

Francesca draws the most general representation of the syllogism, but shows confusion. Now consider her protocol for syllogism (67), given in (73), which occurred immediately *before* the above protocol.

(73)   FRANCESCA (8B)

All of the teetotalers are reporters
Some of the artists are not reporters

PROTOCOL: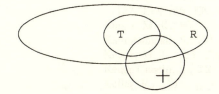

"so if all of the teetotalers are reporters then they're inside then that that's a smaller subset of reporters then some of the artists are not reporters that means if some of them are not reporters then there are definitely some artists that are not teetotalers"

CORRECT CONCLUSION:

"Some of the artists are not teetotalers"

We see, then, that Francesca very easily solves syllogism (67), which has *All* premises first, and that even though the very next syllogism has the same structure, except for the ordering of the premises, she has great difficulty with it. It may be that the syllogisms (67) and (68) differ in difficulty depending on which premise the subject deals with first. For syllogism (67) there were no instances where subjects said they would consider the premises in reverse order. However, for syllogism (68) there were 2 instances where specific mention was made of reversing the order of the premises. (Ford, 1995, pp. 62–67)

The Ford Research into Syllogistic Reasoning: Conclusion

Ford presents the following succinct conclusion to the protocol-based research into the complexities of modes of representation and problem solving in syllogistic reasoning.

The present study has shown that the data on syllogistic reasoning are far more complex than previously realized. First, there are two very different ways in which people reason about the syllogisms—there are those who reason verbally, manipulating the verbal form of the syllogism, and those who reason primarily spatially, though they keep the verbal tag of the premises in mind. Data from the different types of reasoners cannot be lumped together. Second, within each of these two manners of reasoning there are many subtleties leading to different syllogisms that differ in complexity. Neither the spatial nor the verbal reasoners give evidence of developing mental models that are structural analogues of the world where one finite set of individual tokens is mapped into another finite set of individual tokens. The spatial reasoners could be said to provide evidence of developing a model and reasoning by manipulating the model, but the nature of the representation they use is one specifically rejected by Johnson-Laird—it is a model where the class itself and not the finite members of the class is represented. The verbal subjects give no evidence of reasoning by the manipulation of mental models. Their reasoning processes rely on principles which guide the substitution of terms in syllogisms and these principles, it turns out, are equivalent to the well known rules of inference logic—modus ponens and modus tollens. It is only when the two groups of reasoners is recognized and the subtleties of their reasoning processes is realized that the data on syllogistic reasoning can be understood. (Ford, 1995, pp. 69–70)

COMMENTARY

Ford identifies verbal and spatial representations in syllogistic reasoning and contrasts these with the theory of mental models advocated by Johnson-Laird. It is not difficult to show that these three modes of representation as well as that of elementary algebra are expressions of the logic of modus ponens and modus tollens. Ford has pointed this out for verbal representations, but it also holds for spatial representations, as can be seen by the advances of Venn diagrams that use combinations of shading in the Euler circles and their partitions to represent the negations of modus tollens and the two negative syllogistic figures. Regarding mental models, Johnson-Laird describes a matching and non-matching of sets of tokens, but these scanning operations are themselves but the product of the implicit logic of modus ponens and modus tollens.

9

Commonsense Reasoning

THE ROBUST THEORY OF COMMONSENSE REASONING

Commonsense reasoning has posed problems for artificial intelligence. On the one hand, there appear to be rules of thumb in commonsense reasoning, but there also appears to be pragmatic flexibility, permitting adaptation to the special circumstances of situations. Therefore, computational models of commonsense reasoning would appear to require a combined mechanism that would capture patterns in commonsense reasoning by the judicious integration of rules that provide dependable consistency in reasoning and similarities in cases, analogies, or patterns that are useful where flexibility is required. These requirements have been met by Ron Sun (1995) who has developed both a theory and a computational model: CONSYDERR. The interesting research of Sun (1995) will be considered in this section, and, then a brief commentary will be offered.

Robust Commonsense Reasoning: Overview

Sun (1995) presents the following summary account of his research.

The paper attempts to account for common patterns in commonsense reasoning through integrating rule-based reasoning and similarity-based reasoning as embodied in connectionist models. Reasoning examples are analyzed and a diverse range of patterns is identified. A principled synthesis based on simple rules and similarities is performed, which unifies these patterns that were before difficult to be accounted for without specialized mechanisms individually. A two-level connectionist architecture with dual representations is proposed as a computational mechanism for carrying out the theory. It is shown in detail how the common patterns can be generated by this mechanism. Finally, it is argued that the brittleness problem of rule-based models can be remedied in a principled way, with the theory proposed here. This work demonstrates that combining rules and similarities can result in more robust reasoning models, and many seemingly disparate patterns of commonsense reasoning are actually different manifestations of the same underlying process and can be generated using the integrated architecture, which captures the underlying process to a large extent. (Sun, 1995, p. 241)

Domain-Independent Commonsense Reasoning

In the following section, Sun (1995) offers a definition of the nature of commonsense reasoning and proposes the interesting idea that there are patterns of commonsense reasoning that are domain independent.

Commonsense reasoning is somewhat structured yet flexible, and usually reliable but sometimes fallible [Davis, 1990; McCarthy, 1968; Zadeh, 1988]. It has been extremely difficult for AI programs to capture such commonsense knowledge and reasoning in all its power and flexibility. Even the very concept, commonsense reasoning, is difficult to characterize: we cannot define what commonsense reasoning is, just as it is hard to define what intelligence is, or what knowledge is. Roughly speaking, however, commonsense reasoning can be taken, at least for the kind of commonsense reasoning explored in this work, as referring to informal kinds of reasoning in everyday life regarding mundane issues, where speed is oftentimes more critical than accuracy.

The study of commonsense reasoning as envisaged here is neither about the study of a particular domain, nor about idiosyncratic reasoning in any particular domain. It deals with commonsense reasoning *patterns*; that is, the recurrent, domain-independent basic forms of reasoning that are applicable across a wide range of domains (as we believe that such forms do exist).

The question of whether there exist any domain independent, recurrent common patterns in reasoning, especially in commonsense reasoning, is open (cf. [Davis, 1990; McCarthy, 1968]). It is somewhat related to the debate between instance-based reasoning models and rule-based reasoning models (see e.g., [Riesbeck and Schank, 1989; Smith, Langston, and Nisbett, 1992]).

Allan Collins collected a large number of protocols of commonsense reasoning [Collins, 1978a; Collins and Michalski, 1989] in the area of elementary geography and the like. Noticing the inadequacy of traditional logic in explaining the reasoning patterns exhibited by the protocols, he argues for alternative formalisms for patterns found in various commonsense reasoning tasks. Collins and Michalski [1989] believe in the existence of common patterns (versus domain specific and/or ad hoc processes) that are widely applicable across domains (thus they actually developed a generalized logical formulation of them). This standpoint and the data on which it is based is also the starting point of studying commonsense reasoning in this work. (Sun, 1995, pp. 241–242; italics added)

Protocols of Commonsense Reasoning

In the following section, Sun (1995) presents a number of examples of human commonsense reasoning and considers the problem of understanding them from a computational point of view.

Let us look into a set of examples, most of which are protocols from Collins [Collins, 1978a; Collins and Michalski, 1989], though somewhat simplified. The goal here is not psychological data modeling, but a computational understanding.

(1) The first example shows uncertain, evidential reasoning:

Q: Do you think they might grow rice in Florida?

A: Yeah, I guess they could, if there were an adequate fresh water supply, certainly a nice, big, warm, flat area.

There is a rule in this example: if a place is big, warm, flat, and has an adequate fresh water supply, then it is a rice-growing area. The person answering the question deduced an uncertain conclusion based on partial knowledge, although a piece of crucial information (i.e., the presence of fresh water) is absent.

(2) The second example is as follows:

Q: Is the Chaco the cattle country?

A: It is like western Texas, so in some sense I guess it's cattle country.

Here because there is no known knowledge, an uncertain conclusion is drawn based on similarity with known knowledge.

(3) The third example is:

Q: Are there roses in England?

A: There are a lot of flowers in England. So I guess there are roses.

Here the deduction is based on *property inheritance*. Formally, England HORTICUL-TURE flower; rose IS-A flower; so England HORTICULTURE rose (to use the jargon of the inheritance theory; see [Sun, 1993]). The conclusion is only partially certain and is drawn because there is no information to the contrary (i.e., no *cancellation* of properties).

(4) The fourth example is:

Q: Is that [Llanos] where they grow coffee up there?

A: I don't think the savanna is used for growing coffee. The trouble is the savanna has a rainy season and you can't count on rain in general [for growing coffee].

This example shows a chain of rules in reasoning: Llanos is a savanna, savanna has a rainy season, and rainy seasons do not permit coffee growing.

(5) The fifth example is:

Q: Is Uruguay in the Andes Mountains?

A: It's a good guess to say that it's in the Andes Mountains because a lot of the countries [of South America] are.

Here there is no rule stating whether Uruguay is in the Andes or not. However, since most South American countries are in the Andes, the *default* is therefore *in the Andes*. Uruguay just "inherits" this default value (though incorrectly).

(6) The sixth example is:

Q: Can a goose quack?

A: No. A goose—well, it's like a duck, but it's not a duck. It can honk, but to say it can quack. No. I think its vocal cords are built differently. They have a beak and everything. But no, it can't quack.

More than one pattern is present here. One is based on similarity between geese and ducks, independent of knowledge regarding geese, yielding the conclusion that geese may be able to quack. Another pattern is a rule: since geese do not have vocal cords built for quacking, they cannot quack.

(7) The seventh example is:

Q: Is Florida moist?

A: The temperature is high there, so the water holding capacity of the air is high too. I think Florida is moist.

In this example the concepts involved are not all-or-nothing, but somehow graded, so the conclusion must be graded, in correspondence with the confidence values of known facts and rules.

(8) The eighth example is:

Q: Will high interest rates cause high inflation rates?

A: No, high interest rates will cause low money supply growth, which in turn causes low inflation rates.

This example shows a chaining of rules: high interest rates will cause low money supply growth, and low money supply growth will cause low inflation rates, so high interest rates will cause low inflation rates.

(9) The ninth example is:

Q: What kind of vehicles are you going to buy?

A: For carrying cargo, I have to buy a utility vehicle, but for carrying passengers, I have to buy a passenger vehicle. So I will buy a vehicle that is both a utility and a passenger vehicle. For example, a van.

This example shows the additive interaction of two rules: if carrying cargo, buy a utility vehicle, and if carrying passengers, buy a passenger vehicle. The result is the combination of the two rules: something that is both a utility vehicle and a passenger vehicle.

(10) The tenth example is:

Q: Do women living in that [tropical] region have short life expectancy?

A: Men living in tropical regions have short life expectancy, so probably women living in tropical regions have short life expectancy too.

This is another case of using similarity because of the lack of direct knowledge.

(11) The eleventh example is:

Q: Are all South American countries in the tropical region?

A: I think South American countries are in the tropical region, Guyana is in the tropical region, Venezuela is in the tropical region, so on and so forth.

Although the conclusion is incorrect, this example illustrates *bottom-up inheritance* (a form of generalization). Since there is no knowledge directly associated with the super-class "South American countries" as to whether they are in the tropical [region] or not, subclasses are looked at, and a conclusion is drawn based on the knowledge of the subclasses.

One can observe from these examples that (cf. [Collins and Michalski, 1989]):

- *The same patterns are present in many different situations (see e.g. Examples 2, 6, and 10).*

- *People are more or less cértain about their conclusions depending on their certainty of information (including rules and facts; see e.g. Examples 1 and 7).*

- *People have some means of applying existing knowledge, and some means of performing similarity matching when there is no matching existing knowledge (many examples above indicate the existence of the two processes, individually or intermixed together).*

A methodological note is in order here: in describing different patterns, we use rules if conditions are explicitly mentioned and manipulated; we use similarity matching if none of the relevant features or conditions is mentioned explicitly (it is thus suggestive of a holistic process); when in similarity matching, once concept is a superclass (or subclass) of the other, it is a case of inheritance. (Sun, 1995, pp. 244–246; italics added)

Commonsense Reasoning: General Issues

Sun (1995) raises a set of basic issues concerning the nature of commonsense reasoning in the following section.

There are some important unanswered questions about commonsense reasoning. For example, what are the basic patterns in commonsense reasoning? What notions can be used to best characterize these patterns? What is the most fundamental problem underlying the difficulty in producing commonsense reasoning as in these data? We will try to answer (tentatively) some of these questions. (Sun, 1995, p. 247)

Commonsense Reasoning: Rules

In the following section, Sun (1995) asserts that the knowledge contained in commonsense reasoning is best represented by rules.

First of all, there is the question of the proper form of knowledge representation for applying existing, directly-applicable knowledge (such as that in examples 1 and 7). Although there are many alternatives available, by all accounts, *rules* seem to be the best choice as an appropriate or even necessary form for expressing various kinds of knowledge, for a number of reasons. First of all, phenomenological evidence for the existence of rules in reasoning is mounting: Smith et al. [1992] present eight criteria for the existence of rules in cognition; detailed experimental results are analyzed which show that the eight criteria can be satisfied by various data; so the conclusion is drawn that rules are an intrinsic part of cognition. Fodor and Pylyshyn [1988] argue that linguistic and other processes require systematicity which only symbol manipulation and rule-based reasoning can provide; Pinker and Prince [1988] show that phonological performance can be better modeled by utilizing rules, at least as a part of the mechanism. Rule-based reasoning and symbolic manipulation provide some of the rigor and flexibility that are necessary in developing robust reasoning capabilities in commonsense reasoners.

Secondly, examining the examples discussed above, there are clear indications of the existence of rules; for example, in the Florida case, there is undoubtedly a rule with four conditions (big area, warm area, flat area, and fresh water supply) and one conclusion (rice-growing area). Conversely, examining all the examples . . . , although there may be more than one way for encoding some knowledge, all directly applied knowledge can be captured (computationally) in rules rather naturally, as discussed earlier at length.

In addition, at the computations level, the following reasons support the use of rules:

- Rules are the most common form of knowledge representation, used widely in all kinds of AI systems.

- It has been convincingly argued that other knowledge representation schemes can be transformed into logic (rule) based schemes [Chomsky, 1980; Hayes, 1977; Nilsson, 1980].

- Rules are precise but allow incorporation of confidence measures, uncertain knowledge, and plausible inference processes [Pearl, 1988; Zadeh, 1988].

- Rules ensure modularity in representation, making the representation easy to construct and manipulate and making it easy to incorporate new knowledge and change existing ones (the detail of this aspect is not addressed in this paper).

- Representation with rules facilitates explanation generation (explaining inferential processes) and improves human comprehensibility in many other ways.

Next, back at a phenomenological level, we can see that commonsense reasoning processes are *evidential*, which means that the existing knowledge, or rules, are not deterministic, a priori, or transcendentally true. Rather, they are empirical, inexact, and uncertain. Based on the observations [regarding the examples], we further conjecture the following in rule representation:

- Concepts or propositions involved in reasoning processes are often graded, that is, not all-or-nothing but fuzzy, possibilistic, or probabilistic [Dubois & Prade, 1988]. For example, "warm" is a fuzzy concept and there is no fixed boundary as to what is warm and what is not; similarly, the proposition "raining causes flooding" is a probabilistic rather than deterministic proposition. We can associate with each of those concepts and propositions a generic confidence that can be used to facilitate reasoning processes.

- As suggested by data (e.g. Example 6), different pieces of evidence are often weighted, that is, each of them may have more or less impact, depending on its importance or salience (see Osherson et al. [1987] for additional evidence and arguments). We need a way of combining evidence from different sources with different weights, without incurring too much computational overhead (such as in probabilistic reasoning or Dempster-Shafer calculus [Pearl, 1988; Shafer, 1976]).

- The evidential combination process may be cumulative, or in other words, it tends to "add up" various pieces of evidence to reach a conclusion, with a confidence that is determined from the "sum" of the confidences of the different pieces of evidence. Knowing two conditions in a rule results in a larger confidence than knowing only one. For example, in the example regarding whether Florida is a rice-growing area, if we know all the four conditions, warm, flat, big, and fresh water supply, we can make the conclusion with full confidence; when we know only three of the four conditions, we reach the same conclusion with less confidence. A cumulative evidential combination procedure is therefore necessary in rule representation. (Sun, 1995, pp. 247–248)

Commonsense Reasoning: Similarities

In the following section, Sun (1995) discusses the role of similarities in commonsense reasoning from phenomenological and computational viewpoints.

The above data also clearly indicate the need for similarity matching and some form of analogy in reasoning: in situations where there is no directly applicable knowledge (such as in examples 2 and 6), one can find similar concepts, propositions or situations, within the current context, and come up with some plausible conclusions based on the degree of the similarity. Phenomenologically, the comparison process that determines similarities is an intuitive, holistic and unstructured process, for the above protocols and examples do not indicate anything deliberative or analytical. This phenomenon is also recognized by e.g. Dreyfus and Dreyfus [1987], Hinton [1990], and Smolensky [1988], based on theoretical and experimental observations. Computationally, however, similarity can be implemented as rules [Collins and Michalski, 1989] and thus only one process (rule application) is left. Such an approach creates two problems:

(1) one concept is similar to many other concepts, and thus too many rules will have to be added into a system to capture all of these similarities; this tends to make systems for any reasonably large domain unwieldy (to say the least) because of the existence of too many rules;

(2) it will be difficult then to distinguish between strong rule-governed reasoning and mere associations based on similarities, whereas the distinction is rather clear commonsensically.

It is evident that rule application and similarity matching are intrinsically mixed together; for example, in the protocol about geese, the application of a rule regarding vocal cords is intertwined with the similarity matching with ducks. By combining the two processes, many interesting inferences can be made with relative ease. In other words, it is the interaction between the two processes that creates those interesting reasoning patterns (for example, top-down inheritance, bottom-up inheritance, and cancellation ...). Therefore it is important to study their interaction and come up with a computational model within which the interaction can be utilized.

There is evidence suggesting that reasoning processes with similarity matching (comparison of analogous knowledge) are massively parallel and spontaneous (i.e., automatic) (see e.g. [Waltz, 1989]), which should be taken into account in any theory of commonsense reasoning. This is also the case with rule application, which is oftentimes also parallel and spontaneous (see e.g. [Dreyfus and Dreyfus, 1987; Holland et al., 1986] for some arguments). (Sun, 1995, pp. 248–249; italics added)

Commonsense Reasoning: Summary of Patterns

In the following section, Sun (1995) summarizes the diversity of patterns found in the protocols of commonsense reasoning.

We can summarize the patterns of commonsense reasoning in the examples ... as follows (cf. [Sun, 1991, 1992]):

• Partial information (e.g., the first example), in which not all relevant information is known but a conclusion has to be drawn.

- Uncertain or fuzzy information (e.g., the first example again), in which information is not known exactly and with absolute certainty, but a plausible conclusion has to be drawn based on what is known.

- Similarity matching (e.g., the second example), in which rules describing similar but different situations are used due to the lack of exact matching rules (in case of novel input).

- Combinatorial rule interactions (e.g., the ninth example; see [Sun, 1994a] for complete details regarding this aspect), in which conclusions and conditions of multiple rules combine to produce strengthened, weakened, or entirely new results, made possible by the lack of consistency and completeness resulting from a fragmented rule base.

- Top-down inheritance (e.g., the third example), in which information regarding superclasses is brought to bear on the subclasses.

- Bottom-up inheritance (e.g., the eleventh example), in which information regarding subclasses is brought to bear on the superclasses.

Although these patterns seem disparate, a theoretical synthesis below will show their commonalities. (Sun, 1995, pp. 249–250; italics added)

Theory of Robust Reasoning: Definitions

Sun (1995) proposes a theoretical analysis, beginning with definitions, of the possibility of unifying the diverse patterns summarized in the previous section.

To perform a precise theoretical analysis, we need some definitions. A rule is defined here to be a structure consisting of some conditions and a conclusion; a numerical weight is associated with each condition. Whenever conditions are activated (to a degree commensurate with the confidence of the corresponding facts), the activation of the corresponding conclusion can be determined by multiplying the activation values of the conditions of the weights. This computation is commonly used (see [Shultz, Zelazo, and Engelberg, 1989; Sun, 1994a]) and adopted here for its intuitive appeal and simplicity. ... We will denote a rule by $A \rightarrow B$. And if A is activated, the activation of B due to A is denoted as $A * (A \rightarrow B)$.

Similarity can be defined here (a little simplistically) as a measure of the amount of overlap between the corresponding feature sets of the source and target concepts or propositions (taking into consideration the sizes of the source feature set ...). We will denote similarity by $A \sim B$. So if A is activated, the activation of B due to A is denoted as $A * (A \sim B)$, that is, the activation of A times the similarity measure between A and B. (See [Sloman, 1996] for some psychological evidence and arguments for a similar definition.) (Sun, 1995, pp. 249–250)

Theory of Robust Reasoning: Analysis

In the following section, Sun (1995) applies the definitions of rules and similarities to the identified patterns in an attempt to achieve synthesis.

(1) When we have inexact information, the inexactness can be quantified with a confidence value, and the value can be used in reasoning. Given

$$A \rightarrow B$$

if A is activated to a degree commensurate with its confidence level, then

$$B = A * (A \rightarrow B)$$

where A and B represent respective activations, $(A \rightarrow B)$ represents the weight from A to B (i.e., the rule strength, a number), and "*" is multiplication.

(2) When we have incomplete information (that is, when we do not have all the requisite conditions to apply a rule), we can still deduce a conclusion, although with less confidence; for the confidence of a conclusion is determined based on the vector multiplication computation (i.e. the inner product, a simple extension of scalar multiplication). Suppose we have rules

$$A \ B \ C \rightarrow D$$

When given confidence values of A and B with C unknown (zero activation), D is deduced with less confidence than when given full confidence values of all of A, B and C:

$$D = (A \ B \ 0) * (A \ B \ C \rightarrow D)$$

where $(A \ B \ C \rightarrow D)$ represents a vector of the three weights, and they are applied to the activation values of the conditions of the rule, $(A \ B \ C)$, to get the weighted-sum (the inner product).

(3) The similarity matching situation (due to the lack of any exactly matching rule when encountering novel input) can be described as:

$$A \sim B,$$
$$B \rightarrow C$$

and A is activated (i.e. the activation $A \neq 0$); that is, we want to know about A (e.g. Chaco), but there is no rule directly applicable beside a similarity with B (e.g. western Texas). So we utilize the similarity between A and B, and the knowledge C associated with B (e.g. cattle-country):

$$B = A * (A \sim B)$$

where A represents the activation of the concept, $(A \sim B)$ represents the similarity between A and B, and "*" is multiplication; so

$$C = B * (B \rightarrow C) = A * (A \sim B) * (B \rightarrow C)$$

where $(B \rightarrow C)$ represents the weight (the rule strength) from B to C.

(4) For top-down inheritance, suppose A is a subclass of B, A's property value is unknown, B has a property value C, and we want to know the corresponding property value of A, that is,

$$A \sim B,$$
$$B \rightarrow C.$$

When A is activated, C will be activated accordingly, i.e.

$$C = A * (A \sim B) * (B \rightarrow C).$$

(5) For bottom-up inheritance, suppose B is a superclass of A, B's property value is unknown, and A has a property value D, and we want to know the corresponding property value of B, that is,

$$B \sim A,$$
$$A \rightarrow D.$$

When B is activated, D will be activated accordingly, i.e.

$$D = B * (B \sim A) * (A \rightarrow D).$$

(6) For cancellation of inheritance, suppose A is a superclass (or subclass) of B, A has a property value D, and B has a property value C, then

$$A \sim B,$$
$$B \rightarrow C,$$
$$A \rightarrow D.$$

When A is activated, D will be activated more than C.
   (7) In case of rule interaction, we can describe the situation as

$$A \rightarrow C,$$
$$B \rightarrow D,$$
$$C \sim D.$$

When A and B both are activated, the interaction of C and D might result in something else being strongly activated, depending on their mutual similarity (see example 9).
   The above synthesis of these different patterns provides on one hand the rigor and precision . . . , and on the other hand the flexibility, which underlies most patterns of commonsense reasoning. A proper balance and mixture of the two in a theory of commonsense reasoning is our main goal. (Sun, 1995, pp. 250–252)

CONSYDERR: A Connectionist Mechanism for Robust Reasoning

In the following section, Sun (1995) presents the rationale and description of CONSYDERR, a unifying mechanism in the theory of robust reasoning that integrates the operation of rules and similarities in commonsense reasoning.

   I will outline below a unifying mechanism for carrying out the basic processes of rule-based reasoning and similarity-based reasoning. This mechanism, a connectionist architecture, consists of two levels: the first level, called CL, utilizes local representation, that

Figure 9.1
The Architecture

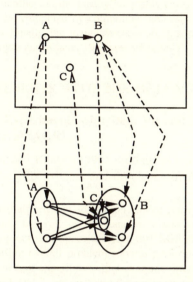

Phase I: top-down
links enabled

Phase II: intra-level
links enabled

Phase III: bottom-up
links enabled

Note: The top level is CL, and the bottom level is CD. A, B, and C are concepts, and the link
between A and B represents a rule A → B. For example, A = Chaco, B = Cattle-country,
and C = Western-Texas.

Source: Sun, R. (1995). Robust reasoning: Integrating rule-based and similarity-based reasoning.
Reprinted from *Artificial Intelligence, 75*, p. 256, copyright 1995, with permission from Elsevier Science.

is, one node for each domain concept; the other level, called CD, is more fine-grained,
utilizing distributed representation with fine-grained feature (interpretable or uninterpret-
able) into which all domain concepts can be decomposed. By dividing the architecture
into two levels, we can utilize the interaction between the two representations of different
granularity to make the architecture more effective and computationally more efficient.
[Figure 9.1] shows a sketch of the architecture. We will call this architecture CONSY-
DERR, which stands for CONnectionist System with Dual representation for Evidential
Robust Reasoning.

The reason for explicit localist representation in CL is the need to explicitly implement
rule applications in a connectionist network. We assume that this network carries out
reasoning at the *conceptual level*; so the representation has to be explicit and individu-
ated, in order for the concepts and reasoning processes to be consciously accessible and
linguistically expressible, without extra matching networks or decoding networks (which
is the case with distributed representations); we want explicitness, so that activated concepts can be easily identified, reasoning processes can be traced, and explanations can
be generated. . . . This leads directly to the idea of local representation: each concept or

proposition in a domain is represented by a single node in a network of nodes [Sun, Bookman, and Shekhar, 1992]; rules are then implemented by links between nodes representing conditions and nodes representing conclusions.

With rules being represented by links between nodes, reasoning can be done with only local computation—rule activations can be calculated within one or a few nodes, in place, without the need to perform indexing, retrieval, reorganization and updating of large databases of facts. Although there are various heuristics for reducing search time in large knowledge bases, none of them succeeded significantly. The overhead of selecting and moving data around can be avoided by directly connecting together those pairs of facts that are related by rules so that only local computation for passing on activations is necessary. This design thus has a computational advantage over more traditional rule-based systems. This design also has an advantage cognitively: the speed in human commonsense reasoning can be better matched [Collins and Loftus, 1975].

Commonsense reasoning by nature is evidential, cumulative, and graded (as has been discussed before), which rule encoding in CL has to deal with. One possibility is to use graded and continuous activations (representing confidence values or certainty values) and weighted-sum combinations functions (representing evidential combination in rule firing) for this purpose; thus rule encoding coincides with the operation of typical connectionist models and consequently has an easy implementation in a connectionist network. . . .

To carry out similarity matching, a distributed representation (based on features) is needed, which must be at a different level because of its distributed character; thus the CD level comes into play. The nature of distributed feature representation decides that it is *similarity-based*: the amount of overlap between two sets of nodes representing two different concepts is proportional to the degree of similarity between these two concepts or propositions. On the other hand, the links in CD are the replications of the links in CL (which represent rules); that is, if there is a link between two nodes (or the two concepts they represent) at the CL level, then we will add a link between each node in the feature set of the first concept and each node in the feature set of the second concept, replicating diffusely the original link at CL (having the full cross-product connection between the two feature sets). This corresponds to the idea of incorporating analytical knowledge (which can be represented by a localist network) into intuition (which can be partially captured by a similarity-based distributed connectionist network; see [Dreyfus and Dreyfus, 1987]), although we will not discuss the learning process per se here.

For more flexibility, interactions between the two levels have a top-down path and a bottom-up path separately. Also, the operation of the system is in cycles; in other words, the interaction of the two levels is not ever-present, and each part is independent to a certain extent. One cycle can be divided into three phases: the top-down phase, the settling phase, and the bottom-up phase, in which top-down flows only occur during the top-down phase and bottom-up flows only occur during the bottom-up phase; in other words, the two levels have *phasic* interactions [Sun, 1994b]. The computational utility of cycles (and the two-level structure on which they operate), as will become clear later on, is avoiding time and space complexity as in e.g. Hopfield networks and other common types of connectionist networks [Barnden, 1988], which requires ever-present global connectivity and thus results in slow settling. *This structure may also be partially justified cognitively by the phenomenon of multiple streams of thoughts (see [Norman, 1977].* (Sun, 1995, pp. 254–255; italics added)

CONSYDERR: First Example of Its Application

In the following section, Sun (1995) provides an illuminating example of the application of CONSYDERR to a protocol of commonsense reasoning.

Let us look at the following example:

Q: Do you think they might grow rice in Florida?

A: Yeah. I guess they could, if there were an adequate fresh water supply, certainly a nice, big, warm, flat area.

The rule used is:

big-area warm-area flat-area fresh-water-supply → rice-growing-area.

This can be handled by CONSYDERR: Each node in CL represents a concept, including "big-area", "warm-area", "flat-area", "fresh-water-supply", and "rice-growing-area". The rules are represented by links between nodes. The weights on the links reflect degrees of confidence in the respective implications, as well as positiveness/negativeness of the implications. The reasoning process is as follows: First three out of four conditions are activated to certain degrees (which reflect the corresponding confidence in these facts), then they send their activation to the node representing the conclusion ("rice-growing-area") and activate that node. Because of one missing condition, the activation, calculated with weighted-sum, will be less than one, but still greater than zero. Therefore we conclude that it *might* be a rice-growing area.

CONSYDERR: Second Example of Its Application

Another example is as follows:

Q: Is the Chaco the cattle country?

A: It is like western Texas, so in some sense I guess it's cattle country.

Here, because there is no direct knowledge regarding Chaco, an uncertain conclusion is drawn based on similarity. The knowledge is expressed in a rule:

Western-Texas → cattle-country

represented in CL by the two nodes, one for "Western-Texas" and the other for "cattle-country", and the link between the two nodes. The similarity between the two areas

Chaco ~ Western-Texas

is implemented through feature overlapping in CD. And the CL links are diffusely replicated in CD. The reasoning process is as follows: first the node for Chaco is activated; in the top-down phase the CD representation of Chaco is activated and because of shared

Figure 9.2
The Reasoning Process for Protocol 2

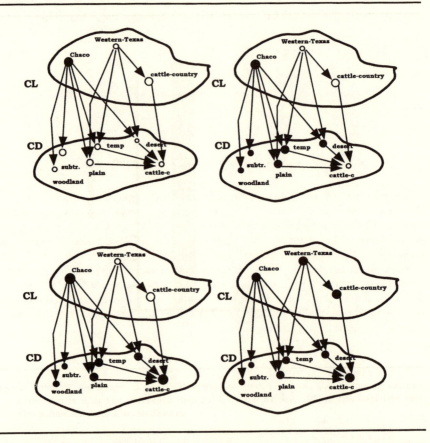

Note: Black circles represent activated nodes. (1) Receiving inputs, (2) top-down, (3) settling (rule application), and (4) bottom-up.

Source: Sun, R. (1995). Robust reasoning: Integrating rule-based and similarity-based reasoning. Reprinted from *Artificial Intelligence, 75*, p. 260, copyright 1955, with permission from Elsevier Science.

features, the CD representation of Western-Texas is activated partially to a degree proportional to the similarity measure; then in the settling phase, the links representing rules take effect in CD, so the CD representation of cattle-country is partially activated; finally in the bottom-up phase, the partially activated CD representation of cattle-country percolates up to activate the node representing cattle-country in CL. See [Figure 9.2]. (Sun, 1995, pp. 258–260)

CONSYDERR: Third Example of Its Application

Whereas the first example demonstrated the operation of rules and the second the operation of similarities, the third example is concerned with inheritance.

The following example involves inheritance, handled by a combination of both rule application and similarity matching.

Q: Are there roses in England?

A: There are a lot of flowers in England. So I guess there are roses.

It can be described by

England → *flower*,
flower ~ *rose*

and we have *flower* $\supset$ *rose* and, in turn, $F_{flower} \subset F_{rose}$. The same way as before, this can be implemented in CONSYDERR with the two-level dual representation and their interaction. See [Figure 9.3] for details of the reasoning process. Overall, CONSYDERR deals successfully with inheritance (see [Sun, 1993] for complete treatments of inheritance). (Sun, 1995, p. 261)

CONSYDERR: Brittleness and Robustness

In the following section, Sun (1995) provides an interesting account of how CONSYDERR avoids brittleness and ensures robustness in solving commonsense reasoning problems.

The term *brittleness* has been around for quite a while for describing some fundamental flaws of existing rule-based approaches [Holland, 1986; Waltz, 1988]. Though different authors have ascribed somewhat different meanings to the word, basically, "brittleness" (the opposite of robustness) suggests being easily broken: the slightest deviation in inputs from what is exactly known about a system can cause a complete breakdown of the system. Specifically, it can be qualified as the inability of a system to deal, in a systematic way within a unified framework, with some important aspects in reasoning, including the following aspects (which have been identified for a long time):

• partial information,
• uncertain or fuzzy information,
• similarity matching,
• rule interactions,
• generalization,
• inheritance (i.e. top-down inheritance),
• percolation (i.e. bottom-up inheritance),
• changing contexts and learning new rules.

Figure 9.3
The Reasoning Process for Protocol 3

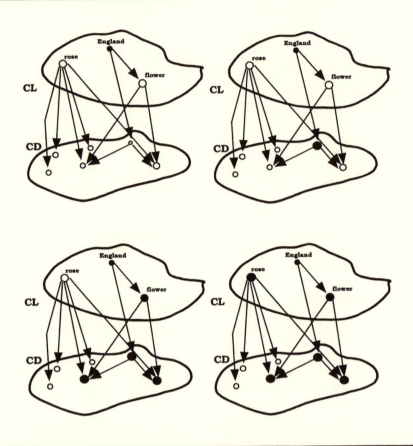

Note: Black circles represent activated nodes. (1) Receiving inputs, (2) top-down, (3) settling (rule
application), and (4) bottom-up.

Source: Sun, R. (1995). Robust reasoning: Integrating rule-based and similarity-based reasoning.
Reprinted from *Artificial Intelligence, 75*, p. 262, copyright 1995, with permission from Elsevier Science.

They overlap substantially with the 7 patterns identified [earlier], which are exemplified
in the 11 examples.

The brittleness problem is pervasive. With the exception of some extremely specialized
narrow domains, it shows up in all kinds of reasoning in various domains: for example,
the brittleness problem exists in *decision-making*: when there are no precisely specified
preconditions and actions (e.g. there exist different values, not just missing values), a
typical rule-based system cannot proceed without further information regarding the sit-

uation or without additional mechanisms (cf. [Hayes-Roth, Waterman, and Lenat, 1983]), due to the lack of aforementioned flexibility in such a system. To circumvent this brittleness problem, a brute force approach can be taken in such a system: every possible scenario of combinations of conditions and decisions is analyzed beforehand and structured into the system, which is not always possible, especially for large systems. The brittleness problem exists also in *diagnosis*, in real world *planning*, and in *control* with expert systems, and many other domains. The difficulty of conventional rule-based reasoning in dealing with all of these commonsense reasoning domains signifies the range and importance of the problem, so it is paramount to address this problem, in order to develop systems capable of robust reasoning.

The idea of robust reasoning is meant to capture the kind of reasoning that occurs in commonsense domains, and both the flexibility and the rigor associated with it; or more precisely, it is meant to be reasoning free from the problem of brittleness. The theory of robust reasoning is able to deal with the requisite flexibility: fuzzy, partial, or incomplete information, inexact knowledge or inexact matches between knowledge in store and situations at hand, generalization from known instances, similarity-based reasoning, and other kinds of flexibility. Among all aspects of the brittleness problem, learning new rules is a separate issue (quite different from the representational issues) and should be so dealt with. (Although the study of their interaction would be interesting, it is beyond the scope of this paper to cover them all.) *While the remaining aspects of the problem still look like a disparate set of problems, they are all characterized in the present theory as rule-based reasoning coupled with similarity-based reasoning. Thus the present theory provides a promising avenue towards robust reasoning.*

The significance lies in the fact that, based on this theory, a connectionist architecture with a simple two-level structure can deal with brittleness (to a certain extent) and solve a certain range of representation and reasoning problems effectively and computationally efficiently in a massively parallel manner; notably, the task is accomplished within a unified framework. (However, it is not a complete solution to all the problems within the scope but a solution to a subset of the most common reasoning problems that can be solved with a simple computational mechanism.) (Sun, 1995, pp. 276–277; italics added)

CONSYDERR: Comparison with Collins and Michalski's Theory

Sun (1995) provides an interesting comparison of the theory of robust reasoning with the Collins and Michalski theory of plausible reasoning in the following account.

Collins and Michalski [1989] present an interesting analysis of patterns in commonsense reasoning. I will not attempt to discuss the theory completely, except to point out some connections to this work. The six categories in [Collins and Michalski, 1989] are of particular interest:

(1) derivation from mutual implication,

(2) derivation from mutual dependence,

(3) generalization-based transformation,

(4) specialization-based transformation,

(5) similarity-based transformation,

(6) dissimilarity-based transformation.

According to the present analysis, they can be reduced as follows: the first two categories have little difference (computationally) and both can, to a large extent, be dealt with by rule application (with contextual effects handled by the context module as discussed before); the rest of the categories are similarity-related, that is, generalization and specialization are special cases of similarity, and therefore they can be dealt with by similarity matching. Dis-similarity based inference is not covered here.

In Collins and Michalski's theory, the confidence of the conclusions reached depends on a number of parameters: conditional likelihood, degree of certainty, degree of typicality of a subset within a set, degree of similarity of one set to another, frequency of the referent in the domain of the descriptor, dominance of a subset in a set, multiplicity of the referent, and finally, multiplicity of the argument. According to the present analysis, a smaller set of parameters can be identified: rule weights and similarity measures. These two parameters can subsume the above parameters used in Collins and Michalski: the first two, conditional likelihood and degrees of certainty, can be easily captured by rule weights [Sun, 1994a]; the rest can be accounted for by similarity measures or a combination of rule weights and similarity measures.

Finally, although the theory of Collins and Michalski [1989] is consistent and justified, the existing implementations of it seem to be a juxtaposition of different techniques within a rule-based framework. A problem with such implementations, I believe, is that they still suffer from the brittleness problem: similarity is handled by rules, and one rule is used for each pair of similar concepts; therefore, there may be too many rules around, because there are too many things similar to any one particular thing, in many different ways and under many different contexts, as pointed out before; such systems will not be free from brittleness in any reasonably large domain, considering the difficulty of this brute force method of putting every pair of similar things into rules. The computational complexity is tremendous, given the number of rules needed. A more integrated mechanism capable of dealing with similarity matching and other types of flexible reasoning in a massively parallel fashion (also cf. [Golding and Rosenbloom, 1991]) is preferred. (Sun, 1995, pp. 277–278; italics added)

Theory of Robust Reasoning: Limits and Developments

Sun (1995) presents the following interesting view of the limitations of his theory of robust reasoning and its computational embodiment in CONSYDERR and related developments.

We shall further refine the theory and the CONSYDERR architecture proposed here. There are several aspects worth pursuing further. One aspect that may be of great importance for further development is automatically developing distributed representation, which is currently underway. It has been suggested that this can be done through grounding high-level processes into low-level processes (i.e. symbol grounding [Harnad, 1990]), and through mapping syntactic representation into semantic representation by learning algorithms [Dyer, 1990]. Features developed in this way (which may not be conceptually interpretable) may better capture the similarity between concepts involved in given situations, and may lead to more accurate models of commonsense reasoning based on similarity matching.

In addition, it is important to study in greater detail the interaction between the feature representation and the more explicit local representation, especially with regard to the exploration of the synergy which interaction generates.

Backward chaining and goal-directed inference are not treated in this paper. Nevertheless, they are important issues and should be addressed in subsequent work.

More experimental work shall be carried out as the next step in this research, which shall include examinations of system dynamics with complex rule structures and feature structures, detailed verifications with quantitative data, and explorations of other representational and reasoning types, such as temporal reasoning, backward chaining, and recursive rule structures. (Sun, 1995, p. 278; italics added)

Theory of Robust Reasoning: Conclusion

Sun (1995) provides the following succinct conclusion to his important research.

The theory advanced here is meant to be an *integrated* model that can deal effectively with a (seemingly disparate) set of important problems in commonsense reasoning (i.e. the basic elements of commonsense reasoning): rule application, evidential combination, similarity matching, inheritance in both directions, and so on. The key point is that these problems are handled in a single unified framework that has no special provision for any single one of these problems. Through data analyses, these problems are reduced to a single process; thus a theory of robust reasoning is proposed, combining the rigor and flexibility needed in commonsense reasoning. The theory is carried out by CONSYDERR, a connectionist architecture, which thus serves as a unifying mechanism. CONSYDERR integrates rule-based reasoning into connectionist networks and couples localist networks with similarity-based distributed representation. (Sun, 1995, pp. 278–279)

COMMENTARY

Sun (1995) claims that his robust theory represents six transforms or patterns and is complete. However, dissimilarity is not included in his theory of transforms and therefore is missing from the CONSYDERR program. Yet, as pointed out in Collins and Michalski (1989), the dissimilarity transform, both by itself and in conjunction with the similarity transform, is frequently found in commonsense reasoning where the overall pattern of similarities and dissimilarities can be evaluated and a judicious decision with an appropriate amount of certainty-uncertainty can be reached.

It is not clear why Sun (1995) left out the dissimilarity pattern since he includes the example of "ducks versus geese" and "quacking versus honking" from Collins and Michalski (1989) in his list of protocol of examples of commonsense reasoning. Certainly, it would seem essential to include dissimilarity in his theory of robust reasoning. Such an inclusion would make his theory more typical of commonsense reasoning and should be included both as part of his "similarity-based" and "rule-based" components of his unified theory of robust reasoning.

10

Temporal Reasoning

The nature of time has preoccupied intellectual history from Plato down to the twenty-first century. For Plato, time possessed an unchanging absolute character, but for Aristotle time was simply the measure of motion or change. Newton viewed time as absolute, as a kind of container into which events could be fitted. Leibniz debated Newton's view and asserted that time was relational to events or changes. Contemporary cosmology proposes that time began with the big bang creation of the universe.

Mathematically, time is considered the independent variable in the relationship $Y = f(t)$. The derivative dy/dt expresses the rate of change in some quantity with respect to a change in time. In many ways, the mathematical conception of time is an advance over the philosophical and psychological views of time. It offers decision concerning change, no change, positive change, and negative change in the relation of events or quantities to time.

Cognitive psychology points to limitations in human processing capacity. Yet, the management of time as in clinical protocols that involve many complex events in the course of a medical treatment regimen requires temporal abstractions between and among past, current, and planned events, together with changes resulting from unexpected effects on patients' improvement or lack of improvement. Difficulties in cognitive abstraction and management of time have prompted research for expert systems that could assist physicians, often confused by the complexities of reasoning with temporal abstractions. Yuval Shahar (1997) has developed a theory of the necessary knowledge and mechanisms required for artificial temporal abstraction and embodied the theory in the expert system, RÉSUMÉ. Shahar's research and development will be described in this chapter, and, then, a brief commentary will be offered.

CONCEPTS AND METHODS OF TEMPORAL ABSTRACTION

The Temporal Abstraction Task

Shahar (1997) summarizes the general purposes of a knowledge-based temporal abstraction method in the following section.

The *temporal abstraction (TA) task*—formation of meaningful, context-sensitive, interval-based abstractions from time-stamped data—is important in many time-oriented domains. The interval-based abstractions that are the output of the TA task can be used for selection and instantiation of plans; for monitoring plans during execution; for creation of high-level summaries of time-stamped data; for explanation purposes; and for critiquing the execution of a plan by one agent when the plan's overall and intermediate goals can be described in terms of creating, maintaining, or avoiding certain temporal patterns. (Shahar, 1997, pp. 121–122)

Temporal Abstraction and the Knowledge Level

Shahar (1997) provides the rationale for a knowledge-level approach to the task of temporal abstraction in the following account.

The knowledge requirements for performance of the TA task are implicit in traditional domain-style applications. This lack of explicit representation prevents using general principles common to performance of that task in different domains, and sharing of knowledge common to several tasks in the same domain.

Our approach embodies a *knowledge-level* view of the TA task. We emphasize the importance of enabling *reuse, sharing, maintenance, and acquisition* of TA knowledge for sizable knowledge-based systems that are applied to time-oriented domains. Our goal has been to elucidate the nature of the knowledge that is required for solving the TA task by a knowledge-based method. (Shahar, 1997, p. 122)

The Knowledge-Based Temporal Abstraction Method

Shahar (1997) describes the hierarchical structure of the knowledge-based temporal abstraction method in the following section.

We presented a specific knowledge-based approach to the TA task: the *knowledge-based temporal abstraction (KBTA) method*. The KBTA *method* decomposes the TA *task* into five *subtasks*, each of which is solved by a different TA *mechanism* (see [Figure 10.1]): temporal context restriction (creation of relevant interpretation contexts crucial for focusing and limiting the scope of the inference); vertical temporal inference (infer-

Figure 10.1
The Knowledge-Based Temporal Abstraction (KBTA) Method

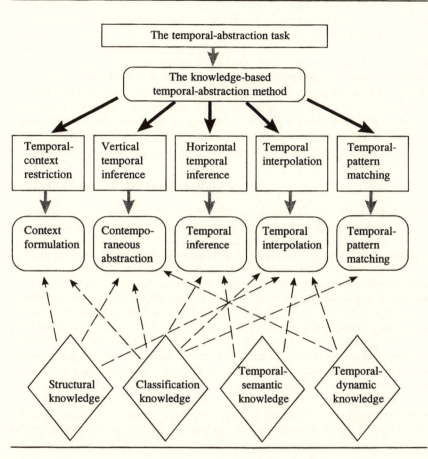

Note: The TA task is decomposed by the KBTA method into five subtasks. Each subtask can be performed by one of the five TA mechanisms. The TA mechanisms depend on four domain- and task-specific knowledge types. Rectangle = task; ellipse = method or mechanism; diamond = knowledge type; arrow = DECOMPOSED-INTO relation; shaded arrow = PERFORMED-BY relation; dashed arrow = USED-BY relation.

Source: Shahar, Y. (1997). A framework for knowledge-based temporal abstraction. Reprinted from *Artificial Intelligence, 90*, p. 84, copyright 1997, with permission from Elsevier Science.

ence from contemporaneous propositions into higher-level concepts); horizontal temporal inference (inference from similar type propositions attached to intervals that span differ- ent periods); temporal interpolation (joining of disjoint points or intervals, associated with propositions of similar type); and temporal pattern matching (creation of intervals by matching patterns over disjoint intervals, associated with propositions of various types). Four *knowledge types* are required for instantiating the temporal abstraction mechanisms in any particular domain (see [Figure 10.1]):

(1) structural knowledge (e.g., IS-A and PART-OF relations in the domain, QUALITATIVE DEPENDENCY relations, SUBCONTEXT relations);

(2) classification knowledge, mostly functional (e.g., mapping of Hemoglobin level ranges into LOW, HIGH, VERY HIGH; joining of INC and SAME into NONDEC; matching of temporal patterns);

(3) temporal semantic, mostly logical, knowledge (e.g., relations among propositions attached to intervals, and propositions attached to their subintervals, such as the *downward heredity* property); and

(4) temporal dynamic knowledge, mostly probabilistic (e.g., local forward and backward persistence (ρ) functions; global, maximal gap (Δ) functions; significant change functions).

The four knowledge types are sufficient to instantiate the five domain-independent TA mechanisms for any particular application area. The knowledge types form a declarative interface for a knowledge engineer developing a new TA system, and support automated acquisition of knowledge from domain experts.

The RÉSUMÉ system implements the KBTA method's inference structure and, in particular, the five TA mechanisms. We used the RÉSUMÉ system to model TA knowledge in several different clinical and engineering domains, and to form in those domains temporal abstractions comparable to those of experts. (Shahar, 1997, p. 122)

THE RÉSUMÉ SYSTEM

The General Characteristics of RÉSUMÉ

Shahar (1997) sets forth the general characteristics for the RÉSUMÉ system for the temporal abstraction task in the following descriptive account.

The KBTA method and TA mechanisms . . . have been implemented as a computer program: the RÉSUMÉ system (Shahar, 1994; Shahar and Musen, 1993/1994, 1996). The RÉSUMÉ system generates temporal abstractions, given time-stamped data, events, and the domain's TA ontology of parameters, events, and contexts. The RÉSUMÉ system is composed of a temporal reasoning module (the five TA mechanisms), a static domain knowledge base (the domain's TA ontology), and a dynamic temporal fact-base (containing the input and output parameter points and intervals, event intervals, and context intervals). The temporal fact base is loosely coupled to an external database, where primitive time-stamped patient data and clinical events are stored and updated, and where abstractions can be stored by the RÉSUMÉ system for additional analysis or for use by other users. The TA mechanisms iterate alternately, activated by the currently available data and by the previously derived abstractions. (Shahar, 1997, p. 116)

The Parameter Ontology

In the following section, Shahar (1997) describes how domain knowledge is incorporated in RÉSUMÉ's parameter properties ontology.

Figure 10.2
A Portion of the Parameter Properties Ontology in the Domain of Protocol-Based Care

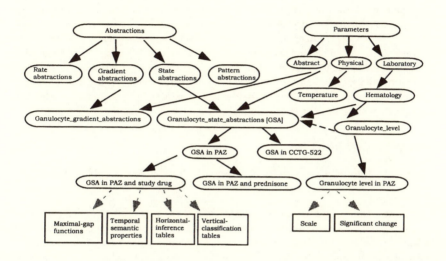

Note: Shown in the figure is a specialization of the temporal abstraction properties of the Granulocyte state abstraction (GSA) parameter in the context of the prednisone azathioprine (PAZ) experimental protocol for treating chronic graft-versus-host disease, and in the context of each part of that therapy protocol. Ellipse = class; rectangle = property; arrow = IS-A relation; shaded arrow = PROPERTY-OF relation; dashed arrow = ABSTRACTED-INTO relation.

Source: Shahar, Y. (1997). A framework for knowledge-based temporal abstraction. Reprinted from *Artificial Intelligence, 90*, p. 117, copyright 1997, with permission from Elsevier Science.

Most of the domain-specific knowledge required by the TA mechanisms is represented in an implementation of the parameter ontology called the domain's *parameter properties ontology*. The parameter properties ontology represents the parameter entities in the domain (e.g., Hemoglobin, Granulocyte state), their properties (e.g., temporal semantic properties, such as *concatenable*), and the relations among them (e.g., ABSTRACTED-INTO). [Figure 10.2] shows a small part of the parameter properties ontology used for the task of managing patients who are being treated by clinical protocols.

The parameter properties ontology is an IS-A frame hierarchy that specializes parameters mainly by increasingly specific interpretation contexts (e.g., classification tables for the Hemoglobin level parameter might be different during administration of a certain protocol or medication). The four knowledge types (including structural relations) are represented as parameter properties.

An important feature of the representation scheme shown in [Figure 10.2] is organization of abstract parameters by four output abstraction types (STATE, GRADIENT, RATE, and PATTERN). Thus, the Granulocyte_gradient_abstraction parameter is a gradient abstraction and inherits slots such as the default set of values and interpolation inference table for gradient abstractions, whereas state abstractions include properties such as their defining classification functions (mapping tables). This structure proved flexible for representation and modification of TA knowledge in several domains.

Pattern parameters are represented as first-class entities in the parameter ontology. This uniformity allows the TA mechanisms, at runtime, to perform further temporal reasoning using the derived pattern intervals, and preserves the logical dependencies of these pattern intervals on the other parameters (and contexts) from which they were derived. Maintaining these dependencies allows updates to the past and present data to be propagated to all abstractions, including the temporal patterns. Furthermore, representing patterns as first-class entities in the ontology of the domain permits the use of uniform methods for acquisition, maintenance, sharing, and reuse of knowledge. (Shahar, 1997, pp. 116–117)

Evaluation of RÉSUMÉ

The performance of the RÉSUMÉ system is evaluated in the following section.

We tested various aspects of the RÉSUMÉ system in several different clinical and engineering domains: protocol-based care (and three of its subdomains) (Shahar, 1994; Shahar and Musen, 1993/1994), monitoring of children's growth (Kuilboer et al., 1993; Shahar, 1994), therapy of insulin-dependent diabetes patients (Shahar and Musen, 1996), and monitoring of traffic-control actions (Shahar and Molina, 1996). We applied the RÉSUMÉ methodology to each domain in varying degrees. Sometimes, our focus was evaluating the feasibility of knowledge acquisition (including acquisition by another knowledge engineer), knowledge representation, and knowledge maintenance (i.e., modifications to the resultant knowledge base). In other cases, we emphasized application of the resultant instantiated temporal abstraction mechanisms to several clinical test cases. In one domain, we applied the RÉSUMÉ system, instantiated by the proper domain ontology, to a larger set of clinical data. We have therefore demonstrated most of the expected lifecycle in the development and maintenance of a TA system.

In the subdomains of protocol-based care, we have focused mainly on the representation of knowledge relevant for experimental therapy of patients who have AIDS, for therapy of patients who have graft-versus-host disease, and for prevention of AIDS-related complications, in each case, working with domain experts (Shahar, 1994; Shahar and Musen, 1993/1994). Typical abstractions included patterns such as "the second episode of Bone-marrow toxicity grade II that lasts more than three weeks" (see [Figure 10.3]). As we expected, we were able to reuse easily both general TA knowledge (e.g., gradient abstractions) and parameter-specific TA knowledge (e.g., Hemoglobin level abstractions) using explicit parameter properties ontology. Maintenance involved mainly adding or modifying classes that represent abstractions specialized by interpretation contexts.

In the domain of monitoring children's growth, we collaborated with a pediatric endocrinologist to form and maintain a growth monitoring TA ontology (Kuilboer et al., 1993). Running RÉSUMÉ on a few clinical test cases produced most of the relevant abstractions (Shahar, 1994). The goal in the growth monitoring domain was not to reach

Figure 10.3
Temporal Abstraction of Platelet and Granulocyte Values during Administration of a Prednisone/Azathioprine (PAZ) Clinical Protocol for Treating Patients Who Have Chronic Graft-Versus-Host Disease (CGVHD)

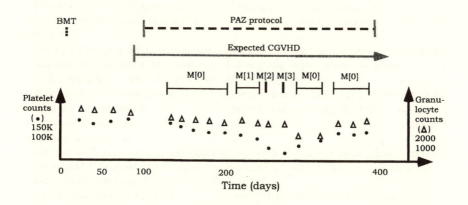

Note: The time line starts with a bone-marrow transplantation (BMT) external event. The platelet and granulocyte count parameters and the PAZ and BMT external event are typical inputs. The abstraction and context intervals are typically part of the output. • = platelet counts; △ = granulocyte counts; dashed interval = event; shaded arrow = open context interval; ⊢⊣ = closed abstraction interval; M[n] = myelotoxicity (bone-marrow toxicity) grade n.

Source: Shahar, Y. (1997). A framework for knowledge-based temporal abstraction. Reprinted from *Artificial Intelligence, 90*, p. 82, copyright 1997, with permission from Elsevier Science.

a final diagnosis, but rather was only to decide whether there was any abnormality in the growth chart that might fit a set of predefined internal patterns, or to answer multiple user-defined external temporal queries regarding relevant intermediate level abstractions. An abnormality detected by an internal or external query can call the physician's attention to the need for further monitoring of a particular child.

In the diabetes domain, we collaborated with two endocrinologists, acquiring within several meetings a TA ontology from one of the experts (Shahar and Musen, 1996). The two experts formed (independently) temporal abstractions from more than 800 points of data, representing two weeks of glucose and insulin data from each of eight patients. The RÉSUMÉ system created 132 (80.4%) of the 164 temporal abstractions noted by both experts. Examination of the output for the first three cases by one of the experts showed that the expert agreed with almost all (97%) of the produced abstractions—a result similar to the one we found in the domain of growth monitoring (Shahar, 1994). We expected this high predictive value, since the domain's TA ontology directly reflected that expert's knowledge about these low-and intermediate-level abstractions. Although these results are encouraging, we noted several difficulties in the representation and detection of cyclical (e.g., diurnal) patterns; in the matching of absolute time to task-specific time; in the integration of statistical and temporal queries; and in querying for patterns of events rather than for patterns of parameters (Shahar, 1994). Most difficulties can be solved by extensions to the language of the temporal pattern matching mechanism.

In the traffic-control domain, the RÉSUMÉ system was used to model the task of monitoring traffic-control actions, and to create a prototype for solving that task (Shahar and Molina, 1996). The task of monitoring traffic-control actions receives as input recent values of different road parameters (speed, flow, and occupancy) measured by sensors located along several highways, and a set of recent control actions (e.g., traffic diversion) undertaken by traffic controllers. It returns an evaluation of the adequacy of the control actions. Performance of this task requires both *temporal* reasoning (e.g., about durations, rates, and trends of traffic parameters over time, for a given location) and linear *spatial* reasoning (e.g., about queue lengths along the highway, at a given time). We used the RÉSUMÉ problem solver to model and solve *both* tasks. First we defined a *spatial abstraction ontology*, using the TA ontology knowledge structures, to describe properties of spatial parameters, such as Congestion, along the highway distance dimension. We used this ontology to create linear spatial abstractions in each highway zone, such as Saturation_level. Second, we created a TA ontology to describe properties of spatial abstractions of each location or highway zone over time. We used this ontology to form and detect crucial traffic-control spatiotemporal patterns. (Shahar, 1997, pp. 118–119)

Nonmonotonicity and Temporal Inference

Shahar (1997) discusses RÉSUMÉ's temporal inferences that take into account the effect of past and present events in the following section.

The five TA mechanisms create state, gradient, rate, and pattern abstractions. Unlike input data, however, the inferred parameter intervals are potentially refutable by any modification or addition to the known data points or events. The need to update past or present abstractions when older (but formerly available) data arrive was noted by Long and Russ (Long and Russ, 1983; Russ, 1989). We refer to this activity as a *view update*. The activity of updating former conclusions and of revising assessments of former decisions given new, present time data is referred to as *hindsight* by Russ (1989). In the first case, we need to evaluate precisely that part of our interpretation and abstraction of the former data that is affected by the newly added old data, such as laboratory reports that are returned a few days after the initial assessment was done. Thus, the *past* influences the interpretation of the *present*. In the second case, we need to bring to bear our current understanding of the situation on the interpretation of the former events, even if no direct additional information about the past has been uncovered; usually, that understanding is a function of current developments, such as the effect of a therapy plan. Thus, the *present* influences the interpretation of the past.

The effects of updates to input parameter and event intervals, which might cause deletion of existing, previously concluded contexts and abstractions, are mediated in the RÉSUMÉ system through a truth maintenance system (Shahar and Musen, 1993/1994). (The dynamic temporal fact base is thus essentially a *historic* database [Snodgrass and Ahn, 1986].) In addition, the temporal semantic properties of parameter propositions are used not only for the task of deriving further conclusions, but also for the task of detecting contradictions in existing conclusions. For instance, using the *downward hereditary* semantic property, the temporal inference mechanism not only can create new conclusions for subintervals of parameter intervals, but also can notice that parameter values for similar type parameter propositions within those subintervals (e.g., LOW(Hemoglobin)) actually differ from the parameter value of the parameter subinterval (e.g., HIGH (Hemoglobin)—a longer interval that was created when the included interval was unknown). Such a difference is a contradiction (due to an explicit assumption of a mutually exclusive set of values for the same parameter, time, and interpretation context) and requires retraction of at least one of the intervals. When a contradiction is detected (i.e., the result of the inference is FALSE), the RÉSUMÉ system uses several heuristics to decide *which* of the parameter intervals, if any, should be retracted (e.g., primitive input data might never be retracted, versus abstract conclusions, which might no longer be true). Finally, the results of retracting one or more parameter intervals should be propagated to previous conclusions that are logically dependent on the retracted conclusions. Similarly, when an event interval is modified, or a context interval that depended on a no longer valid event or abstraction is retracted, the modification is propagated to the rest of the temporal factbase. Conclusions that are no longer valid are retracted and new conclusions are asserted. (Shahar, 1997, pp. 120–121)

COMMENTARY

The architectonics of the knowledge-based temporal abstraction method and its embodiment in the RÉSUMÉ system have several important advantages and implications.

Conceptual and computational advantages include the following:

1. Increased flexibility in the representation and use of input and output data.
2. Enablement of nonmonotonic behavior.
3. Emphasis on context-sensitive interpretation.
4. Support of automated planning.
5. Facilitation of acquisition, representation, sharing, and reuse of TA knowledge (Shahar, 1997, p. 124).

Implications include the issue of the essential nonmonotonicity of temporal abstraction in both its static and dynamic aspects. In particular, there is a problem with coordinating RÉSUMÉ data with an external database. Whereas RÉSUMÉ will update its conclusions, the database lacking RÉSUMÉ's truth maintenance capacity will continue to report older and incorrect conclusions. The problem of how mutual updating might occur so as to achieve reliable consistency while maintaining flexibility will require conceptual advances and extensive experimentation. The problem is not merely computational for there are unresolved issues of temporal reasoning under conditions of nonmonotonicity.

11

Similarity-Based Reasoning

Reasoning from previous cases is common to everyday reasoning and to specialized reasoning in the profession such as case law and medical and surgical
case exemplars. Sometimes the similarity that holds between existing cases and
the problematic case is sufficiently deep that the drawing of valid conclusions
is not difficult. Sometimes, however, reasoning proceeds all too quickly on the
assumption that superficial similarity between source and target case is sufficient.
Thus, the similarity assumption can be misleading. The issue is important in
cognitive psychology and artificial intelligence and has been investigated experimentally with the aid of a computer program Déjà Vu by Smyth and Keane
(1998). In this chapter, the research of Smyth and Keane (1998) will be presented, and then a brief commentary will be offered.

THE SIMILARITY ASSUMPTION IN REASONING

Smyth and Keane (1998) recognize the importance of discerning similarity in
attributes between established case solutions and confronting cases whose solutions are sought, but they assert that mere surface similarity will not suffice
unless surface similarity is supported by deeper similarity in theoretical structure.
Smyth and Keane (1998) set forth their views in the following account:

> One of the major assumptions in Artificial Intelligence is that *similar* experiences can
> guide future reasoning, problem solving and learning: what we will call, the *similarity
> assumption*. The similarity assumption is used in problem solving and reasoning systems
> when target problems are dealt with by resorting to a previous situation with common

conceptual features (see e.g., [Aamodt & Plaza, 1994; Aha, Kibler, & Albert, 1991; Carbonell, 1986; Kambhampati & Hendler, 1992; Quinlan, 1979, 1986; Stroulia & Goel, 1994; Winston, 1980]). In machine learning, such common features are grist to the mill of inductive learners and concept classifiers based on the assumption that situations with shared features reflect critical distinctions between different classes of situation (see e.g., [Cheeseman et al., 1988; Domingos, 1995; Hunt, Marin, & Stone, 1966; Porter, Bareiss, & Holte, 1990; Quinlan, 1986; Stanfill & Waltz, 1986]). However, the similarity assumption in its usual form may not be warranted and may only approximate the real correspondence between situations.

In cognitive psychology, there has been a growing tide of questions about the sufficiency of simple, feature-based similarity as an explanation of human thinking and categorization (see e.g., [Keane, 1988, 1994; Medin, Goldstone, & Gentner, 1993; Murphy & Medin, 1995; Schyns, Goldstone, & Thibaut, 1998]). These criticisms have been based on the growing recognition that similar features are only indicative, that the similarity assumption really only holds when feature similarity directly reflects deeper similarities in the domain theories of two systems of concepts. Indeed, in AI, the development of explanation-based techniques (e.g., explanation-based generalization, EBG) also recognizes that feature similarity needs to be informed by deeper, theoretical knowledge (see e.g., [Aamodt, 1994; Bento et al., 1995; Cain, Pazzani, & Silverstein, 1991; DeJong & Mooney, 1986; Ellman, 1989; Minton et al., 1989; Mitchell, Keller, & Kedar-Cabelli, 1986]).

In this article, we question the similarity assumption in the context of case-based reasoning (CBR) (see also [Smyth & Keane, 1994, 1995a, 1996a, 1996b]). In CBR, the similarity assumption plays a central role when new problems are solved by retrieving similar cases and adapting their solutions. The success of any CBR system is contingent on retrieving a case that is *relevant* to the target problem; that is, the case that can be most easily related to the target problem so as to provide a suitable target solution. We show that it is *sometimes* unwarranted to assume that the most similar case is also the most relevant to the target problem. In many application domains traditional measures of similarity must be augmented by deeper domain knowledge. In particular, in many CBR systems the primary success criterion is whether or not the selected case can be adapted to solve the current target problem. With this in mind, we propose augmenting traditional measures of similarity with adaptation knowledge about whether a case can be easily modified to fit a target problem. We implement this idea in a new technique, called adaptation-guided retrieval (AGR), which provides a direct link between retrieval similarity and adaptation requirements; this technique uses a specially formulated adaptation knowledge which, during retrieval, facilitates the computation of a precise measure of a case's adaptation requirements. We show experimentally, that AGR improves the retrieval accuracy of a CBR system for automated programming (i.e., the Déjà Vu system) while preserving retrieval efficiency and improving overall problem solving efficiency. Moreover, this modified CBR architecture has several other beneficial features as its retrieval mechanism is more robust to changes in adaptation knowledge, and new learning opportunities arise for fine-tuning system performance. (Smyth and Keane, 1998, pp. 249–250)

CRITIQUE OF THE SIMILARITY ASSUMPTION IN CASE-BASED REASONING

CBR and the Similarity Assumption

Smyth and Keane (1998) place CBR operations in the abstract context of symbol spaces. Whereas retrieval is related to the specification space, adaptation is related to the solution space.

It is useful to consider CBR as operating within two distinct symbol spaces, a specification space and a solution space. Retrieval operates in the specification space, whose elements are pairings between the specification features of the target problem and the specification features of cases. Adaptation operates in the solution space, whose elements are transformational pairings between the necessary parts of the target solution and the available parts of the case solutions. From this perspective, retrieval is a search in the specification space for the right set of matches between target and case specification features. On the other hand, adaptation is a search in the solution space for the right set of transformations from a case solution to the target solution.

To select a case for retrieval some way of grading the matches between case and target problem is needed. At this point, most retrieval approaches assume that a case, which is similar to the target problem, will also be easy to adapt (i.e., the similarity assumption). For example, many CBR systems use the statistical concept of *predictiveness* during indexing and retrieval (see [Kolodner, 1993]). The idea is to compute correlations between specification features and solutions, and to grade individual features as more or less predictive of different solution types. While these methods work well in applications with single feature (atomic) solutions, and simple case-bases, they are less impressive in more complex tasks (e.g., [Birnbaum et al., 1991; Leake, 1992; Veloso & Carbonell, 1991]). In particular, since these methods bring only statistical knowledge to bear on the retrieval process they are often misled by common or coincidental similarities between cases. Thus, they frequently fail to recognize important matches that may make the difference between retrieving a case that can or cannot be adapted. The main problem underlying such approaches is graphically illustrated in [Figure 11.1]. There is no link between the specification space and the solution space, and hence no real communication between retrieval and adaptation. (Smyth and Keane, 1998, pp. 251–252)

Approaches to the Retrieval of Adaptable Cases

Smyth and Keane (1998) review attempts to strengthen the usefulness of the similarity assumption in retrieval, including heuristics, domain knowledge, and hierarchical derivation from first principles.

So far we have argued that standard notions of case similarity can lead to problems in more sophisticated CBR systems, especially those that support adaptation in a complex domain. This, of course, should come as no surprise as many researchers have shown simple models of "surface" or "superficial" feature similarity to be somewhat lacking in all but the most basic of retrieval tasks (see, e.g., [Birnbaum, et al., 1991; Cain, Pazzani,

Figure 11.1
Conventional Approaches to Retrieval Separate the Retrieval and Adaptation
Stages, Assuming That Specification Space Similarity Can Be Used to Predict the
Usefulness of a Case

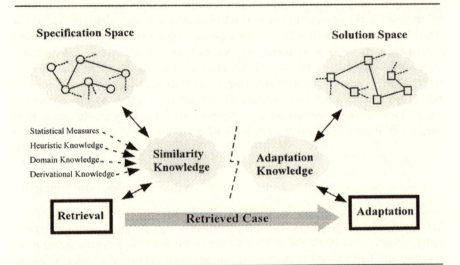

Note: Due to failure of this similarity assumption, more recent approaches have attempted to compensate for poor retrieval performance by considering other factors during retrieval, factors such as domain knowledge or heuristics for estimating the adaptability of cases.

Source: Smyth, B., and Keane, M. T. (1998). Adaptation-guided retrieval: Questioning the similarity assumption in reasoning. Reprinted from *Artificial Intelligence, 102*, p. 252, copyright 1998, with permission from Elsevier Science.

& Silverstein, 1991; Smyth & Keane, 1995a]). Much recent research has been concerned with the investigation of more sophisticated forms of similarity by suggesting methods for coding and exploiting "deeper" (semantic or pragmatic) knowledge during retrieval [Aamodt, 1994; Bento et al., 1995; Bergmann, Pews, & Wilke, 1994; Birnbaum, et al., 1991; Cain, Pazzani, & Silverstein, 1991; Fox & Leake, 1995a, 1995b; Goel, 1989; Kolodner, 1989; Leake, 1992].

Kolodner (1989), for example, proposed that some mappings between a target problem and a candidate case should be preferred over others if they are, for example, more *specific* or *goal-directed*. She has also argued that "easy-to-adapt" matches should be preferred over "hard-to-adapt" matches. Goel's KRITIK system (Goel, 1989) also considers a type of adaptability by preferring design-cases that satisfy the functional specifications of the target. He argues that such matches are, by definition, easily adapted. Of course, the main problem with both of these approaches is that they propose little more than a pre-classification of features as more or less adaptable, and still use only limited heuristic knowledge during retrieval. While this strategy might prove successful in the short term, its long-term utility is in doubt. It is important to emphasize that true adaptability depends on the problem solving context (both the base case context and the target context) and cannot be accurately assigned to individual features on a *a priori* basis.

Cain et al. (1991) have combined ideas from case-based reasoning and explanation-based learning in order to allow explicit domain knowledge to influence retrieval. Explanation-based learning (EBL) uses domain knowledge to judge the relevance of features by explaining the contribution that they make to an example's solution. On its own EBL is brittle when domain knowledge is incomplete, but by integrating it with CBR it is possible to provide a more robust technique, allowing the domain knowledge to *influence* (but not *determine*) similarity computation. A parameterized similarity metric allows the impact of the EBL decisions to be adjusted according to domain-knowledge completeness. If domain knowledge is complete, then the EBL contribution is highly influential; otherwise, traditional CBR similarity plays the dominant role. Obviously, the success of this technique depends on the availability of high-quality domain knowledge, whereas AGR depends on already available adaptation knowledge. In addition, there is no direct link between domain and adaptation knowledge, and so it is difficult to see how domain knowledge can be used to accurately predict adaptation requirements. Indeed, at the end of the day, the domain knowledge is supplying additional relevance estimations to an already heuristic similarity metric.

A different approach is adopted in the use of the so-called *footprint similarity metric* by the Derivational Analogy system, PRODIGY/ANALOGY [Veloso, 1992, 1994; Veloso and Carbonell, 1991]. One of the benefits of Derivational Analogy is that each case contains specialized problem solving knowledge in the form of a derivational trace that describes the reasoning steps taken during the construction of a given solution along with justification for these steps. In the footprint similarity method this derivational knowledge is used to provide an important *implicit* link between the specification space and the solution space by describing how certain specification features act as conditions and goals for the case solution, and thus how specification features impact on the solution derivation process. The technique is used to decide which specification features are goal-relevant and thus which features are likely to be relevant from a solution generation and adaptation viewpoint. In essence, this is an alternative solution to the limitations introduced by the similarity assumption. However, it differs from the AGR approach by using first-principles derivational knowledge, rather than actual adaptation knowledge, to provide the all-important link between retrieval and adaptation. In addition, footprint similarity does not allow judgements to be made about relative relevance of specification features or their relative adaptability. . . .

In summary, all of these approaches to similarity assessment have led to greatly improved retrieval algorithms for CBR. They attempt to improve retrieval performance by supplementing similarity-based methods with additional deeper (semantic or pragmatic) knowledge that may go some way to predicting the true adaptability of a case. However, none use actual adaptation knowledge, and this ultimately limits the accuracy of their predictions. AGR is novel in its explicit use of existing adaptation knowledge during retrieval, leading to a more accurate assessment of case adaptability, and consequently improved retrieval accuracy. (Smyth and Keane, 1998, pp. 252–254)

The Logic of Adaptation-Guided Retrieval

Smyth and Keane (1998) present a conceptual analysis and justification of their adaptation-guided retrieval (AGR) method in the following account.

Figure 11.2
Adaptation-Guided Retrieval Links the Specification and Solution Spaces by Using Adaptation Knowledge and Thereby Provides a Direct Channel of Communication Between Retrieval and Adaptation

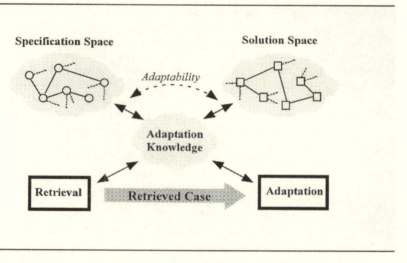

Note: In brief, during retrieval, adaptation knowledge is used to predict the need for change.

Source: Smyth, B., and Keane, M. T. (1998). Adaptation-guided retrieval: Questioning the similarity assumption in reasoning. Reprinted from *Artificial Intelligence, 102*, p. 254, copyright 1998, with permission from Elsevier Science.

Obviously, one of the central tenets of CBR is that there is a correspondence between the specification features of a case and its solution features. If we accept that the basic goal of retrieval is the selection of an adaptable case, then to achieve this we must be able to determine which solution space transformations correspond to a given set of specification space matches. In other words, we need to know how matches constructed during retrieval relate to adaptation operations; only then can we truly determine whether a case can be adapted (easily or at all) to fit the target problem. There must be an explicit relationship between specification space matches and solution space transformations, linking the retrieval and adaptation phases (see [Figure 11.2]).

The uniqueness of AGR stems from its use of adaptation knowledge during retrieval to link the specification and solution spaces (see [Figure 11.2]). Basically, as well as being used during adaptation to carry out particular changes, adaptation knowledge is also used during retrieval to predict the need for such changes. At retrieval time, matches between the specification features of a case and target are constructed only if there is enough evidence (in the form of adaptation knowledge) that such matches can be catered for during adaptation. This makes it possible to prioritize retrieval matches according to their overall adaptation cost. This in turn makes it possible to guarantee, not only the retrieval of an adaptable case, but the retrieval of that case which is the easiest to adapt to the target situation.

In the past, researchers have considered the possibility of grading specification features according to their adaptation difficulty (e.g., [Bento, et al., 1995; Goel, 1989; Kolodner, 1989]). However, these techniques have been based on coarse-grained numerical gradings of local specification features, leading to only moderate improvements in retrieval performance. Problems occur because different groups of case features can affect the adaptability of a case in complex ways, and local measurements of adaptability, based on individual features, may not be sufficient. AGR differs significantly from these approaches by using adaptation knowledge to organize case features into meaningful groups with respect to adaptation. It is not a matter of assigning degrees of adaptability to individual case features, but rather a matter of identifying how sets of related case features can impact on adaptation by linking these feature sets to relevant units of adaptation knowledge. In general, it is difficult to assess the adaptability of individual features. However, in practice the adaptation complexity of a particular unit of adaptation knowledge can be readily assessed and an accurate measure of adaptability for its corresponding feature set can be computed. (Smyth and Keane, 1998, pp. 254–255)

THE DÉJÀ VU SYSTEM

Déjà Vu and Adaptation Knowledge

Smyth and Keane (1998) discuss the essential functions of the adaptation knowledge in Déjà Vu in the following section.

The primary role of adaptation in CBR is to make changes to the solution of a retrieved case. Adaptation knowledge structures and processes can take many forms, from the use of declarative rules for substitutional adaptation (e.g., [Hanney & Keane, 1996, 1997; Smyth & Cunningham, 1993]) to the use of more complex operator-based or derivational knowledge in the first-principle approaches (e.g., [Carbonell, 1986; Kambhampati & Hendler, 1992; Veloso, 1994]); for a comprehensive review of adaptation knowledge see [Hanney, et al., 1995a, 1995b]. In Déjà Vu, adaptation means changing the details and structure of a plant-control solution chart to fit a new target solution. Therefore, adaptation knowledge must contain, in some shape or form, instructions about how to transform solution structures. Déjà Vu's adaptation knowledge is distributed over a collection of adaptation *agents* called *specialists* and *strategies*. The former are designed to offer specialized adaptation procedures related to specific plant objects or tasks, while the latter encode more general transformations. The link between retrieval and adaptation that is central to AGR stems from the availability of these specially formulated adaptation specialists and strategies, from their explicit coding of adaptation *capability knowledge* (alongside conventional *action knowledge*), and in particular from their use of this capability knowledge during retrieval to anticipate adaptation success or failure.

Traditionally in case-base reasoning, adaptation knowledge has taken the form of collections of solution transformation rules (what we have termed *action knowledge*; for reviews see [Hanney, et al., 1995a, 1995b]). Déjà Vu goes one step further by providing so called *capability knowledge* alongside the transformation rules. This capability knowledge characterizes the type and function of a particular set of transformation rules and allows the system to predict the potential for various forms of adaptation at an early stage during retrieval. . . . In Déjà Vu adaptation strategies are used in two basic ways: (1) for co-ordinating the adaptation actions of groups of interacting specialists; (2) for resolving conflicts that arise due to interactions between groups of specialists.

Figure 11.3
The Figure Shows How the Adaptation of a Move Case Can Result in a Violation of the Balance Condition Between the Diameter of the Load Being Transported and the Coil-Car Lifter Height

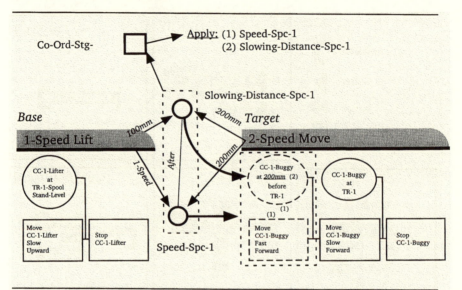

Note: The condition is violated when the load changes during reuse, from an empty spool (with a small diameter) to a large-diameter coil of steel. The balance between load diameter and the lifter height is only restored when a new abstract operator is added to lower the lifter platform. In the figure, individual adaptation is numerically labeled to indicate the responsible specialist.

Source: Smyth, B., and Keane, M. T. (1998). Adaptation-guided retrieval: Questioning the similarity assumption in reasoning. Reprinted from *Artificial Intelligence, 102*, p. 260, copyright 1998, with permission from Elsevier Science.

Strategies are used to co-ordinate specialists. When a retrieved case has to be adapted by more than one specialist, each working on different parts of the solution, the specialists may have to be applied in a particular sequence (see also [Hanney & Keane, 1996, 1997]). The *co-ordination strategy* recognizes ordering constraints between specialists and uses these constraints to schedule the affected specialists for application during adaptation. For example, consider the adaptation of a single speed lift case to a two-speed move case (see [Figure 11.3]). Two of the specialists needed to adapt the base solution are a speed specialist (SPEED-SPC-1) and a slowing-distance specialist (SLOWING-DISTANCE-SPC-1). The former adds the extra solution nodes to cope with the speed difference, while the latter replaces the base slowing-distance with the target slowing-distance. However, the speed specialist must perform its actions *before* the slowing-distance specialist, because it will be adding partially completed nodes which will be further elaborated by the slowing-distance specialist. In the knowledge-base there is an order-dependency (an "after" link) link joining the speed specialist and the slowing-distance specialist. During problem solving, if *both* of these specialists are needed, then this order-dependency link will signal the need for the co-ordination strategy. Obviously,

Figure 11.4
Two Interaction Problems: (a) the BLOCKED-PRECONDITION Problem and (b) the BALANCE-INTERACTION Problem

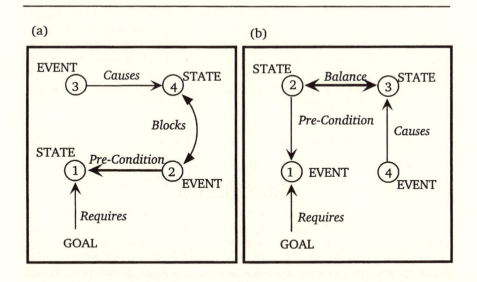

(a)   (b)

Note: Both problems are handled by adaptation strategies.

Source: Smyth, B., and Keane, M. T. (1998). Adaptation-guided retrieval: Questioning the similarity assumption in reasoning. Reprinted from *Artificial Intelligence, 102*, p. 261, copyright 1998, with permission from Elsevier Science.

the same strategy can be used to co-ordinate the activity of many specialists in a wide range of adaptation settings. When this strategy is applied to a set of specialists it returns an execution schedule to ensure that each specialist is executed at the correct time.

Strategies deal with conflicts between specialists. Sometimes conflicts between specialists will be so serious that they cannot be resolved by simply co-ordinating the action of specialists. In fact, even when there is no immediate conflict, it can happen that the action of one specialist will introduce a totally new conflict that will have to be resolved. For example, an interaction problem occurs when one required event prevents the occurrence of some necessary later event. [Figure 11.4a] depicts this situation: a goal event (1) is prevented by the disablement of one of its preconditions (2), the precondition having been blocked by some earlier event (3) causing a conflicting state (4). This *blocked-precondition* interaction can occur when the speed of a coil-car is increased (during adaptation), causing a power availability problem that results in the coil-car running out of power (power is a precondition of movement). This interaction can be repaired by adding an event before the blocking event (3), that prevents its blocking effect: for example, recharging the coil-car before initiating the move operation. The blocked-pre-condition adaptation strategy contains this repair action.

A second type of interaction is the *balance-interaction*, which can occur when the value of one state is proportionally dependent on another (see [Figure 11.4b]). In this situation, some necessary goal-achieving event (1) has a precondition (2) that depends on another state (3) that has resulted from some other event (4). Specifically, adapting the pre-condition feature can have an adverse effect on the validity of the dependent feature. For example, during move tasks, there is a balance condition between the coil-car lifter height and the diameter of the content being carried; before moving the coil-car across the factory floor, the height of its lifter platform must be adjusted to accommodate the load being transported. If this balance is not properly maintained then a failure can occur; for example, the coil-car may collide with an overhead obstacle. These are just some of the ways in which adaptation is used in Déjà Vu (see [Smyth, 1996] and also Appendix B for a complete summary of Déjà Vu's adaptation knowledge). (Smyth and Keane, 1998, pp. 257–261)

Adaptation Capability Knowledge in Déjà Vu

Smyth and Keane (1998) present the rationale for their innovative adaptation capability mechanism within the retrieval structure in the following account.

An important innovation in this work is the idea that adaptation knowledge has a key role to play during retrieval as well as during adaptation. For this reason adaptation capability knowledge is represented alongside the more conventional action knowledge. Capability knowledge makes an explicit statement about the type of adaptation that a particular specialist or strategy carries out; for example, it might indicate that a specialist changes the speed or the direction of a move case. In many ways it is a form of *precondition* knowledge, as to a large extent the capability of structures define the conditions under which adaptation specialists and strategies operate.

Each capability knowledge structure is made up of two main components, features and tests. The feature information describes the target and base features that predict the need for a certain adaptation and includes task information, specification features, and derived features. The capability tests perform certain checks to distinguish between different adaptation requirements. For example, the direction specialist introduced above has capability information that specifies two important features, the task and the move-direction (see [Figure 11.5a]), but has no capability tests. Thus, it is activated between a target problem and cases that perform a type of position-change-task operation (that is, move, lift, align etc.), and where there are directional differences.

Compared to the direction specialist, the adaptation knowledge to cope with speed differences is more complex since different adaptations will be needed depending on the type of speed difference encountered. For example, adapting a one-speed case to perform a two-speed move task involves adding extra nodes to the case solution (see [Figure 11.3]). However, adapting a two-speed case to perform a one-speed task means removing nodes. So there are at least two different specialists to cope with speed adaptations, each differentiated by different capability tests; [Figure 11.5b] shows the capability knowledge of the SPEED-SPC-1 specialist for transforming one-speed cases into two-speed cases. (Smyth and Keane, 1998, pp. 261–262)

Adaptation-Guided Retrieval and Déjà Vu

Smyth and Keane (1998) describe the functioning, within Déjà Vu, of the adaptation-guided retrieval operations in the following section.

Figure 11.5
The Capability Information for Two Different Specialists: (a) The Capability Information of the DIRECTION-SPC-1 Specialist Indicates That It Is Designed to Cope with Any Direction Changes That Occur Between POSITION-CHANGE-TASKS (This Includes Move, Lift, and Align Tasks); (b) The Capability Information for the SPEED-SPC-1 Specialist Indicates That It Is Designed to Adapt a One-Speed Case into a Two-Speed Case

(a)   (b)

```
Direction-Spc-1                    Speed-Spc-1

Capability                         Capability
:TASK   Position-Change-Task       :TASK   Position-Change-Task

:FEATURES  Move-Direction          :FEATURES  Move-Speed

                                   :TARGET-TEST (= Target-Move-Speed '2-Speed)
                                   :BASE-TEST   (= Base-Move-Speed   '1-Speed)
Action
                                   Action
(Adapt-Substitute
   :NODE-FRAME  Move-Device ...       (Adapt-Insert  :BEFORE
      :            :                     :NODE-FRAME  Move-Device ...
                                            :            :
```

Source: Smyth, B., and Keane, M. T. (1998). Adaptation-guided retrieval: Questioning the similarity assumption in reasoning. Reprinted from *Artificial Intelligence, 102*, p. 262, copyright 1998, with permission from Elsevier Science.

In the previous section, we outlined the adaptation knowledge used by Déjà Vu and showed how that knowledge is applied during the adaptation stage of the CBR cycle. In this section, we consider how this adaptation knowledge can be integrated into the retrieval stage of the cycle. This adaptation-guided retrieval technique is our answer to the problems that arise with the standard similarity assumption: showing that notions of similarity based on superficial features need to be augmented by deeper knowledge about the significance of those features in a particular problem solving context.

The AGR procedure [Figure 11.6] takes four inputs (the target specification, the case-base, the adaptation specialists, and the adaptation strategies) and outputs the most adaptable case, along with the specialists and strategies that will be needed during its adaptation. AGR has four basic stages:

Stage 1. Feature Promotion. The target specification is analyzed to identify relevant features, these can be specification features, or they can be newly derived features that are known to be important; this act of identifying relevant features is what we call *feature promotion*. The features are relevant with respect to adaptation. In other words, they are the capability features found in the adaptation knowledge of the system (both specialists

Figure 11.6
The Adaptation-Guided Retrieval Algorithm

Inputs:

Target	: The target specification
CB	: The case-base
Spc	: The adaptation specialists
Stg	: The adaptation strategies

Outputs:

Base-Case	: The retrieved case
Adaptability	: The adaptability rating of this case
Spc'	: The relevant adaptation specialists
Stg'	: The relevant adaptation strategies

Procedure **RETRIEVE** (Target-Spec, CB, Spc, Stg)
Begin
1   Promote-Specialist-Capability-Features (Target)
2   Promote-Strategy-Capability-Features (Target)
3   Candidates ← Candidate-Selection (Target, CB, Spc)
4   Local ← Local-Adaptability (Target, Candidates, Spc)
5   Global ← Global-Adaptability (Target, Local, Stg)
6   Return (Global)
End

Source: Smyth, B., and Keane M. T. (1998). Adaptation-guided retrieval: Questioning the similarity assumption in reasoning. Reprinted from *Artificial Intelligence, 102*, p. 263, copyright 1998, with permission from Elsevier Science.

and strategies). They describe those solution components ultimately required by the target problem. The presence of these capability features in the target specification results in the activation of relevant adaptation specialist and strategies.

Stage 2. Candidate selection. At this point, cases in the case-base are implicitly linked to the target problem by promoted specification features that are found in the adaptation specialists and strategies. Even at this early stage, it is possible to identify cases that cannot be adapted to solve the current target problem. By definition a case that shares no active specialists with the target cannot be properly adapted and therefore is eliminated from further consideration. The remaining candidate cases are known to be adaptable, at least in part, to the needs of the target problem.

Stage 3. Local adaptability assessment. During this stage the set of candidate cases is further reduced. All candidates have been chosen because they are at least *partially adaptable* with respect to the target problem. That is, each case can meet at least some of the target specification requirements. However, only some of these cases can meet all of the target requirements. Such cases are identified during this stage, and all other candidates are removed from further consideration. These fully adaptable cases are, in theory, *locally adaptable*, but in practice may turn out to be difficult to adapt if there are conflict problems.

Stage 4. Global adaptability ranking. Adaptation strategies are used to recognize adaptation conflicts in the locally adaptable cases. The *global adaptation cost* of each case can then be computed by combining the costs of all relevant adaptation specialists and strategies. Finally, the adaptable cases are rank ordered according to increasing adaptation cost. (Smyth and Keane, 1998, pp. 263–264)

EXPERIMENTS WITH THE DÉJÀ VU SYSTEM

Four Experiments with Déjà Vu and Adaptation-Guided Retrieval (AGR)

Smyth and Keane (1998) present an overview of four experiments designed to test the effectiveness and efficiency of AGR in the following section.

We have argued that adaptation-guided retrieval is an advance on conventional CBR architectures that rely on the standard similarity assumption. In particular, we have argued, using our state-space analysis, that AGR should improve retrieval accuracy, as well as benefitting overall problem-solving performance. In this section, we test these hypotheses in four experiments that examine three different performance measures. In Experiments 1 and 2, we compare the retrieval accuracy of different versions of Déjà Vu; one version using standard similarity-based retrieval and the one using AGR. In experiment 3, we measure the retrieval efficiency of AGR with a particular emphasis on how retrieval time increases with the size of the case-base. Finally, in Experiment 4, we go beyond retrieval to look at overall problem solving efficiency of Déjà Vu using AGR, again comparing it with the version that uses standard similarity. The case-bases used in the experiments were based on random selections from a large corpus of plant-control cases (see Appendix C for details on different layouts used). (Smyth and Keane, 1998, pp. 274–275)

Experiment 1: Rationale

Smyth and Keane (1998) set forth their expectations for a comparative test of the standard similarity model and the adaptation-guided retrieval model in the following summary.

In this experiment, we tested the hypothesis that AGR produces more accurate retrievals than a standard similarity-based technique (SS). A nearest-neighbor retrieval method was used in the SS model of Déjà Vu, which matches the features of target problems against the cases in the case-base (i.e., features like MOVE-DEVICE, MOVE-DESTINATION, and MOVE-SPEED). The AGR model of Déjà Vu makes use of the exact same features, except that it has access to extra knowledge about the adaptability of these features. Our expectation was that the SS version would tend to be less accurate in its retrievals, that it would fail to retrieve the most adaptable case for a presented target problem. It should be said that this test is kind to the SS model because all the problems and cases are based on the same plant layout. As we shall see in Experiment 2, the retrieval difficulties facing the SS model become much more pronounced when cases from a variety of plant layouts are introduced. (Smyth and Keane, 1998, p. 275)

Experiment 1: Method

In the following section, Smyth and Keane (1998) describe their experimental design and measures.

Design and measure. The experiment had two conditions, the AGR condition in which the AGR model of Déjà Vu was run on the test problem and the SS condition in which the SS model of Déjà Vu was run on the same test problems. The case-base used was identical in both conditions. For each test problem, it was possible to identify the case in the case-base which was the most relevant to it (i.e., the case that could be most easily adapted to solve it). The measure used was the number of times a given model accurately retrieved the best case to the presented problems, expressed as a percentage of the total set of problems (i.e., % Accuracy).

Case-base and test problems. The case-base contained 45 randomly selected cases from the SIDING plant-model covering all of the main plant-control task categories. The same set of test problems was used in both conditions. It consisted of 45 randomly chosen problems, all of which were based on the Siding plant-model, covering the main plant-control tasks. (Smyth and Keane, 1998, pp. 275–276)

Experiment 1: Results and Discussion

Smyth and Keane (1998) set forth their experimental results in the following account.

[Figure 11.7] shows that the AGR model successfully retrieves the best case for each of the 45 target problems, whereas the SS model is only accurate 66% of the time. That is, one third of the time the SS model retrieves cases that are not as easily adapted as the best case. These results confirm that adaptation-guided retrieval is more accurate in its retrievals than a standard-similarity method. The SS technique is misled by surface-feature similarities that disguise underlying adaptation problems, whereas AGR can recognize and assess these problems. (Smyth and Keane, 1998, p. 276)

Experiment 2: Rationale

Smyth and Keane (1998) summarize their expectations for a comparison of the SS model with the AGR model with respect to retrieval accuracy in a complex case-base in the following section.

In Experiment 1, the AGR model was compared to the SS model using a case-base and test problem set that contained cases from a single plant-model. Retrieval becomes much more difficult with a more complex case-base that contains cases based on a range

Figure 11.7
The Retrieval Accuracy Results for AGR and SS Models of Déjà Vu in
Experiment 1

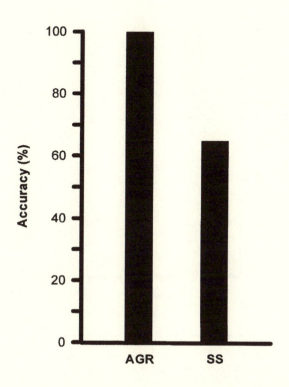

Source: Smyth, B., and Keane, M. T. (1998). Adaptation-guided retrieval: Questioning the similarity assumption in reasoning. Reprinted from *Artificial Intelligence, 102*, p. 276, copyright 1998, with permission from Elsevier Science.

of plant models. We predict that the accuracy of standard, similarity-based retrieval will further degrade relative to AGR with such a case-base. This should occur because the SS model will be much more likely to be misled by features of the problem that are similar, in the presence of radically different plant layouts, that cannot be adapted. (Smyth and Keane, 1998, p. 277)

Experiment 2: Method

Smyth and Keane (1998) describe their experimental design and measures in the following account.

Figure 11.8
The Retrieval Accuracy Results for AGR and SS Models of Déjà Vu in
Experiment 2

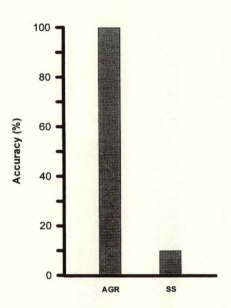

Source: Smyth, B., and Keane, M. T. (1998). Adaptation-guided retrieval: Questioning the similarity assumption in reasoning. Reprinted from *Artificial Intelligence, 102*, p. 278, copyright 1998, with permission from Elsevier Science.

Design and measure. As in Experiment 1, there were two conditions each of which ran a different model of Déjà Vu (the AGR or the SS model) on the same set of test problems with the same case-base.

Case-base and test problems. The test case-base contained 120 cases taken from the 8 different plant models (see Appendix C). The cases were randomly chosen to cover all of the plant-control task categories. The set of test problems consisted of 45 problems randomly chosen from a corpus involving the same 8 plant-models and plant-control, task types. (Smyth and Keane, 1998, p. 277)

Experiment 2: Results and Discussion

In the following section, Smyth and Keane (1998) present and discuss the results of the experiment.

[Figure 11.8] shows that, again, the AGR model successfully retrieves the best case more often than the SS model. Indeed, the SS model's performance is considerably worse in this experiment, whereas the AGR model retains its high level of performance. The AGR model manages to select the most adaptable case for every one of the target problems, while the SS retrieval method only succeeds 12% of the time.

These results again confirm the hypothesis that the retrieval accuracy of AGR is superior to that of a standard similarity method. In addition, it is clear that the AGR model's accuracy is affected by a larger and more diverse case-base. Again, the 100% success rate found in this experiment can be attributed to the completeness of the adaptation knowledge used. In contrast, the performance degradation in the SS model shows how it is misled by surface similarities from competing cases based on different plant-models. This occurs because when a target problem and a case are from the same plant-model a large number of exact matches will be found, whereas few exact matches will be found if the target and case models differ, even if this case is easier to adapt. (Smyth and Keane, 1998, pp. 277–278)

Experiment 3: Rationale

In Experiment 3, Smyth and Keane (1998) focus on retrieval performance and the utility problem.

In the previous experiments, we dealt with the effectiveness of AGR rather than its efficiency. The retrieval stage of AGR is clearly more costly and complex than standard similarity methods. In this experiment, we assess whether this complexity results in utility problems for AGR. In Experiment 4, we determine whether AGR's inefficiency at retrieval is balanced by greater efficiency during adaptation (affording it more efficiency in overall problem solving).

The complexity of retrieval in AGR means that it may not scale well as case-bases increase in size, rendering it prone to the utility problem (see [Francis & Ram, 1993, 1994; Minton, 1990; Smyth and Cunningham, 1996; Smyth and Keane, 1995b]). In CBR systems, the utility problem manifests itself when the cost of retrieval is directly proportional to the number of cases in the case-base; so, as a case-base grows overall problem solving performance can degrade. One solution to this problem is to limit retrieval time so that the best case located within some fixed time-limit might be retrieved (see, e.g., [Brown, 1994; Veloso, 1992]). However, this solution invariably results in the retrieval of sub-optimal cases that may be difficult or impossible to adapt.

In this experiment, we examined the scalability of AGR by varying the size of the case-base used. Apart from varying the case-base size, we also varied the number of adaptable cases present in the case-base for a given target problem. Since AGR is, by definition, sensitive to adaptation constraints, it should be more affected by the presence of multiple adaptable cases (to a given target problem) in the case-base, than by case-base size *per se*. Finally, we also examined a bounded version of AGR to assess its performance. If AGR falters in these tests, relative to the SS model, then the demonstrated accuracy of the technique is irrelevant. In short, all bets are off on AGR's adequacy. (Smyth and Keane, 1998, pp. 278–279)

Experiment 3: Method

Smyth and Keane (1998) describe their experimental design and measures in the following account.

Design and measure. Three conditions were run in the experiment reflecting differing constraints on the system; the *standard, constant, and bounded* conditions. In all conditions, the AGR model of Déjà Vu used in previous experiments are run on a target set of problems while increasing the size of the case-base from 30 to 120 cases. The measure used was the average time taken by the system to retrieve a case that could be adapted to solve a given target problem. In the *standard condition* the case-base was expanded by randomly selecting previously-constructed cases. This random selection has the effect of increasing both case-base size and the number of adaptable cases to a given target problem in the case-base. In the *constant condition*, we separated these two factors by ensuring that as the case-base size increased, the average number of adaptable cases for each target problem remained constant. Finally, the *bounded condition* was identical to the standard condition with the added constraint that retrieval was halted when the first adaptable case was retrieved for a given problem.

Case-base and test set. Four distinct case-bases varying in 30 case increments, were constructed ranging in size from 30 to 120 cases, for the standard and bounded conditions. A separate set of four case-bases was constructed for the constant condition, in which the adaptability of cases to the test problems was controlled. A test of 20 target problems was used. Both the cases and problems were a subset of those used in Experiment 2. (Smyth and Keane, 1998, p. 279).

Experiment 3: Results and Discussion

Smyth and Keane (1998) present and discuss the results of the experiment in the following account.

[Figure 11.9] shows the average retrieval-time performance of AGR as the case-base increases in size for the three experimental conditions. In general, the results show that unadulterated AGR appears to display retrieval complexity that is comparable to that of SS systems. However, on closer inspection a more encouraging observation can be made as retrieval complexity is recognized to be a function of the number of adaptable cases present in the case-base, rather than case-base size *per se*. This bodes very well for the scalability of AGR as the utility problem in CBR is strongly influenced by retrieval costs. More importantly, the results show that bounded versions of AGR do considerably better irrespective of increases in case-base size or the number of adaptable cases in the case-base.

As in SS techniques, retrieval time for AGR increases linearly with the case-base size (see standard condition). However, as we said earlier, this condition confounds increases in case-base size with increases in the number of adaptable cases in the case-base; in the case-base with 30 cases there are only 3 adaptable cases for each problem but by the time it has risen to 120 cases there are 6 adaptable cases per problem. When the number-of-adaptable-cases variable is controlled in the constant condition, we find that retrieval time is constant as the case-base increases. Thus, the retrieval cost in AGR is a function of the number of adaptable cases in the case-base rather than the overall case-base size. From a scaling perspective, we would argue that this finding makes AGR much more promising than SS techniques because the constant condition is more representative of CBR systems than the standard condition. In general, a CBR system that shows an increase in the number of adaptable cases (with respect to some set of target problems),

Figure 11.9
The Average Retrieval Time Taken by AGR Déjà Vu as Case-Base Size Increases in the Three Conditions of Experiment 3

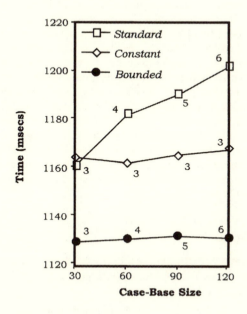

Note: The number of adaptable cases in the case-base per target problem is shown by the numbers annotating the graph's nodes.

Source: Smyth, B., and Keane, M. T. (1998). Adaptation-guided retrieval: Questioning the similarity assumption in reasoning. Reprinted from *Artificial Intelligence, 102*, p. 280, copyright 1998, with permission from Elsevier Science.

will also be one that has an increasing number of redundant cases. If genuinely new cases are being added to a system then the average number of adaptable cases should remain constant. This means that if case-bases are scaled up correctly, then the retrieval time for AGR will remain fixed, potentially avoiding the utility problem altogether.

However, to quiet any objections to the linear time increase observed for the standard condition, the bounded condition proves that even with the standard condition case-bases, retrieval time can be kept constant by stopping retrieval once an adaptable case is found. In the bounded condition, retrieval time for AGR is constant when both case-base size and the number of adaptable cases increase. Of course, bounded AGR may not retrieve the best case (the most easily adapted case to solve the problem), but the one chosen will at least be adaptable. This is important, as most existing bounded-retrieval approaches do not provide such a guarantee [Brown, 1994; Veloso, 1992].

This constant-time characteristic of the bounded condition may seem confusing at first.

Surely there is still the need to do a full pass through the case-base when identifying candidate cases, thereby introducing a case-base size factor into the cost of the algorithm? This is not true. The important thing to remember about AGR is that it exploits a memory structure that explicitly links cases, target problems and adaptation knowledge. In particular, while the current target must be linked to adaptation knowledge at retrieval time, the same is not true for the cases; each case is linked to its relevant adaptation specialists and strategies at the time the case is added to the case-base, not during retrieval. Thus candidate cases are readily selected by examining those specialists that have been activated by the current target problem. The cases themselves do not have to be examined on an individual basis. Hence, it is more accurate to think of retrieval time as a function of the size of the adaptation knowledge-base rather than the case-base.

SS retrieval times (not shown in [Figure 11.9]) are marginally better than AGR times, due to the extra retrieval work AGR must perform in locating relevant adaptation knowledge. However, we do not comment further on SS retrieval times here because we believe it only makes sense to consider SS efficiency in the context of overall problem solving efficiency. In particular, for AGR the extra work carried out at retrieval time pays dividends during adaptation. Hence, the reader is referred to the next experiment where a more meaningful efficiency comparison between AGR and SS is presented. (Smyth and Keane, 1998, pp. 279–281)

Experiment 4: Rationale

In the following section, Smyth and Keane (1998) discuss the evaluation of overall system performance as revealed by Experiment 4.

Even though AGR delivers effective retrieval, its retrieval stage is more complex than SS approaches. The utility of AGR could be challenged if this extra burden at retrieval time finds its way through to overall problem solving performance. However, we expect these extra costs at retrieval to be balanced by lower costs at adaptation because not only is the AGR technique more likely to retrieve a case that is more easily adapted, but also much of the normal adaptation work is dealt with as a natural side-effect of retrieval (for example, locating relevant adaptation knowledge). (Smyth and Keane, 1998, p. 281)

Experiment 4: Method

Smyth and Keane (1998) summarize the design and measures of Experiment 4 in the following account.

Design and measure. As in Experiment 1, two models of the Déjà Vu system were used, the AGR and SS model. In this experiment, we were concerned with retrieval and adaptation, so an adaptation component was added to the SS retrieval system; this component was identical to the adaptation part of the AGR model. The performance measure used was the time taken by the systems to solve target problems.

Case-base and test problems. The case-base contained 100 randomly chosen cases based on 8 different plant-models, covering all the main plant-control task categories. Forty-five test problems from Experiment 2 were used. They were ordered in ascending

Figure 11.10
Cumulative Time to Solve Problems in the Two Conditions of Experiment 4

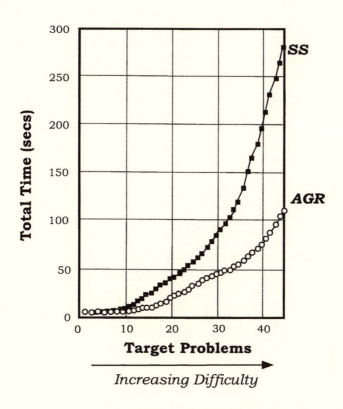

Source: Smyth, B., and Keane, M. T. (1998). Adaptation-guided retrieval: Questioning the similarity assumption in reasoning. Reprinted from *Artificial Intelligence, 102*, p. 282, copyright 1998, with permission from Elsevier Science.

complexity, with the least complex problem being tested first. (Smyth and Keane, 1998, p. 281)

Experiment 4: Results and Discussion

In the following section, Smyth and Keane (1998) present and discuss the results of Experiment 4.

[Figure 11.10] is a graph of the cumulative problem solving time taken by the SS and AGR models. On the whole, the AGR model performs much better than the SS model and the performance gap between the systems is more pronounced the more complex the problem to be solved.

Looking at the total time to solve the 45 test problems, the AGR model was significantly faster (120s) than the SS model (280s). On less complex problems, the performance of both models are [*sic*] roughly equivalent; the cost of solving very simple problems is actually marginally greater in the AGR model than in the SS model. However, as the problems become more complex the SS model has longer solution times, whereas the AGR model remains more constant.

There are two main reasons for the better overall problem solving performance found in the AGR model. First, the AGR model is more likely than the SS model to retrieve cases that are easy to adapt. Indeed, adaptation in the SS model was found to be consistently more costly than in the AGR model. Second, in the AGR model the relevant adaptation knowledge is located as a by-product of the retrieval process, whereas in the SS model there is still a search for appropriate adaptation rules after retrieval is carried out. (Smyth and Keane, 1998, pp. 281–282)

IMPLICATIONS OF ADAPTATION-GUIDED RETRIEVAL

The Generality of Adaptation-Guided Retrieval

In the following section, Smyth and Keane (1998) discuss the applicability of adaptation-guided retrieval in a range of domains.

As far as Déjà Vu is concerned, we have shown that AGR has clear performance benefits. However, this is just one demonstration within a particular application domain. What is the status of the generality of these claims?

Since first proposing these ideas, several other researchers have successfully applied AGR in a variety of domains. Most notably, Collins and Cunningham [1996] have shown that it works well in example-based machine translations (EBMT), while Hanney and Keane [1996, 1997] have used AGR in a property-valuation system designed to automate the creation of adaptation knowledge. In addition, AGR-inspired techniques have been applied to case-based, parametric design problems [Zdrahal and Motta, 1996] and bioprocess planning [Rousu and Aarts, 1996].

Collins and Cunningham [1996] describe an EBMT system called ReVerb to perform English to German translation. A case-base of translation examples is derived from a corpus of bilingual English/German *Corel* Draw-6 manuals. Thus, each translation case or example consists of aligned sentences/clauses which have been extracted from this corpus; each case contains a sentence for the source language (English) and its translation to the target language (German). A fundamental problem for EBMT in general, and ReVerb in particular, is that translation divergences are brittle in reuse. In other words, structural differences between the current translation problem and a previous example may introduce significant adaptation problems after retrieval. An AGR policy has been used in order to recognize significant adaptation problems early on during retrieval so that only cases which can be adapted *safely* are retrieved. ReVerb's implementation of AGR differs from Déjà Vu's in that adaptability information is encoded within individual cases rather than within a separate adaptation corpus. Essentially this adaptation information quantifies just how "dependent" elements of a translation example are on each other. An element with a high dependency is penalized and receives a low adaptability score because a mismatch between such an element during retrieval is likely to impact not only on the adaptation of this element but also on the adaptation of other translation elements. ReVerb has been able to use this form of adaptation knowledge to successfully grade cases for retrieval to favor the selection of an adaptable case. In fact it has been shown that there is a good correspondence between ReVerb's adaptability predictions and a true measure of adaptability as indicated by a human expert.

Hanney and Keane [1996, 1997] implement adaptation-guided retrieval in a property valuation system. The case-base is composed of residential property cases, described in terms of features such as "number of bedrooms", "location", "age", etc. The task is to estimate the value of a target property by retrieving a similar case and by adapting its price to account for differences between it and the target. Adaptation knowledge is represented as a collection of rules that relate feature differences to changes in price. During retrieval, candidate cases are assessed by considering those adaptation rules that apply to these cases in the context of the current target problem. Each case is associated with a collection of rules that can cater for the mismatches between it and the target; each rule collection defines an *adaptation path* from the case to the target. The final choice of which case to reuse is determined by grading the adaptation paths of candidate cases. Each case and path is graded according to a number of factors which measure the specificity, concreteness, and correctness of the constituent rules in order to estimate the adaptability of the case in question. Interestingly, the focus of this research work is how such rules can be automatically learned, and the real success for Hanney and Keane is that they have proposed a technique for automatically learning adaptation rules by examining cases in the case-base. Very briefly, their technique involves making pair-wise comparisons between cases to evaluate how feature differences correlate with solution differences. These correlations are converted into adaptation rules. This work bodes well for adaptation-guided retrieval since now there is evidence that it may be possible to automatically learn the type of adaptation knowledge required by AGR.

The problem of automatically acquiring adaptation knowledge and adaptation costs is also the topic of work by Leake et al. [1997]. They describe a procedure for determining current adaptability based on the cost of similar prior adaptations, using a library of learned adaptation cases. In fact, this technique is very much in the spirit of CBR as it offers a case based approach to adaptation (see also [Leake, 1995a, 1995b]).

Zdrahal and Motta [1996] describe a case-based system for parametric design problems which integrates case-based reasoning with heuristic search. An AGR approach is described in which, during retrieval, an upper and lower bound on adaptation cost is computed to guide final case selection. These adaptation costs are based on worst and best case scenarios for repairing constraint violations that exist between the cases and the target problem. Like Déjà Vu this information is made available as part of the adaptation knowledge which is designed to repair these violations.

Finally, Rousu and Aarts [1996] propose a case-based planning method that combines similarity-based retrieval with an evaluation based on adaptation cost which is very much in the spirit of AGR. Their approach is implemented in a system for bio-process planning. Like Déjà Vu there are three basic adaptation operators for manipulating atomic solution elements (substitution, insertion, and deletion) and adaptation cost is calculated based on their individual costs. However, the current system only represents a partial AGR implementation in that true adaptability prediction is not supported during retrieval. A more complete implementation can be envisaged however by augmenting their adaptation operators with capability knowledge that can be accessed directly during retrieval. (Smyth and Keane, 1998, pp. 283–284)

Implications for Case-Based Reasoning

Smyth and Keane (1998) discuss the implications of AGR for CBR in the following account.

As well as greater accuracy, AGR delivers improved flexibility and robustness compared to traditional models of retrieval. One implication is that perhaps the overall architecture of CBR should be changed in response to these benefits. In other words, that a CBR architecture which traditionally de-couples retrieval and adaptation should be modified to account for a greater integration of their knowledge and algorithmic resources.

Many of the advantages of AGR are based on its partial synthesis of retrieval and adaptation. Conventional systems separate retrieval and adaptation, and the knowledge that they use. As a result any change to the adaptation knowledge of a conventional CBR system must be accompanied by a corresponding change to its similarity metric, so that the new adaptation possibilities can be recognized during retrieval. However, because AGR uses the same knowledge during retrieval and adaptation, any changes are immediately apparent at retrieval time, without any further adjustments.

Obviously many conventional retrieval methods could be improved to respond more closely to the adaptation requirements of cases. For instance, by carefully weighting description features and carefully training a similarity metric, it may be possible to reproduce the retrieval accuracy of adaptation-guided retrieval. However, we doubt whether any such systems could better the accuracy results found for AGR, and furthermore, the likelihood is that these systems would be merely trying to mimic AGR within the confines of standard approaches. In addition, these finely-tuned conventional systems would be extremely sensitive to changes in either the adaptation knowledge or the case-base, and if new adaptation knowledge is added or additional cases are learned, further training would generally be necessary.

The assumption at the heart of adaptation-guided retrieval is that the adaptability of cases should be accurately measured at retrieval time by using adaptation knowledge; the AGR technique represents one particular implementation of this idea. During the development of AGR a number of questions have arisen concerning this basic assumption. For instance, often adaptability is not such a critical retrieval constraint, hence limiting the applicability of AGR; there are applications where criteria such as "elegance of design", "maintainability" and "safety" are crucial. Obviously, this is in no way a shortcoming of AGR. It has been developed to measure adaptability, not elegance, or maintainability, or safety, and clearly if other measures are also required during retrieval, then AGR can still usefully contribute to some overall measure of case suitability.

Another common question is concerned with the reality of predicting adaptation costs during retrieval. Certainly, there exist application domains and tasks where there is very little relationship between case specification and their subsequent adaptation possibilities, and so, it is claimed, there is little of accurately predicting adaptation cost. However, one can argue that such domains go against a basic assumption of case-base reasoning, namely that there is a measurable relationship between case specification features and case solution features, and that problems with similar specifications will also have similar solutions. If this assumption does not hold then neither CBR nor AGR is likely to be useful.

The final question queries the specifics of AGR and asks whether formulating adaptation knowledge as specialists and strategies is a realistic objective, especially from a scaling-up perspective. First of all, most CBR systems that support adaptation do so by using some set of adaptation rules or heuristics, which is strong evidence that in many domains specialist-type rules can be formulated. As a system is scaled-up to deal with more complex problems it is likely that adaptation knowledge will have to change. In our approach this means adding new specialists. However, adaptation strategies are much more robust to change, and existing strategies will cope with a wide range of new situations that become important as a result of scaling. Indeed, even if the application domain changes, it should be possible to reuse the existing strategies since similar conflict and interaction problems occur in most domains. (Smyth and Keane, 1998, pp. 284–285)

Implications for Artificial Intelligence

Smyth and Keane (1998) discuss the tenability of the pervasive similarity assumption in artificial intelligence research in the following section.

While the core of this paper has been concerned with investigating adaptation-guided retrieval in a case-based reasoning setting, the technique has wider implications for the AI community as a whole. There is good reason to believe that the traditional similarity assumption made in AI is quite limited in its usefulness, and that similarity assessment is more complex than previously thought. In particular, "true similarity" appears to depend on a deeper analysis of knowledge than is seen in conventional approaches. In response to this insight, several AI techniques have emerged, for instance, Derivational Analogy (e.g., [Carbonell, 1986; Veloso, 1994]) and Explanation-Based Generalization (e.g., [DeJong and Mooney, 1986; Ellman, 1989]), which, along with adaptation-guided retrieval, illustrate different ways in which the similarity assumption needs to be adjusted. Each of these techniques makes explicit use of some form of domain knowledge during the determination of similarity and each is geared towards more sophisticated problem solving applications than traditional similarity-based techniques appear to follow. (Smyth and Keane, 1998, pp. 285–286)

COMMENTARY

Knowledge-based theories of deductive reasoning and formal logic theories of deduction constitute two of the three current contending theories of deductive reasoning in cognitive psychology (the third is mental models). It is, therefore, of interest that the cognitive architecture of Déjà Vu depends on formal logic, while its problem-solving performance depends on case knowledge and adaptation knowledge. The knowledge goes beyond surface similarity to deeper layers of similarity in theoretical structure. It may be, therefore, that the theory and performance of Déjà Vu directed toward applications in Artificial Intelligence can be extended to improve understanding of the nature of human deductive reasoning.

Appendix A: The n-Factor Problem

SOLUTION TO THE THREE-FACTOR PROBLEM

Problem: Factor $a^3 + b^3 + c^3 - 3abc$ into 3 factors.

Source: *Higher algebra* by Hall and Knight (1898)

Factoring this expression into two factors:

$a^3 + b^3 + c^3 - 3abc = (a + b + c) (a^2 + b^2 + c^2 - ab - ac - bc)$

The problem is factoring $a^2 + b^2 + c^2 - ab - ac - bc$ into two factors

There are 3 cube roots of 1 they are: 1, $\omega = (-1 + i\sqrt{3})/2$, $\omega^2 = (-1 - i\sqrt{3})/2$

From this we develop that $\omega^3 = 1$, $1 + \omega + \omega^2 = 0$ $\omega + \omega^2 = -1$

Solution to factors of $(a^2 + b^2 + c^2 - ab - ac - bc) = (a + \omega b + \omega^2 c)$

$\quad (a + \omega^2 b + \omega c)$

Solution to the final problem:

$a^3 + b^3 + c^3 - 3abc = (a + b + c) (a + \omega b + \omega^2 c) (a + \omega^2 b + \omega c)$

NATURE OF THE N-FACTOR PROBLEM

The three-factor problem was discussed in the previous section. The two-factor problem has a well-known solution: $a^2 + b^2 - 2ab = (a - b) (a - b)$.

The question arises whether there might be solutions to a four-factor, a five-factor, . . . , n-factor problem. This n-factor problem has the form:

Mathematical notation for problem of patterns of solutions to patterns of problems.

$\sum a^3 + b^3 + c^3 - 3\Pi abc$

$\sum a^4 + b^4 + c^4 + d^4 - 4\Pi abcd$

$$\Sigma \ a^5 + b^5 + c^5 + d^5 + e^5 - 5\Pi abcde$$

$\dots$

$\dots$

$$\sum_{i=1}^{n} a_i^n - n \prod_{i=1}^{n} a_i$$

Prove that: The expression beginning a^3 has three factors, the expression beginning a^4 has four factors, the expression beginning a^5 has five factors, ..., the expression beginning a_i^n has n factors.

Conceivably, mathematical software might be employed to locate solutions for n = 4, 5, ..., n. Such solutions may or may not exist.

It would be preferable to prove the conjecture: there are no solutions to the n-factor problem for n greater than 3.

The conjecture is somewhat similar to Fermat's last theorem (where x, y, and z, are integers, the equation $x^n + y^n = z^n$ has no solutions for values of n greater than 2) and as with the proof of that theorem (established by Andrew Wile in 1993; see Kolata [1993]), the proof of the conjecture will probably require sophisticated mathematical research.

It may be that the proof, as with the proof of the four-color problem (Appel and Haken, 1979), will require a contribution of both the mathematician and the computer.

It should be noted that the reason for seeking a solution of the n-factor problem is the establishment of the deep coherence between the number of factors and the number of roots of unity.

Sherman Stein (personal communication, September 2000) has developed proofs that for values of n equal to 4 or greater, there are no solutions to the n-factor problem.

Demonstration That in the Case of n = 4 There Can Be No Solution

Professor Sherman Stein, Department of Mathematics, University of California, Davis, writes:

It is well known that the polynomial $x^3 + y^3 + z^3 - 3xyz$ is the product of three first-degree factors,

$$x^3 + y^3 + z^3 - 3xyz = (x + y + z)(x + wy + w^2z)(x + w^2y + wz) \tag{1}$$

Here w denotes a primitive cube root of unity. (A primitive nth root of unity is a complex number whose nth power is 1, but no lower positive power of w is 1.) Equation (1) can be verified by multiplying the three factors, using the equations $w^3 = 1$ and $1 + w + w^2 = 0$, hence $w + w^2 = -1$. Later we will see how such a factorization could be found.

In view of the factorization (1) and the fact that $x^2 + y^2 - 2xy = (x - y)(x + y)$, Prof. Wagman asked me whether the pattern continues for more than three variables. That is, for which values of the positive integer n is the polynomial

$$x_1{}^n + x_2{}^n + \ldots + x_n{}^n - nx_1x_2 \ldots x_n \tag{2}$$

the product of first-degree factors? The following theorem shows that n equal to 2 or 3 are the only cases for which the answer is yes.

Theorem 1. For $n \geq 4$ polynomial (2) has no first-degree factor.

Proof. Let P be polynomial (2) and assume that F is a first-degree factor of P, P = FG, for some polynomial G and F $= a_1x_1 + a_2x_2 + \ldots + a_nx_n$, where the a_i are complex constants.

Each coefficient a_i must be non-zero. To show this, assume otherwise, say, that $a_i = 0$. Replace all x_j except x_i by 0 and x_i by 1. For these values of the variables, P = 1 and F = 0, contradicting the assumption that P = FG.

If the first $n - 1$ coefficients in F are not distinct, we shall alter them so that they are. To do this, choose $w_1, w_2, \ldots, w_n$ to be nth roots of unity such that $w_1 = 1$, $w_2a_2 \neq a_1$, $w_3a_3 \neq a_2w_2$ or $a_1, \ldots, w_{n-1}a_{n-1} \neq w_{n-2}a_{n-2}, w_{n-3}a_{n-3}, \ldots, w_2a_2, a_1$, and w_n equal to $1/(w_1w_2 \ldots w_{n-1})$.

Replace each x_i, by w_ix_i in the equation P = FG. P remains unchanged by this substitution, and F becomes a first degree polynomial F* whose first $n - 1$ coefficients are distinct, and G becomes G*. We have P = F*G*.

Any permutation of the first $n - 1$ variables leaves P unchanged and transforms F* to another factor of P. Because of the way F* was constructed, F* is transformed into a polynomial distinct from F and not a constant times F. Each of these $(n - 1)$! polynomials is also distinct from any other of them.

Each of these $(n - 1)!$ polynomials must appear in the prime factorization of P, by the unique factorization theorem. Hence $(n - 1)$! is no larger than n. This forces n to be at most 3 and completes the proof.

Note that the proof shows much more, namely, that for any integer n at least 4 and any constant c, $x_1{}^n + x_2{}^n + \ldots + x_n{}^n - cx_1x_2 \ldots x_n$ has no first degree factor.

In the proof of Theorem 1 two operations that left P unchanged were used. Because the coefficients of the powers $x_i{}^n$ are all equal, P is unchanged when the variables are permuted. Also P is unchanged when each variable x_i is replaced by w_ix_i, where w_i is an nth root of unity, and $w_1w_2 \ldots w_n = 1$.

As the proof of the following more general theorem shows, the second operation is all we need, and we may remove the assumption that the coefficients of the powers are all equal.

Theorem 2. Let $c_1, c_2, \ldots, c_n$ be non-zero constants and n at least 4. Then the polynomial

$$P = c_1x_1{}^n + c_2x_2{}^n + \ldots + c_nx_n{}^n - cx_1x_2 \ldots x_n \tag{3}$$

has no first-degree factor.

Proof. Let F $= a_1x_1 + a_2x_2 + \ldots + a_nx_n$ be a factor of P. One may show that each a_i is non-zero, as in the proof of Theorem 1. This uses the assumption that each c_i is not zero.

Let $w_1 = 1$ and $w_2, w_3, \ldots, w_n$ be nth roots of unity such that their product is 1. There are n^{n-2} such choices, and, for each such choice, replacing x_i by w_ix_i takes P into itself and F to another factor of P. Moreover, these n^{n-2} factors are distinct from each other. As in the proof of Theorem 1, all these factors must appear in the prime factorization of P. Hence

$$n^{n-2} \leq n$$

This implies that n is at most 3, and completes the proof.

The proof of Theorem 2 suggests a proof for the following theorem concerning cubic polynomials.

Theorem 3. Let

$$P = x_1^3 + c_2 x_2^3 + c_3 x_3^3 - c x_1 x_2 x_3 \qquad (4)$$

where c_2, c_3, and c are constants. If P has a first-degree factor, then there are constants k_2 and k_3 such that $c_2 = k_2^3$, $c_3 = k_3^3$, and $c = 3\, k_2 k_3$

Proof. Again assume P has a first degree factor F, which we may assume is $x_1 + k_2 x_2 + k_3 x_3$ for suitable constants k_2 and k_3.

Let w be one of the two primitive cube roots of unity. The other is $1/w$, which equals w^2. Recall that $w + w^2 = -1$.

As in the proof of Theorem 2, replacing x_2 by $w x_2$ and x_3 by $w^2 x_3$, changes F to another factor of P. So does replacement of x_2 by $w^2 x_2$ and x_3 by $w x_3$. F and these two factors are distinct, since each has x_1 as a term. Their product is P,

$$P = (x_1 + k_2 x_2 + k_3 x_3)(x_1 + w k_2 x_2 + w^2 k_3 x_3)(x_1 + w^2 k_2 x_2 + w k_3 x_3) \qquad (5)$$

Multiplying the right side of (5) out, and using the facts that w^3 is 1 and $w + w^2$ is -1, we see that the product of the three factors is

$$x_1^3 + k_2^3 x_2^3 + k_3^3 x_3^3 - 3\, k_2 k_3 x_1 x_2 x_3$$

Comparing this expression with (4) shows that

$$c_2 = k_2^3,\ c_3 = k_3^3,\ and\ c = 3\, k_2 k_3$$

As a special case of Theorem 3 we have the factorization (1) quoted in the first paragraph. Moreover, the only real value of c for which $x^3 + y^3 + z^3 - cxyz$ has a first-degree factor is $c = 3$.

The proof of Theorem 2 does not apply to the more general polynomial

$$P = c_1 x_1^n + c_2 x_2^n + \ldots + c_n x_n^n - c x_1^{e_1} x_2^{e_2} \ldots x_n^{e_n} \qquad (6)$$

where n is at least 4, the constants c_i are not 0, the exponents e_i are non-negative, and at least one of them is positive. The following proof, due to Dean Hickerson, disposes of this more general case.

Theorem 4. For n at least 4, the polynomial (6) has no first-degree factor.

Proof. It is no loss of generality to assume that e_n is positive. Replace $x_4, x_5, \ldots, x_n$ all by 0, changing P to

$$Q = c_1 x_1{}^n + c_2 x_2{}^n + c_3 x_3{}^n$$

and a first-degree factor of P to a factor Q, which we may assume is $F = x_1 + k_2 x_2 + k_3 x_3$. For any choice of two nth roots of unity, w_2 and w_3, $x_1 + w_2 k_2 x_2 + w_3 k_3 x_3$ is also a factor of Q. Since these factors are distinct, we must have

$$n^2 \leq n$$

violating our assumption that n is at least 4.

The proof of Theorem 4 shows that for n at least 2, the polynomial $x_1{}^n + x_2{}^n + x_3{}^n$ has no first degree factor. However, $x_1{}^n + x_2{}^n$ factors completely as the product of first-degree factors. This follows from the factorization of $x^2 + 1$ as the product of n factors of the form $x + w$, where $w^n = -1$. Replacing x by x_1/x_2 and clearing denominators produces the factoring of $x_1{}^n + x_2{}^n$.

Up to this point we have been concerned only with first-degree factors. The same methods used so far show that there are no factors at all, as Theorem 5 illustrates.

Theorem 5. For n at least 3 and non-zero constants c_2 and c_3 the polynomial

$$P = x_1{}^n + x_2{}^n + x_3{}^n$$

has no factors other than the trivial factors of degree zero or n.

Proof. Let F be a factor of P. If there is a non-trivial factor, there is a prime factor. We assume that F is prime. It can be shown that all the terms in F are of the same degree, which we denote d. We assume that $1 \leq d \leq n - 1$. Moreover F must contain terms of the form $k_1 x_1{}^d$, $k_2 x_2{}^d$, and $k_3 x_3{}^d$, where each constant k_i is not zero. Hence

$$F = k_1 x_1{}^d + k_2 x_2{}^d + k_3 x_3{}^d + Q$$

where Q is a polynomial of degree d.

Now let w_2 and w_3 be nth roots of unity, and replace x_2 by $w_2 x_2$ and x_3 by $w_3 x_3$ in F. This substitution leaves P unchanged. It may also leave F unchanged, in contrast to the situation in the earlier proofs. However, we will show that for many choices of w_2 and w_3, F is transformed into distinct polynomials.

To show this, let w be a primitive nth root of unity. Then $(w_i x_2)^d = (w_j x_2)^d$ only if $id \equiv jd \pmod{n}$. Equivalently, $i \equiv j \pmod{n/(n, d)}$, where (n, d) denotes the greatest common divisor of n and d. Thus there are $n/(n, d)$ distinct coefficients of $x_2{}^d$ formed by these substitutions. The same holds for replacement of x_3 by $w_3 x_3$.

Thus there are at least

$$\frac{n}{(n, d)} \frac{n}{(n, d)}$$

distinct factors of degree d of the given polynomial of degree n. The total degree of these polynomials is

$$d \frac{n}{(n, d)} \frac{n}{(n, d)}$$

If d is less than n, then (n, d) is less than n. Moreover, (n, d) is no larger than d. Hence

$$d \, \frac{n}{(n, d)} \, \frac{n}{(n, d)} \geq n \, \frac{n}{(n, d)} \geq n$$

As in previous proofs, the total degree of the factors in the prime factorization of the given polynomial exceeds its degree. This contradiction shows that the given polynomial has no factors other than trivial ones.

Other related questions come to mind, such as: For n at least 4 does $x_1^n + x_2^n + x_3^n + cx_1x_2x_3$ have any non-trivial factors? I leave this for the reader to settle. (Stein, personal communication, September 2000)

COMMENTARY

The establishment of mathematical proofs of theorems often extends over considerable periods of time. Three centuries elapsed before the proof of Fermat's last theorem, and a century has elapsed since Bertrand Russell's work on the three-factor problem to the generalization and proof of the n-factor problem.

The proofs presented in this appendix by Stein and Hickerson and a proof proposed by Rosovsky for the case where n = 4 (see Wagman, 1999, pp. 142–143) demonstrate conceptual advances that are characteristic of mathematics as a quasi-empirical science. The proofs presented by Stein for n factors contained theorems that explain at an abstract level demonstrations of Russell and Rosovsky.

Readers of this book who wish to comment on the proofs or who wish to propose solutions to Stein's research problem (see final paragraph of Stein's personal communication, above) are encouraged to communicate with the author.

Appendix B: Adaptation Knowledge

ADAPTATION SPECIALISTS

In Déjà Vu, adaptation specialists are organized along two dimensions: the solution task and the task details. For example, there are specialists for modifying the vehicles used in Unload or Insert tasks and for modifying the vehicles used in Move, Lift, or Align tasks. In total there are 40 specialists, and these are summarized below. (The interested reader is referred to Smyth [1996] for a complete listing of specialists, including a detailed account of their specifications and actions.)

Unload/Insert Specialists

These specialists are designed to modify Unload and Insert solutions by changing features such as the vehicle, the content, the collection and delivery containers, and the park location.

Load-Vehicle-Spc-1 & 2—substitute the target vehicle in place of the base vehicle throughout an Unload/Insert solution.

Load-Content-Spc-1—substitute the target content for the base content throughout the Unload/Insert solution.

Collect-Container-Spc-1—substitute the target collection container for the base collection container.

Deliver-Container-Spc-1—substitute the target delivery container for the base delivery container.

Collect-Location-Spc-1—substitute the target collection location for the base collection location.

Park-Location-Spc-1—substitute the target parking location for the base parking location.

Park-Location-Spc-2—insert a new node to accommodate parking in the target.

Park-Location-Spc-3—delete the base parking node if there is no parking operation needed in the target.

Collect/Deliver/Park Specialists

These specialists are designed to modify Collect, Deliver, and Park solutions by changing features such as the container, the container level, the content, and the collect/deliver location.

Collect-Vehicle-Spc-1—substitute target vehicle for base vehicle. Additional replacements must be made for corresponding vehicle-empty and vehicle-reset levels.

Collect-Container-Spc-2—substitute target collection container for base collection container across by making changes to Move, Align, Engage, Disengage, and Release nodes in a collection solution.

Collect-Content-Spc-1—substitute target content for base content across Engage, Disengage, and Release node.

Collect-Locations-Spc-1—substitute target location for base location.

Similar specialists are defined for Deliver and Park solutions.

Move/Lift/Align Specialists

These specialists are designed to modify Move, Lift, and Align solutions by adapting features such as the direction of motion, the vehicle, the speed of motion, the start and destination locations (or height levels), and the slowing distance.

Move-Device-Spc-1—substitute the target move vehicle for the base vehicle.

Move-Destination-Spc-1—substitute the target destination location for the base destination location.

Slowing-Distance-Spc-1—substitute the target slowing distance for the base slowing distance.

Speed-Spc-1—convert a one-speed solution into a two-speed solution by inserting the necessary nodes to accommodate the speed increase and the slowing down check.

Speed-Spc-2—convert a two-speed solution into a one-speed solution by removing the unnecessary nodes for performing the speed increase and the slowing down check.

There are additional Speed specialists for coping with a range of speed-types not discussed in this paper.

Direction-Spc-1—substitute the target direction for the base direction.

Engage/Disengage Specialists

These specialists are designed to modify Engage and Disengage solutions by adapting features such as the vehicle, the vehicle socket, the vehicle brake, and the vehicle clearing distance and direction.

Connection-Vehicle-Spc-1—when the target connection vehicle differs from the base connection vehicle, this specialist makes the appropriate changes to solution features such as the vehicle brake, vehicle lifter pressure, and connection socket.

Connection-Socket-Spc-1—this specialist makes changes to the container connection sockets.

Clearing-Details-Spc-1—this specialist is relevant if the connection task is for a tension-reel. In this situation, different tension-reels require adaptations to deal with vehicle clearing distances and clearing directions.

Disengage-Vehicle-Spc-1—if the disengage is between a coil-car and a tension-reel, then adaptations related to the particular coil-car being used are needed.

Release Specialists

These specialists are designed to modify Release solutions by changing solution features such as source and target containers, container clamps, container tilt delays, and the content being released.

Source-Container-Device-Spc-1—when the source container is a skid or a coil-car, this specialist can make substitutive adaptations to a release solution to accommodate different coil-cars and skids.

Target-Container-Device-Spc-1—this specialist adapts the containment check at the end of a release operation to ensure that the appropriate load has been acquired.

Source-Container-Clamp-Spc-1—this specialist controls adaptations related to the connection clamp of the source container of a release task.

Target-Container-Clamp-Spc-1—this specialist controls adaptations related to the connection clamp of the target container of a release task.

Source-Tension-Reel-Release-Spc-1—release operations from a tension-reel require a special sequence of actions and checks. This specialist adapts this solution sequence for different tension-reels.

ADAPTATION STRATEGIES

While adaptation specialists are domain dependent and many in number, adaptation strategies are designed to be domain independent, and their level of generality allows a wide range of interaction problems to be captured by relatively few strategies. Déjà Vu's adaptation strategies are summarized below.

Blocked-Precondition Strategy

A solution interaction problem occurs when one required solution event prevents the occurrence of some necessary later event. In particular, the Blocked-Precondition interaction occurs when a goal is prevented by the disablement of one of its preconditions, the precondition in question having been blocked by some earlier event causing a conflicting state. . . . This *blocked-precondition* interaction can occur, for example, when the speed of a coil-car is increased (during adaptation), causing a power availability problem that results in the coil-car running out of power (power is a precondition of movement). This type of interaction can be repaired by adding an event before the blocking event that prevents its blocking effect—for example, recharging the coil-car before initiating the move. The *blocked-precondition* adaptation strategy contains this repair action.

Balance Interaction Strategy

A *balance-interaction* occurs when the value of one state is proportionally dependent on another. . . . In this situation, some necessary goal-achieving event has a precondition that depends on another state, which in turn resulted from another event. Specifically, adapting the precondition feature can have an adverse effect on the validity of the dependent feature. Essentially, there are two solution features that must be balanced against one another. The balance interaction strategy ensures that any change made to one of the balanced features, during adaptation, is met by a corresponding change to the other feature, thereby ensuring that the appropriate balance is maintained. . . .

Co-ordination Strategy

Adaptation specialists make small, local, and independent changes to a case solution. However, while the success of adaptation may depend on executing specialists in the correct order, the independent nature of specialists renders them blind to any ordering constraints. . . . [T]he ordering task is managed by the Co-ordination Strategy.

The job of this strategy, then, is to take a given collection of active adaptation specialists and to produce a valid execution schedule. The strategy uses a standard topological sorting procedure on specialists' before and after links. . . .

Undesirable-Side-Effect Strategy

This strategy is designed to recognize the presence of undesirable states or actions in an adapted solution, and ensures that they are removed. One concrete example occurs when adapting a Release case for different loads. Release programs control the release of spools or coils of steel from a tension-reel or a skid onto a waiting [coil-car and] raises the coil-car lifter pressure so that it can safely accommodate the weight of a full coil of steel. However, if the target program is for a spool release, then this command is not necessary (its side-effect, namely increased lifter pressure, is undesirable), and this strategy will see that the offending node is removed. (Smyth and Keane, 1998, pp. 287–290)

Appendix C: Plant-Control Models

Figure C.1
Outline Plant-Model Specifications Highlighting Track Layouts, Machinery, and Devices

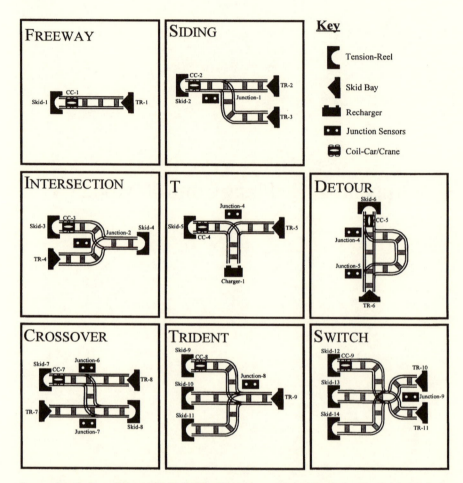

Source: Smyth, B., and Keane, M. T. (1998). Adaptation-guided retrieval: Questioning the similarity assumption in reasoning. Reprinted from *Artificial Intelligence, 102*, p. 286, copyright 1998, with permission from Elsevier Science.

Bibliography

Aamodt, A. (1994). Explanation-driven case-based reasoning. In S. Wess, K.-D. Althoff, and M. M. Richter, eds., *Topics in Case-Based Reasoning*. Berlin: Springer, 274–288.

Aamodt, A., and Plaza, E. (1994). Case-based reasoning: Foundational issues, methodological variations, and system approaches. *AI Communications, 7 (1)*, 39–52.

Aha, D. W., Kibler, D., and Albert, M. K. (1991). Instance-based learning algorithms. *Machine Learning, 6*, 37–66.

Ajzen, I. (1977). Intuitive theories of events and the effects of base-rate information on prediction. *Journal of Personality and Social Psychology, 35*, 303–314.

Alba, M., Chromiak, W., Hasher, L., and Attig, M. S. (1980). Automatic encoding of category size information. *Journal of Experimental Psychology: Human Learning and Memory, 6*, 370–378.

Allais, M. (1953). Le comportement de l'homme rationnel devant le risque: Critique des postulats et axiomes de l'Ecole Américaine [The behavior of rational man with respect to risk: A criticism of the postulates and axioms of the American school]. *Econometrica, 21*, 503–546.

Allen, S. W., and Brooks, L. R. (1991). Specializing the operation of an explicit rule. *Journal of Experimental Psychology: General, 120*, 278–287.

Amble, T. (1987). *Logic Programming and Knowledge Engineering*. Reading, MA: Addison-Wesley.

Anderson, J. R. (1982). Acquisition of cognitive skill. *Psychological Review, 89*, 369–406.

Anderson, J. R. (1985). *Cognitive Psychology and Its Implications*, 2nd ed. New York: W. H. Freeman and Co.

Anderson, J. R. (1990). *Cognitive Psychology and Its Implications*, 3rd ed. New York: W. H. Freeman and Co.

Anderson, J. R. (1993). *Rules of the Mind*. Hillsdale, NJ: Erlbaum.

Appel, K., and Haken, W. (1979). The four color problem. In L. A. Steen, ed., *Mathematics Today: Twelve Informal Essays*. New York: Springer-Verlag, 153–180.

Atran, S. (1990). *The Cognitive Foundations of Natural History*. New York: Cambridge University Press.

Attig, M., and Hasher, L. (1980). The processing of frequency of occurrence information by adults. *Journal of Gerontology, 35*, 66–69.

Bar-Hillel, M. (1980). The base-rate fallacy in probability judgements. *Acta Psychologica, 44*, 211–233.

Barker, J. A. (1992). Lind and limeys. *Journal of Biological Education, (1) & (2)*, 45–53, 123–129.

Barnden, J. (1988). The right of free association: Relative-position encoding for connectionist data structures. In *Proceedings, Tenth Annual Conference of the Cognitive Science Society*, Montreal, Quebec, 503–509.

Baron-Cohen, S. (1994). *Mindblindness on Autism and Theory of Mind: An Essay*. Cambridge, MA: MIT Press.

Baron-Cohen, S., Ring, H., Moriarty, J., Schmitz, B., Costa, D., and Ell, P. (1994). The brain basis of theory of mind: The role of the orbito-frontal region. *British Journal of Psychiatry, 165*, 640–649.

Barsalou, L. W., and Ross, B. H. (1986). The role of automatic and strategic processing in sensitivity to superordinate and property frequency. *Journal of Experimental Psychology: Learning, Memory, and Cognition, 12*, 116–134.

Bartlett, F. C. (1958). *Thinking*. New York: Allen and Unwin.

Bayes, T. (1763). An essay towards solving a problem in the doctrine of chances. *Philosophical Transactions of the Royal Society of London, 53*, 370–418.

Begg, I., and Denny, J. P. (1969). Empirical reconciliation of atmosphere and conversion interpretations of syllogistic reasoning errors. *Journal of Experimental Psychology, 81*, 351–354.

Bento, C., Exposto, J., Francisco, V., and Costa, E. (1995). Empirical study of an evaluation function for cases imperfectly explained. In J.-P. Haton, M. Keane, and M. Manago, eds., *Advances in Case-Based Reasoning*. Berlin: Springer, 45–59.

Bergmann, R., Pews, G., and Wilke, W. (1994). Explanation-based similarity: A unifying approach for integrating domain knowledge into case-based reasoning for diagnosis and planning tasks. In S. Wess, K.-D. Althoff, and M. M. Richter, eds., *Topics in Case-Based Reasoning*. Berlin: Springer, 182–196.

Bernard, J. (1994). History of concept and dogmas. *Blood Cells, 19*, 549–553.

Birnbaum, L., Collins, G., Brand, M., Freed, M., Krulwich, B., and Prior, L. (1991). A model-based approach to the construction of adaptive case-based planning systems. In *Proceedings, DARPA Case-Based Reasoning Workshop, Washington, DC*. San Mateo, CA: Morgan Kaufmann, 215–224.

Bonatti, L. (1994). Propositional reasoning by model? *Psychological Review, 101*, 725–733.

Boole, G. (1854). *An Investigation of the Laws of Thought on Which Are Founded the Mathematical Theories of Logic and Probabilities*. New York: Macmillan.

Borgida, E., and Brekke, N. (1981). The base-rate fallacy in attribution and prediction. In J. H. Harvey, W. J. Iekes, and R. F. Kidd, eds., *New Directions in Attribution Research*. Hillsdale, NJ: Erlbaum, 66–95.

Bottini, G., Corcoran, R., Sterzi, R., Paulesu, E., Schenone, P., Scarpa, P., Frackowiak,

R.S.J., and Frith, C. D. (1994). The role of the right hemisphere in the interpretation of figurative aspects of language. *Brain, 117,* 1241–1253.

Bourbaki, N. (1964). *Elements de mathematique.* Paris: Hermann.

Braine, M.D.S., Reiser, B. J., and Rumain, B. (1984). Some empirical justification for a theory of natural propositional logic. In G. H. Brown, ed., *The Psychology of Learning and Motivation.* Orlando, FL: Academic Press.

Brewka, G., Dix, J., and Konolige, K. (1997). *Nonmonotonic Reasoning: An Overview.* Stanford, CA: CLSI Publications, Stanford University.

Brown, M. (1994). An under-lying memory model to support case retrieval. In S. Wess, K.-D. Althoff, and M. M. Richter, eds., *Topics in Case-Based Reasoning: First European Workshop,* PWCBR '93, Kaiserslautern, Germany, November 1–5, 1993: Selected Papers. Berlin: Springer, 132–143.

Brumfitt, J. H., and Hall, J. C. (1973). *The Social Contract.* Translated from the French and introduction by G.D.H. Cole. Revised and augmented by J. H. Brumfitt and J. C. Hall. London: Dent.

Bruner, J. S., Goodnow, J. J., and Austin, G. A. (1956). *A Study of Thinking.* New York: Wiley.

Brunswik, E. (1939). Probability as a determiner of rat behavior. *Journal of Experimental Psychology, 25,* 175–197.

Brunswik, E. (1955). Representative design and probabilistic theory in a functional psychology. *Psychological Review, 62,* 193–217.

Burton, A., and Radford, J. (1991). Thinking. In J. Radford and E. Gover, eds., *A Textbook in Psychology.* London: Routledge.

Byrne, R.M.J. (1989). Suppressing valid inferences with conditionals. *Cognition, 31,* 61–83.

Cain, T., Pazzani, M. J., and Silverstein, G. (1991). Using domain knowledge to influence similarity judgement. In *Proceedings, DARPA Case-Based Reasoning Workshop, Washington, DC.* San Mateo, CA: Morgan Kaufmann, 191–202.

Carbonell, J. G. (1986). Derivational analogy: A theory of reconstructive problem solving and expert acquisition. In R. S. Michalski, J. G. Carbonell, and T. M. Mitchell, eds., *Machine Learning,* vol. 2. San Mateo, CA: Morgan Kaufmann, 371–392.

Carbonell, J. G., and Collins, A. (1973). Natural semantics in artificial intelligence. In *Proceedings of the Third International Joint Conference on Artificial Intelligence.* Stanford, CA: Stanford University Press, 344–351.

Carey, S., and Gelman, R., eds. (1991). *The Epigenesis of Mind: Essays on Biology and Cognition.* Hillsdale, NJ: Erlbaum.

Carpenter, K. J. (1986). *The History of Scurvy and Vitamin C.* Cambridge, MA: Cambridge University Press.

Casscells, W., Schoenberger, A., and Grayboys, T. (1978). Interpretation by physicians of clinical laboratory results. *New England Journal of Medicine, 299,* 999–1000.

Chang, C. L., and Lee, R. C.-T. (1973). *Symbolic Logic and Mechanical Memory.* Hillsdale, NJ: Erlbaum.

Chapman, L. J., and Chapman, J. P. (1959). Atmospheric effect reexamined. *Journal of Experimental Psychology, 57,* 220–226.

Charniak, E. (1983). Passing markers: A theory of contextual influence in language comprehension. *Cognitive Science, 7,* 171–190.

Charniak, E., and McDermontt, D. (1985). *Introduction to Artificial Intelligence.* Reading, MA: Addison-Wesley.

Cheeseman, P., Self, M., Kelly, J., Taylor, W., Freeman, D., and Stutz, J. (1988). Bayesian classification. In *Proceedings, Seventh National Conference on Artificial Intelligence [AAAI-88], August 21–26, St. Paul, Minnesota, USA*. Cambridge, MA: MIT Press, 607–611.

Cheng, P. W., and Holyoak, K. J. (1985). Pragmatic reasoning schemas. *Cognitive Psychology, 17*, 391–416.

Cheng, P. W., Holyoak, K. J., Nisbett, R. E., and Oliver, L. M. (1986). Pragmatic versus syntactic approaches to training deductive reasoning. *Cognitive Psychology, 18*, 293–328.

Cheng, P. W., and Novick, L. R. (1990a). Where is the bias in causal attribution? In K. Gilhooly, M. Keane, R. Logie, and G. Erdos, eds., *Lines of Thought: Reflections on the Psychology of Thinking*. Chichester: Wiley, 181–197.

Cheng, P. W., and Novick, L. R. (1990b). A probabilistic contrast model of causal induction. *Journal of Personality and Social Psychology, 58*, 545–567.

Cheng, P. W., and Novick, L. R. (1991). Causes versus enabling conditions. *Cognition, 40*, 83–120.

Chomsky, J. (1980). Rules and representation. *Behavioral Brain Science*, 1–16.

Christensen-Szalanski, J.J.J., and Beach, L. R. (1982). Experience and the base-rate fallacy. *Organizational Behavior and Human Performance, 29*, 270–278.

Church, A. (1956). *Introduction to Mathematical Logic*. Princeton, NJ: Princeton University Press.

Clark, K. L. (1978). Negation as failure. In H. Gallaire and J. Minker, eds., *Logic and Databases*. New York: Plenum Press, 293–322.

Clocksin, W. F., and Mellish, C. S. (1981). *Programming in PROLOG*. Berlin: Springer.

Cohen, L. J. (1981). Can human irrationality be experimentally demonstrated? *Behavioral Brain Sciences, 4*, 317–370.

Cohen, L. J. (1986). *The Dialogue of Reason*. Oxford: Clarendon Press.

Collins, A. M. (1978a). Fragments of a theory of human plausible reasoning. In D. Waltz, ed., *Theoretical Issues in Natural Language Processing II*. Urbana: University of Illinois, 194–201.

Collins, A. M. (1978b). *Human Plausible Reasoning*. Report No. 3810. Cambridge, MA: Bolt Beranek and Newman.

Collins, A. M. (1985). Component models of physical systems. In *Proceedings of the Seventh Annual Conference of the Cognitive Science Society*. Hillsdale, NJ: Erlbaum, 80–89.

Collins, A. M., and Gentner, D. (1982). Constructing runnable mental models. In *Proceedings of the Fourth Annual Conference of the Cognitive Science Society*. Hillsdale, NJ: Erlbaum, 86–89.

Collins, A. M., and Gentner, D. (1983). Multiple models of evaporation process. In *Proceedings of the Fifth Annual Conference of the Cognitive Science Society*. Hillsdale, NJ: Erlbaum.

Collins, A. M., and Gentner, D. (1987). How people construct mental models. In N. Quinn and D. Holland eds., *Cultural Models in Language and Thought*. New York: Cambridge University Press, 243–265.

Collins, A. M., and Loftus, E. F. (1975). A spreading-activation theory of semantic processing. *Psychological Review, 82*, 407–428.

Collins, A. M., and Michalski, R. (1989). The logic of plausible reasoning: A core theory. *Cognitive Science, 13*, 1–50.

Collins, A. M., Warnock, E. H., Aiello, N., and Miller, M. L. (1975). Reasoning from incomplete knowledge. In D. Bobrow and A. Collins, eds., *Representation and Understanding: Studies in Cognitive Science*. New York: Academic Press, 383–415.

Collins, B., and Cunningham, P. (1996). Adaptation-guided retrieval in EBMT: A case-based approach to machine translation. In I. Smith and B. Faltings, eds., *Advances in Case-Based Reasoning*. Berlin: Springer, 91–104.

Conover, W. J. (1980). *Practical Non-Parametric Statistics*. New York: Wiley.

Copi, I. M. (1967). *Symbolic Logic*. New York: Macmillan.

Cornford, F. MacDonald (1945). *The Republic of Plato*, translated with Introduction and Notes. New York: Oxford University Press.

Corruble, V., and Ganascia, J. G. (1994). Aid to discovery in medicine using formal induction techniques. *Blood Cells, 19*, 649–659.

Corruble, V., and Ganascia, J. G. (1996). Discovery of the causes of leprosy: A computational simulation. In *Proceedings of the Thirteenth National Conference on Artificial Intelligence [AAAI-96] and the Eighth Innovative Applications of Artificial Intelligence Conference*. Menlo Park, CA: AAAI Press, 731–736.

Corruble, V., and Ganascia, J. G. (1997). Induction and the discovery of the causes of scurvy: A computational reconstruction. *Artificial Intelligence, 91*, 205–223.

Cosmides, L. (1989). The logic of social exchange: Has natural selection shaped how humans reason? Studies with the Wason selection task. *Cognition, 31*, 187–276.

Cosmides, L., and Tooby, J. (1996). Are humans good intuitive statisticians after all? Rethinking some conclusions from the literature on judgement under uncertainty. *Cognition, 58*, 1–73.

Darley, J. M., Glucksberg, S., and Kinchla, R. A. (1988). *Psychology*. Englewood Cliffs, NJ: Prentice Hall.

Darwin, C. (1872, 1936). *On the Origin of Species by Means of Natural Selection*, 6th ed. New York: Modern Library.

Daston, L. J. (1981). Mathematics and the moral sciences: The rise and fall of the probability of judgements, 1785–1840. In H. N. Jahnke and M. Otte, eds., *Epistemological and Social Problems of the Sciences in the Early Nineteenth Century*. Dordrecht, The Netherlands: D. Reidel, 287–309.

Daston, L. J. (1988). *Classical Probability in the Enlightenment*. Princeton, NJ: Princeton University Press.

Davis, E. (1990). *Representations of Commonsense Knowledge*. San Mateo, CA: Morgan Kaufmann.

de Groot, A. (1965). Thought and choice in chess. *Psychological Studies, 4*. The Hague: Mouton, 441–446.

de Groot, A. (1966). Perception and memory versus thought: Some old ideas and recent findings. In B. Kleinmuntz, ed., *Problem Solving*. New York: Wiley.

DeJong, G., and Mooney, R. (1986). Explanation-based learning: An alternative view. *Machine Learning, 1 (2)*, 145–176.

Denny, J. P. (1986). Cultural ecology of mathematics: Ojibway and Inuit hunters. In M. Class, ed., *Native American Mathematics*. Austin: University of Texas Press.

Domingos, P. (1995). Rule induction and instance-based learning: A unified approach. In *Proceedings of the Fourteenth International Joint Conference on Artificial Intelligence (IJCAI-95), Montreal, Quebec*. San Mateo, CA: Morgan Kaufmann, 1226–1232.

Dominowski, R. L. (1995). Content effects in Wason's selection task. In S. E. Newstead and J. St. B.T. Evans, eds., *Perspectives on Thinking and Reasoning: Essays in Honour of Peter Wason*. Hove, England: Erlbaum, 41–65.

Dreyfus, H., and Dreyfus, S. (1987). *Mind over Machine*. New York: The Free Press.

Dubois, D., and Prade, H. (1988). An introduction to possibilistic and fuzzy logics. In P. Smets et al., eds., *Non-Standard Logics for Automated Reasoning*. San Diego, CA: Academic Press.

Duda, R. O., Gashnig, J. G., and Hart, P. E. (1980). Model design in the Prospector consultant system for mineral exploration. In D. Michie, ed., *Expert Systems in the Microelectronic Age*. Edinburgh, Scotland: Edinburgh University Press, 153–157.

Dyer, M. (1990). Distributed symbol formation and processing in connectionist networks. *Journal of Experimental Theory in Artificial Intelligence*, 2, 215–239.

Earman, J. (1992). *Bayes or Bust? A Critical Examination of Bayesian Confirmation Theory*. Cambridge, MA: MIT Press.

Eddy, D. M. (1982). Probabilistic reasoning in clinical medicine: Problems and opportunities. In D. Kahneman, P. Slovic, and A. Tversky, eds., *Judgement under Uncertainty: Heuristics and Biases*. Cambridge: Cambridge University Press, 249–267.

Edwards, W. (1968). Conservatism in human information processing. In B. Kleinmuntz, ed., *Formal Representation of Human Judgment*. New York: Wiley, 17–52.

Edwards, W., and von Winterfeldt, D. (1986). On cognitive illusions and their implications. In H. R. Arkes and K. R. Hammond, eds., *Judgement and Decision Making*. Cambridge: Cambridge University Press.

Eisenstadt, S. A., and Simon, H. A. (1997). Logic and thought. *Minds and Machines*, 7, 365–385.

Ellman, T. (1989). Explanation-based learning: A survey of programs and perspectives. *ACM Comput. Surv.*, 21 (2), 164–219.

Engel, P. (1989). *The Norm of Truth: An Introduction to the Philosophy of Logic*. Toronto: University of Toronto Press.

Erickson, J. R. (1974). A set analysis of behavior in formal syllogistic reasoning tasks. In R. Solso, ed., *Theories in Cognitive Psychology: The Loyola Symposium*. Hillsdale, NJ: Erlbaum.

Erickson, J. R. (1978). Research on syllogistic reasoning. In R. Revlin and R. E. Mayer, eds., *Human Reasoning*. Washington, DC: Winston.

Ericsson, K. A., and Simon, H. A. (1984). *Protocol Analysis: Verbal Reports as Data*. Cambridge, MA: MIT Press.

Ervin, S. M. (1964). Imitation and structural change in children's language. In E. H. Lenneberg, ed., *New Directions in the Study of Language*. Cambridge, MA: MIT Press.

Evans, J. St. B.T. (1977). Linguistic factors in reasoning. *Quarterly Journal of Experimental Psychology*, 29, 297–306.

Evans, J. St. B.T. (1982). *The Psychology of Deductive Reasoning*. London: Routledge & Kegan Paul.

Evans, J. St. B.T. (1993). The mental model theory of conditional reasoning: Critical appraisal and revision. *Cognition*, 48, 1–20.

Evans, J. St. B.T. (1998). Matching bias in conditional reasoning: Do we understand it after 25 years? *Thinking and Reasoning*, 4, 45–82.

Evans, J. St. B.T., Barston, J. L., and Pollard, P. (1983). On the conflict between logic and belief in syllogistic reasoning. *Memory & Cognition, 11*, 295–306.

Evans, J. St. B.T., Clibbens, J., and Rood, B. (1995). Bias in conditional inference: Implications for mental models and mental logic. *Quarterly Journal of Experimental Psychology, 48A*, 644–670.

Feather, N. T. (1967). Evaluation of religious and neutral arguments in religious and atheist student groups. *Australian Journal of Psychology, 19 (1)*, 3–12.

Fenichel, O. (1945). *The Psychoanalytic Theory of Neurosis.* New York: W. W. Norton.

Feynman, R. (1967). *The Character of Physical Law.* Cambridge, MA: MIT Press.

Fiedler, K. (1988). The dependence of the conjunction fallacy on subtle linguistic factors. *Psychological Research, 50*, 123–129.

Fisher, R. A. (1955). Statistical methods and scientific induction. *Journal of the Royal Statistical Society, Series B, 17*, 69–78.

Fodor, J. A., and McLaughlin, B. P. (1990). Connectionism and the problems of systematicity: Why Smolensky's solution doesn't work. *Cognition, 35*, 183–204.

Fodor, J., and Pylyshyn, Z. (1988). Connectionism and cognitive architecture: A critical analysis. In S. Pinker and J. Mehler, eds., *Connections and Symbols.* Cambridge, MA: MIT Press.

Fong, G. T., Krantz, D. H., and Nisbett, R. E. (1986). The effects of statistical training on thinking about everyday problems. *Cognitive Psychology, 18*, 253–292.

Fong, G. T., and Nisbett, R. E. (1991). Immediate and delayed transfer of training effects in statistical reasoning. *Journal of Experimental Psychology: General, 120*, 34–45.

Ford, M. (1985). Review of P. N. Johnson-Laird's "Mental models: Towards a cognitive science of language, inference, and consciousness." *Language, 61*, 897–903.

Ford, M. (1995). Two modes of mental representation and problem solution in syllogistic reasoning. *Cognition, 54*, 1–71.

Fox, S., and Leake, D. B. (1995a). Modeling case-based planning for repairing reasoning failures. In *Proceedings, AAAI Spring Symposium on Representing Mental States and Mechanisms.* Stanford, CA, 31–38.

Fox, S., and Leake, D. B. (1995b). Using introspective reasoning to refine indexing. In *Proceedings of the Fourteenth International Joint Conference on Artificial Intelligence (IJCAI-95), Montreal, Quebec.* San Mateo, CA: Morgan Kaufmann, 391–397.

Francis, A. G., and Ram, A. (1993). Computational models of the utility problem and their application to the utility analysis of case-based reasoning. In *Proceedings Workshop on Knowledge Compilation and Speedup Learning.* Amherst, MA.

Francis, A. G., and Ram, A. (1994). A comparative utility analysis of case-based reasoning and control-rule learning systems. In *Proceedings, AAAI Case-Based Reasoning Workshop.* Menlo Park, CA: AAAI Press, 36–41.

Frege, G. (1879). Begriffsschrift, a formal language modeled upon that of arithmetic, for pure thought. In J. can Heijenoort, ed., *From Frege to Godel: A Source-book in Mathematical Logic, 1879–1931.* Cambridge, MA: Harvard University Press.

Freud, S. (1966). *Psychopathology of Everyday Life.* Edited by J. Strachey. New York: W. W. Norton.

Freyd, J. J. (1987). Dynamic mental representations. *Psychological Review, 94*, 427–438.

Gallistel, C. R. (1990). *The organization of learning.* Cambridge, MA: MIT Press.

Galotti, K. M. (1989). Approaches to studying formal and everyday reasoning. *Psychological Bulletin, 105*, 331–351.

Ganascia, J. G. (1987). AGAPE et CHARADE: Deux techniques d'apprentissage symbolique appliquées à la construction de base de connaissances. Ph.D. Thesis (Doctorat d'Etat), Université Paris-Sud, Centre d'Orsay.

Ganascia, J. G. (1991). Deriving the learning bias from rule properties. In J. E. Hayes, D. Michie, and E. Tyuga, eds., *Machine Intelligence*, vol. 12. Oxford: Oxford University Press, 151–168.

Gavanski, I., and Hui, C. (1992). Natural sample spaces and uncertain belief. *Journal of Personality and Social Psychology, 63*, 766–780.

Genesereth, M. R. (1983). An overview of meta-level architecture. In *Proceedings of the National Conference on Artificial Intelligence, August 22–26, 1983, Washington DC, AAAI–83*. Los Altos, CA: AAAI/distributed by Wm. Kaufmann, 119–124.

Gentner, D. (1983). Structure-mapping: A theoretical framework for analogy. *Cognitive Science, 7*, 155–170.

Gentner, D., and Collins, A. (1981). Studies of inference from lack of knowledge. *Memory & Cognition, 9*, 434–443.

Gentner, D., and Toupin, C. (1986). Systematicity and surface similarity in the development of analogy. *Cognitive Science, 10*, 277–300.

Giarratiano, J., and Riley, G. (1989). *Expert Systems: Principles and Programming*. Boston: PWS-KENT Publishing Co.

Gigerenzer, G. (1991). How to make cognitive illusions disappear: Beyond "heuristics and biases." *European Review of Social Psychology, 2*, 83–115.

Gigerenzer, G. (1993). The bounded rationality of probabilistic mental models. In K. I. Manktelow and D. E. Over, eds., *Rationality: Psychological and Philosophical Perspectives*. London: Routledge, 284–313.

Gigerenzer, G., and Hoffrage, U. (1995). How to improve Bayesian reasoning without instruction: Frequency formats. *Psychological Review, 102 (4)*, 684–704.

Gigerenzer, G., Hoffrage, U., and Kleinbölting, H. (1991). Probabilistic mental models: A Brunswikian theory of confidence. *Psychological Review, 98*, 506–528.

Gigerenzer, G., and Murray, D. J. (1987). *Cognition as Intuitive Statistics*. Hillsdale, NJ: Erlbaum.

Gigerenzer, G., Swijtink, Z., Porter, T., Daston, L., Beatty, J., and Krüger, L. (1989). *The Empire of Chance: How Probability Changed Science and Everyday Life*. Cambridge: Cambridge University Press.

Goel, A. (1989). Integration of case-based reasoning and model-based reasoning for adaptive design problem solving, Ph.D. Thesis, Ohio State University, Columbus, OH.

Golding, A., and Rosenbloom, P. (1991). Improving rule-based systems through case-based reasoning. *Proceedings AAAI-91*. Anaheim, CA, 22–27.

Gould, S. J. (1992). *Bully for Brontosaurus: Further Reflections in Natural History*. New York: Penguin Books.

Green, D. W. (1997). Hypothetical thinking in the selection task: Amplifying a model-based approach. *Cahiers de Psychologie Cognitive, 16*, 93–102.

Green, D. W., and Larking, R. (1995). The locus of facilitation in the abstract selection task. *Thinking and Reasoning, 1*, 183–199.

Green, D. W., Over, D., and Pyne, R. (1997). Probability and choice in the selection task. *Thinking and Reasoning, 3*, 209–235.

Grice, H. P. (1975). Logic and conversation. In P. Cole and J. L. Morgan, eds., *Syntax and Semantics, Vol. 3: Speech Acts*. New York: Academic Press.

Griggs, R. A. (1983). The role of problem content in the selection task and THOG problem. In J. St. B.T. Evans, ed., *Thinking and Reasoning: Psychological Approaches*. London: Routledge, 16–43.

Griggs, R. A., and Cox, J. R. (1982). The elusive thematic-materials effect in Wason's selection task. *British Journal of Psychology*, *73*, 407–420.

Griggs, R. A., and Ransdell, S. E. (1986). Scientists and the selection task. *Social Studies of Science*, *16*, 316–330.

Guyote, M. J., and Sternberg, R. J. (1981). A transitive-chain theory of syllogistic reasoning. *Cognitive Psychology*, *13*, 461–525.

Hall, H., and Knight, H. (1898). *Higher Algebra*. London: Macmillan.

Hammerton, M. (1973). A case of radical probability estimation. *Journal of Experimental Psychology*, *101*, 252–254.

Hammond, K. J., Siefert, C. M., and Gray, K. C. (1991). Functionality in analogical transfer: A hard match is good to find. *The Journal of the Learning Sciences*, *1*, 111–152.

Hammond, K. R. (1990). Functionalism and illusionism: Can integration be usefully achieved? In R. M. Hogarth, ed., *Insights in Decision Making*. Chicago: University of Chicago Press, 227–261.

Hanney, K., and Keane, M. T. (1996). Learning adaptation rules from a case-base. In I. Smith and B. Faltings, eds., *Advances in Case-Based Reasoning*. Berlin: Springer, 178–192.

Hanney, K., and Keane, M. T. (1997). The adaptation knowledge bottleneck: How to ease it by learning from cases. In D. B. Leake and E. Plaza, eds., *Case-Based Reasoning Research and Development*. Berlin: Springer, 359–370.

Hanney, K., Keane, M. T., Smyth, B., and Cunningham, P. (1995a). When do we need adaptation? A review of current practice. In *Adaptation of Knowledge for Reuse: Papers from the 1995 AAAI Fall Symposium, November 10–12, Cambridge, Massachusetts*. Menlo Park, CA: AAAI Press; Boston: MIT Press, 41–46.

Hanney, K., Keane, M. T., Smyth, B., and Cunningham, P. (1995b). Systems, tasks, and adaptation knowledge. In M. Veloso and A. Aamodt, eds., *Case-Based Reasoning: Research and Development*. Berlin: Springer, 461–470.

Harnad, S. (1990). The symbol grounding problem. *Physica D*, *42*, 335–346.

Hasher, L., and Chromiak, W. (1977). The processing of frequency information: An automatic mechanism? *Journal of Verbal Learning and Verbal Behavior*, *16*, 173–184.

Hasher, L., and Zacks, R. T. (1979). Automatic and effortful processes in memory. *Journal of Experimental Psychology: General*, *108*, 356–388.

Haviland, S. E. (1974). Nondeductive strategies in reasoning. Ph.D. dissertation, Department of Psychology, Stanford University, Stanford, CA.

Hawkins, J., Pea, R. D., Glick, J., and Scribner, S. (1984). Merds that laugh don't like mushrooms: Evidence for deductive reasoning by preschoolers. *Developmental Psychology*, *20*, 584–594.

Hayes, P. J. (1977). In defence of logic. In *Proceedings of the Fifth International Joint Conference on Artificial Intelligence, Cambridge, Massachusetts, August 22–25, 1977*, volume I. Pittsburgh, PA: IJCAI [International Joint Conference on Artificial Intelligence].

Hayes-Roth, F., Waterman, D. A., and Lenat, D. B., eds. (1983). *Building Expert Systems*. Reading, MA: Addison-Wesley.

Hellman, D. (1993). Dogma and inquisition in medicine: Breast cancer as a case study. *Cancer, 71 (7)*.

Henle, M. (1962). On the relation between logic and thinking. *Psychological Review, 69*, 366–378.

Heron, W. T., and Hunter, W. S. (1922). *Studies of the Reliability of the Problem Box and the Maze with Human and Animal Subjects*. Baltimore, MD: Williams and Wilkins.

Hinton, G. (1990). Mapping part-whole hierarchies into connectionist networks. *Artificial Intelligence, 46*, 47–76.

Hintzman, D. L. (1976). Repetition and memory. In G. H. Bower, ed., *The Psychology of Learning and Motivation*, vol. 10. New York: Academic Press, 47–91.

Hintzman, D. L., and Stern, L. D. (1978). Contextual variability and memory for frequency. *Journal of Experimental Psychology: Human Learning and Memory, 4*, 539–549.

Hobbes, T. (1651). Leviathan. In Sir William Molesworth, ed. (1839–1945), *The English Works of Thomas Hobbes of Mathersbury*, vol. 3. London: John Bohn.

Hoch, S. J., and Tschirgi, J. E. (1983). Cue redundancy and extra logical inference in a deductive reasoning task. *Memory and Cognition, 11*, 200–209.

Holland, J. (1986). Escaping brittleness. In R. Michalski, J. Carbonell, and T. Mitchell, eds., *Machine Learning*, vol. 2. San Mateo, CA: Morgan Kaufmann, 593–625.

Holland, J., Nisbitt, N., Thagard, T., and Holyoak, J. (1986). *Induction: A Theory of Learning and Development*. Cambridge, MA: MIT Press.

Holyoak, K. J. (1984). Analogical thinking and human intelligence. In R. J. Sternberg, ed., *Advances in the Psychology of Human Intelligence*, vol 2. Hillsdale, NJ: Erlbaum.

Holyoak, K. J. (1991). Symbolic connectionism: Toward third-generation theories of expertise. In K. A. Ericsson and J. Smith, eds., *Toward a General Theory of Expertise: Prospects and Limits*. Cambridge: Cambridge University Press.

Holyoak, K. J., and Koh, K. (1987). Surface and structural similarity in analogical transfer. *Memory and Cognition, 15*, 332–340.

Holyoak, K. J., and Thagard, P. (1989). Analogical mapping by constraint satisfaction. *Cognitive Science, 13*, 295–355.

Hume, D. (1739/1951). *A Treatise of Human Nature*. Edited by L. A. Selby-Bigge. Oxford: Clarendon Press.

Hunt, E. B., Marin, J., and Stone, P. T. (1966). *Experiments in Induction*. San Diego, CA: Academic Press.

Janis, I. L., and Frick, F. (1943). The relationship between attitudes toward conclusions and errors in judging logical validity of syllogisms. *Journal of Experimental Psychology, 33*, 73–77.

Jepson, C., Krantz, D. H., and Nisbett, R. E. (1983). Inductive reasoning: Competence or skill? *Behavioral and Brain Sciences, 6*, 494–501.

Johnson-Laird, P. N. (1969). Reasoning with ambiguous sentences. *British Journal of Psychology, 60*, 17–23.

Johnson-Laird, P. N. (1975). Models of deduction. In R. J. Falmagne, ed., *Reasoning: Representation and Process in Children and Adults*. Hillsdale, NJ: Erlbaum.

Johnson-Laird, P. N. (1980). Mental models in cognitive science. *Cognitive Science, 4*, 71–115.

Johnson-Laird, P. N. (1982). Thinking as a skill. *Quarterly Journal of Experimental Psychology, 34A*, 1–29.

Johnson-Laird, P. N. (1983). *Mental models.* Cambridge, MA: Harvard University Press.

Johnson-Laird, P. N. (1986). Reasoning without logic. In T. Myers, K. Brown, and B. McGonigle, eds., *Reasoning and Discourse Processes.* London: Academic Press.

Johnson-Laird, P. N., and Bara, B. G. (1984). Syllogistic inference. *Cognition, 16*, 1–61.

Johnson-Laird, P. N., and Byrne, R. (1991). *Deduction.* Hove, England: Erlbaum.

Johnson-Laird, P. N., Legrenzi, P., and Legrenzi, M. S. (1972). Reasoning and a sense of reality. *British Journal of Psychology, 63*, 305–400.

Johnson-Laird, P. N., and Steedman, M. (1978). The psychology of syllogisms. *Cognitive Psychology, 10*, 64–99.

Kahneman, D., and Miller, D. T. (1986). Norm theory: Comparing reality to its alternatives. *Psychological Review, 93*, 136–153.

Kahneman, D., Slovic, P., and Tversky, A., eds. (1982). *Judgement under Uncertainty: Heuristics and Biases.* New York: Cambridge University Press.

Kahneman, D., and Tversky, A. (1972). Subjective probability: A judgement of representativeness. *Cognitive Psychology, 3*, 430–454.

Kahneman, D., and Tversky, A. (1973). On the psychology of prediction. *Psychological Review, 80*, 237–251.

Kahneman, D., and Tversky, A. (1982). The psychology of preferences. *Scientific American, 246*, 160–174.

Kahneman, D., and Tversky, A. (1984). Choices, values, and frames. *American Psychologist, 39*, 341–350.

Kaiser, M. K., Jonides, J., and Alexander, J. (1986). Intuitive reasoning on abstract and familiar physics problems. *Memory & Cognition, 14*, 308–312.

Kambhampati, S., and Hendler, J. A. (1992). A validation-structure-based theory of plan modification and reuse. *Artificial Intelligence, 55 (2)*, 193–258.

Keane, M. T. (1988). *Analogical Problem Solving.* Chichester, England: Ellis Horwood.

Keane, M. T. (1994). Analogical asides on case-based reasoning. In S. Wess, K.-D. Althoff, and M. M. Richter, eds., *Topics in Case-Based Reasoning.* Berlin: Springer, 21–32.

Kleiter, G. D. (1994). Natural sampling: Rationality without base rates. In G. H. Fischer and D. Laming, eds., *Contributions to Mathematical Psychology: Psychometrics and Methodology.* New York: Springer, 375–388.

Koehler, J. J. (1996). The base-rate fallacy reconsidered: Descriptive, normative, and methodological challenges. *Behavioral and Brain Sciences, 19 (1)*, 1–53.

Kolata, G. (1993). At last, shout of "eureka" in age-old math mystery. *New York Times,* June 24, p. A1.

Kolodner, J. L. (1983). Reconstructive memory: A computer model. *Cognitive Science, 7*, 281–328.

Kolodner, J. L. (1989). Judging which is the "best" case for a case-based reasoner. In *Proceedings, DARPA Case-Based Reasoning Workshop, FL.* San Mateo, CA: Morgan Kaufmann, 77–81.

Kolodner, J. L. (1993). *Case-Based Reasoning.* San Mateo, CA: Morgan Kaufmann.

Kosslyn, S. M., and Pomerantz, J. R. (1977). Imagery, propositions, and the form of internal representations. *Cognitive Psychology, 9*, 52–76.

Kuilboer, M. M., Shahar, Y., Wilson, D. M., and Musen, M. A. (1993). Knowledge reuse: temporal-abstraction mechanisms for the assessment of children's growth. In C. Safran, ed., *Proceedings of the Seventeenth Annual Symposium on Computer Applications in Medical Care*. New York: McGraw-Hill, 449–453.

Langston, C., Nisbett, R., and Smith, E. E. (1991). *Priming Contractual Rules*. Unpublished manuscript, University of Michigan, Department of Psychology, Ann Arbor.

Laplace, P.-S. (1814/1951). *A Philosophical Essay on Probabilities*. F. W. Truscott and F. L. Emory, trans. New York: Dover.

Larkin, J., and Simon, H. A. (1987). Why a diagram is (sometimes) worth ten thousand words. *Cognitive Science, 11*, 65–99.

Larrick, R. P., Morgan, J. N., and Nisbett, R. E. (1990). Teaching the use of cost-benefit reasoning in everyday life. *Psychological Science, 1*, 362–370.

Larrick, R. P., Nisbett, R. E., and Morgan, J. N. (1993). Who uses cost-benefit rules of choice? *Organizational Behavior and Human Decision Processes, 56 (3)*, 331–347.

Leahey, T., and Wagman, M. (1974). The modification of fallacious reasoning with implication. *Journal of General Psychology, 91*, 277–285.

Leake, D. B. (1992). Constructive similarity assessment: Using stored cases to define new situations. In *Proceedings of the 14th Annual Conference of the Cognitive Science Society, Bloomington, IN*. Hillsdale, NJ: Erlbaum 313–318.

Leake, D. B. (1995a). Combining rules and cases to learn case adaptation. In *Proceedings of the 17th Annual Conference of the Cognitive Science Society, Pittsburgh, PA*. Hillsdale, NJ: Erlbaum.

Leake, D. B. (1995b). Becoming an expert case-based reasoner: Learning to adapt prior cases. In *Proceedings of the 8th Annual Florida Artificial Intelligence Research Symposium*. Melbourne, FL, 112–116.

Leake, D. B., Kinley, A., and Wilson, D. (1997). A case study of case-based CBR. In D. B. Leake and E. Plaza, eds., *Case-Based Reasoning Research and Development*. Berlin: Springer, 371–382.

Lee, G., and Oakhill, J. (1978). The effects of externalization on syllogistic reasoning. *Quarterly Journal of Experimental Psychology, 36A*, 519–530.

Lehman, D. R., Lempert, R. O., and Nisbett, R. E. (1988). The effects of graduate training on reasoning: Formal discipline and thinking about everyday life events. *American Psychologist, 43*, 431–443.

Lehman, D. R., and Nisbett, R. E. (1990). A longitudinal study of the effects of undergraduate education on reasoning. *Developmental Psychology, 26*, 952–960.

Leslie, A. M. (1987). Pretense and representation: The origins of "Theory of Mind." *Psychological Review, 94*, 412–426.

Lichtenstein, S., Fischhoff, B., and Phillips, L. D. (1982). Calibration of probabilities: The state of the art to 1980. In D. Kahneman, P. Slovic, and A. Tversky, eds., *Judgement under Uncertainty: Heuristics and Biases*. Cambridge: Cambridge University Press, 306–334.

Lind, J. (1753). *A Treatise of the Scurvy*. Edinburgh: Millar.

Lindley, D. V., Tversky, A., and Brown, R. V. (1979). On the reconciliation of probability assessments. *Journal of the Royal Statistical Society, 142*, 146–180.

Long, W. J., and Russ, T. A. (1983). A control structure for time dependent reasoning. In *Proceedings of the Eighth International Joint Conference on Artificial Intel-*

ligence [IJCAI-83], 8–12 August 1983, Karlsruhe, West Germany. Los Altos, CA: IJCAI/Morgan Kaufmann, 230–232.

Lopes, L. L. (1991). The rhetoric of irrationality. *Theory and Psychology, 1*, 65–82.

Love, R., and Kessler, C. (1995). Focusing in Wason's selection task: Content and instruction effects. *Thinking and Reasoning, 1*, 153–182.

Lukasiewicz, J. (1967). Many-valued systems of propositional logic. In S. McCall, ed., *Polish Logic*. Oxford: Oxford University Press.

Lyon, D., and Slovic, P. (1976). Dominance of accuracy information and neglect of base rates in probability estimation. *Acta Psychologica, 40*, 287–298.

Mackie, G. L. (1973). *Truth, Probability, and Paradox*. New York: Oxford University Press.

Macnamara, J. (1986). *A Border Dispute: The Place of Logic in Psychology*. Cambridge, MA: MIT Press.

Mahé, J. (1880). Le scorbut. In *Dictionnaire Encyclopédique des Sciences Médicales, Série 3, Tome 8*. Paris: Masson, 35–357.

Marcus, G. F., Ullman, M., Pinker, S., Hollander, M., Rosen, T. J., and Xu, F. (1990). *Overextensions*. (Occasional Paper No. 41). MIT, Center for Cognitive Science.

Marcus, S. L., and Rips, L. J. (1979). Conditional reasoning. *Journal of Verbal Learning & Verbal Behavior, 18*, 199–223.

Markovits, H. (1984). Awareness of the "possible" as a mediator of formal thinking in conditional reasoning problems. *British Journal of Psychology, 75*, 367–376.

Markovits, H. (1988). Conditional reasoning, representation, and empirical evidence on a concrete task. *Quarterly Journal of Experimental Psychology, 40A*, 483–495.

Markovits, H., and Nantel, G. (1989). The belief-bias effect in the production and evaluation of logical conclusions. *Memory & Cognition, 17*, 11–17.

Markovits, H., and Vashon, R. (1989). Reasoning with contrary-to-fact propositions. *Journal of Experimental Child Psychology, 47 (3)*, 398–412.

Marr, D. (1982). *Vision: A Computational Investigation into the Human Representation and Processing of Visual Information*. San Francisco: Freeman.

Martin-Lof, P. (1982). Constructive mathematics and computer programming. In *Logic, Methodology, and Philosophy of Science VI: Proceedings of the Sixth International Congress of Logic, Methodology, and Philosophy of Science, Hanover, Germany, 1979*. Amsterdam, Netherlands: North-Holland.

Mazoyer, B. M., Tzourio, N., Frak, V., Syrota, A., Murayama, N., Levrier, O., Salamon, O., Dehaene, S., Cohen, L., and Mehler, J. (1993). The cortical representation of speech. *Journal of Cognitive Neuroscience, 5 (4)*, 467–479.

McCarthy, J. (1968). Programs with common sense. In M. Minsky, ed., *Semantic Information Processing*. Cambridge, MA: MIT Press.

McCarthy, J. (1988). Mathematical logic in artificial intelligence. *Daedalus, 117*, 297–311.

McDermott, D. V., and Doyle, J. (1980). Nonmonotonic logic I. *Artificial Intelligence, 13*, 41–72.

Medin, D. L., Goldstone, R. L., and Gentner, D. (1993). Respects for similarity. *Psychological Review, 100*, 254–278.

Medin, D. L., and Ross, B. H. (1989). The specific character of abstract thought: Categorization, problem solving, and induction. In R. J. Sternberg, ed., *Advances in the Psychology of Human Intelligence*, vol. 5. Hillsdale, NJ: Erlbaum.

Medin, D. L., and Smith, E. E. (1981). Strategies and classification learning. *Journal of Experimental Psychology: Human Learning and Memory, 7,* 241–253.

Meehl, P. (1954). *Clinical versus statistical prediction.* Minneapolis: University of Minnesota Press.

Meehl, P., and Rosen, A. (1955). Antecedent probability and the efficiency of psychometric signs, patterns, or cutting scores. *Psychological Bulletin, 52,* 194–216.

Michalski, R. S. (1980). Pattern recognition as rule-guided inductive inference. *IEEE Transactions on Pattern Analysis and Machine Intelligence, PAMI-2,* 349–361.

Michalski, R. S. (1983). A theory and methodology of inductive learning. *Artificial Intelligence, 20,* 111–161.

Michalski, R. S., and Winston, P. H. (1986). Variable precision logic. *Artificial Intelligence, 29,* 121–146.

Michener, E. R. (1978). Understanding understanding mathematics. *Cognitive Science, 2 (4),* 361–383.

Mill, J. S. (1874). *A System of Logic.* New York: Harper.

Miller, G. A. (1962). Some psychological studies of grammar. *American Psychologist, 7,* 748–762.

Minton, S. (1990). Qualitative results concerning the utility of explanation-based learning. *Artificial Intelligence, 42 (2–3),* 363–391.

Minton, S., Carbonell, J., Knoblock, C., Kuakko, D., Etzoni, O., and Gil, Y. (1989). Explanation-based learning: A problem solving perspective. *Artificial Intelligence, 40 (1–3),* 63–118.

Mitchell, T. M. (1982). Generalization as search. *Artificial Intelligence, 18,* 203–226.

Mitchell, T. M., Keller, R., and Kedar-Cabelli, S. (1986). Explanation-based generalization: A unifying view. *Machine Learning, 1 (1),* 47–80.

Morgan, A. B. (1956). Sex differences in adults on a test of logical reasoning. *Psychological Reports, 2,* 227–230.

Morris, M. W., Cheng, P., and Nisbett, R. E. (1991). *Causal Reasoning Schemas.* Unpublished manuscript. University of California, Department of Psychology, Los Angeles.

Murphy, G. L., and Medin, D. L. (1995). The role of theories in conceptual coherence. *Psychological Review, 92,* 289–316.

Newell, A. (1980). Reasoning, problem solving and decision processes: The problem space as a fundamental category. In R. Nickerson, ed., *Attention on Performance VIII.* Hillsdale, NJ: Erlbaum, 693–718.

Newell, A., and Simon, H. A. (1972). *Human Problem Solving.* Englewood Cliffs, NJ: Prentice-Hall.

Nickerson, R. (1996). Hempel's paradox and Wason's selection task: Logical and psychological puzzles of confirmation. *Thinking and Reasoning, 2,* 1–31.

Nilsson, N. J. (1980). *Principles of Artificial Intelligence.* Palo Alto, CA: Tioga.

Nilsson, N. J. (1986). Probabilistic logic. *Artificial Intelligence, 28,* 71–87.

Nisbett, R. E., ed. (1993). *Rules for Reasoning.* Hillsdale, NJ: Erlbaum.

Nisbett, R. E., Fong, G. T., Lehman, D. R., and Cheng, P. W. (1987). Teaching reasoning. *Science, 238,* 625–631.

Nisbett, R. E., Krantz, D. H., Jepson, D., and Kunda, Z. (1983). The use of statistical heuristics in everyday inductive reasoning. *Psychological Review, 90,* 339–363.

Nisbett, R. E., and Wilson, T. D. (1977). Telling more than we know: Verbal reports on mental processes. *Psychological Review, 8,* 231–259.

Norman, L. (1977). *Human Information Processing*. San Diego, CA: Academic Press.

Nosofsky, R. M., Clark, S. E., and Shin, H. J. (1989). Rules and exemplars in categorization, identification, and recognition. *Journal of Experimental Psychology: Learning, Memory, and Cognition, 15,* 282–304.

Oakhill, J. V., and Johnson-Laird, P. N. (1985). The effects of belief on the spontaneous production of syllogistic conclusions. *Quarterly Journal of Experimental Psychology, 37A,* 553–569.

Oaksford, M., and Chater, N. (1994). A rational analysis of the selection task as optimal data selection. *Psychological Review, 101,* 608–631.

Oaksford, M., and Chater, N. (1996). Rational explanation of the selection task. *Psychological Review, 103,* 381–391.

O'Brien, D. P., Costa, G., and Overton, W. F. (1986). Evaluations of causal and conditional hypotheses. *Quarterly Journal of Experimental Psychology, 38A,* 493–512.

Oden, G. C. (1987). Concept, knowledge, and thought. *Annual Review of Psychology, 38,* 218.

Osherson, D. (1975). Logic and logical models of thinking. In R. Falmagne, ed., *Reasoning: Representation and Process*. New York: Wiley.

Osherson, D., Smith, E., and Shafir, E. (1987). Some origins of belief. Technical Report 3, Cognitive Science and Machine Intelligence Lab, University of Michigan, Ann Arbor.

Pearl, J. (1986). Fusion, propagation, and structuring in Bayesian networks. *Artificial Intelligence, 29,* 241–288.

Pearl, J. (1987). Embracing causality in formal reasoning. In *Proceedings Sixth National Conference on Artificial Intelligence*. Los Altos, CA: Morgan Kaufmann.

Pearl, J. (1988). *Probabilistic Reasoning in Intelligent Systems*. San Mateo, CA: Morgan Kaufmann.

Petrides, M., Alivisatos, B., Evans, A. C., and Meyer, E. (1993). Dissociation of human mid-dorsolateral from posterior dorsolateral frontal cortex in memory processing. In *Proceedings of the National Academy of Sciences USA, 90,* 873–877.

Phillips, L. D., and Edwards, W. (1966). Conservatism in a simple probability model inference task. *Journal of Experimental Psychology, 72,* 346–354.

Piaget, J. (1949). *Traite de logique; essai du logistique operatoire* [Treatise on logic: essay on operative logistics]. Paris: Armand Colin.

Piaget, J., and Inhelder, B. (1951/1975). *The Origin of the Idea of Chance in Children*. New York: Norton.

Piattelli-Palmarini, M. (1994). *Inevitable Illusions: How Mistakes of Reason Rule Our Minds*. New York: Wiley.

Pinker, S., and Bloom, P. (1990). Natural language and natural selection. *Behavioral and Brain Science, 13,* 707–784.

Pinker, S., and Prince, A. (1988). On language and connectionism: Analysis of a parallel distributed processing model of language acquisition. *Cognition, 28,* 73–194.

Platt, R. D., and Griggs, R. A. (1993). Facilitation in the abstract selection task: The effects of attentional and instructional factors. *Quarterly Journal of Experimental Psychology, 46A,* 591–613.

Polk, T. A., and Newell, A. (1995). Deduction as verbal reasoning. *Psychological Review, 102,* 533–566.

Pollock, J. L. (1987). Defeasible reasoning. *Cognitive Science, 11,* 481–518.

Polya, G. (1968). *Patterns of Plausible Inference*. Princeton, NJ: Princeton University Press.

Popper, K. (1959). *The Logic of Scientific Discovery*. New York: Basic Books.

Porter, B. W., Bareiss, R., and Holte, R. C. (1990). Concept learning and heuristic classification in weak theory domains. *Artificial Intelligence, 45 (1–2)*, 229–263.

Pylyshyn, Z. W. (1973). What the mind's eye tells the mind's brain: A critique of mental imagery. *Psychological Bulletin, 80*, 1–24.

Pylyshyn, Z. (1984). *Computation and Cognition: Toward a Foundation for Cognitive Science*. Cambridge, MA: MIT Press.

Quillian, M. R. (1968). Semantic memory. In M. Minsky, ed., *Semantic Information Processing*. Cambridge, MA: MIT Press.

Quinlan, J. R. (1979). Discovering rules from a large collection of examples: A case study. In D. Michie, ed., *Expert Systems in the Micro-Electronic Age*. Edinburgh, Scotland: Edinburgh University Press.

Quinlan, J. R. (1986). Induction of decision trees. *Machine Learning, 1 (1)*, 81–106.

Real, L. A. (1991). Animal choice behavior and the evolution of cognitive architecture. *Science, 253*, 980–986.

Real, L. A., and Caraco, T. (1986). Risk and foraging in stochastic environments: Theory and evidence. *Annual Review of Ecology and Systematics, 17*, 371–390.

Reiter, R. (1978). On reasoning by default. In TINLAP-2. New York: Association of Computing Machinery, 210–218.

Reiter, R. (1980). Logic for default reasoning. *Artificial Intelligence, 13*, 1–132.

Revlin, R., and Leirer, V. (1978). The effects of personal biases on syllogistic reasoning: Rational decisions from personalized representations. In R. Revlin and R. E. Meyer, eds., *Human Reasoning*. Washington, DC: Winston-Wiley, 51–82.

Revlin, R., Leirer, V., Yopp, H., and Yopp, R. (1980). The belief-bias effect in formal reasoning: The influence of knowledge on logic. *Memory & Cognition, 8*, 584–592.

Revlis, R. (1975). Two models of syllogistic reasoning: Feature selection and conversion. *Journal of Verbal Learning and Verbal Behavior, 14*, 180–195.

Riesbeck, C., and Schank, R. (1989). *Inside Case-Based Reasoning*. Hillsdale, NJ: Erlbaum.

Rips, L. J. (1983). Cognitive processes in propositional reasoning. *Psychological Review, 90*, 38–71.

Rips, L. J. (1986). Mental models. In M. Brand and R. M. Harnish, eds., *Problems in the Representation of Knowledge and Belief*. Tucson: University of Arizona Press.

Rips, L. J. (1990). Reasoning. *Annual Review of Psychology, 41*, 321–354.

Rips, L. J. (1994). *The Psychology of Proof*. Cambridge, MA: MIT Press.

Rips, L. J. (1997). Goals for a theory of deduction: Reply to Johnson-Laird. *Minds and Machines, 7*, 409–424.

Rips, L. J., and Marcus, S. L. (1990). Suppositions and the analysis of conditional sentences. In J. R. Anderson, *Cognitive Psychology and Its Implications* (3rd ed.). New York: W. H. Freeman and Co., pp. 185–220.

Roberts, M. J. (1993). Human reasoning: deduction rules or mental models? *Quarterly Journal of Experimental Psychology, 46A*, 569–589.

Robinson, J. A. (1965). A machine oriented logic based on the resolution principle. *Journal of the Association for Computing Machinery, 12*, 23–41.

Roddis, L. E. (1951). *James Lind, Founder of Naval Medicine*. London: William Heinemann.

Ross, B. H. (1987). This is like that: The use of earlier problems and the separation of similarity effects. *Journal of Experimental Psychology: Learning, Memory and Cognition, 13*, 371–416.

Rouanet, H. (1961). Études de décisions expérimentes et calcul de probabilitiés [Studies of experimental decision making and the probability calculus]. In *Colloques Internationaux du Centre National de la Recherche Scientifique*. Paris: Éditions de Centre National de la Recherche Scientifique, 33–43.

Rousu, J., and Aarts, R. J. (1996). Adaptation cost as a criterion for solution evaluation. In I. Smith and B. Faltings, eds., *Advances in Case-Based Reasoning*. Berlin: Springer, 354–361.

Rumelhart, D. E., and McCelland, J. L. (1987). Learning the past tenses of English verbs: Implicit rules or parallel distributed processing. In B. MacWhinney, ed., *Mechanisms of Language Acquisition*. Hillsdale, NJ: Erlbaum.

Russ, T. A. (1989). Using hindsight in medical decision making. In L. C. Kingsland, ed., *Proceedings of the Thirteenth Annual Symposium on Computer Applications in Medical Care*. Washington, DC: IEEE Computing Society Press, 38–44.

Russel, S., and Grosof, B. (1990). Declarative bias: An overview. In P. Benjamin, ed., *Change of Representation and Inductive Bias*. Boston: Kluwer Academic.

Sahlin, N. (1993). On higher order beliefs. In J. Dubucs, ed., *Philosophy of Probability*. Dordrecht, The Netherlands: Kluwer Academic, 13–34.

Salter, W. (1983). Tacit theories of economics. In *Proceedings of the Fifth Annual Conference of the Cognitive Science Society*. Rochester, NY: University of Rochester.

Schaffner, K. F. (1993). *Discovery and Explanation in Biology and Medicine*. Chicago: University of Chicago Press.

Schank, R. C. (1982). *Dynamic Memory: A Theory of Reminding and Learning in Computers and People*. London: Cambridge University.

Scholz, R. W. (1987). *Cognitive Strategies in Stochastic Thinking*. Dordrecht, The Netherlands: D. Reidel.

Schyns, P. G., Goldstone, R. L., and Thibaut, J.-P.(1998). The development of features in object concepts. *Behavioral Brain Sciences, 21 (1)*, 1–54.

Scribner, S. (1984). Studying working intelligence. In B. Rogoff and J. Love, eds., *Everyday Cognition: Its Development in Social Context*. Cambridge, MA: Harvard University Press, 9–40.

Sedlmeier, P., Hertwig, R., and Gigerenzer, G. (1995). *Is "R" More Likely in the First or Second Position? Availability. Letter Class, and Neural Network Models*. Manuscript submitted for publication.

Sells, S. B. (1936). The atmosphere effect, an experimental study of reasoning. *Archives of Psychology, 200*, 72.

Shafer, G. A. (1976). *A Mathematical Theory of Evidence*. Princeton, NJ: Princeton University Press.

Shafer G., and Tversky, A. (1983). *Weighing Evidence: The Design and Comparisons of Probability Thought Experiments*. Unpublished manuscript, Stanford University.

Shahar, Y. (1994). A knowledge-based method for temporal abstraction of clinical data. Ph.D. dissertation, Program in Medical Information Sciences, Stanford University School of Medicine. Stanford, CA; also Knowledge Systems Laboratory Report No. KSL-94-64.

Shahar, Y. (1997). A framework for knowledge-based temporal abstraction. *Artificial Intelligence, 90*, 79–133.

Shahar, Y., and Molina, M. (1996). Knowledge-based spatiotemporal abstraction. In *Proceedings AAAI-96 Workshop on Spatial and Temporal Reasoning*. Portland, OR, 21–29.

Shahar, Y., and Musen, M. A. (1993/1994). RÉSUMÉ: A temporal-abstraction system for patient monitoring. *Computers and Biomedical Research, 26* (1993), 255–273; reprinted in J. H. van Bemmel and T. McRay, eds., *Yearbook of Medical Informatics 1994*. Stuttgart: F. K. Schattauer and the International Medical Informatics Association, 443–461.

Shahar, Y., and Musen, M. A. (1996). Knowledge-based temporal abstraction in clinical domains. *Artificial Intelligence in Medicine, 8 (3)*, 267–298.

Shallice, T., Fletcher, P., Frith, C. D., Grasby, P. M., Fracowiak, R.S.J., and Dolan, R. J. (1994). Brain regions associated with the acquisition and retrieval of verbal episodic memory. *Nature, 368*, 633–635.

Shanks, D. (1991). A connectionist account of base-rate biases in categorization. *Connection Science, 3 (2)*, 143–162.

Shanteau, J. (1989). Cognitive heuristics and biases in behavioral auditing: Review, comments and observations. *Accounting Organizations and Society, 14 (1/2)*, 165–177.

Sharma, K. N. (1960). Analysis of a test of reasoning ability. *Journal of Educational Psychology, 17–18*, 228–240.

Shepard, R. N. (1984). Ecological constraints on internal representation: Resonant kinematics of perceiving, imagining, thinking, and dreaming. *Psychological Review, 91*, 417–447.

Shortliffe, E. H. (1976). *MYCIN: Computer-Based Medical Consultations*. New York: Elsevier.

Shultz, T., Zelazo, P., and Engelberg, D. (1989). Managing rule-based reasoning. In *Proceedings, Eleventh Annual Conference of the Cognitive Science Society*. Ann Arbor, MI, 227–234.

Simon, H. A. (1956). Rational choice and the structure of the environment. *Psychological Review, 63*, 129–138.

Simon, H. A. (1982). *Models of Bounded Rationality*, vols. 1, 2. Cambridge, MA: MIT Press.

Simon, H. A. (1991). Cognitive architectures and rational analysis: Comment. In K. VanLehn, ed., *Architectures for Intelligence: The 22nd Carnegie Mellon Symposium on Cognition*. Hillsdale, NJ: Erlbaum.

Simpson, M. E., and Johnson, D. M. (1966). Atmosphere and conversion errors in syllogistic reasoning. *Journal of Experimental Psychology, 72 (2)*, 197–200.

Sloman, S. A. (1993). Feature-based induction. *Cognitive Psychology, 25 (2)*, 231–280.

Sloman, S. A. (1996). The empirical case for two systems of reasoning. *Psychological Bulletin, 119*, 3–22.

Slovic, P., Fischoff, B., and Lichtenstein, S. (1976). Cognitive process and social risk taking. In J. S. Carroll and J. W. Payne, eds., *Cognition and Social Behavior*. Hillsdale, NJ: Erlbaum.

Smith, E. E., Langston, C., and Nisbett, R. E. (1992). The case for rules in reasoning. *Cognitive Science, 16*, 1–40.

Smolensky, P. (1988). On the proper treatment of connectionism. *Behavioral Brain Sciences, 11*, 1–59.

Smyth, B. (1996). Case-based design. Ph.D. Thesis, University of Dublin, Trinity College, Dublin, Ireland.

Smyth, B., and Cunningham, P. (1993). Complexity of adaptation in real-world case-based reasoning systems. In *Proceedings of the 6th Irish Conference on Artificial Intelligence and Cognitive Science*. Belfast, Ireland, 229–240.

Smyth, B., and Cunningham, P. (1996). The utility problem analysed: A case-based reasoning perspective. In I. Smith and B. Faltings, eds., *Advances in Case-Based Reasoning*. Berlin: Springer, 392–399.

Smyth, B., and Keane, M. T. (1994). Retrieving adaptable cases: The role of adaptation knowledge in case retrieval. In S. Wess, K.-D. Althoff, and M. M. Richter, eds., *Topics in Case-Based Reasoning*. Berlin: Springer, 209–220.

Smyth, B., and Keane, M. T. (1995a). Experiments on adaptation-guided retrieval in a case-based design system. In M. Veloso and A. Aamodt, eds., *Case-Based Reasoning: Research and Development*. Berlin: Springer, 313–324.

Smyth, B., and Keane, M. T. (1995b). Remembering to forget: A competence preserving case deletion policy for CBR systems. In *Proceedings of the Fourteenth International Joint Conference on Artificial Intelligence [IJCAI-95], Montreal, Quebec, Canada, August 20–25, 1995*. San Mateo, CA: IJCAI/Morgan Kaufmann.

Smyth, B., and Keane, M. T. (1996a). Design a la Déjà Vu: Reducing the adaptation overhead. In D. B. Leake, ed., *Case-Based Reasoning: Experiences, Lessons, and Future Directions*. Cambridge, MA: MIT Press, 151–166.

Smyth, B., and Keane, M. T. (1996b). Using adaptation knowledge to retrieve and adapt design cases. *Knowledge-Based Systems, 9*, 127–135.

Smyth, B., and Keane, M. T. (1998). Adaptation-guided retrieval: Questioning the similarity assumption in reasoning. *Artificial Intelligence, 102*, 249–293.

Snodgrass, R., and Ahn, I. (1986). Temporal databases. *IEEE Computing, 19 (9)*, 35–42.

Spencer, H. (1896). *The Principles of Sociology*. New York: D. Appleton and Co.

Sperber, D., Cara, F., and Girotto, V. (1995). Relevance theory explains the selection task. *Cognition, 52*, 3–39.

Staddon, J.E.R. (1988). Learning as inference. In R. C. Bolles and M. D. Beecher, eds., *Evolution and Learning*. Hillsdale, NJ: Erlbaum.

Stanfill, C., and Waltz, D. (1986). Towards memory-based reasoning. *Communications of the ACM, 29 (12)*, 1213–1228.

Stanovich, K. E. (1998). *Who Is Rational? Studies of Individual Differences in Reasoning*. Mahwah, NJ: Erlbaum.

Staudenmayer, H. (1975). Understanding conditional reasoning with meaningful propositions. In R. J. Falmagne, ed., *Reasoning: Representation and Process in Children and Adults*. Hillsdale, NJ: Erlbaum.

Stein, S. (2000). Personal communication.

Stephens, D. W., and Krebs, J. R. (1986). *Foraging Theory*. Princeton, NJ: Princeton University Press.

Sterling, L., and Shapiro, E. (1986). *The Art of PROLOG*. Cambridge: Cambridge University Press.

Stevens, A., and Collins, A. (1980). Multiple conceptual models of a complex system. In R. Snow, P. Federico, and W. Montague, eds., *Aptitude, Learning, and Instruction: Cognitive Process Analysis*. Hillsdale, NJ: Erlbaum, 177–197.

Stevens, S. S. (1946). On the theory of scales of measurement. *Science, 103,* 677–680.

Stigler, J. W. (1984). The effect of abacus training on Chinese children's mental calculation. *Cognitive Psychology, 16,* 145–176.

Stroulia, E., and Goel, A. (1994). Learning problem solving concepts by reflecting on problem solving. In *Proceedings European Conference on Machine Learning.* Catania, Italy, 287–306.

Sun, R. (1991). Connectionist models of rule-based reasoning. In *Proceedings Thirteenth Annual Conference of the Cognitive Science Society.* Ann Arbor, MI, 437–442.

Sun, R. (1992). A connectionist model for commonsense reasoning incorporating rules and similarities. *Knowledge Acquisition, 4,* 293–321.

Sun, R. (1993). An efficient feature-based connectionist inheritance scheme. *IEEE Transactions on Systems, Man and Cybernetics, 23 (2),* 512–522.

Sun, R. (1994a). A neural network model of causality. *IEEE Transactions on Neural Networks, 5,* 604–611.

Sun, R. (1994b). *Integrating Rules and Connectionism for Robust Commonsense Reasoning.* New York: Wiley.

Sun, R. (1995). Robust reasoning: Integrating rule-based and similarity-based reasoning. *Artificial Intelligence, 75,* 241–295.

Sun, R, Bookman, L., and Shekhar, S., eds. (1992). *Working Notes of the AAAI Workshop on Integrating Neural and Symbolic Processes.* Menlo Park, CA: AAAI.

Suppes, P. (1964). *First Course in Mathematical Logic.* New York: Blaisdell Publishing Co.

Sutherland, S. (1992). *Irrationality: The Enemy Within.* London: Constable.

Taplin, J. E. (1971). Reasoning with conditional sentences. *Journal of Verbal Learning and Verbal Behavior, 10,* 218–225.

Terrell, D. B. (1967). *Logic: A Modern Introduction to Deductive Reasoning.* New York: Holt, Rinehart, & Winston.

Thagard, P. (1988). *Computational Philosophy of Science.* Cambridge, MA: MIT Press.

Thagard, P., and Nowak, G. (1990). The conceptual structure of the geological revolution. In J. Shrager and P. Langley, eds., *Computational Models of Scientific Discovery and Theory Formation.* Los Altos, CA: Morgan Kaufmann, 27–72.

Thompson, V. A. (1995). Conditional reasoning: The necessary and sufficient conditions. *Canadian Journal of Experimental Psychology, 49,* 1–60.

Tooby, J., and Cosmides, L. (1992). *Ecological Rationality and the Multimodular Mind (Tech. Report No. 92–1).* Santa Barbara: University of California, Center for Evolutionary Psychology.

Turing, A. (1936). On computable numbers, with an application to Entscheudung's problem. *Proceedings of the London Mathematics Society, 52,* 230–265.

Tversky, A., and Kahneman, D. (1977). Causal thinking in judgement under uncertainty. In R. Butts and J. Hintikka, eds., *Basic Problems in Methodology and Linguistics, 3.* Dordrecht, The Netherlands: Reidel, 167–192.

Tversky, A., and Kahneman, D. (1982). Evidential impact of base rates. In D. Kahneman, P. Slovic, and A. Tversky, eds., *Judgement under Uncertainty: Heuristics and Biases.* Cambridge, England: Cambridge University Press, 153–160.

Tversky, A., and Kahneman, D. (1983). Extensional vs. intuitive reasoning: The conjunction fallacy in probability judgement. *Psychological Review, 90,* 293–315.

Utgoff, P. (1986). Shift of bias for inductive concept learning. In R. S. Michalski, J. G.

Carbonell, and T. M. Mitchell, eds., *Machine Learning: An Artificial Intelligence Approach 2*. Los Altos, CA: Morgan Kaufmann, 107–149.

Veloso, M. (1992). Learning by analogical reasoning in general problem solving. Ph.D. Thesis, School of Computer Science, Carnegie Mellon University, Pittsburgh, PA.

Veloso, M. (1994). Flexible strategy learning: Analogical replay of problem solving episodes. In *Proceedings, 12th National Conference on Artificial Intelligence (AAAI-94)*. Seattle, WA, 595–600.

Veloso, M., and Carbonell, J. (1991). Variable-precision case retrieval in analogical problem solving. In *Proceedings, DARPA Case-Based Reasoning Workshop*. Washington, DC, 93–106.

Wagman, M. (1978). The comparative effects of didactic-correction and self-contradiction on fallacious scientific and personal reasoning. *Journal of General Psychology, 99*, 31–39.

Wagman, M. (1980). PLATO DCS, an interactive computer system for personal counseling. *Journal of Counseling Psychology, 27*, 16–30.

Wagman, M. (1984). *The Dilemma and the Computer: Theory, Research, and Applications to Counseling Psychology*. New York: Praeger.

Wagman, M. (1988). *Computer Psychotherapy Systems: Theory and Research Foundations*. New York: Gordon and Breach.

Wagman, M. (1991a). *Artificial Intelligence and Human Cognition: A Theoretical Intercomparison of Two Realms of Intellect*. New York: Praeger.

Wagman, M. (1991b). *Cognitive Science and Concepts of Mind: Toward a General Theory of Human and Artificial Intelligence*. New York: Praeger.

Wagman, M. (1993). *Cognitive Psychology and Artificial Intelligence: Theory and Research in Cognitive Science*. New York: Praeger.

Wagman, M. (1995). *The Sciences of Cognition: Theory and Research in Psychology and Artificial Intelligence*. New York: Praeger.

Wagman, M. (1996). *Human Intellect and Cognitive Science: Toward a General Unified Theory of Intelligence*. Westport, CT: Praeger.

Wagman, M. (1997a). *The General Unified Theory of Intelligence: Its Central Conceptions and Specific Application to Domains of Cognitive Science*. Westport, CT: Praeger.

Wagman, M. (1997b). *Cognitive Science and the Symbolic Operations of Human and Artificial Intelligence: Theory and Research into the Intellective Processes*. Westport, CT: Praeger.

Wagman, M. (1998a). *The Ultimate Objectives of Artificial Intelligence: Theoretical and Research Foundations, Philosophical and Psychological Implications*. Westport, CT: Praeger.

Wagman, M. (1998b). *Cognitive Science and the Mind-Body Problem: From Philosophy to Psychology to Artificial Intelligence to Imaging of the Brain*. Westport, CT: Praeger.

Wagman, M. (1998c). *Language and Thought in Humans and Computers: Theory and Research in Psychology, Artificial Intelligence, and Neural Science*. Westport, CT: Praeger.

Wagman, M. (1999). *The Human Mind According to Artificial Intelligence: Theory, Research Implications*. Westport, CT: Praeger.

Wagman, M. (2000a). *Scientific Discovery Processes in Humans and Computers: Theory and Research in Psychology and Artificial Intelligence*. Westport, CT: Praeger.

Wagman, M. (2000b). *Historical Dictionary of Quotations in Cognitive Science: A Treasury of Quotations in Psychology, Philosophy, and Artificial Intelligence*. Westport, CT: Praeger.

Wagman, M. (2002). *Problem-Solving Processes in Humans and Computers: Theory and Research in Psychology and Artificial Intelligence*. Westport, CT: Praeger.

Wallsten, T. S. (1983). The theoretical status of judgemental heuristics. In R. W. Scholz, ed., *Decision Making under Uncertainty*. Amsterdam: Elsevier (North-Holland), 21–39.

Waltz, D. (1988). Connectionist models: Not just a notational variant, not a panacea. In D. Waltz, ed., *Theoretical Issues in Natural Language Processing*. Norwood, NJ: Ablex, 1–8.

Waltz, D. (1989). Is indexing used for retrieval? In *Proceedings, DARPA Case-Based Reasoning Workshop*. Pensacola Beach, FL, 41–45.

Wason, P. C. (1964). The effect of self-contradiction on fallacious reasoning. *Quarterly Journal of Experimental Psychology*, *15*, 30–34.

Wason, P. C. (1966). Reasoning. In B. Foss, ed., *New Horizons in Psychology*, vol. 1. Harmondsworth, Middlesex, England: Penguin.

Wason, P. C., and Johnson-Laird, P. N. (1972). *Psychology of Reasoning: Structure and Content*. London: Batsford.

Whitehead, A. N., and Russell, B. (1910–1913). *Principia Mathematica*, 2nd ed. Cambridge: Cambridge University Press.

Whitfield, J. W. (1947). Rank correlation between two variables, one of which is ranked, the other dichotomous. *Biometrika*, 292–296.

Wilkins, M. C. (1929). The effect of changed material on the ability to do formal syllogistic reasoning. *Archives of Psychology*, No. 102, 83.

Wilson, M. D., ed. (1969). *The Essential Descartes*. New York: Mentor.

Winston, P. H. (1980). Learning and reasoning by analogy. *Communications of the ACM*, *23 (12)*, 689–703.

Woodworth, R. S., and Schlosberg, H. (1954). *Experimental Psychology*, 3rd ed. New York: Holt, Rinehart, & Winston.

Woodworth, R. S., and Sells, S. B. (1935). An atmosphere effect in formal syllogistic reasoning. *Journal of Experimental Psychology*, *18*, 451–460.

Wos, L. (1983). Automated reasoning: Real uses and potential uses. In *Proceedings of the Eighth International Joint Conference on Artificial Intelligence*. Karlsruhe, West Germany, August 10–12.

Yager, R. (1987). Using approximate reasoning to represent default knowledge. *Artificial Intelligence*, *31*, 99–112.

Zacks, R. T., Hasher, L., and Sanft, H. (1982). Automatic encoding of event frequency: Further findings. *Journal of Experimental Psychology: Learning, Memory, and Cognition*, *8*, 106–116.

Zadeh, L. A. (1965). Fuzzy sets. *Information and Control*, *8*, 338–353.

Zadeh, L. A. (1988). Fuzzy logic. *Computer*, *21 (4)*, 83–93.

Zdrahal, Z., and Motta, E. (1996). Case-based problem solving methods for parametric design tasks. In I. Smith and B. Faltings, eds., *Advances in Case-Based Reasoning*. Berlin: Springer, 473–486.

Author Index

Subject Index

About the Author

MORTON WAGMAN is Professor Emeritus of Psychology at the University of Illinois, Urbana–Champaign. He is the author of 19 books, including *Problem Solving Processes in Humans and Computers* (Praeger, 2001) and *Historical Dictionary of Quotations in Cognitive Science* (Greenwood, 2000).